Strange Tastes

Strange Tastes

Aesthetics and the Public in Latin American and Latinx Feminisms

MONIQUE ROELOFS

Duke University Press
Durham and London 2026

Project Editor: Livia Tenzer
Designed by Courtney Leigh Richardson
Typeset in Minion Pro and Helvetica by
Westchester Publishing Services

Library of Congress Cataloging-in-Publication Data
Names: Roelofs, Monique author
Title: Strange tastes : aesthetics and the public in Latin American and Latinx feminisms / Monique Roelofs.
Other titles: Aesthetics and the public in Latin American and Latinx feminisms
Description: Durham : Duke University Press, 2026. | Includes bibliographical references and index.
Identifiers: LCCN 2025033900 (print)
LCCN 2025033901 (ebook)
ISBN 9781478038658 paperback
ISBN 9781478033752 hardcover
ISBN 9781478062240 ebook
Subjects: LCSH: Aesthetics, Latin American—Social aspects | Aesthetics, Latin American—Political aspects | Feminist aesthetics—Latin America | Feminist theory—Latin America | Women artists—Latin America—Criticism and interpretation | Women authors, Latin American—Criticism and interpretation | Art and society—Latin America
Classification: LCC BH221.L29 R64 2026 (print) | LCC BH221.L29 (ebook) | DDC 111/.85098—dc23/eng/20260116
LC record available at https://lccn.loc.gov/2025033900
LC ebook record available at https://lccn.loc.gov/2025033901

Cover art: Mariángeles Soto-Díaz, *Painting with Fire* (detail), 2017. Multimedia installation. MAK Center for Art and Architecture, West Hollywood, California.

Contents

Acknowledgments

This book owes its existence to a whole collective of people. I'm grateful to Norman Holland for his amazing companionship in thinking and writing. Team teaching courses in Latin American and Latinx literature and cultural theory had me on the edge of my seat. Norm's capacious reading style, his way of innocuously floating a question and then leaving it hanging for everyone to muse on in all of its mind-boggling wondrousness is with me in my current classrooms, an ocean away. Many thanks for the times he pored over these pages, as well as for our collaboration on earlier published versions of parts of chapter 3. His voice is embedded in that chapter.

I thank Carla Damião and Mariana Ortega, dear friends, for dialogues about aesthetics that enriched this book and for vital organizational and editorial projects. The Estéticas No Centro Colloquia and the Latina/x Feminisms Roundtable are exemplary moments of collaborative decolonizing philosophical scholarship. The roundtables Mariana organized were an inspiration for this work. Workshopping central ideas in an integral and sustained manner in the minicourses and lectures that Carla hosted brought increased clarity to the project.

Beate Rössler welcomed me with warmth and friendship in the Department of Philosophy at the University of Amsterdam at the height of the COVID-19 pandemic. In a period when face-to-face conviviality and live philosophical exchange beyond one's immediate circle took recourse to city streets and parks, our walks helped me land in Europe after spending decades in the United States.

It's a pleasure to acknowledge the Critical Cultural Theory group—Katia Hay, Stefan Niklas, Aukje van Rooden, Michael Thomas, Frank Rebel, Niki Hadikoesomo, Marieke van der Steen, and Jeff Diamant—for their exciting work, for being terrific academic sports, and for the rich perspectives they bring to our university's program in philosophical aesthetics.

The Film and Philosophy doctoral seminar that Patricia Pisters, Sudeep Dasgupta, and I organized for several years at the Amsterdam School of Cultural Analysis has been a treasured home for reflection. Many thanks to Patricia and Sudeep for their friendship, for sharing their thinking, and for our mind-opening (and mind-altering) exchanges.

During the writing process I taught at different institutions, most extensively at the University of Amsterdam and Hampshire College in Amherst, Massachusetts, and for intermittent spells at Amherst College and the Netherlands Institute for Cultural Analysis. I thank my students, past and present, for the energy and questions they bring to our work together. I learn endlessly from the fascinating projects of my doctoral candidates at the Amsterdam School of Cultural Analysis: Turkuaz Benlioglu, Jack Dignam, Katy McAlary, Martina Flores Mendeville, Fabienne Rachmadiev, Pınar Türer, and Sabahat Zehra. Their courage is contagious.

Conceptual, imaginative, and didactic toggling among philosophy, political theory, film, literature, and the arts has deepened this book's vision. This habit puts me in the company of two extraordinary predecessors. Anecdote: I shared my essay on María Lugones's notion of play from the angle of several stories by the Argentine writer Julio Cortázar with her in 2018 after having a wonderful public exchange about it with her following a talk I gave, and again in the months before her death in 2020. In her last semester of teaching at Binghamton University, she included the essay in her syllabus along with the stories, which she mentioned she had enjoyed in her youth in Argentina. Strikingly, Gloria Anzaldúa names Cortázar as her favorite author (Anzaldúa 2009, 83). She cites Cortázar, who lived in France, as a stylistic influence and mentions his exploration of "in-between places of reality impinging on each other" (Lunsford 1998, 20). The reader will notice the reference to the famed notion of the borderlands. Jorge Luis Borges, another favorite of Anzaldúa's, provides further aesthetic texture to her figuration of liminal experiences. She reworks his renowned figure of the Aleph into an image for the borderlands, rendered as a site that brings together "all dimensions—the sky, spiritual space, the earth, and the underworld" (Anzaldúa 2015, 57). Indeed, the unfinished doctoral dissertation on art, literature, and aesthetic theory she was composing in 1975 was to include an early chapter on Borges and Cortázar, as well as a later one on Lacan and Cortázar (208n15). As late as 2002, she credits Borges for her insight that, "like the real self, the writing self is fictitious" (2015, 197, quoted by AnaLouise Keating). These imaginative crosscurrents point to a web of aesthetic affiliations that animates this book and that I hope to channel toward further social and praxical possibilities, although these reverberations do not necessarily make it in an explicit fashion into the following pages. This resonance is made possible by conditions of aesthetic publicness: universities, literary and artistic institutions, and platforms for theoretical, narrative, and visual exchange, which currently all face vehement cultural, political, and economic pressures. This book is written in a spirit that recognizes the importance of these very public structures, which, as a former first-generation college student and a product of public education systems all the way through, I have everything to thank for.

Ryan Kendall, my editor at Duke University Press, supported this project with an enthusiasm that invigorated the writing. She offered spot-on editorial suggestions that kept me close to what I was doing and to where the argument was going. I'm grateful for her warm, insightful companionship during the writing process. Two anonymous reviewers offered valuable criticisms and keen suggestions that significantly strengthened this book. I'm deeply indebted to their generous readings. Additional thanks are due to the production team at the press, whose attentive care helped shepherd the project to publication.

I'm fortunate to have had the opportunity to share parts of this book with audiences at different places who helped the project along with their generative remarks. Many thanks to organizers and interlocutors at Amherst College's Center for Humanistic Inquiry; Duquesne University; Penn State University; the Radical Philosophy Association at University of Massachusetts, Lowell; the British Society of Philosophy at Oxford University; the Society for European Philosophy at Cardiff University; the University of Warwick; the Amsterdam School of Cultural Analysis at the University of Amsterdam; Leiden University; Tilburg University; the Dutch Research School of Philosophy at Utrecht University; the Federal University of Goiás, Goiânia; the Federal University of Minas Gerais, Belo Horizonte; the University of Brasília; the European University Viadrina; the German Society for Aesthetics at Leuphana University; the Kunsthalle and City of Nürnberg; the University of Antwerp; the University of Klagenfurt; Zuidpool, Antwerp; and meetings of the American Comparative Literature Association, the American Society for Aesthetics, and the Society for Phenomenology and Existential Philosophy.

I'm grateful to dear colleagues and friends for camaraderie, kindness, laughs, and intellectual sparks—especially Brigitte Adriaensen, Emmanuel Alloa, Christoph Brunner, Kandice Chuh, Katja Diefenbach, Adriana Clavel-Vázquez, Gürsoy Doğtaş, Fábio Ferreira de Almeida, Miguel Gally, Miguel Gualdrón-Ramírez, Jörg Heiser, Yolande Jansen, Eileen John, Michael Kelly, Eloe Kingma, Daniel Kojo Schrade, Jaap Kooiman, Jasmijn Leeuwenkamp, Helen Longino, the late María Lugones, Linda Martín Alcoff, Mari Mikkola, Ben Moore, Eleonora Orlando, Andrea Pitts, Sudha Rajagopalan,

Kati Röttger, Anna Schrade, Falguni Sheth, Ruth Sonderegger, Mariángeles Soto-Díaz, Jutta Sperling, Sanjukta Sunderason, Paul Taylor, Pablo Valdivia Orozco, Tom Viaene, and Manon van Zuylen. Thank you.

For her weekly poetic guidance into immersive planes of silence, quiet, and stillness, I thank my meditation and mindfulness teacher Nancy Lustgarten. For accompanying my personally strange, interchangeably super-slow and superfast voyages into the unthought, I'm grateful to my psychoanalyst, Tara Goldberg.

My family stuck with me during decades of phone calls between continents interspersed with yearly visits. Their support was essential during the writing process. A bit over three weeks after I returned to the Netherlands, my father died. In hindsight, I can't believe the stroke of luck that enabled him, at the end of a mandatory quarantine period, to pay me an overnight visit in my temporary home in Amsterdam South. He enjoyed the conversation, took pleasure in the view from the huge window of the trams and the pedestrians in the street, and even ventured outside for a brief walk. I thank my brother Lex for making this heartwarming visit possible, which wove threads of continuity among different worlds that nourished me as I learned to live with the losses and farewells of those years.

To my mother, Loes Roelofs-Vennekens, thanks for all our sustaining conversations and for your love of art and literature. This book carries the traces not only of your intellectual curiosity and joy but also of your wisdom and magnanimous listening skills to which I owe so much. To my sister, Karin, thanks for our closeness, for your encouragement, and for swapping the occasional story about Dutch and European university life in its stranger and more familiar manifestations. To my brothers, Sjoerd, Camiel, and Lex, thanks for all the good cheer and for being there at crucial moments. To Igor, Mirjam, Nicole, Linda, Peter, Marieke, Nathan, Ruth, Joart, Remco, Tobias, Mila, Sara, and Julie, thanks for sharing your arts of living with me. To all those unnamed interlocutors, friends, and colleagues who touched me and conversed with me in the period that this book was brewing, a big thank you for helping to make life so meaningful and so very strange.

Introduction

Aesthetics, Taste, and Public Inhabitance

A turn to the public whirls through contemporary Latin American and Latinx art and literature, establishing new sites of experience, pleasure, and critique. Aesthetic strategies of publicness permeate cultural productions, enveloping the strange in imaginaries of democratization.

This book contemplates strange tastes with an eye to their public reverberations and the political potentialities they activate within aesthetics. I investigate aesthetic sensibilities that deliberately bewilder by going against the grain of prevailing structures of feeling, forms of agency, and modes of responsiveness. Strange tastes are propelled by curiosity: They circumvent customary narrations and predictable readings with unusual twists of fate and uncanny interventions that lead us to unknown territory. They lodge the unexpected into webs of relationships among people, more-than-human beings, things, and places, where it kindles intimacies that call forth changing selves and transmuting others. An attunement to the weird and wonderful lends itself to perceptions and creations that exceed the bounds of the ordinary and hint at social alternatives. Thus, the strange animates ways of organizing public life. As a dimension of alterity and a catalyst of evolving relations among self and other, it fosters an expanded awareness and inhabitation of the realm of publicness.

Strange tastes that latch on to dust, pings, song, and light are at the center of my analysis. I highlight these tastes in the work of several prominent Latin

American and Latinx women writers and artists—namely Alicia Borinsky, Clarice Lispector, Claudia Llosa, and Diamela Eltit. Featuring sensibilities that are intentionally at odds with reigning intuitions and reactions, these feminist creators forge positions that fall outside common schemas of subjectivity. By endowing their female protagonists with aesthetic dispositions that are eccentric in a manner that is hard to draw a profit from, these artists and writers push back against the dominance of market arrangements. In their works, strange tastes inspired by residual materialities of dust, pings, song, and light activate disinterested play in the public domain. Politics moves, spurred by this aesthetics of the strange. For strange taste heightens the powers of artistic and quotidian imaginaries to awaken singularity, to remake city and nation, and to build human and more-than-human worlds.

How can the strange, which has been influentially construed as a constitutive corporeal, psychic, and social mechanism of subject formation (Kristeva 1991) and critiqued in that capacity for its tendency to efface structural differentiations of race, gender, coloniality, ethnicity, and sexuality (Ahmed 2000, 6, 73; 2005, 96–104, 108–9), realize this kind of effect? Strange tastes are unabashedly aesthetic and historical proclivities. These aspects of the strange have been undertheorized. It is precisely the aesthetic abundance and historical charge of strange taste that the artworks in my archive mobilize as incitements of public life. To clarify this point, I offer an initial description of what I mean by the term *publicness* and, in particular, *aesthetic publicness*. By examining a lecture and a short story by Jorge Luis Borges, I show how the field of aesthetic publicness entwines strangeness with taste and writing, and anchors self-making, while also generating mercurial positionalities. These processes prefigure the aesthetics of public inhabitance and becoming pioneered by the four feminist writers and artists.

Borges weaves the movements of the strange, conceived of as an aesthetic category, into figurations of identity. This gesture is embedded in a broader reflection on the impact of aesthetic forms on registers of social positioning and performance, and vice versa. Borges's proposal emerges in texts that contemplate the links between art and identity while putting forward modes of subjective becoming that give a distinctive role to aesthetic invention in the crafting of selves and the design of cultural positions. Before outlining Borges's vision, let me describe my approach to the markers of social identity and positioning announced by my subtitle, especially the term *Latin American and Latinx feminisms*, and sketch some features of the philosophical method that I bring to this book's archive.

Following commentators in disciplines ranging from philosophy and literary and cultural studies to sociology and the arts, I understand Latin American and Latinx cultures and identities as evolving discursive assemblages shaped by intersecting social forces and categories.[1] The element of discursive construction I highlight resonates with the productive facet of a feminist politics that is also an aesthetics: The feminist part of my subtitle underlines an at once aesthetic and political project that occasions trajectories of subjectivity and encounter with the world.[2] More than that, as revealed by the critical phenomenologies of Gloria Anzaldúa, María Lugones, and Mariana Ortega, it signals how feminist actors who engage in a variety of modes of experience, strategies of critique, and forms of coalitional practice enact embodied stances in relation to other actors and material settings.[3]

Far from positing a unitary cultural frame, in my usage the term *Latin American and Latinx feminisms* speaks to a diversity of aesthetic forms and traditions and an array of social positionings. Because the three categories individually and conjunctively point to manifold, ongoing formations rather than to ahistorical givens, they circumscribe a restless cultural reality of tensions, imbalances, and internal differentiations. Entrenched intersectional power disparities undergird divisions within feminisms and among US Latinx and Latin American cultural positionings (Fusco 2000, 9; Dávila 2020, 4–17; Pérez 2019, 114, 157; Pérez 2020). So the mobile assemblage I take as my framing in this investigation encompasses splits, wounds, injustices, and contradictions. Simultaneously, art and theory have dotted the cultural arena with shards of conversation that are ready to be picked up and amplified into full-fledged dialogues, which then can yield further affiliations and solidarities. As the Latinx studies scholar Claudia Milian observes in her luminous celebration of the creative, nonbinary, often refractory force of the *x* in *Latinx*, distinct pathways of multisensory and imaginative interaction give rise to emerging unknowns as we figure out ways of "navigat[ing] the world" (Milian 2019, 2, 39, 77; Milian and Romera-Figueroa 2024). For Milian, *Latinx* is a sign for these navigations—these behaviors "in a social and ethnoracial world" (2019, 11). In tailoring the Latinx, sped up by *LatinX*'s louder grapheme, to a "philosophical unknown" and open-endedness, to "transitions," to "crossings" (2, 12, 14), she lodges it in public territory: "LatinX synchs up, not so sotto voce, with a multitude of discourses and signifiers already in the *public* eye" (11, emphasis added). Far from static, the public syncings are creative. They make things happen; they stretch desire.

Indeed, it is the *x*'s crossings that, as Milian indicates, make the name "Zeze the X" a site of desirous self-discovery to Sandra Cisneros's young Chicana protagonist Esperanza as she engages intimacies and difficulties coming on her path in her Chicago neighborhood (Cisneros 2009 [1984], 11; Milian 2019, 13–14). Esperanza's longing finds a match in the craving of that other daring crossover type, Julio Cortázar's narrator in "Axolotl," who, switching positions with the creature he had been observing, transforms his visual fixation into the gaze of the enigmatic more-than-human other (Cortázar 1967a). *X*-powered crossings go on, traversing bodies, species, histories, continents, subject-object relations. And so my subtitle signals an aesthetic of naming, feeling, seeing, and reading. In short, I trace a field of multisensory bodily encounter, relationality, and address. Following established yet theoretically and interpretively underexplored artistic ventures, I enter a conversation initiated by Latinx and Latin American feminist voices that exceeds nationalist, regional, and other institutionalized demarcations. The audacious public interlopings and aesthetically reverberant cultural trajectories I sketch belie, as Anzaldúa, Lugones, and Stuart Hall have shown, any possibility of unalloyed separation.[4] Echoing in interwoven voices, transversal anticipations, and untested forms, the aesthetic sensibilities I spotlight partake of the operations of the strange. By seeking out the aesthetic quality of the strange, I swerve from philosophy's more typical strategy of address: Art and literature collaborate on an equal footing with philosophy in theoretical invention.[5] Anzaldúa's and Lugones's strategies of opening up social theory to narrative voice, verbal and bodily performance, and anecdotes that exceed their illustrative roles provide precedents: Philosophy encounters itself in a quotidian strangeness that outstrips the theorist's stated observations. Border crossing enters philosophical address, gender, and sexuality, weaving the strange into the queer in a manner that energizes the imagination beyond what a mere conceptual wrap-up could hope to achieve. At the same time, the notion of publicness, no longer dichotomously split from the domestic sphere or the marketplace, needs theoretical explication and conceptual analysis that I want to offer.[6]

Drawn from the open-ended sphere of imaginative searching spanning the Americas that I have just sketched, my archive in this book is a segment of a broader swath of cultural production. I use a limited but powerful set of creative works to shed light on strange taste and aesthetic publicness. These concepts' generativity stretches beyond the selected cases. Indeed, different sources could have advanced my argument. At the end of the book, I consider several works that bring out further angles in our concepts that may reshape the intersection of the strange and the public.

The variety, multiplicity, and flux of our area of inquiry notwithstanding, distinct continuities arise: The artworks that make up my archive yield a narrative that laces the strange through the public in a manner that opens up unforeseen possibilities for agency, identification, and play. To the notion of the public I now turn.

Publicness, Aesthetic Publicness, and Strange Taste

The domain of the public is a historically emergent, material, and symbolic field of engagements where different constituencies enter into multivoiced, contestatory, and consensual encounters over norms, values, social orders, things, and infrastructures. Its participants form evolving coalitions, assemblies, splinterings, and disaffiliations; specific publics take shape. Emerging in a pluralist field of intra- and cross-species entanglements and affective interactions, dependencies, and mutual vulnerabilities among embodied subjects and things (Anzaldúa 1999 [1987]; Connolly 2005, 2013), publicness involves criteria of participation and belonging, institutionalized social and political procedures, standards of expression and publicization, and principles of legitimation adhered to by discursive communities, which implement contingent forms of societal organization. It is a morphing structure of mutual, multimodal address and responsiveness among individuals and among groups that fuels forms of collective and individual alignment and becoming.[7] More specifically, publicness concerns materially embedded, normatively inflected resources, objects, experiences, practices, and interactions.[8] The material and normative realities of publicness make clear that it constitutes aesthetic territory.

I coin the notion of aesthetic publicness to give expression to the aesthetic forms and structures encompassed by and conditioning public space and to acknowledge the fine-grained aesthetic processes bearing on the creation, development, persistence, and dwindling of distinctive publics. An example from a well-known Borges lecture is useful in clarifying what I have in mind. In noting that a present-day invocation of "the wine-dark sea" recalls not only Homer but also "the thirty centuries that lie between us and him," the Argentine writer (2000, 14) places Homer, himself, and his reader in an overarching constellation of aesthetic publicness. Borges implicitly locates the aesthetic powers and significance of aesthetic publicness in the resulting relational expanse when he contends that beauty can be found everywhere across this experiential province, this realm of address: Beauty "is always with us" (14). Aesthetic publicness makes this transhistorical and cross-geographical ambit of engagement possible. It underlies our ability to detect beauty from "the classics" to its current instantiations (14).[9] Borges's treatment of aesthetic publicness merits further elaboration because he connects this phenomenon with taste and the strange.

Borges's democratization of beauty may please his audience with the promise of an infinite stretch of aesthetic joy and delight. However, in the lecturer's eyes, the realization that beauty is all over the place is not a comforting insight, by far. He associates beauty with deviance. Quoting the poet Robert Browning, he observes that it takes a hold of us "'[j]ust when we're safest'" (14–15). Beauty catches the subject unawares with its hazards, including its erotic lure and its messages of death. Borges amplifies: "[B]eauty is lurking all about us. It may come to us in the name of a film; it may come to us in some popular lyric; we may even find it in the pages of a great or famous writer" (15). Wherever there is language, there is the possibility of beauty. And it pops up in other places, as well. Indeed, Borges extends aesthetic publicness to the natural environment.

Taste supplies the necessary link between letters and physical objects or geographical locations. Borges prefaces a discussion of the metaphysics of taste qualities with an allusion to the aesthetic politics of the American settler-colonial system. Whether at the level of textuality or concrete materiality, in literature or food, taste preserves its transgressive allure. It situates knowledge in an ominous proximity to nature or the land of which continents are made:

> Speaking about Bishop Berkeley (who, may I remind you, was a prophet of the greatness of America), I remember he wrote that the taste of the apple is neither in the apple itself—the apple cannot taste itself—nor in the mouth of the eater. It requires a contact between them. The same thing happens to a book or to a collection of books, to a library. For what is a book in itself? A book is a physical object in a world of physical objects. It is a set of dead symbols. And then the right reader comes along, and the words—or rather the poetry behind the words, for the words themselves are mere symbols—spring to life, and we have a resurrection of the word. (3–4)

A natural object or an agricultural product such as an apple requires an eater who brings her mouth and her poetry into contact with the forbidden fruit to actualize its illicit pleasures, just as the life of the book and the library demands a reader who will free up the poetry nascently concealed "behind" the words. The mouth achieves its contact with the world through physical touch and words. It tastes. And it tastes strangely. Lawless taste lends its life- and death-giving powers to existence in the flesh, to quotidian objects, to the institutions of the book, and, no less ambitiously, to the colonial project.

From this unsetting portrayal of taste, Borges moves on to the faculty's ultimate and transcendent achievements. He offers an instance of apparently uncontested poetic perfection. His example of consummate taste is John Keats's sonnet "On First Looking into Chapman's Homer," which Borges interprets as a commentary on "the poetic experience itself" (4). He quotes the sonnet's final lines:

> Then felt I like some watcher of the skies
> When a new planet swims into his ken;
> Or like stout Cortez when with eagle eyes
> He stared at the Pacific—and all his men
> look'd at each other with a wild surmise—
> Silent, upon a peak in Darien. (4–5)

"Here," Borges observes while mimicking Keats's grand gesture and planetary spectacle, "we have the poetic experience itself" (5). He conjectures that the reader "will never have noticed, perhaps, how strange [this poem] is," for "perfect things in poetry do not seem strange; they seem inevitable" (4). Now we, his audience, are in a position to see through the pinnacle of perfection and spot the strange thing, too: Borges leads the aesthetic of the beautiful and the sublime to that of the strange. He emplaces beauty and sublimity as registers of poetic experience and conceptual determinants of the natural world and a geopolitical system, in a historical, global order of aesthetic publicness, to then leave behind these aesthetic categories and their supremely potent constructive labors—their "surge and thunder" (4)—in favor of an aesthetic of the strange, permeated by foreboding. By peeling off the beautiful and sublime sheathing that had enveloped the strange, surrounding it with an air of necessity and lending it the appearance of self-evidence, Borges uncovers the strange in its historical and political reality. "Cortez . . . stared at the Pacific," he quotes Keats's scrambling of the historical record while calling out the poet's fictionalization of Hernán Cortés and the sublime Panamanian terrain that, albeit rather flat, is supposed to feature mountain peaks.[10] The scene blazons colonialism. In the act of exposing the strange, Borges historicizes it. He doesn't state that Keats bungles truth but reveals the poet's inventive production of history, of geography, of conquest. He highlights his indiscriminate yet conventionally legible conjunction of signifiers. Keats is creating linguistically perpetuated aesthetic inevitabilities: He takes a dip in the wine-dark sea. Silently, Borges invites us to apprehend the poetics and cultural politics the strange enacts. He routes aesthetic publicness through strange taste. True to its name, the strange intimates questions, raises doubts, and hints at unstated forms of knowledge more than that it traffics in explicit answers (2, 19).

Divested from its hull of perfection, "the poetic experience" in its bare, uncamouflaged strangeness exudes perplexity, which is exactly what Borges proclaims to offer his reader with his literature: "I can offer you only time-honored perplexities. And yet, why need I worry about this? What is a history of philosophy, but a history of the perplexities of the Hindus, of the Chinese, of the Greeks, of the Schoolmen, of Bishop Berkeley, of Hume, of Schopenhauer, and so on? I merely wish to share those perplexities with you" (2). More than about beauty or sublimity, Borges cares about animating and participating in aesthetic publicness with his words and touching us with the strange, having us join him in lingering on it. Perplexity enacts a relational aesthetics: It relies on a sharing and a public conditioning, a field of aesthetic publicness. Everyone is part of this realm, sometimes alone, sometimes together, as Borges hints elsewhere, but never wholly solitary or in harmony (1999a, 425).[11] The sharing occasions the threats and promises of perpetuating peculiar metaphorical iterations and detecting curious repetitions hidden by an aesthetic of the beautiful and the sublime. And it rolls further, bobbing up and down on the surf of the strange: Drenched in strangeness's at once perilous and exhilarating aesthetic tidings, the reader soaks up Cortés's soldiers' "wild surmise," their stunned searching for the other's gaze. The strange sinks the body deeply into a performance of coloniality and tosses it out of it again, lugging us above and below the surface.

Language, Borges notes, "is shifting" (2000, 14). "And the reader," he adds, "is shifting also" (14). Imagining language as the changing water coursing through the self-same Heraclitean river that no one can twice step into, he points out that readers who are contemplating this flow, fearfully and "with an emerging sense of awe, . . . feel that we too are changing—that we are as shifting and evanescent as the river is" (14). Strangeness infects the reader, carrying her onward to unsuspected places and dissolving any sense of cultural or political inevitability. Aesthetic publicness and taste are in motion under the influence of the strange. Positionality is in flux. Borges features a versatile, contagious, and highly active strangeness that runs between subject and world, reader/writer and text, and readers and writers. This strangeness stretches from mountaintop views and the philosopher's sense of the Americas' "greatness" to the apple's touch of the taster's mouth, and on to subaquatic consciousness.

Borges's aesthetic world is a masculinized arena, just as the lettered culture that he inhabits and takes for granted was for the longest time an orbit dominated by the preoccupations of male writers of a certain class. The feminist performances of the strange I track in this book exhibit a public logic that is different from the one put forth by Borges's ventures into this quality. Nevertheless, against the backdrop of the aesthetic entanglements and reciprocal provocations between self and world he uncovers, the critical modalities under investigation in the pages that follow can be recognized in their full force and invention. To lay the grounds for this inquiry, I turn to his renowned short story "Borges and I."

Writing Selves, Public Selves

First published in 1966, "Borges and I" has an astonishing pertinence in the age of social media, video games, and digital culture more broadly, owing to the distinction the tale makes between Borges's walking and narrating self and the public persona that this self brings into being.[12] The story begins: "It's Borges, the other one, that things happen to. I walk through Buenos Aires and I pause—mechanically now, perhaps—to gaze at the arch of an entryway and its inner door; news of Borges reaches me by mail, or I see his name on a list of academics or in some biographical dictionary. My taste runs to hourglasses, maps, eighteenth-century typefaces, etymologies, the taste of coffee, and the prose of Robert Louis Stevenson" (Borges 1998a [1966], 324). From the start, the story envisions an intricately layered relation between artist and persona. The two enter into an interplay that encompasses a swirl of entanglements, indirections, displacements, takeovers, and movements toward and away from the local, the national, and the global.

Borges's "I" enters the inside edifice behind the arch and inner door from the outside—the Buenos Aires streets—to meet his public persona via textual materials such as the mail that has arrived, a list, and a reference work. In turn, what appears as the author's intimate assertion of his "I"'s taste is heavily mediated by literate culture and his own texts: This self is characterized by his interest in space, time, language, and, notably, coffee, which locates him in the public and not-quite-public spaces of the Buenos Aires coffeehouses where literary encounters and debates take place. Taste, once again, embraces the strange. It is eccentric and highly singular. It is even stranger than the registers of the idiosyncratic and the intensely particular suggest because of the way Borges's persona "shares" the "preferences" of his "I." The persona has a "vain" way of relating to these shared preferences "that turns them into the accoutrements of an actor." In doubling up, and doing so with a determinate and at once mysterious difference, taste makes itself strange. The tastes of Borges's "I" are no longer straightforwardly his. The persona lays a claim on them, too. This "other one" transforms the tastes in the process, turning them into performative props. The "I" is well aware of "the perverse way" the other one has "of distorting and magnifying everything." Nonetheless, he gradually surrenders "everything to him." For instance, he feeds him the "games with time and infinity" with which the "I" has tried to "free" himself "from him" and "[move] on from the mythologies of the slums and outskirts of the city." It is not as if the "I" is overly enthusiastic about "the other one": "I recognize myself less in his books than in many others', or in the tedious strumming of a guitar," he announces with barely disguised rancor. The aesthetic of the strange, here, establishes a "point-counterpoint, a kind of fugue, and a falling away," coupled with a ready absorption and accumulation by "the other man." Neither of the two can claim taste and writing as in any clear-cut sense his own. Taste and writing carry splits between self and other and between interiority and exteriority that keep shifting. Taste is continually other to itself. Aesthetic publicness holds these alterities, which muddle dualities of public and private, separation and togetherness, giving and taking, being and writing or playacting, and having or making and losing.

While traversing distances and proximities between the "I"'s self and its public persona, the story marks the necessary yet impossible differentiation of the two, culminating in the final punch line: "I am not sure which of us it is that's writing this page" (324). Borges invokes the domain of the aesthetic through registers of performance and taste, artifacts, and visual/literary forms. He shows us how identity is mediated through aesthetic modalities that, as already mentioned, cross public-private and interiority-exteriority rifts and that transgress habitual-unusual/new, individual-tradition, local-global, and self-world divides. More than that, our aesthetic activities are productive of our identities. Indeed, these identities are aesthetic creations in a fundamental sense. In the age of digital avatars, artistic performances modulated by artificial intelligence (AI), and incessant demands for online self-representation and self-personification, the story is a crucial reminder of the complexities identity owes to the jumbled yet vital distinctions it presupposes.

Borges conveniently, though critically, inhabits the global literate world of which the Argentine writer, as he notes in an acclaimed essay, is a full-fledged citizen (Borges 1999a). The expanded global aesthetic field as inhabited in Buenos Aires becomes the territory on which Borges resists the reification, commodification, and stultification of subjectivity, averting a hemming in of both the artist's "I" and his public persona. Identity, whose movements are buoyed by both selves and their shifting disjunctions and similarities, absorbs an aesthetic restlessness. It is not in a definitive manner engirded by categories such as the nation or class.

Borges's abstract cosmopolitanism plays games of "time and infinity" with identity at some distance from the economic forces shaping our globalized contemporary aesthetic culture (1998a [1966], 324).[13] Taste makes identity strange and carries this strangeness into the world, a world that, permeated by disquiet, itself becomes strange, even uncanny. This aesthetic venture, this spillage and self-overturning spreading of alterity, hinges on a literary social bedrock whose foundations have been shaken to the core. The aesthetic dynamics marking identity reflect the rushes of shifting rivers, rising sea levels, and wine-dark flows of spilled blood. While the artist's "I" and his public persona shift in relation to each other, aesthetic publicness morphs, too, in a manner that exceeds the interventions of the games that Borges's "I" plays with time and space and passes on to his public persona. For the cultural bolstering of the lettered enterprise has undergone substantial changes.

Toward a Decolonial Feminist Aesthetics of the Strange

Borges's strange produces formidable coilings, displacements, and sensitivities. However, it does not go far enough. It draws its nourishment from a narrow Western literary canon, which institutes a problematically gendered and racialized constellation of aesthetic publicness and valorizes an overly restrictive experiential ambit and an all too limited agential sphere. If Borges conscripts the strange to solidify an existing edifice of aesthetic publicness and saturate it with disquiet, then the artists and writers who make up my archive use it to tear down his uncanny domicile and design new abodes for cultural practice, even a new house of culture.

Estranging Borges's playlist of literate and quotidian tastes and composing an alternative repertoire, they put strange taste to work to bring into being unprecedented paradigms of aesthetic publicness. They center these models on the aesthetic travails of remarkable female protagonists, whose anomalous tastes mix jarring rhythms and hues into serialities of comfort and crisis. The characters' dissonant, unruly imaginaries rupture given societal templates and the aesthetic investments channeled by these schemes. Flaunting their idiosyncrasy in the face of normalizing desires, liminal figures craft aesthetic stances and forge aesthetic conditions that open up aesthetic publicness to positions of marginality. Equipped with curious sensibilities, they realize temporally disjunctive and narratively compound textures of experience in the fictional worlds they inhabit. In this manner, they uproot aesthetically mediated societal frames that seek to contain them. Strange taste, in my archive, thus informs an expanded orbit of decolonial feminist imagination and social practice and supports projects of critique and world making. Like Borges, the four authors and artists engender intimacies that summon shifting selves and shifting others. In contrast to their predecessor, however, they extend the critical, transformative capacities of the strange to constellations in which coloniality intersects with gender race, and class, among other modalities and, in doing so, orient these formations and the sensibilities with which we meet them toward revised orders of experience and agency.

The strange, accordingly, is a strategy and a conceptual tool of a decolonial aesthetics and an aesthetics that queers itself. Anzaldúa's and Lugones's views of border experience are in the philosophical vanguard of this work. Inspired by their artistic and theoretical/praxical decolonial feminist outlooks alongside the perspectives of a cadre of kindred scholars, I use the term *decolonial aesthetics* to refer to a critical engagement with coloniality in cultural productions and aesthetic and art theory.[14] Coloniality consists of a matrix of ongoing, modern historical formations of space and time in which structures of race, gender, sexuality, and nation, among other social positions, intersect with one another (Anzaldúa 1999 [1987]; Anzaldúa 2015, 73; Lugones 2010; Pérez 2019; Quijano 2007; Wynter 1992, 2003). A decolonial aesthetics is a form of decolonial and postcolonial critique that is alert to the specificities of the aesthetic. Because the dimension of the "post-" in postcoloniality refers to an ongoing process of critical reading rather than a temporal designation, the postcolonial and the decolonial overlap significantly.[15] In two previous books, I theorize the aesthetic in a manner that affirms its specificity, while acknowledging its links to configurations of experience, power, and social identity and difference, including coloniality. The aesthetic, in my view, concerns activities that lend organization to perception, affect, and meaning, suffusing them with a dimension of normativity that ties into various kinds of promises and threats, among other forms of address and relationality (Roelofs 2014, 2020). The organizational devices of the aesthetic include so-called aesthetic categories, such as the beautiful, the fine, the detailed, the subtle, the grotesque, and, importantly, the strange. Aesthetic practice, sensibility, and judgment navigate—and, in the process, often destabilize while also reinstalling—dualities such as reason and emotion, mind and body, imagination and sensation, form and content, public and private, individual and community.[16] As Anzaldúa's (1999 [1987]) and Lugones's (2003, 2010) philosophies of culture underscore, a decolonial feminist aesthetics engages in productions and analyses that critically tune in to the experiential and social operations of these polarities. It resists reifying binaries of coloniality and postcoloniality/decoloniality (Spivak 2012, 2) and conqueror and conquered, while in the same act questioning gender dichotomies and other intersecting dualities, such as heterosexuality and homosexuality or the queer.

Coloniality is marked by reciprocal mediations between local situations (such as a nation's music education system) and global arrangements (including musical diasporas with a worldwide reach, such as Black, Latin American and Latinx, African, Asian, and European sonic traditions).[17] As a set of practices that crisscross the domains of theory, institutional existence, and the everyday, a decolonial aesthetics interrogates these formations at all three levels, which interact with one another. Part of a decolonial aesthetics is then a critical, self-reflexive engagement with the relationships among theory, ongoing institutional histories, and day-to-day life (Anzaldúa 1999 [1987]; 2015, 47–64). In the realm of contemporary artistic and cultural production, a decolonial aesthetics creates objects, forms, norms, performances, experiences, traditions, and collaborations that unsettle or take a measure of distance from neocolonial modalities of power and sociality. In the theoretical domain, a decolonial aesthetics calls into question and rethinks socially entrenched conceptual structures that support (neo)colonial conditions of aesthetic meaning and normativity.

Creative and theoretical impulses, meanwhile, typically are part of each other: Artworks, as is widely recognized, engage in theory. On an autobiographical note, I'd like to share that Latin American and Latinx art, thought, and culture have been of immense philosophical significance to me. The notion of the aesthetic I elaborate in my previous works is fundamentally indebted to the writings of Pablo Neruda, Lispector, Anzaldúa, and Lugones and the paintings of Remedios Varo, among others. This book carries on in this critical lineage because quite a few Latin American and Latinx artists invent astoundingly generative kinds of play and bring them to bear on the forms and possibilities of publicness and the intertwinements of aesthetics and politics. Thus, they engage in vital theoretical explorations from which philosophy has much to learn. Part of this learning is to elaborate conceptual frames that recognize these inquiries as philosophy. Pushing back against certain disciplinary conventions, a decolonial aesthetic philosophy/practice thus operates at this self-reflexive level, where disciplinary and transdisciplinary modes are under construction.

Neither indexing an endpoint in a process of interpretation or design nor on a quest for unblemished moral and political excellence, a decolonial aesthetics, at a structural level, adopts a conjectural mode of address that acknowledges elements of indeterminacy, uncertainty, and opacity.[18] In short, it amounts to a multivalent, critical cultural politics of reading, making, and encounters that incites further readings and rereadings, further makings and remakings (Anzaldúa 2009, 190–91; Anzaldúa 2015, 60, 64; Lugones 2003, 219, 229; Rooney 2017, 446–49), and further encounters and reencounters (Ahmed 2000, 13–17). The notion as well as the practices of strange taste are part of this process.

As it happens, taste has gone out of favor in influential quarters of aesthetic theory.[19] Yet cultural life is more massively conditioned by it than ever. Social media provide spaces for the articulation of people's aesthetic likes and dislikes. Digital platforms encourage the creation of aesthetic personas that mediate our encounters with the world and that we can identify with. Content providers track consumer habits and choices to fine-tune recommendations and relay the resulting profiles back to producers. Matters of taste thus constitute a huge driving force in our algorithmic ecosystem. This has a mainstreaming effect, owing to the sway of ratings, which privilege popularity and allow items that enjoy mass appeal to crowd out productions sought after by smaller constituencies of consumers. Media and entertainment industries, fed by consumer data, exercise control over what sees the light. Commentators attest in this context to a flattening and diminishment of culture (Chayka 2024) and a reduction of political discourse (Dean 2009). Given that the attention economy conjoins trials posed by overexposure, echo chambers, information bubbles, fake news, and nonstop vigilance with exhilarating and pathbreaking possibilities for connectedness fostered through technology, communication networks occasion a mixed bag of aesthetic and cultural effects. Nonetheless, questions of taste and the public take on a new form and urgency in contemporary societies, as algorithmically produced information exerts growing measures of control and as transformed patterns of self-expression and response tie into democratic decline and fuel rising and intensifying authoritarianisms.[20]

Most of the strange tastes threading through this book's archive are radically different from what the market prizes. In addition, they tend to be at variance with strategies of aesthetic homogenization and cultural blunting or dilution. The realm of strangeness is actually broader than my cases bear out. For instance, I imagine that it includes certain fixations on friendship bracelets or semiautomatic rifles that, though strange, may feed smoothly into the regular organization of things, especially when these items are all the rage in some segments of the population in a manner that reflects distinct economic interests. The strange, thus, is not insulated from the marketplace. It extends beyond the genres of strangeness that I discuss. My focus on strange elements that fly in the face of mainstream economic interests is a consequence of my choice to zero in on feminist art and literature that casts an intersectional light on commodification processes and finance and venture capital.

Strange tastes, as already indicated, are sensibilities. They are bodily, socially, and ecologically emplaced modes of comportment toward the world. A whole slew of these capacities are worth cultivating. This does not imply that they are unqualified moral and political goods. Rather, they carry ambivalences. We need to be alert to their treacherous potentialities. Nevertheless, as I hope to show, these ambiguous predilections sustain life-enhancing, culturally and politically vital activities and perceptions.[21]

The strange is often queer. In her last, posthumously published book, the cultural critic Eve Sedgwick defines the queer in terms of the strange (2011, 188–89). The strange, I would propose, animates the motion of the queer, the fluctuations, multiplicities, and vagaries of the "across" she predicates of it while performing it: "Queer is a continuing moment, movement, motive—recurrent, eddying, *troublant*" (188). Strange taste keeps alive this anarchic queering. It suffuses the life-sustaining and simultaneously harrowing, excruciating social and personal journeys and transformations that scholars such as Anzaldúa (1999 [1987]), Lugones (2003, 2006), Ortega (2016), and Milian (2019) associate with nonbinary, queering Latinx liminalities, carnalities, and border crossings.[22]

In line with Borges's and Sedgwick's suggestions, read in the context of Latinx feminist philosophies of culture, my archive highlights the logics and potentialities accruing to the strange as an aesthetic category. The strange resonates with discourses of shock, rupture, wonder, excess, abjection, disquietude, restlessness, estrangement, defamiliarization, alienation, astonishment, the absurd, the neutral, the eerie, the weird, the grotesque, the monstrous, the horrific, the surreal, and the uncanny that frequently accompany it. Each notion holds specificities. The strange must be given its due alongside these other aesthetic categories, which have commanded concentrated theoretical attention. Strangeness is worth examining in its own right and for the impetus it lends processes of aesthetic interpretation, making, doing, questioning, and critique.

While sustaining distinctive logics, aesthetic categories often approximate aspects of one another. They typically carry elements that they share, and that support and feed into one another, sometimes to the point of being virtually inseparable.[23] The strange, thus, tends to display features that characterize, or even are prominent aspects of, other qualities. For instance, it may dovetail with forces of estrangement and alienation. Many an instance of the strange is illuminatingly seen as an aesthetic experience and intimation of a condition of estrangement or alienation. At the same time, the strange commonly pursues paths and patterns of its own and diverges from trajectories outlined by, notably, Marxist, Existentialist, Surrealist, or Lacanian traditions. The sharing of contents and the interactions among aesthetic categories do not detract from the significance of any one of them individually. Overlap, cross-fertilization, and porosity indicate that strangeness offers portions of a story about other qualities, just as other qualities offer portions of a story about strangeness. It's a two-way street. Given the protean collaborations and volatile differentiations that characterize the life of any given aesthetic quality, we need to peer into manifold directions to see where we're going or coming from. In this spirit, I look to the strange side.

Another prominent attribute of aesthetic categories is that their meanings and connotations are likely to shift depending on the discursive, communal, and experiential contexts of their instantiations. This context-dependence can also be expected in the case of the strange. Relatedly, it is unlikely that all instances of strangeness have a single feature or set of features in common with one another that makes them strange. Again, this point is not unique to the strange but obtains for aesthetic categories generally—notably, beauty (Korsmeyer 2006, 52–56; Sibley 1959, 424–37). The variability and breadth of scope of the strange, which encompasses cultural elements that range from highly particular moments to general tendencies, are compatible with the concept's relevance. Apart from the inevitable assortment of difficult cases, furthermore, the strange emerges in uncontroversial instances that are readily recognizable as such.

Surpassing the expected and embracing the peculiar, strangeness is never insulated from the exotic. On occasion, strange taste shrouds itself in the garb of the calculatingly marvelous, the reliably outlandish, to make room for more surprising fascinations that upend entrenched forms of attachment and valuation. As a critical mode of bodily comportment, strangeness runs athwart established aesthetic scripts, including schemas of magical realism and transculturation; routinized registers of resistance; and patterns of euphoria and hope, disaffection and negativity, absorbed by existent cultural hierarchies.[24] The residual characters who cultivate these refractory sensibilities assert their humanity in the face of a racial and colonial apparatus that employs gender, sexuality, and class, among other forms of difference, as modes of production and dismissal.

Taste has a long history in Western philosophy as a practice of individuality and human worthiness. For David Hume, writing in the eighteenth century, it is a means by which subjects can assert their relative autonomy in a world of accidental, happenstance occurrences. Thus, we can take charge of our own happiness. He holds that "we are pretty much masters of what books we shall read, what diversions we shall partake of, and what company we shall keep" (1998c, 11). Taste, for him, is the capacity that enables us to do this. It grants us a measure of independence from the eventualities of existence. Hume thought that this was a good thing, something that every "wise man" would try to achieve insofar as possible (11). Of course, not all of us are wise men, and in concocting this view of the matter, Hume lost sight of the conditioning factors that tend to facilitate or detract from the aesthetic autonomy of the subject of taste. He avoids examining the logic taste assumes when books are not permitted, diversions are ruled out, and company is reduced to a handful of relatives in a rigorously surveilled household that places one at the bottom. In short, Hume suffuses taste with the preoccupations of a white, propertied, heterosexual male intent on expanding his sphere of influence and enriching his interior world. There is much to question about Hume's views. Yet he ventured a notion of taste that has a great deal of pertinence in an era when societies are subjected to algorithmic rewiring and experience and agency undergo intensifications, as well as reductions, as a result.

Taste is a sensibility that can occasion a singular way of experiencing and responding to the world.[25] A culturally trained habitus, it is a faculty that permits relative, not unqualified, aesthetic self-determination, for our interdependences are constitutive of who we are. More generally, taste must be seen as an aesthetic position that we attain in consequence of a process of living. As an aesthetic stance, it involves a whole array of activities and states: Imagination, sensation, perception, emotion, understanding, questioning, desire, and fantasy are all part of it. These elements are components of taste. In exercising taste, we bring these elements to our encounters with what we seek out or have in front of us and to our interactions with people, more-than-human animals, things, and places. In sum, taste amounts to an acquired disposition to experience and relate to the world in a certain manner.

I have not yet mentioned taste's aspect of judgment, the dimension that has commanded most of the attention by far that philosophy has lavished on the propensity. Taste is so powerfully associated with the good and bad that it is hard to think about apart from these predicates. But I want to loosen this evaluative apparatus to bring into focus the potentialities of the strange as an operation of taste. For if habitual proclivities we acquire over time establish a baseline of what counts as normalcy to us, then this inevitably engenders a zone of the uncommon, the unusual, that defies expectation. And if the forcefully and immediately evaluative language of good and bad freezes the temporality of taste to roll out judgments of performative achievement and failure, then the vocabulary of the strange points to the dialectical unfoldings of the ordinary and the extraordinary, where a new normal becomes the jumping-off point for a new strangeness that swerves around what happen to be the subject's approbations and condemnations of the moment. So the temporality of the strange, while lodging in the very moment, also sweeps that instant up in an ongoing movement. As an acquired predilection, taste can respond and change—for better or worse, to be sure, but no less powerfully for stranger or less strange. Taste shifts, propelled by the strange, as we saw in Borges's lecture. The ensuing vagaries affect the criteria of applicability for the predicates of the strange and the ordinary that are in effect. What does this dynamical, norm-changing aesthetics of the strange look like?

This book takes up this question by following a cast of recalcitrant types who wield taste as an antidote to aesthetically reductive social designs in which they are embroiled. Equipped with highly eccentric tastes, a troupe of contrarian characters populating novels, poems, and films go against the grain of a colonial system of racial capital that regards aesthetic meaning as one more area of expropriation and gain. Taste's capacities to encode a person's unique way of being and distinctive perceptual and interpretive outlook do not confine it to the sphere of the individual. By contrast, as we rely on our tastes to sift through headlines, videos, portraits, podcasts, performances, databases, websites, and the like, we participate in publics. These publics we bring into being as makers and recipients of cultural productions. Taste is a way of navigating our presence in these publics. It not only binds us to the materiality of objects, ecologies, and substances but locates us as sentient beings in a collective social reality, a world we share with other people and more-than-human living creatures. As subjects of taste, we are members of publics. Hume concurs enthusiastically. Indeed, aesthetic publicness was first theorized by Enlightenment philosophers. Invoking the eighteenth-century heritage, the next section lays out this notion in greater detail and highlights its contemporary generativity by way of two examples.

Aesthetic Publicness: Enlightenment Visions and Twenty-First-Century Artistic Tendencies

The European Enlightenment gave rise to a field of practices I call *aesthetic publicness*. This term denotes aesthetic conditions and forms that index a public domain. I have in mind aesthetic constellations that posit a sphere of public interactions as a structural ground for varieties of normativity and relationality that they put forth and presuppose. More than a pattern of incidental exchanges, aesthetic publicness is a systemic phenomenon. It involves institutional arrangements that employ aesthetic norms and forms. It engenders experiential stances and distributions of power. Aesthetic publicness pertains to the aesthetically suffused structural organization that shapes encounters among artists, cultural artifacts, and audiences and leaves its marks on modes of cultural production and reception. It thus concerns the societal conditioning and infrastructural scaffolding of cultural practices and productions. Publics come into being to gather collectively around architectural sites, image flows, and sound repertoires by building on multivalent and disjointed histories. Aesthetic publicness yields forms and materials that make this possible. The public, meanwhile, permeates the private, and vice versa, for rather than binary opposites, these notions are mutually implicated in each other.

The field I am sketching encompasses social forces and technological developments surrounding the ways in which art-audience relations take shape and presuppose or contribute to the engendering of artistic stances and audience identities. Aesthetic publicness revolves around the platforms or forums in which aesthetic encounters and experiences occur. Besides the historical production and emergence of different kinds of publics, it undergirds the workings of aesthetic norms, codes, and strategies in the culture, within and beyond the artwork.[26] At issue are the ways in which artworks reach into such structural and normative elements and give them form.

Enlightenment philosophy forged a genre of aesthetic publicness based on the figure of the general observer. By reference to this idealized perceiver, concrete aesthetic norms and relationships could be construed on a universalist model, where experiences, values, and modes of creation and reception aspire to validity for everyone, regardless of their social position, geographical location, or place in history.[27] A problem with this paradigm, as many have recognized, is that what were taken to be a universal forum for aesthetic meaning making and a generally accessible faculty of taste are actually sites of fundamental exclusions. The ideal public is less than ideal. Should philosophy, hence, discount the notion of the public as a realm of aesthetic production and reception? And might we in the final reckoning do well to hold off from thinking about taste as a capacity that endows us with ways of navigating this field? I believe these notions have an enduring significance today that must be acknowledged. Let's consider two actual instances.

In 2019, the Chilean feminist art collective Las Tesis took the world by storm with its protest performance *Un violador en tu camino* (A rapist in your path) (figure I.1). In a mode of direct confrontation, the activists chanted and danced truth to power, contesting gender violence at all levels of the society. "Y la culpa no era mía, ni dónde estaba, ni cómo vestía" (It wasn't my fault, neither where I was, nor what I wore), they sang. The joyful lyrics deployed the sayings of their abusers, underwritten by taste and decorum, against them. Furthermore, they shifted the violence against women onto the state. The initial performance was held in front of a police station in Valparaíso. Reenactments followed in Santiago, first on the International Day for the Elimination of Violence Against Women and later outside the National Stadium, which served as a detention and torture center during the dictatorship. Social media worked its magic following the second performance, and soon public assemblies formed in about two hundred sites across Latin America and worldwide, before state and governmental institutions such as courthouses and parliaments. The performance's energetic corporeal synchronies and percussive sociality resonated online and offline. Public spaces became sites of critical and affective solidarities (Butler 2015; Serafini 2020). Collaborative participation in aesthetic publicness engendered incantatory scenes that provoked further collective aesthetic affiliations. Public territory marked by systemic gender domination and its authorizing procedures rolled out feminist mobilizations demanding change. Feminists aesthetically claimed public space as a domain where a reconfiguration of gendered existence should occur.

Dance squats during which the performers folded their arms behind the neck alluded to invasive body searches carried out routinely by police officers. Green scarves tagged the Latin American reproductive rights movement. Alongside the locations of their rendering, these aesthetic forms and histories were constitutive elements of the performance. By drawing on, implying, and activating existing frames of meaning and matrices of cultural production and reception, the performance enacted a structure of address that amounted to a formation of aesthetic publicness. The public extension of the happening also spoke from the lyrics' riff on a Chilean police slogan: "Un amigo en tu camino" (A friend in your path).[28] Clearly, publicness was in action. It supplied an aesthetic infrastructure against the backdrop of which the performance could assume its meanings and resonance. Seen from one angle, aesthetic publicness conditioned the performance.

Considered from another angle, aesthetic publicness was enacted and shaped by the performers, who redirected common sayings and recognizable gestures in public spaces toward public institutions. Las Tesis's performance exemplifies a broader phenomenon: Aesthetic publicness is a setting where cultural actors can create and communicate affirmations of their coalitional, female, and LGBTQIA+ embodiment in its manifold

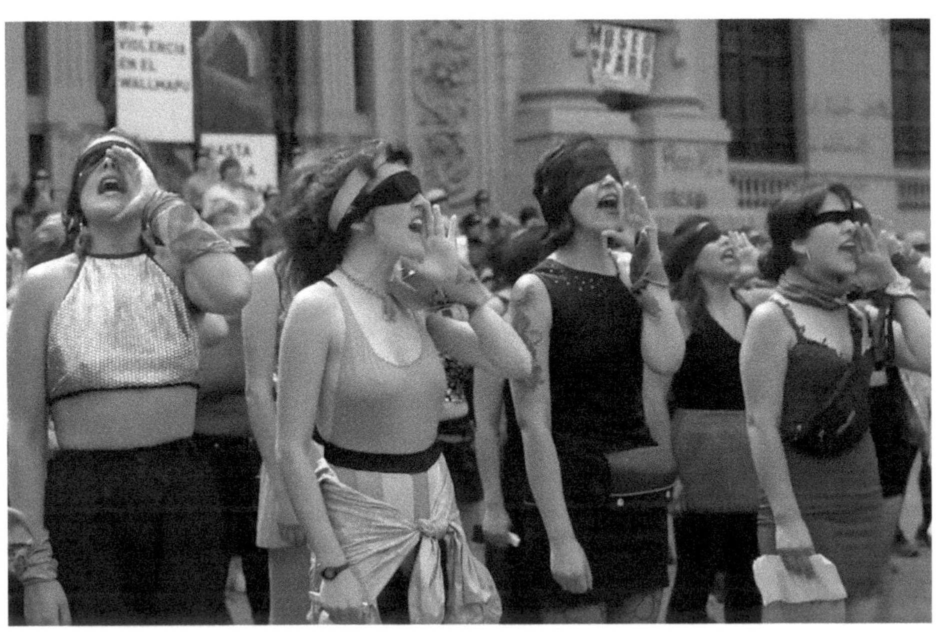

FIGURE I.1. Las Tesis, *Un violador en tu camino* (A rapist in your path). Santiago, Chile, November 25, 2019. Video still, Colectivo Registro Callejero.

interconnections. Hosting at once desirous and vulnerable corporeal and performative realities, this forum yields crucial capacities for collaborative political intervention (Butler 2015).

The Las Tesis performance burst onto the public scene by using a very direct form of address: the *je t'accuse* of the mantra "El violador eres tú" (The rapist is you), thrown with a pointed finger at a state apparatus. The catchy song and the dance's rapid, rhythmic pace articulate an unabashedly polemical sensibility, intent on transparency and broad communicability. Taste is in play here, and must hence be recognized as such. It is not exactly what I would call strange, although somewhat strange, puzzling elements, such as blindfolds, might give the bystander or the viewer pause and slow down reading, alluding to areas of experience that are not immediately legible, zones of devastating pain, concealed domains of brutality and suffering—affective and relational fields that necessitate the claim on publicness made by the performers. The strange in the sense I have in mind, consequently, is not absolutely strange but sufficiently mystifying and peculiar to mark a space where legibility is restricted. In this space, aesthetic practice and experience can provoke questions and push back against criteria of expected bodily comportment and social behavior.

My second case is Consuelo Jimenez Underwood's 2024 multimedia wall installation *Everything All at Once* (figure I.2). A migrant family is on the run, the crisp, brown-red strips schematically defining them overlaid onto a cartographic grid whose fiery orange-yellow lines partition the land. A spiky, triply painted and threaded, winding line reminiscent of barbed wire and carrying pins, necklaces, and sundry items is in turn superimposed over the human figures. *X*s mark places of presence and existential possibility, as well as of heightened surveillance. The border crossers find their existence reduced to bare parameters of speed and direction of movement by a long arrow piercing the adults' hearts, having swished by just above the trailing little girl. The family image, a recurring presence in the artist's work, is derived from a road sign cautioning Californian motorists from the early 1990s through 2018 against undocumented trespassers they might encounter on the highway.[29] Pen-drawn paper cutouts bookend the installation with two female deities who are watching over the scene, which is framed by multicolored abstractions and patterns of cactus leaves, oak leaves, and wiry stretches of woven fabric suggestive of fences. Maps of the Americas are embroidered into the chicken netting of nopal leaves below. Other leaves reveal open hands or hold a flower. Whereas the arrow abstracts the three migrants' existence into a ruthless path of banishment or coerced flight, a central hoop replenishes and

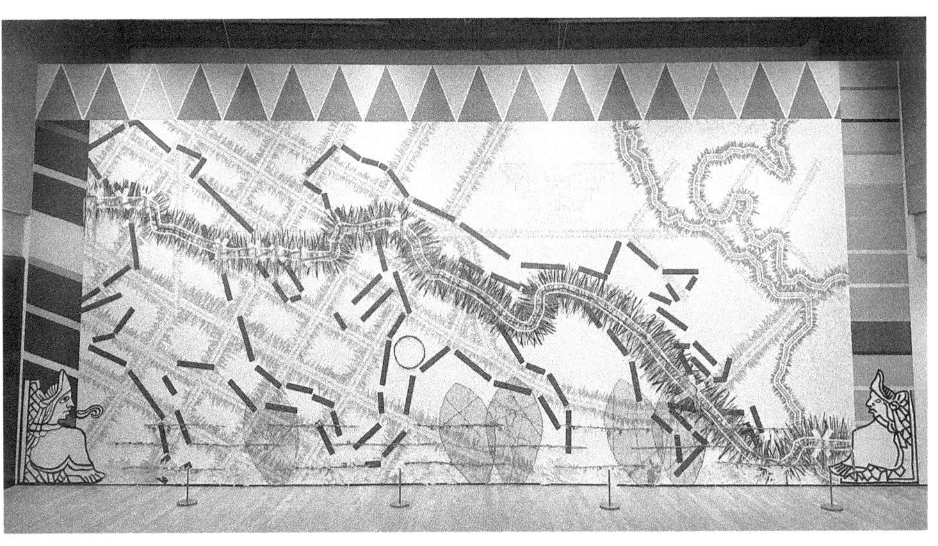

FIGURE I.2. Consuelo Jimenez Underwood, *Everything All at Once*, 2024. Mixed media installation, 27 × 40 ft., Oakland Museum of California. Photograph courtesy of Oakland Museum of California.

affirms their lifeworld. It declares that undocumented people who are being pushed out of their longstanding places of residence belong in their fullness to the geographical and cultural locations they inhabit, connected as they are to concrete imaginaries and experiences of the land, to spiritual and material ecosystems that foster participating in the strength and courage of an eagle, and to the nourishment a meandering river or resilient plants may bring.

By reworking the highway safety sign, *Everything All at Once* transforms an official public space of terrorization into one where Latinx migrant and Indigenous communities can find revitalization, notwithstanding vehement forces of reduction. Publicness, the work's title stresses, encompasses "everything," both in its terribleness and in its delicate powers of sustenance. Rather than jettisoning the lexicon of the public, philosophy needs to rethink it, consonant with current tendencies in culture and the arts.

Publicness and the Arts: Three Feminist Models

Aesthetic publicness is an active register of sociality that pervades all of life. Surrendering it comes at a price. A loss is incurred. Agency shifts. We pass over control to market forces determined to incorporate it into societal cycles ruled by profit principles. Influence is ceded to authoritarian impulses that evince not the least hesitation about bolstering the sway of small groups of actors over others. Neither art nor the vast majority of people stand to gain from this arrangement. The benefits are stacked against those on the receiving ends of oppression by race, gender, ethnicity, sexuality, coloniality, and ability. Current practices of violent accumulation and extractivism rooted in historical structures demand a reply in terms of substantive figurations of the public. To be sure, publicness need not amount to a replica of the phenomenon that the Enlightenment made it out to be. And neither is it necessary to construe taste along the lines proposed by philosophers such as Hume and Immanuel Kant, who elevate this sensibility to the status of an adjudicating mechanism that issues distinctions between life-forms celebrated as human and worthy of existing and ones written off as nonhuman and deserving of eradication or curtailment.[30] Different notions of taste and the public can be devised and exercise their effects in the culture. The body of work by Latin American and Latinx women artists and writers assembled for this book enables us to imagine such formations.

By turning the lens of publicness onto this literary and visual archive, I'm following in the footsteps of several feminist scholars. In their writings on contemporary literature and performance and installation art in the Americas, the artist-theorist Coco Fusco, cultural critic Nelly Richard, and literary historian Jean Franco stress the significance of public space as a site of artistic intervention. Fusco connects this public orientation in the Americas with the dual need to provide artistic responses to strategies of institutional control, including modalities of state power, and to sidestep conservative, culturally nationalist demands for authenticity (2000b, 5–6). In an analysis that speaks volumes about the era of Javier Milei and Donald Trump, Fusco points to hegemonic exercises of power that extend across the Americas and brings out how artists in the region turn to public arenas as sites of critical engagement with these forces (9). She observes that a focus on public formations characterizes both the responses of Latin American artists to realities of state-inflicted violence that persist during transitions from dictatorial regimes to democracy and the responses of Latinx artists to issues such as the operations of immigration and border patrol authorities, endemic exploitative labor practices, neofascist mobilizations, and racially segregated communities. While opposing any reduction of cultural expression to its political valence and meaning, Fusco underscores the political and symbolic import of art's use of public space in the Americas. Indeed, marking through lines in the work of Latinx and Latin American artists, she highlights aesthetic forms and choices that purport to foil certain institutional forces, to widen and reestablish "civic space," and to intervene into "public space" by marking its "absence" or "call[ing] it into being" (6, 10, 14). Publicness here is a register through which artists critically address social imaginaries in the Americas and participate in the making of culture.

Richard has long emphasized the public dimension of the happenings and activities organized by the Chilean experimental art group Colectivo Aciones de Arte (Art Action Collective [CADA]). In CADA's artistic practice, which includes events such as the distribution of milk in working-class sections of Santiago and the blazoning of "No+" throughout the city—a gesture cited by Las Tesis (see figure I.1)—the public constitutes, in Richard's words, the "scene of art production" (2000 [1986], 207). In her discerning reading of founding member Lotty Rosenfeld's 1979 performance *Una milla de cruces sobre el pavimento* (*A Mile of Crosses on the Pavement*), she notes the work's address to the "anonymous spectator (virtually anyone)," which provokes the viewer to "critically restructure their schema of daily experiences" (2009, 116). Richard here signals the form of address that lies at the core of Enlightenment constructions of publicness. The starting point for the reorganization of quotidian frames is the "insolent . . . orientation" of the stripes Rosenfeld affixes to the surfaces of roads, initially in Santiago and subsequently in other places across the Americas and beyond, and that run perpendicular to the regular lines guiding the flow of traffic in a forward direction. For Richard,

Una milla de cruces exemplifies CADA's investment in public engagement, its strategy to make interventions into "public space" (116). The "+" signs, in her reading, inaugurate "a new, rebelliously creative relationship with signs and codes" that exposes and counters totalitarianism with a "multiplicative plurality" of meaning (117).

Richard spots an analogous turn to the public in Rosenfeld's later multimedia installation *Moción de orden* (*Point of Order* [2002]). In this combined three-channel video work and site-specific action, the artist's strategy of publicness is to interrupt and displace a flattened global mediascape and its concomitant institutionalized dynamics of othering. Mapuche voices enter news flows. Crawling ants traverse city surfaces, passing through museums and galleries. Insinuating themselves into icons of the fossil fuel and financial industries, these dispersive, at once orderly and disorderly, border crossers enact an "art of the streets" that creates small disturbances in technologically mediated patterns of socioeconomic and cultural control (Richard 2009, 124). In this way, the installation targets aesthetically saturated forms of power channeled in the field of aesthetic publicness.

The public, here, is not a province of heroic monumentalism but a space where "strange" forms (Richard 2004b, 6) elude cultural binaries and upend ideological, institutional, and symbolic stratifications and closures (Richard 2004a, 18, 130; 2004b, 4–6). Artworks fulfill a public role by answering figurations of white, heterosexual masculinity of the middle classes, regimes of ableism, and sexual and gender oppression with a desirous, imaginative, and playful embrace of the as yet unknown (2004a, 119–27, 139–42, 160–76). Thus, the public is a site of confrontations among tastes and among other sensibilities that hosts unceasing negotiations between "margins" and "institutions" (122–23, 130, 173; 2004b, 32–33). Regarding the horrors of the dictatorship of Augusto Pinochet and the forgetful, mass-mediated neoliberal order it installed, this ongoing contestation attests to the need to animate our "powers of public invocation and convocation" in the name of direly pressured cultural memories and alternative imaginaries (Richard 2019, 103). Publicness, for Richard, is a key site of collective, creative world making and an antidote to destructive authoritarian mobilizations.

In a discussion of the work of Latin American women writers in the context of social movements of the 1980s and 1990s, Franco signals the problematic gendered nature of historical public-private divides and argues for a reorganization of existent gender constellations. Literature, she notes, must contend with the hegemony of a pluralism that renders everything commodifiable, including political engagement and difference (1992, 69, 79–80).

As many have observed in the wake of Gayatri Chakravorty Spivak's famous treatment, an unproblematic enunciative stance in the margins is not available to the cultural and political actor. Indeed, the aporias of this position necessitate alternative forms and structures of address. Whereas Argentina's Mothers of Plaza de Mayo could gather "in a public place" and "reclaim the *polis*" from a position of marginality while "making public both their children's disappearance and the disappearance of the public sphere itself" and testifying to their own anomalous presence "in the symbolic center of the nation," according to Franco, this strategy is no longer available in the same way to the contemporary woman writer because of literature's changed societal status (67). In response to this predicament, she advocates for a form of literary critique: "The imperative for Latin American women is . . . not only the occupation and transformation of public space, the seizure of citizenship, but also the recognition that speaking as a woman within a pluralistic society may actually reinstitute, in a disguised form," various relations of privilege (80). Women writers, consequently, must "broaden the terms of political debate by redefining sovereignty and by using privilege to destroy privilege" (80). In Franco's assessment, literature thus faces the twofold task of engendering a transformative participation in public space and producing an intersectional mode of aesthetic and political engagement that reconstructs what we mean by autonomous agency and avoids the traps of single-axis gendered aesthetic politics.

In her subsequent book-length study *The Decline and Fall of the Lettered City* (2002), Franco spells out in greater detail what this option implies for the societal role of contemporary cultural production. Tracing the shifting positions of Latin American and Latinx art and literature, she exposes the untenable, internally contradictory claims to direct public participation of the Mexican muralists, who in various ways were in cahoots with the state apparatus and an art market that they purported to challenge in the name of the people (67–69). Analogous contradictions undermine, in her view, the pose of the iconic poet of the streets (in contrast to libraries or diplomatic and political chambers) Pablo Neruda, who used to read his work at public gatherings—notably, union meetings (72–85). Franco situates these artists in a large narrative span. Placed under this arc, Borges becomes a stand-in for an imaginative rehearsal of "the end of the social" (176), notwithstanding his uncanny investigation of the categories of the universal and the particular.[31] And Cortázar epitomizes a dematerialization of public space achieved through the fantastic projection of a white masculinist coterie onto a sphere of actual social complexities (Franco 2002, 116–17), notwithstanding his unsettling inquiry into the relation between art and politics. Franco's narrative privileges a social-realist mode of reading.

Despite the limitations of her literary analyses, Franco offers a cultural history that usefully documents shifts in the status of art and literature from a position of autonomy that she believes mimics national sovereignty, through a violent reordering effected by military repression, to an ambiguous state of immersion in a globalized economy, where established registers of domination persist in newly emerging forms and put shifting pressures on the political aspirations of the aesthetic (1–18). Literature generates aesthetic fissures whose ties to social classes and groups have become severed (219). Economic change accompanies a curtailment of the public space where popular demands can receive political articulation (272–73). Literary writing has lost its purchase on tastes, which are assimilated by commodity culture and its criteria and ratings (5, 50, 186, 263–64). Pronouncing "'literature'" today "an uncertain category," Franco tells a story of attrition. She chronicles the "founder[ing]" of artistic utopianism and the prevalence of the marketplace over the literary institution and its practices. Under the rubric "What's Left of Literature?" she refers to aesthetic modes of negation and rupture whose links with the social and the collective are unclear (274–75).

Yet while Franco assigns the artist to a cultural position that is decidedly fraught, ambivalent, and complex, the final decades of the twentieth century and the beginning of the twenty-first century reveal for her "reenactments in new circumstances of demands for the not-yet-realized universal" (18). She attends to forms of art and cultural criticism that "expose strategies of containment" and push back against the "geopolitics of domination" (18). Indeed, she ends her account on a hopeful note, for "among the rubble" of utopian visions and literary projects of world making, "something is still alive": Planetary "stirrings" are heard (275). This detection of sustained aesthetic life and the voicing of demands for a yet-to-be-actualized universal and for a caring, responsible fulfilment of social needs require the public space that, she argues, women writers have been and should be entering in a transformative manner. The reciprocal structure of address that she hints at necessitates a forum in which stirrings occur and demands are made and can be registered, interpreted, and responded to.

Franco's cultural charting delineates a profound, tremendously jolting problematic. Aside from certain interpretive worries, I find her argument highly generative. It pinpoints a dynamic of aesthetic publicness that constitutes a pivotal reality but is simultaneously in turmoil, if not in crisis. By scrutinizing the works of four Latin American and Latinx women writers and artists—two of whom inform Franco's overview and two of whom remain unmentioned—I intend to further the theorization of this fundamental concept.

An Archive of Tense Multiplicities; an Archive of Pleasure

In curating the works at the core of this investigation, I aim to respond to three principal concerns. First, the Enlightenment heritage to date puts its stamp on institutionalized settings, such as governance models and other societal infrastructures. Smaller-scale phenomena, such as encounters among racialized and gendered bodies and modes of cultural creation and interpretation, are likewise affected. The enduring cultural influence of Enlightenment paradigms makes it imperative to conceptualize forms of aesthetic publicness that surpass historically entrenched exclusions, which seep through all levels of experience.

Second, taste exerts an ongoing impact on the culture as a register of self-fashioning and world making. In this capacity, it engenders aesthetic enjoyments and aspirations. Regardless of what objects the propensity fastens on, as human beings we tend to hold dear certain tastes we cultivate. In exercising them, we shape them. Partaking of waves of information, we daily hone our individual and collective sensibilities. An awareness of taste's productive functioning should factor into our understanding of the social realm. My first two points speak to each other: By reflecting on taste, we can recognize how this propensity nourishes or detracts from publicness.

The third driving force for this investigation revolves around the nature and contours of aesthetic practices broadly conceived. It is crucial that we conceptualize the aesthetic domain and the notion of the aesthetic in a manner that is up to par with the current day and age. Aesthetics needs to reckon with contemporary cultural and economic developments, which speak to its fundamental presuppositions. This philosophical endeavor stretches to the frames of the public: Publicness must be considered in light of the conditioning powers and functioning of the aesthetic even as we need to think through how shifts in registers of publicness bear on the aesthetic.

These three lines of reflection delineate an intricate orbit of entanglements. It is here that, as the works in my archive demonstrate, we can open up ways of thinking, feeling, sensing, and making and devise trajectories of aesthetic being at the edge of what has been thought. I investigate aesthetic facets of publicness that resist rapid legibility, engaging in a significant stretch of interpretive labor. This is precisely what the four artists and writers are calling for. Their works do not give away their insights on first blush. These strategies of paced aesthetic elaboration are deliberate. They establish a dialectic between an aesthetics of opacity and clarity, lightness and depth, giving and withholding, satire and seriousness that is part of what the aesthetic brings to the field of cultural agency and the public.

Meanwhile, the aesthetic is of key relevance to the propensity of taste. This sensibility, after all, juggles and traverses the polarities just mentioned. Taste is a quintessentially aesthetic phenomenon. It harbors a vortex of tense multiplicities. The archive assembled here enables us to explore the manifold potentialities of taste in light of changes that are happening with regard to the organization of our aesthetic lives, broadly speaking.

Philosophy and cultural criticism, as already indicated, are of a piece in my approach to my archive. The cultural objects that fuel the discussion engage at once in aesthetic theory and forms of institutional intervention and quotidian practice. A writer such as Lispector wrestles with theoretical and existential questions about aesthetic, moral, and political life. These interweavings also mark contemporary Latinx feminist philosophy and cultural theory, ranging from Anzaldúa and Lugones to more recent analyses by Laura Pérez (2019), Ortega (2025), and other scholars (Pitts et al. 2020). My readings, motivated by the three considerations that drive the selection of my archive, thus are philosophical inquiries in the same act that they are investigations of artistic productions. So this book embraces a realm of pleasure.

Indeed, were we to single out the aesthetic for one achievement only, an admittedly absurd but nonetheless instructive venture, I submit this would be pleasure. We may care all we want about imagination, ethics, politics, insight, and critical questioning and other facets of the aesthetic, but apart from the enjoyment that comes with them, aesthetics rapidly loses allure. Here I am thinking of profound and possibly enduring pleasures (which are not necessarily the same) as well as of thin and fleeting ones that remain on the surface. The question of pleasure—its effusiveness, its compulsions, its orientations—is a vital preoccupation in my archive and informs my engagement with this archive throughout these pages. As aesthetic practitioners and theorists have known for many centuries, by seeking out pleasure, by getting us to go where pleasure proposes to take us, worlds open up. Accordingly, I am guided by the directions into which my artists and writers travel propelled by pleasure.

Following their cues, we find gratification in dust, pings, song, and light. These entities lend their structures to the sensibilities they awaken in the cultural objects under consideration. They activate contingent relationalities. Siding with pleasure, we go after materiality and give ourselves over to the ways things feel. We may be present to the body, in intimacy with ourselves, with others. We sense twinges of desire. We march in lockstep with repetition. But we also trail off in flights of fancy, drawn to remote corners of the imagination. These journeys give us a sense of the states of subjectivity, collectivity, and agency that we inhabit as we slip into and out of pleasure. Pleasure, meanwhile, encounters displeasure typically not in some sort of standoff. Their relation is more complex than that. Indeed, these experiences often nourish each other. They are commonly part of one another.

Thinking about the rich categorical repertoire through which we apprehend our pleasures and about the manifold forms in which we enjoy them calls to mind tinges of adventure and possibility we likely sense when at play. For play can be a quite pleasurable activity. It involves freedoms in ways that alert us to unfreedoms. A playful comportment rests on disinterest in a manner that speaks to our interests. Disinterest here is not the rigorously nonconceptual, non-purpose-bound mode of attention theorized by Kant, but a more qualified concern for experiences in their own right and qualities that are intrinsically valuable. Thus, it is mixed with elements Kant would count under the umbrella of interest, as acknowledged by theorists as diverse as Theodor Adorno (1997, 9–13), John Dewey (1934, 257–66), Jerrold Levinson (1996, 16–18), Peg Brand (1998), and Amelia Jones (2003, 78–79, 82–84).

From another angle, play ties into the stories we tell about ourselves and other people and that we enact as a matter of our day-to-day living. Playfulness has a seemingly inexhaustible narrative and performative generativity. Children's games make this clear: "I'm the murderer, you were the corpse; you kept watch over the bridge, I was the thief; you were the pirate, I was the dancer; the princess had been kidnapped but we didn't know it yet." These ludic hints can precipitate dramatic happenings that carry on for entire afternoons.

Pleasure is interlaced with a whole array of adjacent aesthetic occupations. How might aesthetic existence harness these sundry practices in response to contemporary information circuits and socioeconomic conditions? One reply rings loudly from the artworks under discussion in this book: by making a turn to the public.

As noted before, my analyses in the following chapters zero in on the work of four Latin American and Latinx woman artists and writers. These creators investigate aesthetic life with an eye to the possibilities and limits of publicness. In a corporatist epoch when consumerism is massively promoted as an answer to the challenges the world faces at the same time that growth has become caught up in catastrophic cycles that cry out for intensified regulation, the four artists and writers confront our investments in market-boosted pleasures with stories, modes of play, and trajectories of subjective and collective being that exert traction, resisting capture by instrumental reasoning. The aesthetic forms and strategies enacted by the works that constitute this book's archive carry seeds of recalcitrant relationalities, alternative intimacies.

I commence with poems in the collection *Frivolous Women and Other Sinners / Frívolas y pecadoras* (2009), by the Argentine-born fiction writer and scholar Alicia Borinsky. Then I caper back in literary history to linger over the Brazilian writer Clarice Lispector's last novel, *A hora da estrela* (*The Hour of the Star* [1998 (1977); 2011]). Next, I leap forward to the Peruvian filmmaker Claudia Llosa's feature film *La teta asustada* (*The Milk of Sorrow* [2009]), before ending with two late twentieth-century novels by the Chilean writer and performance artist Diamela Eltit: *Lumpérica* (*E. Luminata* [1997a (1983)]) and *El cuarto mundo* (*The Fourth World* [1995 (1988)]). Each work (or set of works) initiates orientations toward the notion of the public while self-reflexively probing the question of the aesthetic, intent on teasing out its conceptual underpinnings and reverberations.

Through the juxtaposition of these works I make visible fundamental facets of historically embedded, corporeal, decolonial feminist agency: An embrace of publicness enables us to participate in practices of seduction, intimacy, and play in a manner that incorporates a self-conscious gender politics into our aesthetic actions and gestures, as I indicate in reading Borinsky's poetry. Publicness is also a terrain where all manner of love stories play out and where we may find ourselves enacting stories that don't really work for us, stories we don't even want to read or write. Institutions of art, such as literary and musical traditions, may trap us in narratives from which we want to steer clear. Historical structures of aesthetic need, desire, and demand are realities to be reckoned with in reflecting on the social functioning of art and literature and the possibilities of decolonial feminist aesthetic agency, as we observe when perusing Lispector's novel and Llosa's film. And while individuality and collectivity bear relations to each other, these relations can take different forms depending on the specific genres of aesthetic publicness that are in effect in our communities. When economic and political pressures have a heavy hand in public life in a manner that threatens to submerge us, as we learn in Llosa's movie and Eltit's novels, aesthetic publicness in all of its richness and shortcomings may just be an ambit where, following our imagination and sensibilities, we can realize and access the resources we need to embark on different subjective and collective paths—ones that open up possibilities of aesthetic flourishing, notwithstanding the barriers and procedures that stand in its way.

Through figurations of strange taste and disinterest, the four artists and writers that make up my archive probe aesthetic publicness. With Borinsky, I reflect on aspects of gendered desire that revolve around storytelling and that point to a generative form of aesthetic publicness driven by disinterested play. This practice needs to contend with the power of entrenched aesthetic politics, as I demonstrate in my reading of Lispector, which enables us to see how the lines between positions inside and outside modern aesthetic institutionality are becoming blurred and dislodged. Present-day aesthetic constituencies and publics work with and against these ambivalent and oscillating positionings to enact decolonial alternatives at a communal level, as I find in Llosa's case. While the aesthetic affordances and demands of the marketplace are a constant theme in my archive, they raise questions about technology, which, reading Eltit, I fold into my evolving reflections on current trajectories of subjectivity and collectivity. Aesthetic publicness is marked by complex entanglements between technological mediations and political and economic constellations and can be activated, responded to, tweaked, and reconfigured in multiple registers of intercorporeal existence and feminist sensibility.

My archive's conjectures about the public become visible if we read the works from a fully fledged, unabashedly aesthetic perspective, which to my knowledge has not yet been done. From this perspective, neglecting publicness is not an option. Indeed, society requires aesthetic publicness to grapple with the very concerns about differential structures of power and being that tend to lead present-day critical discourses away from the public domain in a substantive sense of the notion. In addition to building this case through my readings, I underscore the need to construct aesthetic publicness on new terms. My analyses of the different cultural productions thus highlight facets of these works that gesture toward such alternative constellations.

To clarify the philosophical grounds for this project, I give a brief overview of Hume's and Kant's basic understandings of taste and aesthetic publicness that brings out these entities' imbrications with coloniality and race and attendant forms of difference. Then I describe two contemporary takes on questions of the public that constitute further starting points for this inquiry.

Philosophical Interlocutors on Taste and the Public

How can aesthetic judgment be both a matter of the perceiver's subjective feelings and a phenomenon that permits clear-cut valorizations of some artistic oeuvres over and above others? In his essay "Of the Standard of Taste," Hume famously answers this question by centering a notion of aesthetic normativity around the figure of the ideal critic and the joint verdict of a panel of such critics (1998e, 147). Their aesthetic judgment is determinative of beauty or goodness in art. With his invocation of the ideal critic, Hume posits a general observer whose aesthetic experience is shaped by five appreciative propensities, or, in other words, marks of taste. These proclivities are delicacy of taste or imagination, freedom from prejudice, good sense, and an interpretive skillfulness honed by both practice with relevant kinds of art and a history of making aesthetic comparisons. I briefly walk through these criteria.

The first characteristic, called delicacy of taste or imagination, amounts to a sensitivity to fine feelings that, when all is good and well, indexes "clearly and distinctly" what is "universally found to please" in the field of perception (137–38, 143). Confirmation that we are on the right track in this regard can be derived from the "durable admiration" enjoyed by great works and the "rules of art" we can base on them, which guide the observer toward works of "universal" goodness or beauty, functioning as a kind of benchmark for our experience (138–39).[32] Taste, thus, is fundamentally an appreciative propensity. But this perceptual disposition needs some shaping to do its work properly, which the other four characteristics help to ensure. The second criterion of taste, freedom from prejudice, mandates judgment from the standpoint of "man in general" (145). This requirement calls for a gesture of abstraction. In Hume's words, "[W]hen any work is addressed to the public, though I should have a friendship or enmity with the author, I must depart from this situation, and, considering myself as a man in general, forget, if possible, my individual being, and my peculiar circumstances" (145). Certain "interests," such as the appreciative concerns one has "as a friend or enemy, as a rival or commentator" need to be ignored (146). In response to such biases, "[c]omprehension" must be adequately "enlarge[d]" (146). Moreover, "a proper violence" should be "imposed" on the observer's "imagination" (146). The observer is expected attain "a certain point of view," which is "conformable to that which is required by the performance" (145). In the case of works that originate in a different era or geographical location than the observer's, the observer is asked to make "allowance" for the interpretive barriers this engenders by letting go of "his natural position" and "placing himself in that point of view which the performance supposes" (145). So the second criterion explicitly foregrounds the figure of the general observer and his disinterested stance.

To proceed to Hume's third criterion, good sense concerns an interpretive or reasoning capacity, such as the ability so see the point of certain aesthetic strategies or to follow a character's thinking (146–47). In the fourth and fifth place, practice in judging art and a history of comparing the qualities of artworks with one another are required to sharpen aesthetic judgment and correctly pitch the degree of appreciation it conveys (144–45, 147). Hume allows some sources of legitimate variability in taste, but with the apparatus just laid out, he essentially provides a standard of taste or, in other words, a way of adjudicating between mutually contradictory beauty judgments, both synchronically and across time and space. Now we have a ground on which we can all agree about what is aesthetically good: The judgment of the true critics is decisive. Taste is a normatively inflected appreciative faculty for Hume. Artworks have a place in a public sphere.

Structural racial and colonial difference enters Hume's theory of taste by way of two direct paths, along with a whole array of more intricate trajectories. I consider the direct ones first. One, the criteria of practice and comparisons blatantly lock out from the realm of taste a whole group of observers who lack access to the relevant kinds of art, for these observers cannot obtain the required experiential training.[33] Two, Hume's writings are rife with dismissive remarks about the mental faculties and productive skills of different populations, such as Amerindian people, Black people, white women, and women of other races. The presumed subject of taste, accordingly, is a white, male European of the middle classes. Besides these two quite clear-cut senses in which Hume construes taste and the public domain in which it is enacted in racial and colonial terms, there are many tricky ways in which coloniality and race reverberate within the culture he envisions.[34]

To get a handle on the interlacing of race, taste, and the public Hume envisions, I want to recall a few terms that point to the depths and range of cultural practices and zones of experience in which these entanglements play out. If we enter the nitty-gritty of his theory, we find that Hume, through socially differential allocations of reason and emotional responsiveness and through conceptions of the cultural functioning of artistic, scientific, and commercial endeavors, forges distinctive webs of *aesthetic relationality*. This term, as suggested earlier, refers to patterns of aesthetically mediated relationships among people, more-than-human animals, things, and places.[35] Hume organizes these structures by way of trajectories of aesthetic racialization and racialized aestheticization and intersecting procedures such as aesthetic gendering and gendered aestheticization. These processes pervade the culture, as Hume construes it. White cultural flourishing is held out as a promise that he attaches to practices of taste. Aesthetic life aspires to whiteness, implementing processes of aesthetic racialization. Whiteness feeds aesthetic life, realizing processes of racialized aestheticization. The world where taste rules is ultimately a white one. Black cultural productions and creativity are construed as threats to this world. They are to be avoided and curtailed. Taste assists in this invidious eradication and diminishment. Aesthetic publicness is simultaneously construed on white terms, by way of white racial delineations (exemplifying racialized aestheticization), and fosters whiteness (enacting aesthetic racialization). These cultural processes fuel each other.

The intersection of aesthetics and race that results from Hume's theory is a zone of entwinements among the two processes. They forge constellations of aesthetic relationships that are institutionalized in practices of art, science, commerce, love, domesticity, national and class development, and publicness.[36] They suffuse cultural life.[37] This, in outline, is Hume's take on aesthetic publicness. Let me turn to Kant.

In theorizing the conditions of possibility for what he regards as the pure judgment of taste, Kant, in his *Critique of the Power of Judgment*, construes aesthetic experience as a mode of disinterested attention—that is, a form of perception devoid of any interest on the part of the observer in the actual existence of the item that is being perceived (Kant 2000 [1790], 90–91). Such interest, in Kant's view, links up with desire, a faculty that distinguishes people from one another (90). By rendering aesthetic experience free from interest, he characterizes it as a contemplative condition, tying it to mental faculties that human beings presumably share with one another. The examples he gives of interested states concern things we like and don't like, such as palaces or cook shops, and items we deem to be worthy or unworthy of the effort of making or imagining them (90). These instances are not altogether univocal, but Kant's point is clear enough: By essentially separating out from aesthetic experience everything that differentiates observers as the culturally situated individuals they are, he renders the experience universally accessible. The perceiver's concepts and goals are prevented from hindering this universality. Indeed, for Kant, pure judgments of taste are nonconceptual. They stay clear of purposes. They are not regular cognitions, valorizations of what is merely agreeable to the senses, or the kind of judgments of the good involved in moral verdicts (91–101). Instead, judgments of taste index what Kant describes as the free play of the faculties of imagination and cognition, capabilities that all human beings can be assumed to share (102–3). Universalizability is attained because all differentiating factors are purportedly bracketed from the beauty experience. Hence, if one of us judges a cultural object aesthetically valuable or beautiful in the manner just sketched, then everyone else has to agree (101). This is what Kant means when he says that the pure judgment of taste has subjective universal validity (100).

Kant's third *Critique* is part of an oeuvre that also includes his apparently more incidental approach to beauty and sublimity along with explicitly anthropological and geographical discourses (Kant 2011 [1764], 2012a, 2012b). In both the *Critique* and these other works, Kant, like Hume, offers comparative assessments of people's capacities for reasoning, for fine feeling, and for aesthetic apprehension. Among others, Black, Native American, Caribbean,

Asian, and Romani people of different genders, as well as white women, fall short by his measures. Taste, accordingly, is an exclusionary phenomenon. So is the public sphere where it is exercised. Not everyone can participate in the presumed universally accessible forum comprising the aesthetic public and the objects produced and received by this public. Conditions of participation reflect formations of structural social difference, belying Kant's attestations of universality.

I analyze relevant Hume and Kant passages elsewhere, and Kant's views of race have been discussed with great critical acumen by other interpreters.[38] I therefore sidestep the details, limiting myself to the observation that Kant, like Hume, theorizes pronounced patterns of aesthetic relationality, which he structures with the help of lineages of aesthetic racialization and racialized aestheticization. In sum, while voicing ideals of human equality that place humans on an equal footing as possible participants in aesthetic practices, both philosophers also develop valorizations of aesthetically produced inequality that applaud culture insofar as it exemplifies white, heterosexual masculinity of the middle classes and deprecate culture insofar as it is associated with male and female Blackness and Indigeneity as well as with, among others, Asian, Native American, and Caribbean positionalities.

While of great significance, the notions of taste and the public we inherit from the Enlightenment are fraught. How should aesthetics approach these problems? The present book aims to reclaim both taste and publicness from the Enlightenment by showing their pertinence to contemporary cultural commitments and encounters and by marking their indispensability to our capacities to deal with algorithmically perpetuated, simultaneously intensified and diluted experiential textures that we enact as inhabitants of currrent consumerist societies. This agenda, however, necessitates that we design alternative constructions of taste and publicness.

In hoping to open up novel conceptualizations of publicness, I flout certain orthodoxies in aesthetics. The current state of the discipline is divided on the question of the public. On the one hand, philosophy in various analytic and continental genres continues to rely on Enlightenment paradigms of aesthetic normativity, experience, and value. Concerns about social difference and hierarchy are kept at a distance from a basic conceptual outlook that is retained, especially with respect to questions of race, gender, and coloniality.[39] On the other hand, a good deal of postcolonial and decolonial scholarship sets aside the issue of publicness by replacing the vexed, timeworn field of aesthetics with the allegedly more salutary practice of aesthesis or, in other words, forms of imagination, emotion and perception.[40] Although these different approaches have important insights to offer, neither is adequate. The difficulties at hand call for a richer conceptual framework. This account I aim to develop through the turn to my archive.

While rejecting the tendency in postcolonial and decolonial thought to step over aesthetic publicness, I also tread in the footsteps of important work in these quarters. I specifically mention Stuart Hall's writings, which incipiently insist on the aesthetic significance of publicness. For Hall, cultural and performance spaces are among the conditions for the realization of an intersectional cultural politics that includes modes of artistic creation and reception (1996c, 467, 471, 474).[41] By revealing how identities arise in "historical and institutional sites" and observing that categories of aesthetic value are not transcendental criteria but must be seen as elements of critical social practices, he makes room for theorizations of aesthetic publicness (1996a, 4; 1996b, 446, 448). Beyond the confines of binary notions of high and low culture and oppression and liberation, Hall attests to the "ordering of different aesthetic morals, social aesthetics, the orderings of culture that open up culture to the play of power" (1996c, 469–70; 1994, 396). Hall here associates modes of aesthetic ordering with evolving power dynamics. The analytic of power and culture he elaborates also rejects binaries such as resistance and incorporation, authentic and inauthentic, experiential and formal. What is especially suggestive about his approach in light of the present inquiry is the notion of aesthetic orderings, which allows him to avoid getting caught in restrictive oppositions that hinder the scope of cultural criticism. These orderings are elements of the social ontology Hall sees in effect. Aesthetic publicness, I submit, must be counted among them.

Hall remains cryptic about what, precisely, he has in mind with the aesthetic orderings he posits. This reluctance is related to the departure that cultural studies, from the late 1960s to the late 1990s, purported to make from philosophical aesthetics. Today, however, these lines are drawn much less sharply, at least from the cultural studies side. It is timely to push the aesthetic side more forcefully in interpreting Hall. Indeed, with the notion of aesthetic orderings, I suggest, he is pointing to structures of aesthetic relationality. This includes differentiations between self and other and belonging and otherness that are stabilized by intersecting oppressions and critically contested by an intersectional cultural politics of difference (Hall 1996b, 445–46). Accordingly, Hall is alluding to a web of aesthetically mediated societal consolidations and displacements, where the mediating items include factors such as "memory, fantasy and desire," intertextual resonances, and technologies (448). The relevant relational structures are fruitfully understood in terms of a framework of aesthetic publicness. So I propose to read Hall as a major advocate of aesthetic publicness.

Because cultural analysis, as brought into being and institutionalized by Hall among other trailblazing scholars, defined itself in stark opposition to philosophical aesthetics, this line of theorization has been left undeveloped. At the current juncture, however, when cultural theory embraces vast swaths of aesthetics, it is illuminating to pursue the path the earlier epoque had shunned. It is all the more intriguing that a scholar such as Hall has been leaving spoors for later scholarship that can be usefully traced and picked up on.

My approach to the aesthetic facets of publicness and the public registers of the aesthetic finds inspiration in the work of another predecessor, whose writings cross the lines of feminist philosophy, critical studies of race and ethnicity, and cultural theory. Anzaldúa combines genres of poetry, storytelling, historiography, and essay writing to create a theoretical perspective that connects with her lived experiences in the borderlands of Mexico, white Anglo-American traditions in the US Southwest, and Nahuatl culture (1999 [1987], 23–32, 44; 2009, 190). She brings to expression hitherto unsuspected intimacies, in their nightmarish as well as joyous dimensions (19, 42, 80–83). Philosophy and art are interwoven in an approach where aesthetics is part of all facets of life—quotidian, functional, spiritual, and political (88–97). Her genre-straddling writerly strategy enters public territory through moments of self-exposure and self-fictionalization and by asking the reader to meet her texts with their own experience (1999 [1987]; 2009, 190, 196). By means of her distinctive auto-poetic mode of address, Anzaldúa intervenes into structures of aesthetic relationality. Accordingly, when she discusses racial and gender restrictions and possibilities inherent in a variety of public spaces, such as museums, classrooms, auditoriums, literary and academic writing, and public culture broadly conceived (1999 [1987], 90; 2002, 185; 2009, 190, 195; 2015, 10, 17–22, 48–49, 154), she is at once querying and rewriting registers of aesthetic publicness.

Salient vestiges of Enlightenment philosophy appear in her texts. In her renowned "Speaking in Tongues" letter, written, as the subtitle indicates, to "Third World Women Writers," on May 21, 1980, she both rejects the "distance" mandated by institutionalized writerly modes and acknowledges that writing allows her "a margin of distance" that is lifesaving (Anzaldúa 2002, 185, 188). Distance, which was so central to Enlightenment aesthetics, is decidedly problematic but can also be invaluable. There is more. A sense of universality suffuses the experience of writing when Anzaldúa is gripped by it: "And more and more when I'm alone, though still in communion with each other, the writing possesses me and propels me to leap into a timeless, spaceless no-place where I forget myself and feel I am the universe. *This* is power" (191). Difference and hierarchy somehow are suspended in the experience to be given a new form that energizes and empowers. Aesthetic experience, it seems, is sometimes characterized by a dimension of universality, not unlike the Enlightenment would have it. Even if aesthetic publicness is not directly on the table for Anzaldúa, her view of individual and social knowledge production, storytelling, and transformation, notably her notion of *conocimiento*, or an expanded, embodied form of awareness, powerfully speaks to it (2015, 117–59). Further theorization of the topic promises to expand our understanding of this poet-scholar's aesthetic and political project.[42]

Anzaldúa's philosophy of culture provides additional entries into questions of publicness. Life in the borderlands, in her account, is weighed down by oppressive cultural norms. It unfolds in regimes of normalcy on which border crossers, "*los atravesados*," infringe as they pass through and move away from "the confines of the 'normal'" (1999 [1987], 25). Living in the borderlands combines feelings of being at home with a constant presence of the strange, which attaches to an animation of a shifting awareness, of capacities that are being "activated, awakened" (19). "In the borderlands," as she puts it in a poem, "you are at home, a stranger" (216). Experience that transgresses the routines of normalization, for Anzaldúa, thus manifests itself in a tense coincidence of the familiar and the strange.[43] I see in this insight an intimation of a public aesthetic of the strange.

Intriguingly, tastes make their appearance in Anzaldúa's letter. She puts faith in the "words" that "germinate in the open mouth of the barefoot child in the midst of restive crowds" (2002, 192). She shares how a craving for an apple Danish pastry hits her just before reaching a crucial insight, getting her to drop her letter for a visit to the store. As familiar as this may sound, perhaps it is also an incursion by strange taste. After all, suffering from diabetes, she had been off sugar for three years (189). Austerity dissipates. We learn how last night's beer weighs on the day, necessitating her bribing herself into writing with pizza (190). She tells her addressees to "*write with your tongues of fire*" (192). Moreover, she wants a thunderbolt effect for her and her fellow feminists of color's texts, a moment of bewitching, incantatory strangeness: "I say mujer mágica, empty yourself. Shock yourself into new ways of perceiving the world, shock your readers into the same" (191). Deep down, there is a voice to be freed: "Find the muse within you. The voice that lies buried under you, dig it up" (192). Necessitating intimacy with the self's bodily substances, a closeness that exacts labor, that is in touch with pain, it takes "blood and pus and sweat" to touch the reader (192). In Anzaldúa's text, taste highlights the corporeality of the writing process.[44] It leans into the social differentiations that shape what is brought to expression and brings the writers' and the readers' bodies into the text and hence into the "public arena" (2015, 154). It refuses to back off from the strange. Taste, it turns out, is a part of *la facultad*, of the shifting and transformative experiential capacities of the border crosser, a sensitivity that is "excruciatingly" and at the same time "exhilarating[ly]" "alive to the world," finely attuned to distance and love (1999 [1987], 19, 60–61; 2009, 182). And it offers the reader a way to connect with this life-sustaining sensibility.

While Borges's games with identity deal quite summarily and incidentally with the body—whether this body is walking through the Buenos Aires streets, toying with hourglasses, or having coffee—Anzaldúa understands the body and its tastes as intercorporeal phenomena.[45] She feels called by taste's demands and responds to them. She also makes demands on the body herself, keeping it in line until the writing is finished and the pizza's time has come. In response to a show of Aztec art, she critically engages the embodied spectatorial position she brings to the work as a citizen of contemporary consumption society, a member of an art public (2015, 58–62). Anzaldúa theorizes Latina and Latinx bodies and the bodies of other women of color at the cross section of public and private spaces and at the point where other dichotomized polarities reveal their mutual participations in each other: mind and body, individual and society, standardization and individuality, and, yes, self and other (1999 [1987], 101–3; 2015, 6, 139–43, 151). The binary of universality and particularity, I suggest, is also among the oppositions that Anzaldúa scrambles with her aesthetics. Aesthetic publicness, from this perspective, is a site of tense potentialities that Anzaldúa reframes by rendering it a gendered, racial, and culturally situated corporeal reality and orienting it toward a more egalitarian condition conducive to the flourishing of women of color, their creative productions, and the planet—a collective, interspecies reality (1999 [1987], 72, 103; 2015, 137–38). While her theory powerfully enriches our understanding of public life, the functioning of aesthetic experiences, categories, productions, and institutions demands further conceptualization for the ways these entities shape people and societies, including the registers Anzaldúa terms *light* and *dark* (1999 [1987], 71; 2015, 10).

The present investigation, then, takes root at the junctures where postcolonial and decolonial thought meets with the ambivalent heritage of Enlightenment social and political philosophy. This terrain is marked by points of convergence that have been unnoticed or wrapped in mutual quiet. By encountering this hesitation with a strategy of philosophical inquiry that at the same time is a mode of aesthetic reading, I intend to strengthen the repertoire of conceptual options and methods we bring to contemporary culture.

Before proceeding to discuss the specifically aesthetic dimensions we have at stake in aesthetic publicness—and that will be foregrounded in this investigation—I want to reap a quick takeaway from the ensemble of approaches just outlined. Hume's and Kant's accounts and Hall's and Anzaldúa's theories trace concrete historical processes.[46] The aesthetic sensibilities and strange tastes this book features are elements of these shifting formations. This bears on the specific forms of strangeness deployed by the artists and writers who make up my archive. The strange qualities of the tastes that jump out from their works are subtle, mutinous instigators of a historical dialectic. They move in and out of evolving pairs of oppositions, such as the extraordinary and the standardized, the out-of-bent and the regular, the norm and the exception, the familiar and the exotic, home and the unhomely, the contemporary and the archaic or futural. The strange here is an operation that unsettles while also creating space for situationally, socially attuned forms of connectedness with places, such as the sites of belonging and nonbelonging we engender through the improvisatory practices Ortega calls "hometactics" (2016, 201–10) or the fluid spaces that make up Lugones's "hangouts" (2003, 220–21). The artists and writers showcased in this book employ strange tastes to realize modes of affective, sensory, and conceptual friction, affiliation, and change. The question then becomes how these modalities link up with structures of publicness.

Given the ambivalent attractions and repulsions that mark stale regimes of exoticization, as well as our mundane attachments to quotidian rites that keep things and people in their place, the strange is dreaded even when desired. Culture often turns this common element into something to be feared while brushing off the enticement. It makes us forget our commonality. Strange tastes return to remind us of our humanity. They find assistance in Sigmund Freud's uncanny. They are not just exotic but stagings of the odd, performances of the queer. They produce uneasy and unruly intimacies that shape our experience of the common, the world, ourselves. Strange tastes exercise curious critical effects, whose logic gives us pause and incites us to think, to feel at the limits of right and wrong, expediency and uselessness. So these remarkable tastes compel us to expand the bounds of what we sense as and understand by feminist and decolonial agency. The run-of-the-mill contrasts are light and dark, and juxtapositions of silence with sound, noise, music, speech, and listening. What happens when we travel from dust by way of pings and song to light? Philosophy tells a strange tale and intimates what it might be like to tell a strange tale.

Four Zones of Aesthetic Meaning

I now turn to the distinctively aesthetic phenomena to be highlighted in my archive in the following chapters. The first phenomenon is playfulness and the kinds of stories for which it casts around. Decolonial feminists value play as an experiential state that fosters travel among worlds separated by lines of oppression. As such, play is key to sustaining selves under domination. It supports coalition making. From the side of postcolonial feminisms, scholars understand play as a state that allows us to maintain in tension antithetical demands we are facing, rather than dropping one polarity in favor of an unambivalent embrace of the other.

Against the backdrop of these two approaches, chapter 1 investigates the capacities of certain kinds of play. What kinds of stories do we produce and reproduce in our games? What happens to gender and intersecting varieties of difference as we fall for certain narrations or hope finally to be done with them? How do these tales occasion freedom or states of captivity? In poems that voice questions of reading and writing, Borinsky teases out intimacies and gatherings, modes of aliveness and forms of the terrible, that skirt the constraints of commodification. Poetry here lingers in public space after the staged spectacle is over, telling tales, making up games, fancying untold endings. The aesthetic functions as a critical resource that yields designs by which we can run athwart of hierarchies of gender, race, and coloniality. In Borinsky's collection, as I show in the chapter, the aesthetic claims publicness as the site for trenchant encounters that keep alive conflict while also promising journeys to other worlds. The text's frivolous poet character incites us to imagine a kind of publicness that pushes the boundaries of literary respectability and market appeal. Floodgates open up to pleasure. Postcolonial and decolonial thought, I argue, needs aesthetic desire and fiction in a richer, more encompassing sense than it had surmised. Crossed through by disinterest, desire in the poems becomes a force of singularity and individuality. At the same time, disinterest and its accompanying condition of autonomy risk slipping into commodification and idealization. A distancing strategy of autonomous self-fashioning may well lose itself in the marketplace. I show how aesthetics can critically respond to this complication by recognizing how disinterested play and the strange tastes that embrace it awaken new intimacies in the margins of publicness, tying into open-ended forms of relationality.[47] Borinsky has us play in the dust, which becomes the ink for unusual writings, fodder for peculiar sensibilities. In reply to overly abstract postcolonial and decolonial appeals to play that end up paring down its messy realities alongside earlier philosophical approaches that, likewise, minimize its problematic workings, I offer a historicizing notion of play that is rich enough to at once push back against troubled constellations of race, gender, and coloniality and cherish its own, inexorable aesthetic situatedness and productivity. With this notion, chapter 1 reclaims disinterested play for decolonial feminism and cultural criticism. My main interlocutors, besides Borinsky, are Lugones, Spivak, and Walter Benjamin.

Disinterest is an Enlightenment asset. Yet it is given over to furtive strolls, stunningly acrobatic feats, and mesmerizing tricks of hide-and-seek that we might not have expected from a policy so devoted to distance, so insistent on holding things at arm's length, so committed to keeping at a remove from life's ordinary hubbub. Indeed, disinterest has prowled into aesthetic canons and the societal structures that uphold them, where it is now solidly implanted. It has lodged its crafty gimmicks at the core of market formations, as already suggested. After considering disinterest in connection with the exigencies of play in chapter 1, I focus on its structural functioning as a register of aesthetic publicness. This is the second kernel of aesthetic and public activity I foreground in this book. We keep playing. Disinterest is responsible for a bounteous array of aesthetic pleasures for which we look to the arts and culture. At the same time, its moral and political record is decidedly equivocal: Our games intuit ample room for playing double binds.

A key tool of Western canon formation, disinterest has served to inoculate aesthetic existence against worries about the social distribution of excellence and power. These concerns, after all, fall outside the autonomous sphere of intrinsic aesthetic value. They threaten to contaminate art's sui generis valorizations with external realities. Historical figurations of disinterest hold these heteronomous conditions at bay by pronouncing them ancillary to the sphere of artistic goodness and truth. Consequently, notions of disinterest, for several centuries, have bolstered Eurocentric canons and their attendant societal institutions, ranging from museums and performance venues to the fields of art history, cultural critique, and education. Yet, as chapter 1 makes plausible, might disinterest gain a different kind of traction when we shift aesthetic attention to societal settings that fall outside the scope of its mainstream formulations?

Incited by Lispector, let's contemplate a young, literally dirt-poor Brazilian woman who encounters her dilapidated urban surroundings with an aesthetic fascination for residual occurrences, such as the pings she hears on the radio or a creaky, rusty gate. And let's dwell on the fact that this character likes to perceive these sonic and visual items for themselves, finding pleasure in them for what they are. Our subaltern perceiver may not be undergoing the rigorously nonconceptual gratification advocated by Kant, but, analogously to the beauty feeling he commended, her viewpoint reflects a bracketing of immediate interest in a host of phenomena. They include the normalized cultural conditions that declare things such as pings and peeling paint irrelevant to the main conduct of societal affairs. Now what kind of narrative can accommodate the aesthetic pleasure that this penniless, barely literate aesthete is enjoying when she is touched to the core by the whistling of the cargo ships passing by the Rio de Janeiro docks? Here we return to the question of linguistic description and storytelling. Animating, like Borinsky, a residual zone of aesthetic practice, Lispector probes the institutional underpinnings of the literary enterprise and scrutinizes its public limits and potentialities. There is a lot of dust to go around. We continue to play with it. There also are stars. We play with them, too, at our peril.

In her final novella, *The Hour of the Star*, as I argue in chapter 2, Lispector tackles the problem of aestheticized poverty—that is, the problem of the complicity of the aesthetic in the hardships of those who barely live hand to mouth. She asks how language and literature can give expression to this imminent catastrophe without looking away from it or assisting the reader in tried and tested ploys of evasion. In reply, she engages a template of aesthetic publicness that dovetails with the Enlightenment paradigm while also reflecting its own cultural logic. By casting the story of the urban travails of her destitute protagonist Macabéa, to whose aesthetic pleasures I have alluded, in the voice of an invented male narrator, Lispector examines the gendered and class dynamics of the so-called lettered city (Franco 2002; Rama 1996 [1985]). This is a constellation of power and knowledge fostered by all manner of lettered practices that have underwritten colonialist positions of authority and modes of epistemic and political legitimation in Latin America since the conquest. Authorship and its attendant symbolic strategies are among them.

By coining the notion of the lettered city, the Uruguayan critic Ángel Rama (1996 [1985]) sought to theorize a sociocultural constellation that entwined letters with the colonial apparatus in Latin America over the previous four centuries and ongoing. This entanglement has engendered an institutionalized system of aesthetic relationality that extends its effects throughout the region. Rama documents literature's contributions to the establishment of a colonialist state order and class society rooted in the occupations of a lettered elite and the control they exercised over the fields of education, bureaucracy, politics, jurisprudence, and the military. More than the operations of a select group, however, he spots a discursive structure organized around historical forms of lettered address. The lettered city, I propose, amounts to a model of aesthetic publicness. It is a framework of aesthetic production and reception that installs capacious patterns of aesthetic relationality, address, and normativity. Rama didn't have too much to say about gender or sexuality. By giving us Macabéa and her male author, Lispector begins to address this omission and advances our understanding of both Rama's guiding conception and aesthetic publicness more broadly. The aesthetic import of her novel reaches yet further than this.

Disinterest, as I already suggested, makes a comeback through the aesthetic perceptions of Lispector's protagonist. Macabéa is a subject of taste. She enacts a decolonial form of aesthetic agency. By interlacing disinterest with a decolonial figuration of time and space, Lispector highlights capabilities of this aesthetic strategy that philosophy, so far, has left unrecognized. Beyond the frame of the proprietary middle-class preoccupations that it is presumed to negate, disinterest, it turns out, takes on roles that Enlightenment philosophers did not foresee, although they may in effect have been building on them, as becomes clear in due course. Outside the ambit of its better-known functions, disinterest, thus, displays operations that expand the repertoire of a decolonial aesthetics and that enhance the range of resources that accrue to the aesthetic, more generally.

My third nexus of aesthetic meaning centers on the collective forms that the aesthetic assumes. Songs, potatoes, and furniture have a place in aesthetic traditions. These traditions exercise callings on the members of the communities and publics that place value on them. Colonial histories of violence and extraction impact these callings. The meeting points between different cultures and different cultural segments give rise to competing demands. A decolonial aesthetics needs to develop a theoretical framework that acknowledges and gives a place to these demands. What if they conflict in a manner that deprives an Indigenous singer of the air she needs to breathe, to live? How can we account for the possibilities for agency and collectivity taking form around the tensions that are her lot?

In her second feature-length film, *The Milk of Sorrow*, which I discuss in chapter 3, Llosa engages these questions from the perspective of a confrontation between colonial Lima and a Quechua worldview beholden to Andean village life. The protagonist Fausta and her family have left the village for a sprawling informal settlement in Lima's outskirts. Indigenous norms dictate that, upon the death of her mother, Fausta bury her in the village. Owing to the conflict that has raged from the 1980s to the present between the Peruvian government and the left-populist, revolutionary movement the Shining Path, the mother suffered a trauma that Fausta ingested with the breast milk that she drank as an infant. The milk of sorrow puts the daughter on a death track. To gain the funds for burial, she takes up employment in the household of a haughty composer in the city center, who, unbeknownst to Fausta, reworks the young woman's songs into her own piano recital. For a moment it looks as if the lettered city remorselessly swallows the distraught Fausta, without suffering the slightest loss or facing any consequences for it. Nonetheless, inspired by the everyday creativity of her community, Fausta invents a way to honor her mother's body and her memory. Singing a new song, she negotiates an Indigenous aesthetic stance of her own devising, which lets her live. Her singular tastes offer her the breathing room to survive. She plays, whether in a muted register that provides solace for her agony or in a loud pitch, propelled by her curiosity, her wish to participate in her social and material surroundings.

Away from a ruinous modernity (perpetuated by the colonialist household and the concert hall) and a confining tradition (the Andean village as a site of resistance), her young town becomes an evocative site of aesthetic publicness. What looks like a grave is a makeshift pool hosting people's laughter, play, and socializing. Llosa supplants official culture and its principles of racialization and gendering by a sociality anchored in Fausta's evolving aesthetic agency and her and others' aesthetic interactions with one another around cultural artifacts, including photographs, TV shows, pool, and potatoes. Fausta answers her predicament with an aesthetics, not a preexisting identity. Tellingly, in the film's final scenes, she receives a flowering potato plant in the vicinity of two dancing children, one of whom is teaching the steps to the other. The aesthetic is key to the life of the community.

For our purposes, several particularly important insights follow. First, aesthetic publicness, I show, not only allows Fausta to tweak the tensions between worlds in accordance with her aesthetic desires but also thrives by her decolonial interventions and the path of becoming she initiates. Indeed, aesthetic publicness is a site of community building that nourishes individual aesthetic agency while, additionally, absorbing lessons from this kind of agency, lessons that it makes available to new generations, who can draw on them as they contend with their own difficulties. Second, the notion of aesthetic publicness offers a framework for theorizing the encounters among cultures and among differentially racialized cultural groups that moves away from paradigms of transculturation, magical realism, and syncretism. These latter models enjoy widespread artistic and theoretical appeal, yet they collude with the global marketplace and end up dulling and quenching strange tastes. More generally, these models elide aesthetic modalities that owe their normative and experiential contours to the evolving structural workings of aesthetic publicness, and they must be understood as such. Third, as a historically embedded propensity, strange taste offers the community a vehicle of cultural memory attuned to a changing world. Both supported by and supporting aesthetic publicness, strange taste embodies a stance that can meet adversity with a trajectory of growth, play, and pleasure rather than primarily destruction, suffering, and withdrawal from life, which would ultimately result in individual and collective collapse.

My fourth and last set of aesthetic considerations revolves around the historical, symbolic, and material underpinnings of trajectories of subjectivity and modes of cultural gathering. In a society awash with technology, where imaginaries and taste often lock into the marketplace, apparently unmoored from the public apparatuses that since the Enlightenment have undergirded forms of creation and identification, it is easy to lose sight of aesthetic publicness. Nonetheless, loops between the aesthetic and the public channel crucial societal lineages in which art and capital, literature and neoliberal entrepreneurship, history and presentism attain reciprocal orientations toward one another. Philosophy needs to develop conceptual frames that acknowledge these routings. To this end it can build on Plato's cautions about itinerant discursive ventures and critical theory's concerns about exploitation and rootlessness. But the aesthetic side of the matter remains insufficiently articulated. While the demands of market rationality are a constant preoccupation in the archive under discussion, chapter 4 places this concern front and center.

At issue are the reverberations of finance and venture capitalism for dynamics of subjectivation and formations of collectivity. The status of literature is in doubt. Is this art form conscripted into symbolic regimes perpetuated by a technologically dominated corporatism hell-bent on overtaking what remains of the Enlightenment public sphere and the lettered city? Or do literature and adjacent artistic endeavors hold out aesthetic and political potentialities that escape consumerist principles and the lure of the latest technological advances?

Chapter 4 addresses these questions from the perspective of two novels by Diamela Eltit that were published during the Pinochet dictatorship. Both *E. Luminata* and *The Fourth World* carry out what philosophy calls a thought experiment. They raise the specter of all-out technologically dominated neoliberal control over the society and incite the reader to critically reflect on this condition. Eltit's thought experiment resonates with an actual socioeconomic experiment that was being carried out to devastating effect at the time of the novel's writing. As many have documented, Chile of the 1970s and 1980s served as a testing ground for neoliberal policies. At massive human cost, the country's trial run laid the ground for significant social and economic overhauling worldwide in subsequent decades. Eltit's polysemous texts engage this overwhelming historical reality, which not only continues to stir right-wing militant zeal in the region but also keeps tearing at deep wounds incurred by survivors and subsequent generations.[48]

We currently live in an era of democratic backsliding. Autocracies and right-wing populisms battling to destroy civic institutions they take advantage of are enjoying a heyday in many countries. These developments are tied up with an explosive ascendance of technologies that generate content that is disassociated from its societal contexts and local modes of production. Aesthetics is barely beginning to reckon with these developments. Eltit's novels speak to them by offering us images of a hegemonic marketplace that reduces language, literature, the cinema, and other symbolic forms to free-floating corporate input and output. Consumerism consumes all and everything. Discourses become evanescent flashes that light up for an instant before disappearing. In a prescient fashion, the two texts bring to a climax long-standing tensions that have only intensified today. They lay out in stark outline choices we have knowingly or unknowingly been making. Yet they are experimental thought images, not realistic documents. They ingeniously make the reader aware of facets of aesthetic life that elude their own guiding premises, inspiring us to take a close look at aesthetic historicity and, more than that, to recall a tradition that champions the agora and light as pillars of democratization.

In *E. Luminata*, her first novel, Eltit literalizes the notion of enlightenment through the image of an advertising sign that casts its projections over the people gathered in a public square in Santiago. The sign endows the Chilean people with an identity in the global marketplace, construing them as a colonial aftereffect and heralding society's total governance by a neoliberal world system. However, through strategies such as counterstatements and temporal disjunctions, the text also makes visible an alternative form of aesthetic agency. Eltit's later novel, *The Fourth World*, develops this approach further by countering a global process of relentless accumulation with critical figurations of taste, race, sexuality, and nation. By juxtaposing Enlightenment constructions of taste and the public with aesthetic readings of crucial aspects of Eltit's two texts, I argue for the importance of aesthetic publicness and agency and signal ways in which we can construct these notions on new terms.

Eltit's metaphors of light and the public plaza recall moments in *The Hour of the Star*, placing her residual characters and their experiences in conversation with Lispector's marginalized protagonist and her aesthetic pleasures. Satirically reimagined, the Enlightenment public sphere and the lettered city disclose their corporeal commitments. Showcasing the previously banished subaltern female body—indeed, celebrating their historical other—these formations can also animate along fresh lines the people's powers of gathering and self-fashioning. Storytelling, far from running out of steam or being doomed to reiterate already known tales, reveals its vitality to pressing questions of our era. In close touch with conditioning factors such as the square, literature and the other arts well exceed their roles as fodder for market designs, search engines, and generative AI bots. The notion of aesthetic publicness sheds light on the aesthetic workings and situatedness of the materials, objects, and content that populate public spaces. It enables us to find in a vibrant sense of aesthetic connectedness an answer to the profound loss of belonging, the slippage of roots and home, experienced on a large scale today, an existential phenomenon that Hannah Arendt in a different context associated with the rise of totalitarianism. Aesthetic publicness, further, concerns the structural underpinnings of aesthetic experience and interaction. Enlightenment philosophers saw this point clearly. Eltit joins their ranks in this regard. She is not alone. As I indicate in the conclusion, a whole range of contemporary artists and writers across different media and genres, champion aesthetic publicness in efforts to rethink the institutional frames in which social existence unfolds, from the house, the plaza, and the concert hall to the milonga and the nation.

The artists and writers in my archive build on contingent relationalities that they give form around the tropes of dust, light, song, and pings. While the first two figures engender a play between counterpoints of idealization and destruction or dissolution, ethereality and the residual, the latter two connote unstable points of, on the one hand, entry into modernity and, on the other, a banishment from or a rebuffing and redoing of these structures. The four items constitute material and figurative nodes in a contemporary critical and imaginative engagement with Enlightenment constructions of subjectivity and publicness. With its extolment of light, as Latinx feminists and other theorists of color have recognized, the Enlightenment posited a darkness, an obscurity, and a messiness that it sought to dispel yet that didn't cease to intrigue. By unsettling the relations between light and dust, we can move with and through the Enlightenment to actualize different aesthetic and social potentialities. While other figures might have been selected, the ones I have chosen articulate a dynamic of idealization and dismissal/repudiation that sheds light on the way in which we experience modernity's contradictions as well as the tensions inherent in projects of critique and revisioning. The four elements sustain an ongoing relational engagement that employs but also goes beyond strata of negative dialectics, to give expression to the manifold, concrete experiential contents and lived concepts that we bring into being through a playful encounter with dust, light, song, and pings and their many analogues.

Cumulatively, the zones of concentrated aesthetic investment this book explores put the aesthetic to the test in domains where, in ever changing colors and forms, it conjures pleasures that entice and impel. Strange tastes and other aesthetic sensibilities run the gamut between the exceptional and the ordinary, the unusual and the routine, without allowing themselves to be caught on either side of these oppositions. Storytelling, disinterested attention, and adjacent subjective and collective aesthetic capacities work their spells to summon into being feminist and decolonial lifeworlds. Key philosophical concepts reveal unsuspected collaborations: Strange taste carries disinterested attention into the territory of aesthetic publicness, enlisting disinterest's energies in support of a vibrant communal existence. Institution-altering shifts come to light in structures of aesthetic relationality.

We play with the stars; we play in the dust. We play with muted hues; we play in loud tonalities. As our four writers and artists enable us to see, the aesthetic, when juggled in certain ways, beckons with a calling: Let's reenchant public inhabitance, and here's how we're going about it.

1

Dust

A Sniff of Getting Together

Aesthetics gives us a place, a time, and materials for play: play with forms, play that invents concepts, play that acts out imaginaries. And it beckons with the allure of fun and games—from imposed to illicit ones, from furtive diversions to rituals that seek the spotlight, from collective fantasies promoted by corporations to residual creations that are too laborious and involved to be of use to anyone besides ourselves. For there are games that, really, only we can play, gambles on life that sustain the contours of a unique way of being us.

What sorts of stories do we welcome into our play? And what sorts of stories might we want to tell about these stories? What does play look like if it absorbs these latter stories, too? This chapter considers play from the angle of the stories it embodies or declines to absorb. I show how narrations seek out strange tastes and other aesthetic sensibilities as a way of enacting our singularity. In this fashion, they give life, personhood, a distinct if transient, form. And while stories and the play they suffuse individualize their creators, they also unfold us in shifting ways in an inextinguishable sociality. Indeed, narration realizes its intimacies in public territory, making this terrain habitable on new terms for the protagonists of play, the tellers of stories.

The conceptual trajectory I design around play and stories extends to our singular cares and concerns and to moments of individuality. I trace out stretches of experience and interaction where we actualize a certain autonomy. With the notion of autonomy, I have in mind a relative condition. This state arises within an ineradicable ontological relationality that renders us vulnerable to one another, albeit in different ways, to different degrees, and with different moral and political implications. My intention is not to reinstall the figure of the sovereign actor who assumes his position in public while sequestering his sustaining dependencies in a private realm. By contrast, I call attention to freedoms that we can and do exercise as inhabitants of fields of intercorporeal engagement. I also wish to invoke the aesthetic dimension of the exposure that, as feminist scholars and critical theorists of race have demonstrated, fundamentally characterizes our lives as bodily creatures. What philosophy has not yet sufficiently accounted for is that this exposure, crucially, takes aesthetic forms, weaving aesthetic norms and values fundamentally into our relational being. The term *aesthetic relationality* denotes this state of interwovenness. Aesthetic sensibility and taste shape the textures of our intercorporeal entwinements. Accordingly, we can work these propensities to forge positions and orientations in this relational fabric. In doing so, we can achieve relative autonomy. Indeed, we can initiate freedoms that become junctures to which we aspire, instances to which we attach. We hold on to them as individual and collective points of identification and address. Of course, the search for elements of freedom involves immersion in practices of unfreedom, as well, and an engagement with forces of restriction and confinement. This, then, is the terrain I plan to chart in this chapter. My principal theoretical interlocutors are María Lugones, Gayatri Chakravorty Spivak, and Walter Benjamin.

Autonomy and freedom tie into strategies of disinterest in the conceptual trajectory I lay out. Accordingly, we enter a philosophical tradition elaborated by thinkers such as David Hume, Immanuel Kant, G. W. F. Hegel, and Friedrich Schiller, which historically has put forth aesthetic figurations of play and freedom, of autonomy and disinterest. At issue is the question of what this conceptual constellation currently has going for it in the aesthetic realm. As noted in the introduction, I associate the aesthetic with a resonant web of relationships that lie at the core of who we are as individuals and a society. What do the four concepts just mentioned have to offer a relational view of the aesthetic? What do these threadbare notions look like in the context of practices that are immanent in day-to-day imaginative and sensory existence? And how do these raggedy conceptions speak to current cultural and economic arrangements, where aesthetic feeling and action inevitably imbricate us in the marketplace? As the reader will have noticed, we have started to play in the dust. So let's see what comes of that play.

Dust may be what the body becomes when a person's life gives out, but as the Argentine-born poet and fiction writer Alicia Borinsky reminds us, such residual materials are also the stuff of which play is made. In her bilingual poetry collection *Frivolous Women and Other Sinners / Frívolas y pecadoras* (2009), dust provides the ink for a new kind of storytelling.[1] The unnamed protagonist of "el espectáculo empieza cuando usted llega / the show starts when you arrive" (62–63) scoops it up "beneath the seats" of the theater when the performance has ended. In her and her friends' perception, it's not the staged production but the acts following in its tail that strike the desired tone. This understanding lures them back into the theater when the official happening is over. The tone is downright insulting. It is unabashedly arrogant. It demands a public setting. With her insolent games, Borinsky's protagonist rethinks the strategies of play through which contemporary critical theorists seek to reckon with an enduring colonial legacy.

The philosopher María Lugones and cultural theorist Gayatri Spivak both hold that play fulfills pivotal roles in the process of decolonizing culture. Notwithstanding the substantial theoretical differences separating a decolonial thinker steeped in contemporary analytical philosophy from a postcolonial critic drawing on poststructuralism and Marxism, the two feminist scholars share an understanding of play that regards it as a central component of societal movements toward formations of critical collectivity. Both theorists invoke aesthetic terminology in their accounts of play, such as the notion of beauty. They engage aesthetic theory—notably, Schiller's views in Spivak's case and Johan Huizinga's and Arthur Danto's ideas in Lugones's. Lugones and Spivak make important contributions to a present-day aesthetic revalorization of play. At the same time, art and aesthetics point up dimensions of play that require further theorization. By juxtaposing Lugones's and Spivak's approaches with the conceptions of play found in Borinsky's collection along with Benjamin's writings, this chapter advances our understanding of play's significance as a component of a decolonial feminist aesthetics. Play, I show, engenders a form of intimacy that summons selves and others and fulfills distinctly public roles. While my observations are not meant to cover all kinds of play, they signal an important cultural capacity that artists deploy to negotiate current cultural conditions. In particular, my analysis spotlights ways in which we can reclaim play from the global marketplace and other institutional forces that threaten to curtail its critical resourcefulness and clamp down on the space for decolonial feminist agency.

Play as a Device of a Decolonial Feminism

According to Lugones, playfulness is a dimension of an attitude and, more than that, of a pattern of social and material interactions that fosters oppositional coalitions in defiance of barriers forged by social difference (Lugones 2003, 26–27, 41, 91–99). It involves imagination, surprise, and an openness to uncertainty and risk. It inspires "world" traveling—that is, the crossing of worlds of sense separated by forms of oppression (26). By *worlds of sense*, she refers to lived constructions of society and life, or what phenomenologists would term *lifeworlds*—that is, worlds of experience. Lugones declines to offer a strict definition of such worlds. She substantiates the notion primarily through philosophical exploration of everyday occurrences and testimonial narratives, including her own, which bear out how people divided along lines of gender, race, coloniality, class, and sexuality, inhabit different worlds.[2] Play assists in the practice of crossing the boundaries between these worlds, a task that overwhelmingly falls to people of color and other individuals subjected to oppression, who are often compelled to travel from subalternized worlds of sense to dominant worlds (17). In facilitating this travel, play is a life-sustaining and life-fostering capacity. Crucially, it nourishes world traveling across barriers of sense that separate people who undergo different forms of oppression and resist such oppression in ways that are specific to their positionalities. An important tenet of Lugones's view of communication is that meaning is opaque across worlds of sense (25; 2006, 83–84). Play is a way of handling these opacities. It implies a surrendering of established ground in favor of an immersion in worlds that are not transparently legible to the self. Lugones thus insists on play's epistemic and corporeal centrality to the building of coalitions that supersede socially enforced groupings based on categories such as gender and race. It is a tool of social connectedness and possibility in a substantially opaque field of meaning and practice.

Play also gains a prominent existential role in Lugones's account of resistance to oppression. It feeds tenderness and love. It spreads throughout far-reaching webs of meaning, relationality, and address (Lugones 2003, 32–33). In this capacity, play is a device through which subaltern subjects navigate multiplicity. With the notion of multiplicity, Lugones essentially indicates that people of color, people who are nonnormatively gendered, and women—to name identities that intersect or, in her terms, "intermesh" with one another—are not exhausted by oppression or by oppressive notions of their positionalities (3, 93). We are always more than what oppression makes of us (97–98). Play is a strategy through which we inhabit this multiplicity. It is a practice that makes possible the multiple subject's enactment (and exposure to others) of her multidimensionality (41, 93).

Various anecdotes Lugones offers about smashing stones, kids' rooftop activities, and maternal gambits with vases and tureens, along with her own, authorial improvisations on metamorphosing tongues across various chapters—tongues that metaphorically travel from people to people, where they enact different kinds of verbal performances and erotic/sexual activities—highlight additional elements of play.[3] These narrative fragments and interventions make visible dimensions of delight, enjoyment, and humor that play can involve. They are instances where philosophy brushes up on its own playful capacities, drawing the reader in and inviting her to linger in the epistemic and connective resources of play. The reader notices facets of creativity, which are a hallmark of play for Lugones (96). These stories and strategies also point to play's often mischievous and potentially rebellious aspects. Resistance, in the mode of play, can be a lot of fun. This, clearly, doesn't mean play is not serious or profound or would be, as Lugones puts it, "frivolous" (26, 33). To the contrary: Play's humorous dimension plausibly signals quite intricate, subtle kinds of engagement.[4] Employing a phrase that stresses the corporeal and intersubjective aspects of playing, Lugones speaks of the "nuances [in the] face" that it can engender (32).[5] Play amplifies the ambit of relational possibility for bodies that encounter one another face-to-face. Playfulness can advance the world traveler's ability to handle the perils and unpredictabilities inherent in the borderlands she traverses (27, 32–33). Writes Lugones, "A playful attitude is a good companion to fear; it keeps one focused on the crossing, on the process of metamorphosis" (27).

Read through the lenses of philosophical aesthetics, Lugones invokes a conception of play that is unconfined by any orientation toward an end or goal. In line with scholars such as Huizinga (1949) and Hans-Georg Gadamer (2000, 103–107, 113), she regards it as a phenomenon that is dissociated from immediate use. One of the anecdotes makes this evident. Lugones and an unnamed "you" are throwing gray stones onto a bedrock of other gray stones. When the stones hit the ground, they break open to reveal luminescent colors. The two go on for hours with this activity, which obeys no rules. There is uncertainty. The players are creating a beautiful spectacle, whose pleasures and thrill are in the doing, in the gazing, and, I suppose, in the sharing. The companions are "*open to self-construction*" (Lugones, 2003, 96). Building on this story, Lugones points out that a playful attitude involves an openness to "construction or re-construction of the 'worlds' we inhabit playfully, and thus openness to risk the ground" underlying conceptions of self and others "as oppressors or oppressed" and in line with domination (96). This dimension of openness, a letting go of given ground, is the feature of play that is responsible for its border crossing, coalitional powers. Playing is an epistemic, existential, and political means of inhabiting liminal zones. As such it is useful, to be sure.[6]

However, the value of the activity being found in no purpose or consideration other than its very practice itself, aestheticians here will spot the telltale marks of a nonteleological notion of play. Lugones's play, like the modes privileged by Huizinga and Gadamer, is disinterested. She employs disinterested play to free up zones of female creativity that have been foiled and censored (Lorde 1984; Rich 1980, 638–40) and to release their collective energies, liberating them from aesthetic regimes of devalorization.

For Lugones, play is a crucial cultural technology. The practice is key to the realization of a more just and equitable society. It is a phenomenologically pivotal source of queer, feminist ingenuity and a decolonial field of experience. How, exactly, does her theory of playful world traveling speak to aesthetic life—this vast field of existence that is so intently invested in the wonders and delights of play? For many centuries, art and aesthetics have scrutinized the powers of play in the arena of the imagination and the realm of societal and political freedom. Several of Lugones's concepts resonate with these lineages. Let's see how her account fares in aesthetic territory, where contemporary artists address questions of creativity and reading that implicate registers of social difference. Indeed, Borinsky's poetry engages intricate gendered and colonial constellations through various playful ploys and mobilizes remarkable strategies of play. Reading her collection in an aesthetic light, I want to meet these poetic designs with the philosophical question: What is it to play? In reply, her texts bring out distinctive angles on play's capabilities, as facets of both ordinary and extraordinary sensibilities. It is to her poetry that I turn.

Play's Treacherous Side

Many of the poems that make up *Frivolous Women* are about the possibilities of reading, writing, and play. The old stories in which the imprisoned princess awaits the liberating kiss of the dashing prince won't do anymore. Poetry, imagined in "poética / on poetry" (Borinsky 2009, 36–37) as a languid seductress whose charms spell distress, is a capricious being:

> she's told us lie after lie
> involved me in her crimes
> managed to imprison me

Poetry's quirky games are not to be trusted. She ensnares the reader in the sham. In "final del juego / end of the game" (40–41), which is titled after a Julio Cortázar story, literature has passed on its deceitfulness to the credulous reader, a young girl referred to as "she" by the first-person poet-narrator:

> she lies when she tells you she was there when sleeping beauty
> woke up and that she herself attended snowwhite's wedding
>   she lies
> she's a girl
>   forlorn girl who only wants to play

Play mires the girl in lies. Aesthetics points up an aspect of play that Lugones elides. Taking note of the gendered dimensions of playful practices embedded in various artistic canons, one realizes that Lugones's conception of play is an idealization. Downplaying play's treacherous side, she sanitizes its social functioning, reaping its feminist effects too rapidly. The oppressive gender and sexual dimensions of play need further probing.

Borinsky's narrator has some creative plans for her clueless reader:

> I've already prepared her apple
> shiny red
> I'll give it to her tomorrow with a smile
> a pirouette and the key to her cell

Is the girl going to use her gifts to lock herself up? Or is she going to pull herself together to venture an escape? Will she smile and dance like the narrator or lie down and wait in captivity for her knockout suitor? The game isn't over just yet. Play carries on. That certainly is the choice of the narrator, who is performing the part of the evil stepmother.[7] She is a mistress of dissimulation. She sides unabashedly with poetry's cravings, whose transformative vitality displays its erotic, feminized irresistibility in the stanza that opens "on poetry":

> disdainful
> sloth
> femme fatale
> vulgar
> her intuitive appetites send us to another world

Poetry is a practice of world traveling. It desires and engulfs the reader in desire. We go where it sends us. But this travel is not solely invested with the salutary effects Lugones attaches to it.[8] Let's continue with "on poetry" and read its closing stanza beyond the lines quoted at the start of this section:

she's told us lie after lie
involved me in her crimes
managed to imprison me
and now arrogant tries another carnival
suggests to me escape voyages around the world in this
room filled with strident murmurs
                                        claptrap

Poetry's response to its own lies is not to stop lying and retreat in silence. It keeps pursuing the turns of its desire, "her intuitive appetites" ("apetitos clarividentes"), giving expression to its clear and more-than-clear perceptions. The poet refuses to be a demure or disoriented reader of past stories—the "forlorn girl" of "end of the game." By the same token, she declines to be outdone by a militant noisiness that, although failing to make sense, dominates the mediascape. Amid these alternatives, the poet is a reader and writer who comes up with her own kind of game. Spurning the "stories of rescued princesses" with which the girl has "fooled us," the frivolous poet of Borinsky's collection tells a story of which the young woman hasn't heard the likes.

Lugones, I have suggested, steps over the power of play to confine us within old narratives of heterosexual bliss. Her notion of play lacks the critical resources that would enable it to shrug off the captivating hold that mainstream stories have over the girl in "end of the game."[9] Borinsky explores the dual senses of this aesthetic captivation, which interweaves enthrallment and entrapment. The princess tales on which the girl has staked her pleasures revolve around gender-conforming female characters who timidly await the initiatives of spiffy, male, heterosexual, cisgendered heroes, who actively move about and travel. Lugones's conception of the playful attitude locks into canonical formations of art and culture, reiterating codes enshrined in social institutions. The girl is playing but her game is not the epistemically and socially transgressive activity advocated by Lugones.

The poet-narrator, as the title suggests, may be pronouncing the end of the literary gamble, that complicit, fraught wager that holds the girl down, perhaps keeps her forever "young." However, the narrator herself is playing another game. Her gambit leaves it open whether the evil stepmother persona she enacts is in turn pulling the wool over the girl's eyes. Play, then, is an ambivalent phenomenon. While taking part in it, we are not sure which side we are on. In one sense, we side with the gendered cultural codes that we are playing with. But other sides likely emerge in this play, for it spills into its surrounding world in a manner awash with indeterminacy, contingent as it is on a profusion of reverberations that issue within concrete contexts of aesthetic production and reception. Borinsky's poem immerses its reader in this well of indefiniteness and its concomitant uncertainties. This state of being and experience is an inexorable component of participation in institutionalized cultural constellations.

Play's Ambivalence

In Borinsky's poetry, as I have indicated, play carries antithetical tendencies that resist tidying. A thickly knotted texture of contradictory forces is also the focus of Spivak's (2012) theory of play, which traces this dynamic to Schiller's (1967) account of the play drive. With that notion, he refers to a culturally honed capacity that bridges the opposing realms of reason and emotion or sensation. Attuned to beauty, which it also fosters, the play drive instigates a process of aesthetic cultivation that culminates in an allegedly egalitarian and democratic society. Spivak's appeal to play resonates with an involved tradition of aesthetic and political thought. Her intent is to update Schiller for our contemporary era. Following explicitly in his conceptual and pedagogical footsteps, she observes that the current epoch of capitalist development necessitates "play training," conceived on the model of an aesthetic education (Spivak 2012, 5). Her turn to play and the aesthetic are part of her retooling, for present-day purposes, of Kantian and Schillerian frameworks. Indeed, she sets out to "ab-use" the European Enlightenment. The aim is to "sabotage" Schiller (2–4).

In a gesture that picks and chooses from Kant as well as Schiller, Spivak theorizes play as a function of the imagination. The imagination, she notes, can shake up epistemic habits and achieve a break within entrenched arrangements of desire (10). Accordingly, play serves for Spivak as an antidote to the intertwined gendered, racialized, and class inequalities fostered by global capitalism to which we bear double binds—at once epistemic, affective, and political. In short, play constitutes an imaginative readerly/interpretive engagement with the contrastive ethical, political, and epistemic commitments and investments that characterize existence in twenty-first-century information society.

The task Spivak discerns here is literally to gain "the skill of playing the double bind" or, in other words, to learn "to live with contradictory instructions" (3). Drawing on Gregory Bateson, she observes that such double binds are all around us, in all territories of action, thought, and reflexivity: "Contradictory instructions come to us at all times. We learn to listen to them and remain in the game" (10–11). Gender is part of this game of juggling conflicting demands without end. As she points out, "[A] gendered access to the Enlightenment, which was often a way out of indigenous gendering, is doubled over a double bind" (11). Spivak, it appears, sketches her notion of double binds in deliberately general terms. In this fashion, she is able to accommodate a variety of mutually countervailing motivational pulls and exigencies. Through play, we handle and give form to a whole web of overlaying double binds.

As another instance of the double binds Spivak has in mind, she discusses opposing attitudes of hope and doubt about the directions contemporary culture is taking. The overall aim of her argument being the goal of understanding and dismantling the progressing machinery of capitalism, she zeroes in on the antitheses between complicity with the marketplace and the realization of critical breaks with systems of commodification and electronically regulated information processing. These stances dovetail in her account with attachments we bear to pragmatic, goal-oriented thought, on the one hand, and noninstrumental rationality, on the other. From her reconstructed Schiller, she adopts the idea that an imaginative, nonteleological playing of the double binds we maintain as participants in the data-saturated global marketplace can incite ethically and politically necessary epistemic changes and engender shifting structures of desire. With the image of wasting time—in particular, wasting time "to parse the desires (not the needs) of collective examples of subalternity" (34)—she provides a metaphor for self-displacing trajectories of "destinerrancy" (28) and "entering another's text" (6) that she associates with this crucial kind of play, which is the sine qua non of the humanities in an epoch when they face devastating economic cramping and minimization. In Spivak's view, we need to keep inhabiting double binds at the level of reading and experience. As necessary supports of epistemic and political change, these double binds then undergo dissolution in the plane of decision making and action (11, 18). At these moments when we briefly put an end to the game, to speak with Borinsky and Cortázar, we cut through indeterminacy to act in the world. In this way, an aesthetic education feeds into politics.[10]

Spivak provides a theoretical frame for acknowledging the ambivalences of play highlighted by Borinsky's poems. While Lugones (2003, 96) at one point affirms play's ambivalence to subsequently leave it aside in her account of its actual societal functioning, Spivak usefully dwells on and amplifies this aspect. To get a clearer grasp on both Lugones's and Spivak's notions of play, I want to take a closer look at their appeals to aesthetics. Thus, I bring to light parallels between their views. Moreover, I signal points at which further inquiry is needed to advance our understanding of play in its at once intimate, individualizing, and public potentialities.

Spivak's and Lugones's Aesthetics of Play: Parallels, Limitations

Although Spivak and Lugones draw on divergent philosophical and artistic heritages, their outlooks reveal undeniable commonalities when we attend to the extensive swathes of aesthetic territory they each invoke. Both theorists connect play along analogous lines with aesthetic dimensions of life while rendering these links in a more or less implicit manner. Perhaps most centrally, they associate play with practices of reading or, in other words, aesthetic interpretation (Lugones 2003, 12–14, 226, 229, 219; Spivak 2012, 6, 10–12, 34). Further, by investigating aspects of the organization of sensory, affective, and imaginative existence, they tread fundamentally aesthetic territory, albeit in largely indirect fashion (Lugones 2003, 3, 77–78, 84, 116–17, 215; Spivak 2012, 2, 34, 72). They consider our intercorporeal movements through space. Attention is paid to the functioning of objects such as stones, vases, cars, and trains. Spivak and Lugones describe moments of beauty, grandeur, the spectacular, the monumental, the grotesque, and the diminutive. They signal dynamics of commodification, consumption, production, exchange, and social performance under capitalist modernity, thus broaching major complexities at the intersection of aesthetics and politics (Lugones 2003, 19, 74, 81, 95, 157, 207–10, 214; Lugones 2007; Spivak 2012, 2, 63, 69–72). Play, for them, takes effect in a social field shaped by aesthetic categories and structures. The two scholars differ on the way in which they take play to be nestled in this field. Nonetheless, they set important, partially overlapping goals for an aesthetic theory of play, aspirations that I heed in the discussion that follows.

Borinsky's poetry and Spivak's postcolonial vision, I have argued, set stock by play as a dimension of feminist critical agency. In this poet's and this scholar's work alike, play is a means through which we navigate mutually opposing forces and ambivalent subjective impulses and stances. It effects epistemic, political, and aesthetic ruptures with established social delineations that revolve around intersecting racial, class, and gender constellations. We are now in a position to offer a reply to my objection that Lugones idealizes play. I suggest that we modify her notion of play in light of her enduring emphasis on the entanglement of subjugation and resistance. With the concept of "oppressing↔resisting," she gives expression to a strained interlacing of various kinds of domination with the manifold oppositional strategies through which relational actors challenge domination (Lugones 2003, 11–13, 208). Lugones sketches practices of nontransparent opposition that enact trajectories from "I→we" (226–29). Epistemic opacity, in this context, demands complex communication practices and other relational tactics that she outlines through key notions for which she is known, such as active subjectivity, world traveling, superimposed forms of address to different audiences, and hanging out (2003, 2006). While the details of these practices exceed the scope of this chapter, what matters for our purposes is that Spivak's notion of double binds resonates deeply with a fundamental tenet of Lugones's: The social field in which subjectivity and collectivity take aesthetically inflected forms is a field of tense multiplicities.[11] By rendering these tense multiplicities internal to play, we can give a place to the facet of idealization I have pinpointed. A view of play as an emphatically double-edged, polyvalent phenomenon does not undermine Lugones's account of world traveling but broadens it to encompass play's treacherous side as exposed by Borinsky, rather than eliding it by reverting to a tidied and thinned understanding of an involved, multidimensional practice. I thus propose to work with my adjusted rendering of Lugones's notion of play, which fits her overall philosophy better than the idealized conception formulated through her explicit remarks on the topic. Meanwhile, the aesthetic line of inquiry we have followed has brought to light previously unsuspected parallels between Lugones's decolonial stance and Spivak's postcolonial approach. These positions prove to be closer than they appear to be at first glance. Let's carry on just a bit further along this path of aesthetic questioning in relation to both theories and see where it takes us.

So far I have used Borinsky's poems and Spivak's views to rethink and amplify Lugones's notion of play. Spivak's perspective is important in that it challenges us to reckon with play's ambivalent aspects. Nevertheless, it falls short for aesthetic purposes. Two sets of limitations are particularly salient. First, her understanding of an aesthetic education fueled by play rides on Paul de Man's fragmentary interpretation of Schiller, which regards Schiller's aesthetics as emblematic of aesthetic ideology, a case of being taken in uncritically by language's symbolic functioning.[12] Through this generic move, Spivak builds her account around an overall anti-aesthetic model of cultural analysis that she in some respects repudiates. However, this model overshoots its mark. It downplays the ethical, societal, and political productivity of the aesthetic, thus hamstringing cultural criticism. Second, her conception of moving out of the aesthetic game to make effects in the world needs further substantiation. Much more is going on in the transition from disinterested play to decisive action than her rudimentary remarks suggest. Experiential, social, and political complexities slip away from the bare-bones ethical dilemmas she outlines. Aesthetic culture is a field in which games imply forms of action, a reality that gains no foothold in her account due to the binary between disinterested attention and pragmatic interest that informs her interpretation of the shift toward political agency.[13] Spivak's aesthetic theory is too schematic. More generally, the aesthetic specificities of processes of epistemic and political transformation surpass what can be captured by reference to the notions of aesthetic experience, change, and action that she adumbrates in terms of the practice of playing double binds and the critical powers of imaginative reading. Her turn to aesthetics hurtles past significant aesthetic resources, hiatuses, and linkages.

An analogous problem marks Lugones's appeal to aesthetics. By extrapolating from her remarks on play and integrating them with other components of her theory, I have offered a reading on which her view can acknowledge play's hazardous side. My interpretation yields an abstract way of accommodating potentially invidious aspects of play. Yet this approach doesn't yet adequately address the experiential field in which idealization takes effect. The problem of idealization arises in the phenomenological plane of day-to-day aesthetic life. To develop a response at this level, it is important to note that playfulness embodies a whole array of aesthetic norms and forms. Furthermore, playfulness activates all manner of narrations, including the restrictive gender parables that seem to be to the liking of Borinsky's young girl and that have percolated to the corners of the society she frequents. These kinds of aesthetic and narrative elements, which we energize and handle when we are at play, call for further attention. The stories Lugones so wonderfully and inspiringly connects with the practice of playful world travel are too one-sided for aesthetic purposes, casting a phenomenon that in many ways is ambivalent in an overall favorable light. Like Spivak, Lugones thus sprints past aesthetic complexities that bear on play's ties to political action. These complexities also characterize play's contributions to the creation of affiliations across categories of difference and to the forging of grounds for coalitional alignments, projects that belong to the core ambitions of Lugones's view of playful world traveling. Both theorists thus shy away from some of the more concrete textures of aesthetic life.[14] And by sidestepping aesthetic intricacies, they also overlook moral and political tendencies. Cultural resources go unheeded that we use for better or worse. We ignore forces that keep us beholden to stifling tales.

Likewise, we neglect impulses that lead us toward more unencumbered, freeing narrations.

Philosophy needs to reflect further where Spivak's and Lugones's vital yet, for aesthetic purposes, relatively abstract accounts of play leave off. To do this, I focus on the activities of Borinsky's frivolous poet. As it happens, this character is superbly adept at the kinds of playful readerly and writerly wanderings Spivak commends—her "destinerrancy." Simultaneously, the frivolous poet spreads her ingenious crafts and bold tastes to the liminal zones where Lugones detects the stomping grounds of the world traveler.

Finding Play's Freedoms

In Borinsky's collection, as I have indicated, the game goes on, with poetry in the business of plotting "crimes" and getting the reader caught up in them. What are these crimes? The poem "por qué lee y escribe / why does she read and write" (2009, 84–85) offers hints:

> everybody has told her that nothing is free
> but she keeps asking for loans
>
> you all know
>   she's in debt

Addressing "you all" ("ustedes") as representatives of "everybody," the narrator (if there is a single narrator) places herself in the same position as them. No one would deny the obvious fact, which hardly needs stating, that "she" who reads and writes owes them big time. Despite everyone's warnings, the frivolous poet keeps violating a financially, governmentally, and juridically supported property system. Her crime: She practices a poetics of freedom. Who does she think she is? Everybody knows even more things about her:

> they're aware she's crafty
> admire her barefaced manner
> this gesture in the storm

Twinges of envy and indignation that are barely contained in the removed admiration in which they hold the poet's demeanor find resolution in the ominous final line just quoted, which concludes this short poem. The one who reads and writes waves off her alleged economic bondage in an act of freedom. Her words are a small sign in the midst of a powerful upheaval. This may be why she reads, why she writes. She, for her part, will find out what she got herself into.

While the storm would appear to denote a weather system, this figure also stretches beyond a metereological event to a historical condition. With her frivolous poet protagonist, Borinsky feminizes Benjamin's famous angel of history, the image through which he conceptualizes the epistemic and political position of the cultural critic within what is often seen as a progressively unfolding modernity, eyes glued to a pile of debris mounting in front of him, back fixed in the direction of what is to come (Benjamin 2003b, 392). The poet is arrogant, as we are told in "on poetry." She is playing. She lies at will and takes for herself what she wants. Play asserts its freedoms. Unlike the philosopher's angel who, driven forth by the wind blowing into his wings, cannot stop flying with his back turned toward the future, the frivolous poet offers her pirouettes in the face of progress's storm, twirling between past and future. She creates her own airflows. She matches the storm with a self-designed turbulence, gyrating where her words take her.

Feminist agency, in Borinsky, counters capitalist, technologically modulated temporality with the resources of play. But what of the relational politics Lugones inscribes into play? The "she" who reads and writes does this at a distance from the "they" who are assumed to know a lot about the way the world is run. Borinsky's playful poet of history, it appears, stands alone.

Engaged in reading and writing, however, she is enacting recalcitrant forms of address, dyed-in-the-wool relational modes. Her "gesture in the storm" is an expression. As a gesture, it partakes of another practice celebrated by Benjamin: children's play, which, for him, foreshadows the workings of the cinema—or, more precisely, "second" technology—as a way to handle the devastation wrought by primary technology, which asserts its domination over nature (Benjamin 2002b, 107–8, 112, 124n10). The child's "gesture," notes Benjamin, is a "signal from another world, in which the child lives and commands" (1999d, 203–4). World traveling and entering another's text can be happening within and around the poet's gesture, depending on how we read, how we write.

The poet's gesture in the storm supports a passage between worlds; it initiates a movement from narrative to narrative, from body to body. While a vast distance separates the poet from those who are in the know, the creation and perception of a gesture constitute points of contact. Participating in a playful capacity shared by adults and children, the poet joins the young girl of "end of the game." However, the poet's elliptical gesture betokens a difference of worlds. It asserts a break between texts. The princess tales burned into the girl's game and, we can assume, delimiting the epistemic and cultural repertoire "everybody" sagaciously regurgitates, remain a far cry from this.

The "they" who are regardful of the poet's cunning may gleefully anticipate her being blown over by the storm. Again, the frivolous poet enters a Benjaminian scene. She is facing the decline of experience owing to conspiring economic, military, and political catastrophes that leaves the subject of modernity, who had previously "gone to school in horse-drawn streetcars" under open sky, exposed to the "torrents" (Benjamin 1999a, 732; 2002a, 144). Storytelling, experience, and play, for Benjamin, have to be reclaimed as critical practices now that the once dependable shelters have been torn to pieces. This, in part, means contending with the protective shields that withdraw shock from consciousness. And, indeed, play is a historically situated collective practice that engenders a form of relationality; it is an emphatically public, material, and knowledge-producing strategy of address that ruptures the edifice of pleasing appearances (also known as "beautiful semblance") in which the white, European bourgeoisie has ensconced itself, while catching the image of beauty in the ruins and reassembling the fragments to form new constellations (Benjamin 1999c, 720; 2002b 107–8, 127–28n22; 2019, 9 12–17, 39, 68–70, 254–58, 269–70).[15] The wiliness of the frivolous poet has not been lost on those who take recourse to received economic wisdom at a time when crisis upon crisis afflicts a global capitalist order. So how is she planning to outsmart the "destructive torrents and explosions" that surround her? In what ways is the "tiny, fragile human body" going to pull off this feat (Benjamin 1999a, 732; 2002a, 144)?

The frivolous poet, I have argued, performs a relational gesture. She makes a pirouette. But what story is she enacting? How does she handle play's gender trouble when assuming the role of the evil stepmother? Mothers, as it happens, are important Benjaminian characters. But his mothers are not playing. Grounding a communal connectedness with the cosmos in the role of "Mother Earth," they hold up the forms of relationality that the aesthetic subject navigates and creates by playing (Benjamin 1996, 486; 1999d, 204; 2002b, 124n10; 2019, 11, 125).[16] Can women play only by becoming evil stepmothers, as the cliché has it, or by reproducing a masculinized ecological comportment delineated in white, middle-class terms?

Borinsky challenges the gender and racial constellation in which Benjamin recruits play and symbolic forms more generally. Adopting the stance of the Benjaminian critical subject of modernity, the frivolous poet equips herself with a historicized, politically crucial, collective faculty of play. At the same time, the distance that separates her from those individuals who find comfort in the already known suggests that her relational politics more closely approximates the roaming of Benjamin's distinctly gendered and racialized flaneur than Lugones's coalitional practice of playful world traveling (Benjamin 2003a, 319–21, 323–26, 338–41).[17] Are the poet's whirls in the wind, after all, the flailing of a forlorn girl who spins from story to story? The difference I underscored earlier lies in the fact that the frivolous poet answers the princess stories with the turns of her own narration. But her poetic performance simultaneously courts an indeterminacy and uncertainty that set them apart from the certitudes circulating as common sense. We have shifted from the end of the girl's game to the open-ended game of the poet. So the question stands of how the poet's—and our own—playful aesthetic wandering can assume a decolonial feminist orientation.

Pinpointing Play's Critical Orientations

To see how the frivolous poet's stories make a break with the tales reenacted by the girl and how we can reclaim play in the face of the gendered and colonial difficulties in which it is embroiled, I turn to several other poems in the collection. Today, "miss poetry," as we learn in the poem by that name (Borinsky 2009, 73 ["miss poesía," 72]), "rides around on a motorcycle." Technology is a prop in her fantasy ploy, which has her "dressed like a vamp." Nature obliges in the form of "two cute lap dogs / and a trained butterfly for special holidays." Indeed, miss poetry alternates vampire fiction and revolutionary motorcycle diaries à la Che Guevara with tinges of magical realist splendor reminiscent of Gabriel García Márquez's infamous trail of fluttering insects. As for pets, she repurposes the ferociously dueling urban lowlife lovers of Alejandro Gonzáles Iñárritu's film *Amores perros* (2000) or even the wretched poet in Mario Vargas Llosa's 1963 novel *La ciudad y los perros* (literally, the city and the dogs; translated into English as *The Time of the Hero* [2011]). Miss poetry puts on aesthetic attire to fashion her own, exceptional pleasures. Strange tastes allow her to assert her singular preferences and to enjoy her individuality while also participating in already written stories.

She invents her games darting through the streets of Buenos Aires. Done up as if she is ready to suck your blood, she doesn't quite fit the mold of Lugones's coalitional project or her stint with stones. Although miss poetry enjoys the company of her pals (including, besides the two dogs and one butterfly, "four respectful sweethearts"), they are rapidly counted. The collective is a far throw away.

Our motor-powered vampire takes cutthroat action in "mujeres tímidas / timorous women" (116–17). A woman touched by art obeys the rituals of already outlined social models:

classical ballerina
cook
discreet adulteress

Art punctures these roles.

a sweetsweet song stabs her
her shoes are sagely polished
glance toward the plaza toward the tree toward whatever is
rising without fear "I want to give you a glance with roots, the
true the dark side
of my love, dear heart, little round jug, jewel"

Rather than outpacing fear and following her desire, however, the woman walks in a way that holds longing back, keeps it hidden, abides by existing literary paradigms. "She reads letters on a bench Arranges the collar of her coat." This reading, these letters, leave intact the public-private divide. This is not a game the frivolous poet likes. Revenge is unhesitating and fierce:

her timorousness flatters me peruses me frightens me
her silences make ready my assassination
her caresses offer me mirror
a knife a lash the pulse of her hunger

Play, for Benjamin, brings to consciousness repressed needs. It awakens forgotten desires (2002b, 117–18, 124n10). The poet's dagger inflicts death but also revivifies a hunger that had gone silent, shrouded behind the collar.

Miss poetry unflinchingly operates in public. Her play takes place in the domain in which, in a sense to be explicated shortly, all the stories play out. This realm is where she pursues her exceptional tastes and acts out her unmatched sensibilities.

Like the timorous woman, the narrator of "te cuido como si fueras mía / i care for you as if you were my own" (50–51) settles for an anemic game that surrenders play's rebellious element:

your stories made me fear the daytime
that's why I wear a mask
receive my friends at night
with oversweet tea
and I say to them: let's play cards
make use of the minutes remaining to us

The friends hold off the poet, whose tales jam up "the soul," preferring to play already conceived games in private. They exchange an unnerving daily reality for a phantasmagoria that appropriates time. The minutes are known, rendered productive on already given terms. The possibility of change is ruled out. The party internalizes the poet as an outsider, "an imposter," a bad dream. Again, the distance separating them from the reader and writer who meets the storm barefaced ("desvergüenza") is vast.

So, let's play a more exuberant game, says the narrator of "poesía de lujo / poetry de luxe" (122–23). Here the poet is taken away from the subway where, "useless to look at," she hangs out "begging for / change smiles stories games." Her preferred area of operation is the residual, what is left over in the margins. She has made her home in daily public places considered irrelevant. These offbeat corners, and the outlandish behavior they host, ruffle good taste. The servants of suitable aesthetic sensibility have nothing to worry about, however. "They"—that is, the guardians of literate culture—recover the poet and do her up. They "put sonnets on her tongue" before granting her a stream of prizes. Emanating pride, she displays "her smile her well-tamed merriment." Vengeance, again, is swift:

> a gang of us follow her we yank out her eyelashes
> we frighten her with shrieks we splotch her books
>
> WE MAKE READY A VOICE HOWL ONLY
>
> A GARDEN SUDDENLY JUNGLE
>
> What deep silence awaits us my poor dear sparrows

Public territory lays traps that spell commodification. The sparrows are the frivolous poet's companions in pronouncing this outcome: the end of the game. The "they" aren't coming any closer to the frivolous poet and her gang. The distance is deliberate and mutual. The poet still vaguely wonders whether pretty artifice won't do for poetry. But as the narrator of "acá también hay poesía qué se creen / believe it there is poetry here too" (102–3) intimates, this takes persuasion. The female character in this poem is looking "smashing":

> everything is delight
> brilliance of painted wood
>
> my star my decked out austere watch

The game she is playing, however, is too guarded, too ascetic for the taste of the frivolous poet. Sensibility is overregulated. One can try to convince oneself that "there is poetry here," but in the final reckoning the poet's game is less abstemious, less inhibited than this woman's performance. The belief doesn't quite stick. Like Benjamin's children at play, the frivolous poet meets beautiful semblance with an irrepressibly subversive gesture. In "On poetry," Borinsky had already made evident that the frivolous poet, as Benjamin says of playing children, is "insolent and remote from the world" (Benjamin 1999b, 101).

Remote but not alone. And now the collective is coming nearer.

The setting is the theater. In the paradoxically titled poem "the show starts when you arrive," the performance has ended. "They" have already "said good-bye." The narrator doesn't care about "what each one thinks / alone at home." Her game is of a different order:

> I go back to the theatre
> search beneath the seats
> sniff smell
> scratch in the carpet
> carry away this dust
> that spider web a perfume

The poet writes with the leftovers of the earlier game, awakening thoughts and desires that have gone unnoticed. She collects the dust to compose a new game. Enacting a residual temporality, away from the marketplace, out of the grip of a defensive posture that surrenders to fear, disinterested play asserts an intimacy that no forlorn girl, no timorous woman has seen the likes of:

> I write you insulting letters
> tell you my secrets
> we laugh at ourselves without reaching the exact note
>   without fuss
>   without rhyme or reason

The letters are insolent ("insolentes"). The secrets are out. A laughter rings that answers to no external standard of normativity. It encounters its desires, its measures, in itself. Taste, again, is joyfully strange, brazenly individual. Borinsky reclaims disinterested play for aesthetics. It follows no form, use, or rationale beyond its own designs.

In the final stanza, just quoted, the formal second-person appellation of the title ("usted") gives way to an informal "you" ("tú"/"te"). Through her play, the frivolous poet creates an intimacy that Benjamin cannot quite fathom through his proliferating figures of play. These images range from children's play, the trance of hashish and gambling, and the flaneur's visions to Mickey Mouse and Charlie Chaplin. They run all the way to a self-displacing, reciprocal mode of relationality known as "innervation."[18] As I have noted above, Benjamin's imaginary of play in significant ways invisibilizes gendered and colonialist pieties.[19] Yet for him, the child "use[s] play to create a world," whereas the adult who flees from an all too frightful reality "removes [the] sting [of the real world] by playing with [this world's] image in reduced form" (Benjamin 1999b, 100). In his assessment, "[W]hat is truly revolutionary is the *secret signal* of what is to come that speaks from the gesture of child" (1999d, 206). Borinsky reimagines these sibylline signs exuded by the actions of the child at play. She gives the mysterious cipher an overt place in a structure of aesthetic relationality. She also highlights the relational effects it makes in this context. Let's stay just a bit longer with the relational setting and productivity of Borinsky's entrancing invocations. This will enable us to push the politics of play beyond its Benjaminian confines and to advance play's theorization beyond the relatively abstract accounts provided by Spivak and Lugones.

With its trope of the enigmatic signal, Borinsky's poem "the show starts when you arrive" gestures toward another world. The sign prefigures a future that is as yet unknown. It is only "when you arrive" that the "show starts" and that we will find out what the show might be. This special foretold yet unforetold event is going to take place "after the performance." The planned game has to end before the frivolous poet's game can commence. Play intervenes at the very moment when public performance threatens to surrender to private action. It desires public territory. It craves history. For the poet at play looks for the substances and creatures left behind when the arranged event has run its course. And "you" have to appear, as well. Once you show up, things will get going. You are not already there, wrapped up in some old game. You are not being consumed by a predestined narrative that is unfolding onstage. Neither are you hiding behind your collar or mask or in cahoots with your prince and princess friends. One way or another, you are somewhere to be found.

Declining self-abnegation in the face of the gender and colonial trouble cast by a whole lot of worn-out games, the frivolous poet invents her very own. Letters follow letters. It's a serial process. "I" finds a "you." They become a "we." The collective is arriving. The show, finally, commences. Selves are summoned; others are called forth, including the writer's and her readers' selves and others. The poet comes by the public she wants. Together, they participate in a collaborative world making. Play unfolds in aesthetic space. It seeks out aesthetic forms and materials. There is desire. Play pursues its distinctively aesthetic rhythms of beginnings and endings. This is how we can hope to tell as yet unwritten stories. The dust is our ink.

Searching for a Public in Public

The theater provides the setting for the game that the frivolous poet is inventing in Borinsky's "the show starts when you arrive." The sheer fact that there are secrets to divulge in this site means that that there is world travel. The frivolous poet traverses worlds. Her reader traverses worlds. These public practices are not without their perils. Publicness can make demands that flatten relationships and agency rather than incite aesthetic life. It can repress individuality and shortcut connectedness and expression. Interiority, as theorists have acknowledged, eludes publicness, not in the sense that it severs its ties to the public, but in the sense that public visibility and legibility never exhaust it (Quashie 2012). It has designs of its own. These designs refuse to obey public norms.

Lugones, indeed, calls attention to the risks of publicity (2003, 15). These risks display an unequal distribution. Publicness is more fraught with danger for some populations than others, depending on what social hierarchies are in effect. Borinsky's frivolous poet meets these dangers with insolence. But she doesn't desire the public for what it just happens to be. Normalized, established aesthetic publicness and the games it foments is not what she is after.[20] Neither does she long to build a close connection with an abstract anyone—that is, the presumed inhabitant of a universal public.[21] A public remains yet to be created and found. The laughter that sounds in the theater is collective laughter. The public is a "we," who are laughing at themselves. The intimacy of this "we" is a reciprocal creation. "You" arrive at some point. "You" are not the "they" who go home after the performance. It's not them,

alone at home
    as they take off their stockings
make tea
beckon the night

who attract the frivolous poet. The "you" to whom she addresses her letters are the ones who return to the theater when the staged spectacle has come to an end. The show that follows is of an order different from the programmed event. The fellow players bring into being the public that they jointly constitute, beyond the reign of preconceived "rhyme or reason." A hitherto unexperienced web of aesthetically mediated relations is in effect. Strange taste awakens unsuspected qualities and sensations in a relational field that it animates. The players find their own and each other's singularity. Public space enlarges itself. Feeling amplifies, intensifies.

The frivolous poet searches out her public within the public arena where, as noted before, all the stories play out. Miss poetry, as I have indicated, is speedily re-motorcycling and revamping the old dog and butterfly stories in the streets. What is it to cocreate and become a nascent public in public territory? What notion of publicness can harbor the emerging intimacies in their uncurbed spunk, their full affront? And why does the "revolutionary" gesture require it?

Multiplicity involves all the stories that have been and can be made. No story can be foreclosed in advance. They all potentially contain shades of meaning that the young girl may want to assimilate into her games or cast off, depending on the circumstances. They all potentially carry enticements that ensnare or enchant her in one way or another. They all hold elements that the girl, among others, can pick up on, reach out to.

With her residual figures of the dust, a cobweb, and a whiff of perfume, Borinsky highlights the multiplicity of publicness. She insists on the many stories, the peculiar tastes that the public sphere can hold. More than a stage-managed, stage-directed production per se, publicness contains signs that have gone unnoticed and are as yet illegible. These signs inspire games whose rules have not yet been engendered or deciphered, let alone enshrined. The games are being concocted in the process of their unfolding. Playing with the dust, the frivolous poet and her associates, who include the reader, are extemporizing their language, inventing furtive protocols, and forging their alliances. As Benjamin emphasized, by picking up the pieces and going on "journeys of adventure" among them, turning them into the props of a game without bounds, we can revive forgotten wishes, including demands for transformation of the society as we know it (2002b, 117; 2003a, 321, 336). Public space holds the tiny shreds and particles that supply the materials for these games.

The Pitfalls of Disinterested Play

Lest we once more idealize play, now under the rubric of public companionship, it is necessary to look at the ways in which the frivolous poet and her accomplices work around certain pitfalls of disinterested attention. I use the term *work* advisedly, for intimacy isn't exempt from toil. It exacts effort. As Tina Campt points out, intimacy often requires the labor of creating and sustaining connections.[22] And with their disinterested games, the accomplices have devised ways to circumvent several aesthetic traps, thus carrying out a vital kind of cultural work and giving disinterested attention and strange taste the room to do their jobs in the field of intimacy. I consider three of these traps.

The first concerns the way disinterestedness can encapsulate ambivalence while simultaneously occluding it. Disinterested play can be part of an attitude toward the poet that incorporates her as an outsider. In "i care for you as if you were my own," as we have seen, the narrator conceals herself behind a mask in fear of what the poet's stories tell her about the daytime. At night, she sits out the time playing cards with her friends. They have retreated from public space. Time has become something to be used and managed. It is neither a source of hope nor an arena where dreams, notions, and intrigues arise that might prefigure societal change. Keeping autonomous art at an arm's length, in this case, results in a paradoxical state of internalized exteriority.[23] As the title makes clear, caretaking ("i care for you" [te cuido]), conceived on an individualist, self-regarding model ("as if you were my own" [como si fueras mía]), plays into a property system that differentiates between what is and isn't owned. A phantasmagoria settles. Awareness of a constitutive alterity is foreclosed. Aesthetic autonomy lends itself to different deployments and as such is invested with divergent societal roles and functions. The friends respect it in relation to the poet's stories and, I assume, as a component of their card game, but they violate it in relation to temporality and the mask, which are instrumentalized. The connection with the "you," the poet, stalls:

let's not keep watch over the dream of that woman
                she's an imposter
a fortune teller from the carnival
a dirty joke
a caramel stuck in the middle of the soul

The narrator's stated intention to refrain from surveilling the poet lays bare that surveillance is exactly what she and her friends are doing and intend to continue doing: to keep a watchful eye on her. They lock her into place. In this way, they block up aesthetic relationality and experience. The poet's dreams and visions for the future are to be held off. This scheme of containment has consequences for the friends' interior lives. Withdrawn from the world, their digestive system balks. Even the "oversweet tea" the narrator serves her friends won't flow past the poet's chunky sweetness, her low-blow humor, and her prognostications for the future.[24] The othered outsider is preserved inside, refusing to go down and glide through, obstructing motion.

Aesthetic autonomy channels a care that doubles as a dismissal. It legitimates the absorption of a being who is in equal measure refused and desired ("as if you were my own"), thus landing the simultaneously repulsive and craved person in the middle of the immobilized soul.[25] But the narrator, at once reader and poet, is in no position to recognize this ambivalence. Her soul is too crammed to swallow anything else. Everyone, everything stays where they are. Disinterested attention is caught in a stalemate between a stagnant interiority and a petrified presence in the world. Nothing budges. The frivolous poet fancies a more vibrant aesthetic practice. The path is not yet clear, however.

A second pitfall of aesthetic autonomy attaches to the price exacted by beautiful semblance. I have already discussed the conflicting convictions surrounding pretty looks in "believe it there is poetry here too." A female character's marvelous appearance implies a guarded demeanor. Her vigilance, however, reins in the exhilaration and shine predicated of her. It may be the case that "everything is delight," but this pleasure is sharply curbed by the heedful attentiveness securing the "brilliance of painted wood." The opening exclamations

how smashing she looks with those curls
how enchanting her smile
how well-starched her petticoat

give expression to the narrator's admiration. This narrator's actual response to the woman's enchanting smile is not enchantment, however, but distant idealization, as the closing line makes clear: "my star my decked out austere watch." Desire once again is contained. The woman holds it back in a hardened, forbidding casing. The cautious, self-bracing adornment safeguarding beautiful semblance reduces interiority, even if incredulously one may detect poetry in this arrangement. As noted earlier, the belief does not quite hold. Autonomous semblance won't do for the frivolous poet. At least, it is not her aspiration to provide a disinterested gaze with a visual hit. Her audience is out of luck in this regard. The distant exultation voiced by the laudatory appraisals is not what she is after. The artist who self-surveils to charm her audience and who plays her games safe in the hope of becoming a star transforms herself into commodity. Vigilant watchfulness implies self-censorship and self-denial, the overwriting of her own aesthetic values and wishes by those of others. Paradoxically, the woman surrenders autonomy at the moment that she realizes it. The gamble of disinterested attention, warns the poem, can play into the cards of a gendered commodity system. The poet has her reservations about this game.

After all, commodification, as "poetry de luxe" demonstrates, means the end of the game. In this poem, the anonymous overseers of literate culture have made the poet over into a trophy. Having previously kicked her out of her domicile, the subway, where she was luxuriating in "the vices of the city," and having carried her off,

> they locked her up to put make-up on her face
> . . .
> they honed her sex to receive literary prizes
> they told her fables in boxed editions.
>
> When she went out they warned her to accept declamations
> happier than a winning football team
> More radiant than a patriotic holiday she showed off
> Her smile her well-tamed merriment

Play is lost. It has been coopted. The adjutants of literary culture have retooled it to the desires of a star system. "They" are making it work in the name of commodity production. The game is over, declares the frivolous poet: Howling remains. Sounds go rogue. Ordered nature turns wild. Silence rings from the gang of poets and their companions, the city birds. Words cease. Just like "believe it there is poetry here too" and many other poems in the collection, "poetry de luxe" ends without a period. But this open-endedness suggests not a continuation of language but an ever deepening silence, a growing inability to speak about what needs to be said. The frivolous poet rejects this lettered game.

Indeed, as I have argued, the frivolous poet encounters history and the technologically regulated marketplace with slyness and shamelessness. She dances in the dust. She performs her pirouettes. She doesn't really have a need for the mask, the painted wood, the saccharine tea of her fearful colleagues. Bitter truths don't have to be sugarcoated, covered up, or concealed. The real wielder of aesthetic autonomy makes a break with the machinery of up and down judgments, credits and debits, and checks and balances propping up the custodianship of entertainment and the administration of literate culture.

The resistance of the frivolous poet to the economic marketplace does not actually imply that "engaged literature" is what she is after, as we learn in the prose poem by that name (55 ["literatura comprometida," 54]). Here, Borinsky alerts us to a third pitfall of disinterested attention. The engaged writer has left the revolution as a result of his toothache. Relieved from his pain and infatuated with a woman who is after his money, he finally settles on a tranquilized poetics, pledging to "cultivate his garden and make poems with instructions that would be followed by poor boys here and there, teeth still perfect, sparkling piss and unselfish sweethearts" ("novias *desinteresadas*" [emphasis added]). Again, disinterested attention sacrifices interiority. It retreats to the private or to a carefully guarded, narrowly delimited relational field. It irremediably falls for the old love stories. It shrinks away from the "torrents and explosions" scourging the public arena. It allows "the vices of the city" to slip away. The frivolous poet turns down this sanitized pact with the reader and the impeccable, risk-aversive, ostensibly disinterested aesthetic experience it foments. She wants her readers sullied, muddled, adventuresome, no less on the edge than she. These reader-friends bite at their peril, perhaps even bite the dust. A dose of tidily regimented disinterestedness directed toward an idealized aesthetic order is distasteful to the frivolous poet.

In several poems, Borinsky, as we have found, shows how disinterestedness can become a trap for artist and audience alike: It can dull interiority, quench multiplicity, ossify relationality, and flip into commodification and idealization. One by one, these effects put the reader and writer in a straitjacket. Impediments arise that prevent disinterested attention from working its magic. The frivolous poet is not enchanted. In each case, however, there is a poetic presence, a voice, that witnesses and outstrips these obstacles. Borinsky's poetry thus highlights the predicaments in which contemporary life embroils disinterested attention and free play while also pointing to ways in which we can endeavor to shrug off and upend these formidable powers.

Less stilted communications become possible when the frivolous poet returns to the theater. In the aftermath of the performance, a more enlivening kind of disinterestedness is set free. The curious poet, sniffing and smelling materials from which she can make new stories, starts to "scratch in the carpet." She recovers some of the items that had gone unnoticed. Her dusty ink does not bother with the rites of the performance. Traces of perfume have detached themselves from the bodies that brought them in, hanging on in the theater, like the poet and her friends. The spider web is a fellow hanger-on, which installs linkages, connections, traps, and sticky spots well beyond the happenings hosted onstage. The curiosity of other beings is piqued. The party grows. An unforeseen covenant connects the frivolous poet and her cross-species friends with her reader. They invent a different game from the one they just attended. They throw off the demands of the literary institution and the theater. Disinterested play, in "the show starts when you arrive," awakens unprecedented intimacies.[26] It also thrives by them. Disinterest is "interesting" to the frivolous poet. Interest, by contrast, is not interesting. A reciprocal flow arises, with disinterested play feeding intimacy and intimacy provoking disinterested play. Relationality is in motion.

The Public as a Site of Disinterested Play and Aesthetic Intimacy

In "the show starts when you arrive," aesthetic intimacy and self-reflection occur within an institutionalized public forum yet outside the constraints of culturally authorized performance. This public space houses a direct address to a public: "I write you insulting letters / tell you my secrets." A space for the generalized "they" (which includes the ones who have left for home) hosts a new public "we" precipitated by this direct address. The movements from "I" to "you" and on to a "we" carry the intemperate possibilities of aesthetic exchange. In these gestures, the provocations of a brazen ambivalence thrive, shot through with promise and threat.[27] Multiplicity flows, for the controls that shut it off have been flipped. Impediments that bar experiential possibility have been suspended. The public space where aesthetic life flourishes undergirds an abundance of ways of making form and meaning. This setting sustains experiments with normativity and value that are open to those who enter.

Publicness is vital in Borinsky's poetry. The city streets, the theater, and the collective space of reading and writing are the habitats of aesthetic production. This public space is a realm where we can work to shake off modern, colonial, and gendered demands for marketability. This effort is part of the labor of intimacy. It is part of the work that allows disinterested play to do its work of realizing intimacy. Places such as the theater and the streets are locations where we can seek to enact liberatory relations between self and other, intrepidly facing our needs for public forms of intimacy and delight. Yielding to these longings and their attendant aggressions, we can enact aesthetic norms that we set for ourselves in contrast to what is imposed by authorized cultural normativity. This doesn't mean a jettisoning of institutionality but a recognition of its multiplicity, two aspects of aesthetic publicness that Borinsky's image of the theater and her figures of the chairs, the carpet, and their leftover treasures ingeniously bring together.

Public connectedness, as desired and incompletely engendered by the frivolous poet-reader, eludes marketable modalities of (self-)distancing and proximity. Rife with inevitable uncertainties, indeterminacies, provisional positionings, and strange tastes, it circumvents dulled and purified modes of address among artist and audience, whether subdued through the mediations of presumed artistic autonomy or the desiderata of engagement.

We are not sure what letters the poet spells out with the dust. Indeed, the intimacy of these compositions is an achievement of opaque designs, necessitating further games between poet and reader. As Borinsky suggests in an earlier poem "nos debemos al público / we owe ourselves to the public" (2007, 180–81), this duo travels "complicated routes" figuring out what the other is about.[28] Her own life, the narrator of this poem divulges, "is a collection of clues that I offer them to be returned to me in secret and in whispers." She listens in on the recipients of the schemes she concocts to have them "follow" her "until after dark and . . . come back to compare signs, suggestions, hypotheses." The intrigue that the poet gets going sustains the intimate pursuit of reader by writer, writer by reader. Interminable mysteries keep both hooked. Meanwhile, the game transmits each of the friends to other worlds. Aesthetic sensibilities are works in progress, as are the intimacies they allow us to craft and that inspire the paths they follow, all the while shaping singularity, specifying individuality, and crafting bonds between self and other from signs scoured for in public territory.

Cultural agency in the public realm, Borinsky makes clear, cannot offer the security of having the right in hand. Poetry, which has uttered "lie after lie," is not about to stop fabricating, to shy away from sending its readers to different worlds, and to give up sharing its inventions with those very worlds. Accordingly, cultural agency needs to face up to a normative ambivalence even as we do our utmost to dispel the devastating lies we inherit, to undo a voracious capitalist apparatus, and to create liberatory identities and coalitions across difference. The aesthetic, as a sphere of publicness, is fundamentally polyvalent, no matter how determinedly we attempt to bring about a better, more sustainable world. Indeed, aesthetic publicness and play, Borinsky's poems make clear, are critical to our ability to collectively inhabit the tensions, antagonisms, intimacies, and visions that we long to give aesthetic form—with a freeing laughter "at ourselves" to supplant the right note as a sign that the show, at last, is beginning.

Coda: The Game Carries On

Play is an activity through which we partake of games, old and new. It mires us in tales already told and tales that are yet to be conceived. It is a practice through which we exercise strange taste and enjoy highly individualized aesthetic sensibilities. Irrespective of how singular or standardized our games may be, they trace an aesthetic orbit, partaking of aesthetic norms, forms, and values that are in effect in the culture. This is part of their historicity. Games make their effects as junctures of patterns of aesthetic relationality. The marketplace and the pantheons of culture are among the institutional settings in which games realize their productivity. While Benjamin purports to historicize play, he leaves its gender, racial, and colonial workings unexamined and uncontested. I have identified elements in Borinsky's poetry that we can activate to circumvent these limitations. Ploys of disinterest and schemes of aesthetic intimacy and publicness are strategies we can mobilize to supersede the restrictions that mark Benjamin's theory of play. Thus, these notions are key to an adequate understanding of the aesthetic politics of play. They also yield a line of response to the problem of abstraction that I have identified in Lugones's and Spivak's conceptions of play. While the modalities of play these theorists advocate substantially proceed in aesthetic territory, Lugones and Spivak, as I have indicated, each overlook the ways in which these designs draw on aesthetic norms, forms, and values. So their favored kinds of play eventually threaten to take recourse to tales of princesses and princes and their like. My reading of Borinsky's poems has pointed up an aesthetically and politically more savvy conception of play. Philosophy cries out for this notion. This is what I have in mind. Play, of a sort that is up to the challenges posed by life's terrible aspects, critically engages the aesthetic determinants it posits and the aesthetic conditioning it puts into effect. Thus, it achieves a rigorously historical stance. It reckons with the inexorable fact that it relies on prior aesthetic formations and occasions further aesthetic effects. Enriched by a register of self-reflexivity, play lends acknowledgment to the formations of aesthetic relationality by which it is partially shaped and to which it, in turn, lends its shape.

When read through the aesthetic lens they call forth from the reader, Borinsky's poems awaken this kind of play. In "the show starts when you arrive," as we have observed, the frivolous poet makes a departure from already given games without jettisoning their concrete materiality. In swapping tales of princesses and princes for stories to be wrought from dust and spiderwebs, she revises existing constructions of alterity to make room for new modalities of aesthetic publicness, new modes of intimate gathering. Analogously, miss poetry embraces concrete aesthetic relationality when she re-motorcycles old tales of butterflies and dogs into a quite different kind of performance. The frivolous poet practices styles of world traveling and world making that are reminiscent of the semiotic and creative modes Benjamin ascribes to children's games, among other figures of play. But the frivolous poet differs from Benjamin, Spivak, and Lugones in that she embraces play's concrete aesthetic entanglements and realities even as she rejects the smothering of our games by oppressive narrations that they assimilate. This is the way in which the politics of play can hope one day, if she catches the taste, to tell a different story to the young girl who, at present, just wants to hear and rehearse the same one over and over again.

For Lugones, play ruptures arrogant perception, which aligns awareness and feeling with entrenched social categories, setting people apart (2003, 97–98). For Spivak, somewhat enigmatically, we can reach from play to action by calling double binds to a halt and owning the ideologically motivated mistake this move implies. A frivolous character myself, following Borinsky and rejoicing in her subterfuge with Benjamin, Cortázar, and her readers, I propose a more radical sort of play. This play affirms its own insolence. Disinterested, unperturbed by the limits of a given world or textual form, at a remove from the standards of time management and goal-oriented conduct prevalent in the marketplace, and in defiance of concomitant proprietary worries, this game enters the margins of publicness to awaken new intimacies.[29] The gestures of the poet at play seek out a "you" that wishes to join up in the emerging twirls of a readerly and writerly "we." Things get going once the official game is over and "you" arrive. Selves may warm to the invitation. Fictions go 'round. No one is telling others what to believe. The young girl can keep waiting all she wants for her prince or pick up a motorbike. Exact notes are nowhere to be heard, for the story is being pieced together as we speak. This is the freedom of disinterested play. Here its critical designs arise.

Why would we want to let go of this freedom when we choose to reflect on it and to think about the conditions of publicness that can foster and enhance it? Once we get the taste of it, why give it up? As Borinsky reveals when her frivolous poet-character assumes the role of the evil stepmother, games shape not only our stories, but also, specifically, the stories we tell about the stories that we tell when we are at play. Freedom, disinterest, and autonomy come with the terrain, as do conformity and imprisonment.

Disinterested play has a rightful place at the heart of critical practices of subjectivity and freedom. However, postcolonial and decolonial theory must also recognize its complexities and pitfalls. By exploring play's aesthetic potentialities in my reading of Borinsky's poems, I have shown how desire, by following and cherishing the impulses of disinterested play, can be a source of singularity and individuality. At the same time, disinterest and autonomy carry the risk of slipping into commodification and idealization. They can sidle into the marketplace. The impulses of desire, as many have recognized, can, of course, have the same effects. There is no way to forestall these risks. They are part of the game. However, we can also make it a part of the game to be alert to these developments. At that point, we are playing a self-reflexive game. Intrepidly carrying on with this game, we may want it to assimilate stories about stories, different stories, stories we haven't heard yet. This is my hope. Therefore, I offer this chapter as part of the game, an extended game I have been playing with some delightful interlocutors and that has me fired up about possibly finding other playmates.

A self-reflexive turn doesn't make disinterested play any less risky. But it can make us aware of turnabouts, reductions, and rigidifications that we might want to avoid. One way in which aesthetics can take note of these complications is by recognizing how disinterested play and the strange tastes embodying it can seek out the residual zones of publicness to engender new intimacies. Sniffing the perfumes, ferreting around in the spiderwebs, and inviting others into the game, after all, we can hope to reopen relationality and give it an unsuspected, not altogether legible, twist that yields yet more smells and spiderwebs and gives us material for further stories.

How should we deal with play's gender havoc, with its colonial and racial mayhem? The frivolous poet replies, "keep playing." Let's go play with the dust underneath the seats. Let's sound out the secret signals.

2

Pings

Sounding Out the City

Aesthetic publicness historically bears powerful, normatively inflected ties to disinterestedness, rendering this mode of perception a substantive determinant of the public organization and conditioning of aesthetic interaction and experience. According to David Hume and Immanuel Kant, aesthetic objects call for disinterested attention on the part of their observers. This form of apprehension is the subjective corollary of the objects' public standing—that is, their place in a public sphere: Aesthetic objects are public entities. To properly experience them as such, the observer's idiosyncratic characteristics must be circumvented. Disinterested contemplation sets them aside.

This chapter investigates disinterest's workings as a structural register of aesthetic publicness. The attitude has been institutionalized as a component of the aesthetic experiences fostered by artistic canons and the societal structures that uphold these canons. As we saw in chapter 1, disinterest also lodges in market formations. Alert to its alliances with play, the present chapter probes its role as an ingredient of a modern lifeworld still imbricated with coloniality.

For several centuries, disinterest has shielded Eurocentric canons and their concomitant societal institutions from incursions by ancillary realities believed to fall outside the domain of artistic beauty, goodness, and truth. Museums and performance venues, art historical protocols, methods of cultural criticism, and educational practices reflect this process. A pillar of artistic autonomy, disinterest served to screen aesthetic experience off from heteronomous factors, such as concerns about inequities of excellence and power. Thus, disinterest could be counted on to prevent art's sui generis valorizations from being tarnished by external conditions. Disinterest erected a buffer zone. Ensconced inside its own domain, art could realize its artistic qualities and engender aesthetic pleasure unhampered by ostensibly extrinsic sources of interference. Although disinterest suffuses vital kinds of play and yields aesthetic experiences that draw us to culture and the arts and that many wouldn't want to do without, this mindset also displays an ambivalent moral and political track record. While brazenly distancing concerns about inequality, disinterest ushers them in by piggybacking on societal disparities.

It is the surreptitious meanderings, glorious acrobatics, and hypnotic hide-and-seek games that we carry out in the form of disinterest that the present chapter scrutinizes. What can we learn about disinterest's contradictory commitments when we consider the imaginaries it supports and the experiences it forges in areas beyond its customary societal settings? What, as Clarice Lispector asks in *A hora da Estrela* (*The Hour of the Star* [1998 (1977), 2011]), might these oscillations have to offer a poor person who has barely any interets to speak of? What can disinterest comfortably negate in this case? At the limits of normalized, embodied consciousness, disinterest at once provides an entry into modernity and withholds such entry, achieving uncanny fluctuations between inside and outside stances. How can aesthetics account for these curious permutations? What should we make of the power imbalances they reflect? Philosophy has work to do when it comes to recognizing the aesthetic pleasures of a person that it banishes from the realm of official culture. It needs to develop adequate ways of dealing with the complicity of the aesthetic in the maintenance of class hierarchy and destitution—the endemic reality of aestheticized poverty. It is not obvious how we can tell a hitherto unheard story about this phenomenon, a tale that, rather than lending support to desperate inequality and immiseration, aspires to rise to the moral and political challenges brought forth by these conditions.

Perhaps we need to keep rummaging in the dust underneath our seats to see whether these residual zones beyond the orbit of official taste offer hints of a solution. This strategy seemed advisable to Lispector, who, casting about to write a story of abject destitution and neglect, resumed the tradition of the found manuscript in the style of Cervantes's *Don Quixote* (2003) and Jorge Luis Borges's story "Pierre Menard, Author of the *Quixote*" (1998b). Perplexingly, she comes upon a narration produced by Rodrigo S. M., the novel's fictional author. Let him find a response to the problem of aestheticized poverty! Let a male, heterosexual narrator show off his powers of invention! Who landed us in this jumble to begin with, anyway?

Again, the scraps and remnants of regular aesthetic form are the go-to place for an aesthetic engagement with marginality. Telling the story, as Rodrigo plans to do, of the indigent, disposable Macabéa, the work's protagonist who is left out of the social imaginary, is a struggle. He ties himself in knots that he ultimately shrugs off. So Lispector steps in on behalf of her abandoned character. She breaks her displacement from the narrative to ensnare the reader in the aesthetic coils Rodrigo vacates. While the found author may get himself off the hook, this option is withheld from the novel's public. Lispector closes off any line of escape to her reader, preventing her audience from turning their backs on the predicament the novel voices. Hence, we continue to play in the dust in the current chapter, now in Lispector's mesmerizing company, although things will turn quite serious, even a bit hazy and tearful, some of the time, as her author-character also intimates (Lispector 2011, 6, 9, 11, 25).

Aesthetics, the novel shows, is rather at a loss when it comes to the job of narrating the strange tastes and aesthetic likes and dislikes of a young, subaltern woman in whom the field historically has encountered its constitutive other. Nonetheless, disinterest, when wielded by Macabéa, reveals an unsuspected side as it swivels spatial and temporal orientations away from the folds of the very colonialist formations it has helped to establish. The strategy, here, plays a critical role that the Enlightenment had not foreseen. In its capacity as an ingredient of strange tastes and unusual aesthetic sensibilities, disinterest displays a remarkable efficacy at transforming an aesthetic system of gendering, nation and class formation, and racial and ethnic subjectivation into a field of expanded possibilities. Change, ultimately, comes too late for Macabéa. But Lispector refuses to let the reader wash her hands of her protagonist's fate. We stay with the dust. Rooting around in it will be our destiny, which replicates the fate held in the stars for the woman writer and her unlucky, expendable character. Let's then consider taste, which the novels spotlights in conventional as well as strange varieties. I start with a taste for pings.

Pings as Props of Taste, Habitual and Quirky

Sonic abstraction is a powerful aesthetic technique of mainstream temporal consciousness. For the longest time, broadcasting organizations used a series of precisely timed consecutive pings to mark the minutes before and after the change of the hour. These insistent pings asserted the order of the day. They corralled the nation into a collective sense of time. The following message rang out: "Think of it what you will, but now we're all here and this is where we are going—indeed, where we should be going." Each ping is the same kind of mediated technological achievement. Nonetheless, every listener can slot a portion of their experience into the moment before a ping arrives, and then likewise with the next ping. To the string of pings, the nature of the experience one brings to it doesn't matter. It could be a tragic instance or a high point. It could be plainly unremarkable. As far as the pings are concerned, it's all the same. These sonic signs parcel out our listening into crisply delineated segments. The same format fits the other experiences that make up the day. Whatever we do or don't do in a twenty-four-hour cycle can in principle be captured in a stint of pings. The idea bears repeating: Standardized time used to make itself known in tidy sound bites over and over again in the course of the day. The society could hook their feelings and desires into the experiential schema the radio provided.

Most of the time, the listener didn't pay too much attention to this obstinate compartmentalization of temporal sensibility. The clean sonic markers were absorbed in a distracted fashion. We may semiconsciously have been awaiting the start of the hour in anticipation of the news. There may have been regret that something was over. Perhaps we were unnerved about being already where we were and things carrying on relentlessly, irresistibly. Or we may have hoped for some indefinite granule of change at the end of a stretch of pings. Making visual and tactile translations, we could align our watches with the sounds, for we had our own ticking and ringing devices that were in or out of sorts with the pinging sessions, at least if we were fortunate to belong to a class that could keep up with the times aided by these individual possessions. More often than not, the listener's dealings with the pings were as routine as the pings themselves.

Not so for Macabéa, the protagonist of *The Hour of the Star*, which was published in 1977, the year of Lispector's death. A poverty-stricken young woman from northeastern Brazil who barely keeps afloat in Rio de Janeiro, Macabéa savors the pings she hears on her favorite radio station. In the novel's perspective, they are a cornerstone of the aesthetic life of city and nation. Through her love of these intimate sonic sprinklings, Macabéa takes part in a public culture that otherwise renders her an irremediable outsider. The pings are her daily point of entry into what the station describes as "'the right time and culture'" (Lispector 2011, 28). They make up her "now"—in all of its ampleness, its generosity, and, by the same token, its very thinness, its emaciation.

This chapter traces the ways in which the novel captures its protagonist's subaltern "now," which arises in the wake of a distinctive kind of authorship. Through the device of the found author and his text, Lispector radicalizes

Cervantes's and Borges's experiments with authorship. Macabéa's tale, as noted before, is told through the eyes of the male writer Rodrigo S. M., who struggles to make narrative sense of a character who is virtually indistinguishable from so many others. Somehow, he gets the story going. Orphaned when very young and raised by an abusive aunt, he tells us, Macabéa moves to Rio de Janeiro to take up employment as a typist while living with four roommates. His narrative listens in on her during her wanderings through the city, her shifts in the office followed by her evenings in the apartment, and an outing on the bus. In earlier novels, including *The Passion According to G. H.* (1964) and *Água viva* (1973), Lispector had voiced a view of aesthetic existence as a relational interfolding of self and other, body and matter, interiority and exposure to continually unsettling alterity, including gender. Her last novel explicitly brings this interest in the reciprocal aesthetic innervation of subject and object, individual and world, to the question of societal inequity. The work places poverty at the forefront of its plot, venturing to find a way to cope with this "state of emergency and . . . public calamity" (xiv).

Lispector approaches this crisis from a perspective that highlights the question of what aesthetics can do about it. With this theme, the novel broaches the colonialist workings of the literary enterprise analyzed by Ángel Rama (1996 [1985]). Rama influentially challenged literature on account of its participation for more than four centuries in the establishment, bolstering, and maintenance of a colonialist state order and class society centered on the practices of a lettered elite and the influence it wielded over a bureaucratic apparatus and an education system, in the realm of politics and the law, and in the domains of the military and the business of war. Rama names this arrangement the lettered city. Privileging a select class of *letrados* (lettered individuals), literature, as a colonialist institution, excludes subaltern subjects such as Macabéa. Structural forces militate against their entry into the cultural field that constitutes literate society. These people, by and large, are barred from participating in the creation and reception of literature. Lettered culture to a significant extent ignores their aesthetic perceptions and interventions or deems them irrelevant or uninteresting. Lispector lodges her narrator Rodrigo from the start in this hegemonic cultural field: He is a *letrado* par excellence. Like Rama, she will then offer a demystification of literature. This, however, couldn't be further from her style, which, even a cursory glance at her texts tells the reader, courts the mysterious, the enigmatic. Voices in her text partake of one another and mingle with other strands of sound. Lispector celebrates the flows of feeling and insight that writing allows in pursuit of the elusive and the unknown. Accordingly, as I reveal, Lispector takes the additional step of renewing literature's potential, whereas Rama and Jean Franco (2002), following him, leave the medium, conceived as a form that has lost its justification if not practical durability, in a state of philosophical disarray. The novel's exploration of philosophical concepts—notably, disinterest—is part of this project.

The Hour of the Star is probably Lispector's best-known text in Brazil, not least due to a successful film adaptation that drew large audiences when it first appeared in the mid-1980s and that continues to grip the popular imagination. The novel's fraught treatment of subaltern subjectivity, which the film straightens out by dropping Rodrigo altogether, has not lost its ability to fascinate. Macabéa recently underwent a makeover as the subject of an illustrated short story by the acclaimed Afro-Brazilian author Conceição Evaristo (2023), which, while reworking images from the novel, poetically envisions Macabéa as an Afro-Brazilian woman.

The text continues to inspire owing to its bewitching protagonist and the deadpan humor with which Lispector subverts truisms that threaten to blunt reflection on tragedy. This gesture is especially compelling in view of a further move: The work brings a feminist lens to the modern operations of coloniality as well as decoloniality. It evinces an aesthetic interplay among these factors by situating them in a dense web of existential, material, and affective forces. The ensuing aesthetic entanglements present conceptual challenges for postcolonial and decolonial studies, for with her focus on the aesthetic dimensions of a life lived in poverty compounded by gender inequity, Lispector underscores intricacies of modern lifeworlds that have not yet received theorization and entail philosophical implications.

Scholars such as Walter Mignolo (2007) influentially propose to supplant Western aesthetics by a form of aesthesis that "delinks" societal realities and epistemological conditions from modernity. I would dispute that aesthesis—that is, affect, sensation, perception, and imagination—yields a critical tool apart from the workings of aesthetics. Aesthesis is not available in a fashion uncompromised by the problematic heritage of the aesthetic. It is neither a zone of critical purity nor a plane of unsullied grassroots agency. Its history is as tarnished as that of aesthetics. This, to be sure, doesn't mean that aesthesis should be jettisoned, but neither should aesthetics. Consequently, the intertwinements of modernity and coloniality observed by Mignolo require a more involved aesthetic methodology than the notion of aesthesis provides. Indeed, the project of epistemic and sociopolitical uncoupling from invidious facets of modernity stands in need of the experiential and critical resources of aesthetics, its creative and political potentialities. Lispector broaches these complexities by probing the role of aesthetic norms, values, and traditions in Macabéa's predicament. The novel investigates the workings of the aesthetic as a register of contemporary societal realities rather than taking this matter to be settled in the abstract and one-sidedly, by ongoing factors of colonialist domination and enduring power imbalances between Global North and Global South. In this respect, the work bears affiliation to the political epistemologies of Édouard Glissant and María Lugones, whose decolonial modes of interpretation and relationality center opacity, and with Gayatri Chakravorty Spivak's notion of reading and inhabiting the double bind.[1] An aesthetic approach, as I show, brings to light decolonial registers that tend to be disregarded on perspectives that overlook the aesthetic.

In reflecting on the aesthetic aspects of existing alliances among modernity, coloniality, and decoloniality, two decisive issues arise that have to be brought to the forefront of critical theorizing. Lispector's novel speaks to them. The first concerns the nature of the aesthetic experiences that emerge in the relevant province of mutual entwinements. Here, strange tastes exercise their magnetism. Dissonant sensibilities exert their unruly effects. Lispector explores the phenomenology of quotidian aesthetic experience by tracing the vicissitudes of Macabéa's disinterested aesthetic affections and engagements and by inviting us to compare these experiences with the aesthetic outlooks of other characters. Because Rodrigo S. M. is the young woman's most prominent fellow character, a fact he boasts of, and because as a fiction writer he stands in for the lettered city at large, we here touch on the second issue: the role of institutions of art. By these institutions, I mean not only, narrowly, spaces such as libraries and museums but also the broader forms of cultural organization connoted by concepts such as literature, the cinema, music/sound art, theater, performance, and the art world. These notions point to a public sphere, a realm of public aesthetic activity, at some distance from state sovereignty and juridical/political normativity, on the one hand, and the capitalist marketplace, on the other. Odd tastes and exceptional aesthetic sensibilities insinuate themselves into public territory, claiming their space alongside more orthodox aesthetic investments. By scrutinizing aesthetic experience in its multivalent entanglements with aesthetic institutionality and publicness, this chapter advances our grasp of the colonial and decolonial operations of the aesthetic.

Through her juxtaposition of a subaltern, female protagonist with the male, middle-class author who is responsible for her creation and fate, Lispector offers a critique of the lettered city. Simultaneously, this forum proves to be a place that gives rise to acute questions about the current "time and culture." The lettered city undergirds its own perplexingly gendered self-criticism, enacting a form of *autohistoría-theoría* (Anzaldúa 2009, 189–90; 2015, 5–6). Here, an additional philosophical strategy takes hold: Reassembling the remnants of the lettered city, *The Hour of the Star* puts forth a constellation of aesthetic publicness that extends to the daily forms and materials that shape Macabéa's pleasures. Further, owing to its embrace of the quotidian experience of its subaltern protagonist, the novel contributes to the field of everyday aesthetics, which has become a prominent optic in twenty-first-century philosophy and cultural analysis (Saito 2007, 2017). This subfield by and large circumvents the realm of strange taste in favor of the commonplace. However, by affirming eccentric sensibilities, the field can take into account quotidian sites of decolonial aesthetic agency that arguably belong to its purview, and that it is vital to acknowledge, as we will see.

Lispector's oeuvre has received substantial philosophical attention in French feminism and new materialism—notably, in the writings of Hélène Cixous and Rosi Braidotti.[2] This work barely registers the implications of coloniality for the questions of gendered embodiment that occupy the novel, and vice versa. Debate on these matters is emerging but still scratches the surface. The trenchant, distinctively aesthetic logics Lispector pinpoints, as well as her assiduous uptake of the category of the aesthetic, clamor for a reading.[3] Indeed, a focused aesthetic lens is required that contends with the ways in which the literary institution desires the subaltern and might accommodate itself to her experiences and desires.

As indicated by her affection for the pings she audits on her borrowed radio, Macabéa simultaneously does and doesn't belong to modernity. This paradoxical position makes for an aesthetic sensibility that is as delicate and razor-edged as it is volatile, as comical as it is heartrendingly devastating. Through her figuration of her character's modes of listening and feeling, Lispector rethinks sonic and adjacent (multi)sensory and affective constructions of identity, the city, and the global.[4] Aesthetics must take note. It is with the dual intention of sparking the sense of aesthetic possibility found in coalescing forces of modernity and coloniality/decoloniality and of acknowledging the philosophical import of a writer who occupies a single league with Toni Morrison, Franz Kafka, and Marcel Proust, and their like, that I turn to Macabéa's uncommon tastes and Rodrigo's attempts to tell a story that gives them their due. My argument proceeds via the two characters' aesthetic outlooks, the entwinements among their visions, Rodrigo's response to this, and Lispector's ultimate critical intervention.

In Praise of the Aesthetic

Lispector lays the ground for Rodrigo's writerly venture with an opening section that reads like a eulogy to the aesthetic. More accurately, it panegyrizes Western avant-garde aesthetics. Labeled "Dedicatória do autor" (Dedication by the author) (Lispector 1998 [1977], 9; 2011, xiii), the paean is cast in a grammatically masculinized voice. A parenthetical clause immediately complicates matters by specifying "Na verdade Clarice Lispector" ("actually Clarice Lispector"). From the start, the novel embroils the reader in an aesthetic world ruled by gendered principles. The reader hears Lispector's voice in Rodrigo's, and vice versa, plunging precipitously into a gender politics that is being fought out at the aesthetic level. Let's look more closely at the ways in which the novel deals with pillars of aesthetic institutionality that become apparent here: gender, authorship, the existential significance of canonized art.

The dedication raises considerable stakes for Rodrigo's artistry: to create a work of literature true to the aspirations of ambitious art, art that searches out the edges, that aspires to the new. Nonetheless, he hardly makes it through his first five words before evincing an attitude toward writing that is decidedly offhanded. He starts the dedication with the conjunction "So" ("Pois" [1998 (1977), 9]; see also 2011, xiii), as if we are overhearing a discourse that has been going on for a while.[5] Moreover, he refers to the novel with the casual expression "this thing here" (2011, xiii). He then begins to pay his respects by dedicating the thing first off to Robert and Clara Schumann, "who today alas are bones." Next, he dedicates it to "the very crimson color scarlet" that looks like his blood "of a man in his prime and so" ("e portanto"), in the same gesture, he dedicates it to his blood. "[A]bove all" ("sobretudo"), however, he dedicates the novel to the "gnomes, dwarfs, sylphs, and nymphs who inhabit [his] life." We have barely commenced. He cites the "memory of [his] former poverty," before he had ever "eaten lobster," along with sonic tonalities ranging from Beethoven's "tempest" to Bach's "neutral colors" to Chopin, "who makes me swoon." Preeminence is given, however, to "the yesterdays of today and . . . today." Various members of the historical European avant-garde are of paramount importance, such as Stravinsky, "who frightened [him] and with whom [he] soared in fire." The same pantheon features Arnold Schoenberg and the serialists. Lispector's contemporary at the time of writing and fellow northeasterner, the composer Marlos Nobre, makes an appearance, as do the "strident cries of the electronic generation." Finally, the group of dedicatees singled out "most of all" ("[s]obretudo") encompasses, as he puts it, "all those who reached the most alarmingly unsuspected regions within me, all those prophets of the present and who have foretold me to myself until in that instant I exploded into: I" (1998 [1977], 9; 2011, xiii). Perhaps this superlative class includes all of the others, for with the doubling rankings that outstrip one another with their claims to dedicatory primacy, ontological categories begin to run through one another. The hierarchies among different kinds of beings, artists, and conditions are mixed up upon their assertion. Their distinctions become fluid. Stravinsky and the sylphs exist in the same plane, just like the Schumann spouses, their bones, and blood. The same goes for Rodrigo, Lispector, the thing Rodrigo is declaring authorship of, and the sonic artists whose work blasted him into being, challenging aspirations to artistic sovereignty he will soon go on to express.

The dedication reads like an encomium to the aesthetic because of the way it conjoins art with daily realities: Existence appears as the whole rigmarole experienced around food, loss of life, bodily parts and substances, fantasy figures, a vortex of feeling, the passage of time, and the imprints of history on the self. Rodrigo invests numerous entities with the power to set alight unrecognized zones of the "I" and spark dimensions of "today," of the present. The notion of the aesthetic covers the territory that couples sources of interiority and self-fashioning with capacities to actualize a contemporary moment. The blurring of ontological distinctions among the different entities and the abundant scope of affective, fantastic, dramatic, and material qualities to which Rodrigo pays homage invoke a notion of aesthetic democracy, where every feeling, every sound, form, object, and person, can potentially participate in the torrent of impulses that go into the making of the subject and the moment.[6] As it pervades items ranging from bodily fluids and densities, even corpses, to the most ethereal, depersonalized sonic forms, the aesthetic exercises a leveling force. It is an aesthetic sensibility in its unrestrained multiplicity that kindles previously unfathomed realms of subjective experience, yielding the present and actualizing the person Rodrigo experiences himself to be.

He goes on to explain that the modus operandi of aesthetic form and the incendiary self-eruption it occasions is relationality. His observation about his explosion into the "I," is followed by a musing on the very "I" with which Rodrigo self-reflexively identifies: "This I that is all of you since I can't stand being just me. I need others in order to get by, fool that I am, I all askew" ("eu enviesado") (1998 [1977], 9; 2011, xiii–xiv). This relational, bent-out-of-shape self who hankers for companionship then sets out to engage "today" and its "yesterdays." Aesthetic relationality is at work, but it is pervaded by fantasies of sovereignty. Rodrigo's flexed, internally torn "I" is gearing itself up for his encounter with the now. The "I" has readied itself by becoming "all" of us, the unnamed "you" mobilized in a direct address to the reader. The slice of today that this ample he—a he that is a we—wants to confront, as mentioned earlier, is undergoing a crisis. A barrage of aesthetic experiences that are constitutive of self lead Rodrigo to a wordless meditation on "the nothing" (2011, xiv). What can you do otherwise, he sighs wistfully, besides sinking into "that full void that you can only reach through meditation"? Self-plenitude and nothingness coincide. Action and contemplation collapse into each other. Meditation, adds Rodrigo, doesn't need to produce results. It "can be an end in itself" (xiv). Disinterest takes root. At a remove from language and immediate consequence, he indicates, extends an atmosphere of still drifting, as filled with meaning as it empties itself of it.

Any feeling of serenity attendant on this charged state of reduction dissipates, however, as Rodrigo continues with his reflections. He has already acknowledged that he needs other people to keep him on his feet ("preciso dos outros para me manter de pé" [1998 [1977], 9]). This joint balancing act, however, is a delicate accomplishment, for there is also writing, which espouses its own ends. And writing, he shares, "trips up [his] life" ("O que me atrapalha a vida é escrever") (1998 [1977], 10; 2011, xiv). The paragraph closes with this remark. He and his fellow human beings may try to hold him upright. Writing pursues its own aims, threatening to knock him over, whamming his existential equilibrium to pieces.

As if to prove the point, his next paragraph goes on to trip up the reader. Prefaced by doubling conjunctions "And—and" ("E—e"), it throws the reader into the middle of an ongoing discourse about the things that "you" know without seeing, perhaps even know without knowing, but that nonetheless impel belief: "Weep and believe." We get an inkling that Rodrigo may be asking a thing or two from his audience. His dip into epistemic territory prepares a final narrative surrender to the stream of things and to the words that are yet to be found, completed in the last paragraph of the dedication: "This story takes place during a state of emergency and a public calamity. It's an unfinished book because it's still waiting for an answer. An answer I hope someone in the world can give me. You? It's a story in Technicolor to add a little luxury which, by God, I need too. Amen for all of us" (2011, xiv). The earlier, highly subjectivized, heated language of a desirous male author who struggles with his needs shifts in this passage to a dramatization of objective conditions. Rodrigo takes a distance from his creation, which he now, in neutral terms, describes as "[t]his story" and "[a] book" ("Esta história," "[t]rata-se de livro inacabado" [1998 [1977], 10]). The formal tone prepares the ground for an animation of a general "you," which, abstractly, open-endedly, serves as a stand-in for the whole human community ("all of us"). He calls on the unnamed addressee we have already encountered several times to deal with the imminent public catastrophe, ultimately entrusting "all of us" with the responsibility to offer a response to this disaster. A hint of apology accompanies his intention to assimilate mass technology into the inner construction of the story's narrative form. Pleasure remains desirable no matter how severe the difficulties that are looming. And although his plaudits center on Western classical and avant-garde music, he eventually includes the mass media and especially cinema in the lateral, de-hierarchized flow of aesthetic world making and self-engendering of which he has just sung praises.

With this tribute to aesthetic life, Lispector sets the stage for a literary uptake of the crisis that she puts in front of the reader. Is the aesthetic ready for this job? How will it handle the problem of aestheticized poverty and inequity? Lispector passes the buck to her stand-in, who, we have seen, waxes lyrically over the powers of the aesthetic before tactfully, and in advance of his literary endeavor, passing it on to us, with his blessing. While he manages to dodge responsibility, Lispector involves the reader.

This hand waving may not make us optimistic about the prospects of the aesthetic in regard to the task ahead. Nonetheless, we, the public, are immediately made present in the text. The emergency concerns us—"all of us." The text is going to do what it takes to bring the emergency home, to have it be the reader's problem to solve.[7] Neither Lispector nor Rodrigo leaves any doubt about it whatsoever.

Tensions, meanwhile, remain. The dedication catapults the reader into the flow of things through its opening and repeating conjunctions, its unsettled temporalities. A lot happens at once, in an ecstatic rush; the reader senses multiplying layers of meaning. Rodrigo offers a paean that praises artists to the sky while also exuding a lackadaisical flavor. A modern cultural hierarchy is established even as it is being undercut. A strand of aesthetic democratization intermingles with a reentrenchment of a Eurocentric cultural canon and a celebration of the Western avant-garde. What resources does this imbroglio have in store to make a response to the calamity that is just around the corner? And how does Rodrigo's star-studded aesthetic compare to his invented character's sensibilities in the multimodal spheres of sound, writing, and quotidian life?

A Story That Is Hard to Tell

Rodrigo, the reader realizes, is not that hopeful, either, about the materials at his disposal. Indeed, the techniques he habitually puts in the service of his process of aesthetic self-formation are recalcitrant when it comes to the character by whose invention he is currently gauging his authorial muscle, the pauperized Macabéa. She is giving him a hard time, for she offends against all stylistic and semantic protocols. How does one even speak of a life when the one who is supposed to live it is barely distinguishable from "thousands like her" and dwells in an atmosphere of unnoticed nothingness (Lispector 2011, 5–6, 28–29, 32)? How does one tell this story? Grappling with this conundrum, Rodrigo shares his ruminations on his poetic choices and his authorial position in the society with the reader. The novel performs the powers of literary narration that it investigates by positioning the reader as a participant in its fictional author-character's dialogue.

As a part of a lengthy process of authorial self-personification, Rodrigo indicates that there is no getting rid of Macabéa, for she sticks to him like molasses or "black mud" ("melado pegajosa ou lama negra") and refuses to let go (1998 [1977], 21; 2011, 13).[8] Worse, "[s]he forced her being upon me," he notes resentfully (2011, 21). He feels that his character is pulling him through the wringer. Whereas he craves the "novelty" attainable by writing, she is all about "repetition" (13, 32). He frets about the "exterior and explicit" tale with which he is "invading" the reader (4–5). Yet he feels obliged, "however artlessly, to reveal her life" (5). There is no other way: "I have to write about this northeastern girl or I'll choke" (9).

One worry tormenting the writer is that he is bound to come up with a story "[o]ut of which . . . blood so pantingly full of life might ooze and instantly congeal in cubes of trembling jelly" (4). A similar fate, he agonizes, could be his as a writer: "Will this story someday become my own congealing?" (4). These anxieties keep popping up: "Will what I'm about to narrate sound treacly? It might but then this very second I'll dry out and harden" (9). The stakes in getting the story right are high for its author.

Rodrigo offers preliminary after preliminary as he wrestles with fear and shame. Only he can write the story, for he is the sole creature in the world who loves Macabéa (21). At least, that is how he understands the matter. To make things happen, he is willing to set aside his usual experimental style: He plots "a beginning, middle and 'grand finale' followed by silence and falling rain" (5). If he gets his act together, the reader wonders, will anyone bother to read the tale?

His status in the society is not helping. He is "left over" and lacks a place "in the world of men" (12). Consequently, his text is by no means guaranteed an audience (10, 22). He decides to practice austerity; he gives on up sex, soccer, "all human contact" (14). He pares down his food intake to fruit and chilled white wine. Literature is exacting. Nonetheless, his strategies seem to work. One way or another he shakes off his inhibitions and by fits and starts rolls out his tale.

The trouble Rodrigo is experiencing reveals how tough it is to open up the lettered city, built from existent and historical premises and aligned with a Western canon, to the subaltern character he loves. The story lets itself be told only with difficulty. To learn how literature might be equipped to deal with the theme of poverty and to find out what philosophical resources this medium can mobilize to overcome a history of aestheticized exclusions, let's see what the story makes of the aesthetic experience of its elusive protagonist.

Sensing "Today"

Macabéa delights in the pings she hears on the radio. They function as a regime of temporal abstraction: Everyone can compress their experiences into the intervals they delineate, taking part in a modernist compartmentalization of time. The pings make up her "now." This is the present that Rodrigo, too, was talking about in the author's dedication: his "today."

The coveted "today" reemerges as an element of Macabéa's self-understanding. "I'm a typist and a virgin, and I like coca-cola," she proclaims (27). The beverage is not just a beverage, Rodrigo had observed earlier, when disclosing his own indebtedness to it: Coca-Cola is "today" (15). Macabéa, in short, sees herself as modern. The city, however, refuses to acknowledge her claims to self-identity. The workplace sees her not as a typist but as a less than skillful copyist. Despite the disciplinary beatings visited on her by her aunt throughout her childhood, her place within the female imaginary is that of a streetwalker, a prostitute. And the marketplace has no patience with her attempts to pass as a consumer. The city declares her superfluous. She is as insignificant as the things that capture her aesthetic desires: a creaky, rusty gate; a rooster's call; the sound of honking cars (22–23, 25, 43). Replete as it is with lack, Macabéa's life, ironically, is filled with disinterested perceptions. Her delight in the pings is one among many such pleasures: She enjoys them for their own sake. Ever starved, she is a voracious seeker of the looks, sounds, feels, and tastes of things in her environment. She has a special fondness for aesthetic occurrences and items found in the margin.

Paradoxically, as attested to by her liking of the pings and Coca-Cola, Macabéa occupies an aesthetic position that is at once modern and nonmodern. Her sonic desire keeps up with the moment-to-moment organization of temporality. This is the modern aspect of her aesthetic sensibility. Simultaneously, her perceptions of the pings give these sonic "drops" (29), which in the normalized symbolic order have at most an instrumental significance, a value for what they are in and of themselves. The "drops of the minutes of time" (41), to her, have meaning in their own right. Her taste for the pings singles out for appreciation incidental occurrences that are ancillary to the phenomena that really count in the run-of-the-mill course of events—namely, the progression and measurement of time. It is a strange taste.

With her penchant for residual matters, Macabéa goes aslant the regular cultural system. Indeed, she valorizes creations that fall outside the scope of modernity. Her experience, in other words, latches on to nonmodern items. It embodies nonmodern qualities. Here we arrive at the crux of the novel: Lispector confronts her reader with the internally refracted aesthetic agency of her protagonist. By means of Macabéa's aesthetic, *The Hour of the Star* demonstrates that modernity and nonmodernity are not mutually exclusive entities. Indeed, Macabéa's modernity, her participation in a regime of abstraction, consists of her nonmodernity—her break with instrumentalized temporal orderings. Conversely, she crafts her nonmodernity, her joyous indulgence in things for no ulterior designs, from modernity—that is, from the materials that uphold modern lifeworlds. No wonder Rodrigo, this other type who is hovering on the cultural sidelines, has his attention piqued.

Craving his own "today," Rodrigo invents Macabéa, who is in tune with it. Disinterested attention is her ticket to modernity. It offers her the joy of the pings and her contemporary identity as a Coca-Cola enthusiast. Whereas the city withholds approval, Rodrigo is spellbound, sighting an opportunity to renew not only his authorship but also his public. "I've experienced almost everything, including passion and its despair. And now I'd only like to have what I would have been and never was" (13). This is literature's chance to put itself back in the center from which it had been displaced by emerging technologies and popular media. Deferred self-actualization is on the horizon.

Rodrigo's relation to the beverage differs from Macabéa's. Presenting himself as an unbiased narrator, he divulges that his narrative is benefiting from the patronage of the Coca-Cola Company:

> I . . . forgot to say that the account that is soon going to have to start—since I can no longer withstand the pressure of the facts—the account that soon is going to have to start is written with the sponsorship of the most popular soft drink in the world even though it's not paying me a cent, a soft drink distributed in every country. Moreover it's the same soft drink that sponsored the last earthquake in Guatemala. Even though it tastes like nail polish, Aristolino soap and chewed plastic. None of this keeps everyone from loving it with servility and subservience. Also because—and now I'm going to say something difficult that

> only I understand—because this drink which contains coca is today. It's a way for a person to be up-to-date and in the now. (14–15)

Having a few pages earlier declared his marginal status, Rodrigo here trumpets his societal relevance. The Coca-Cola Company sponsors him in exchange for the seal of contemporaneity that only the artist can bestow on the commodity. This pays off handily for the firm. Monetizing the artist's unique insight into the present, the global corporation turns a profit on a drink that, apart from the aura of the "now" granted by literature, is fated to repel the consumer's sensorium. Rodrigo can pride himself on quite an accomplishment. Although the actual drink no longer contains any coca, Lispector's reference to the plant underscores how the signature of the new obfuscates a centuries-long, evolving aesthetic history and effaces dimensions of communal existence that carry on well into the present. Coca-Cola's claim on the moment brackets ongoing Indigenous production and consumption practices centered on coca leaves. While the beverage in name preserves the original coca, object of enduring spiritual and agricultural rites, this historical reality slips away under the mark of the now. Rodrigo lends his literary machinations to an alarming aesthetic vanishing trick. Lacing the drink with an unmatched contemporaneity, he is a prized asset in the marketplace. He knows it.

He knows other economic ruses, as well. Capital, he intimates, not only controls many a nation in the Global South but also governs the allegedly natural disasters harrying these regions, crises in whose death toll corporate rule has a hand. A denizen of the Global South, like the majority of the 23,000 persons who died in the 1976 earthquake in Guatemala, he fails to profit from this spot-on diagnosis.[9] Although he lends his energies to the corporate world, his aesthetic labor is taken for granted. It does not gain him a penny, but all the same, austerity has its advantages. Conveniently, for the corporation as well as for himself, his epistemic position is relieved from the risk of being compromised by his authorial endeavors. A conscientious, impartial narrator, he wisely discloses his perceived partiality, safeguarding his capacities for disinterested reportage. He maintains an autonomous outlook on the present. His artistic integrity survives unscathed.

Literature, in what we understand to be a disinterested fashion, assists the Coca-Cola Company in its merchandising of the present. Aside from the aesthetic stage setting that literature has provided for the nation, and absent the centuries-long orchestration of taste that canonized art has put in the service of Western hegemony and the country's social and political order, the populace might just have declined to buy the commodity, grossed out by its unpalatable sensory qualities. Indeed, Lispector reveals how the lettered city historically has been instrumental in rendering modernity aesthetically desirable. It pulls off this feat in virtue of its autonomy, which gives it aesthetic credibility. It also realizes this achievement in spite of its autonomy, which entails a retreat from such deployments. This paradoxical entwinement of autonomy and heteronomy has an extended history in philosophy and the arts.[10] Meanwhile, transnational capital champions authorship; authorship, in turn, secures selling power and a reliable revenue stream. Supplying just the bare minimum of infrastructural scaffolding for the literary effort, the corporate realm withholds further remuneration, lending credence to Rodrigo's disinterested stance. Unsalaried, he is free to take up residence in the "darkness of the night"; he can seek out the "pouring rains or great gusts of wind" bedeviling this nocturnal atmosphere (10). Natural man is a citizen of the lettered city.

I have moved from Macabéa's aesthetic experiences to Rodrigo's "interested" species of disinterest. The interested part of this oxymoronic state is ambiguous between his wish to peek into the life of the protagonist he has invented and his bewildering stance as an author within a market society that accords a confounding, labyrinthine role to the practice of literature. The novel investigates this paradoxical territory, which gives rise to a remarkable aesthetic interdependence between the two characters.

To Rodrigo's skillful description we owe a discerning account of the taste of the beverage that connotes the present. Coca-Cola, he has told us, smacks of nail polish. But how does he come by this aesthetic insight? We get a clue from Macabéa's habits. Our character has an intimate experience of this decorative medium and substance: She habitually colors her fingernails "a tacky red" (27). Regrettably, the glamour is short-lived. Because she chews her nails "almost down to the quick," the "loud color" vanishes in no time, "and you could see black dirt below" (27). Ironically, Rodrigo's authorial voice is infected by Macabéa's aesthetic judgment. For it takes an eater of nail polish like her to detect that special tang of lacquer in the soft drink's flavor. Rodrigo's reading of the material world and its economic conditioning is indebted to Macabéa's perceptions. Whereas he sustains her life, he also depends on her for his aesthetic grasp on the present. Her strange tastes insinuate themselves into his today. Their cheapness, gaudiness, grotesquery, and their nearness to "black dirt" and mass culture infiltrate his sensibility, where they border on the eerie and the monstrous. His incorporation of her strangeness gives away the freakishness and monstrosity limning personhood, authorship, and earthly existence that he, to no avail, struggles to avoid (3, 7, 10).

If literature is both in cahoots with modernity and maintains a distance from it, what follows for aesthetics? Most immediately, the aesthetic proves to be an arena where contrastive cultural strategies and positions enter into contact. What does this imply for Macabéa's and her author's aesthetic attitudes? To develop a reply to these questions, I turn to a set of encounters in the novel that in their own way replicate the frictions that characterize Rodrigo's authorship.

Conflicting Aesthetic Worlds

Macabéa's other admirer is a fellow northeasterner named Olímpico. He wants to become a politician. Her kaleidoscopic aesthetic imaginaries stand out by contrast with the prospective congressman's choices. The tensions in Rodrigo's cultural position, as construed by Lispector, return with redoubled force in Macabéa's relationship with the young man. They have a fling. The proud owner of a stolen watch, he is in a hurry to become rich. At first, he sees Macabéa as a career asset. When she starts to take delight in words, in signs apart from their referents—relishing pings and advertisements on the radio—she threatens his cultural superiority and masculinity. Whereas Macabéa, as we have seen, likes to listen to the radio station emitting the "correct time" (41), Olímpico has no need for these feminized technological mediations. His stolen timepiece serves him well: "I don't need the correct time because I've got a watch" (41). The watch gives him a place in a realm of commodities and professional standing. For her, the pings heard on "Clock Radio" offer a point of access to an aesthetic present, an experiential world. Macabéa's and Olímpico's relations to time diverge dramatically.

The two also have different tastes. Olímpico is heavily invested in his aesthetic preferences. Besides being employed as a "metallurgist" (36), as he describes his post as an assembly line worker in a metal factory, he is an artist. In his free time, he carves statues of Jesus and the saints down to the most graphic detail and draws caricatures of powerful people based on newspaper photographs. His dexterity notwithstanding, our sculptor and draftsman favors an outmoded, literalist notion of artistic production that is impervious to the media dominating his era. Whereas she is a fervent moviegoer, he opts for funerals and bullfights. The term *electronic*, which arouses her curiosity when she catches it on the radio among a wealth of intriguing linguistic items this medium brings her way, leaves him indifferent (41). Macabéa's experiences are solitary. When she recounts them to her rat of a "boyfriend," they do not create a space for solidarity and love. He scoffs at them.

The future politician starts to look elsewhere for companionship. He drops the emaciated, "ugly" Macabéa for her well-fed coworker Glória, who performs more convincingly in the realm of female beautification. He has hit the mark. "From her hips you could tell [she] was made for childbearing. Whereas Macabéa seemed to have in herself her own end" (51). Glória's family background is excellent, too. They are from the city of Rio—they are the real thing: "The fact that she was a carioca made her belong to the longed-for clan from the South" (50). Her father even works in a butcher's shop, where he wields knives that appeal enormously to Olímpico's taste for blood. He has already killed a man. Having his desires tied up with his ambitions for upward mobility, he buys into the marketplace and the promises of modernity. Indeed, his aesthetic interests map unidirectionally onto his plans for social advancement.

Macabéa's perspective couldn't be more different. Her experiences of cultural objects and linguistic concepts subtly question the values these items entail, asking what they mean in human terms. "She knew that there were a lot of things she didn't know how to understand. Did 'aristocracy' mean an answered prayer? Probably. If that's the way things are, that's how they should be" (42). She is the antipode of a politician. Futurity barely registers in her awareness. Resistance is not her forte. Nonetheless, her sensibility includes an acute alertness to societal privileges and rank orders. Her aesthetic is tuned in to small frictions in the normative fabric of the society. From the bus, she observes a rusty gate that squeaks. It leads to a block of houses that carries the number 106 and a name plaque. "It was called 'Sunrise'. A pretty name that also augured good things" (43). A beautiful future may be in the offing behind the "rusted, twisted, creaking, peeling gate" (43). The reader painfully senses how notions of the good life uphold disparities among social classes, ethnicities, genders, and races.

Macabéa's perceptions yield keen aesthetic readings of the city. She is taken with aesthetic elements that for the most part fall below other people's evaluative radars, such as the pings, the docks, and the cargo ships passing through the port. She is also fond of Donizetti's aria "Una furtiva lacrima," sung by Enrico Caruso, which she hears on the radio. When she tries to sing it herself, it brings her to tears first because "her voice was as crude and out of tune as she was" and "because, through the music, she might have guessed there were other ways of feeling, there were more delicate existences and even a certain luxury of soul" (42). Lispector keeps the reader's affect centered on this crucial truth, which, with a sharp pang, apprises the reader of the sadness of the situation. Macabéa belongs to these fine existences; hers is this abundant soul. If only society would recognize and honor this. Market rationality and pragmatic comportments represent no more than a sliver of the worlds that are possible.

Macabéa's tastes appreciate sonic textures and other cultural objects for what they are in themselves. Her aesthetic perceptions resonate in a vibrant sphere of values, emotions, and fantasies. She inhabits an enchanted world, vastly more expansive than the splinter of reality that passes muster by the criteria of her ex-boyfriend's interested gaze. Macabéa sets her own aesthetic compass: "[S]he like a stray dog was guided exclusively by herself (10). She is the aesthetic subject who employs the Surrealist-inspired urban strategy of the *dérive*, or drifting, in exploring the city and the forms of creaturely life it houses: "She had unprompted and stray thoughts because even though she was at random she possessed much inner freedom" (63).

What does she do with her freedom? Macabéa is a cosmopolitan inhabitant of global culture. She lives in a colonial building on Acre Street, among storehouses filled with import and export goods (22). Her neighborhood is a favorite haunt for sailors and hookers. Warehouses containing coal and cement surround her tenement house near the docks. Passing cargo ships give her a longing "for who knows what" (32). She is thrilled when she catches their sporadic whistling on her Sunday stroll (23). Other kinds of noises appeal to her, as well, such as the honking of cars in the night: "They were life" (25). She is a Greta Garbo fan. What she really craves, however, is to be like the less aloof Marilyn Monroe. The star's pink skin inspires her devotion. Roping the actress even more closely into the circle of her daily life, our typist gives her a special name, perhaps taking advantage of one of her characteristic typos: "Marylin" rather than "Marilyn" (45, 53, 55). With Marylin one can have fun; she can be your very own hero. Macabéa's tastes are cosmopolitan: An aficionado of Hollywood films and movie stars alongside the ships and the docks, she is plugged in to a transnational flow of goods.

Her modus operandi, meanwhile, is fantasy. Her participation in the global economy differs in this regard from that of her four roommates. These young women, who all go by the name Maria, are employed in sales at Lojas Americanas, a large department store with joint US-Brazilian origins (21). This line of work is not Macabéa's thing. "One of them sold Coty face powder, if you can imagine" (23). Macabéa stays clear of producing or purveying merchandise. The reader surmises she is living beauty, not a seller of it. Her dreams are not at risk of spilling over into her dealings with some actual commodity. She sticks to desire, which her imagination keeps alive. An avid collector of ads that she cuts out of old newspapers left in her boss's office, she dotes on the image of a delicious-looking cream "for the skin of women who simply were not her" that she has discovered in one of them (30). The imagining is pure joy. But she would never waste this delicacy on her skin. Her idea would be to gulp it down. The choice is sheer speculation. The two options are unlikely to eventuate for our disinterested perceiver, who stares at shiny jewelry and satin clothing through shop windows "just to mortify herself a bit" and visits the butcher's shop to smell the air of meat, wondering contentedly what it might taste like (26, 44).

Awestruck by a rainbow, Macabéa longs for another one and is even eager to see fireworks (27). She is overcome with ecstasy in front of a tree so large that she can't wrap her arms around it. Once a month, on payday, she splurges by visiting the cinema and sometimes buys herself a rose (24, 27, 45). The party she throws for herself after Olímpico jilts her—she for whom nobody ever gives a party—is to treat herself to a bright red lipstick she doesn't really need. To her astonishment, the mirror reflects the grotesque image of someone who has received a punch in the mouth, blood spurting from her lips. Glória laughs at her for having done herself up like the type that sleeps with soldiers. During the row that follows, the two young women hurl accusations of ugliness at each other (53).

Macabéa's disinterested outlook stands in stark contrast to the new couple's aesthetic preferences, which conform to the demands of social and material advancement. Their attitudes are of a piece with the norms of the upwardly mobile, technocratic order that renders Macabéa disposable. The two youngsters abandon her, ugly as she is. Even Rodrigo admits that "poverty is ugly" (13). It's not that Glória is beautiful, but she is blonde, white, even chubby, for she eats well. The other girl cannot compete. Her dry, barren body is a lost cause. Gender wreaks its effects in conventionally ordered, heterosexual society. Glória is impressed with her boyfriend's furious masculinity (56). Deserting Macabéa in favor of the expedient choice, the lovers align their desires with the "technical society," in which, unbeknownst to herself, Macabéa is a "dispensable cog," as Rodrigo puts it (21). With the courtship taking off, Lispector's protagonist remains behind. Modernity dismisses her. Whereas Olímpico uses his new liaison to break with his upbringing in the backlands of the northeast (56–57), Macabéa unwittingly nourishes her bond with the past. Notwithstanding her miserable youth, she misses the manioc flour of her childhood in the dead quiet of her Sunday afternoons (26–27). The periodic, unlikely crowing of a rooster in her urban neighborhood brightens her days on Acre Street, but it also calls to mind nostalgic memories of the "Alagoas backlands," where, in what might have been her words if she were thinking about it, "she sprouted from the soil . . . like an instantly molded mushroom" (21–22). Taste's movements pull her between past and present.

With the normative societal order using its instrumental appraisals to get Macabéa out of the way, this moldy mushroom branches its diaphanous mycelium through the conceptual underpinnings of modernity, preparing a soil from which a different world can spring forth. Her exquisite aesthetic perceptions question cultural arrangements encoded in everyday objects and commodified art. She is curious about the word *mimetism*, which was pronounced on Clock Radio (46). And she is puzzled by *elgebra*, which was discussed in connection with a mathematician who had written *Alice in Wonderland* (41). The verb *designate* emerges from her typewriter as "desiginate" (7). The noun *ephemerides* her boss asks her to copy—or was it *ephemeris*?—is totally mysterious to her (31). She falls in love with it, creating her own connection with the stars and touching their evanescent constellations with her fleeting being. Nature and culture intertwine in her aesthetic experience, for her linguistic affection also keeps her in close contact with the two film stars she venerates.

Her typos stir contrarian states of embodiment that pull in astronomy, aesthetic theory, popular culture, and the philosophy of language to free up linguistic form. When she is overwhelmed by the crowd-pleasing "Una furtiva lacrima" and perturbed by the cacophonous voice with which she tries to echo it, the tears dripping from her eyes give expression to a unique world of feeling and imagining. At the same time, her bawling recognizes the irrevocable distance the society produces between the two sonic performances, her daringly discordant "La-la-la-la-la" and the precious aria that is "the only really beautiful thing" she has ever known, or so the narrator asserts (42). Her disinterested mode of attention activates worlds of sensibility and meaning that leave behind the economic and goal-oriented concerns that dominate Olímpico's and Glória's behavior. Magnificent vistas open up. Social criticism registers in sensory terms, in "loud and dazzling" imaginaries (29). Like the elgebrist before her, Macabéa has invented an aesthetic wonderland.

The strains I have identified in Rodrigo's artistic stance reemerge in sharp outline as a facet of Macabéa's tumultuous relationship with the tragicomic duo that her author has chosen as his sidekicks. The relation between Rodrigo and Macabéa ripens during this subplot, for his tale reveals the mechanisms of abandonment the iniquitous pair Gloría and Olímpico visits on her. Rodrigo, it appears, sides with his residual protagonist against the procedures of aesthetically upheld modernity.

Indeed, his attitude is directly antithetical to the couple's aesthetic disparagement of poverty: "Yes, I'm in love with Macabéa, my dear Maca, in love with her ugliness and total anonymity since she belongs to no one. In love with her weak lungs, the scraggly girl" (59). No longer a strike against the girl, her ugliness is part of her appeal. Rodrigo is drawn to her negligible, skinny body that follows its own devices. With his aesthetic embrace of his character, he upends an exclusionary logic of beauty. Thus, he offers a reply to Macabéa's plight in the society. Is Rodrigo fancying a double love fest, with two pairs mirroring each other? We haven't yet seen how Macabéa feels about this kind of plot. And Rodrigo, as I have indicated, has a parallel authorial agenda going at the same time. He wants his tale to bring him to a place where he would have been but has never been. So this love story falls short as a reply to the emergency driving the novel.

Literature, we have seen, bolsters modernity by investing it with aesthetic allure and simultaneously keeps it at a distance by way of a disinterested comportment. These contrary tendencies mark Rodrigo's cultural position, as the novel figures it. The friction between these polarities cannot be smoothed out by writing off either of them. Rodrigo's authorship, after all, rests on their coupling. Further probing his self-personification to lay bare the novel's construction of the lettered enterprise, let's consider how he navigates these conflicting affiliations as he plods through his tale and mints a fate for this character.

Telling a True Story

Lispector traces the movements of her fictional author-character's self-consciousness. Rodrigo is burning to uncover the truth of his protagonist: "I follow a hidden, fatal line. I have to seek a truth that is beyond me" (12). This goal ensures his necessity. "I'm astonished to know the truth so well. Could it be that my painful task is to guess in the flesh the truth that nobody wants to see?" (48). Thus, he establishes his indispensability. His narrative qualifications are of paramount importance to the society. He can even win the public he currently lacks, for, as he realizes, he is "left over"; he has "no place . . . in the world of men" (12). "Marginalized" as he is, he falls outside the social class system: "The upper class considers me a weird monster, the middle class worries I might unsettle them, the lower class never comes to me" (10). The present story is to make all the difference. He wants to surpass his limits (9). He hopes the story will allow his self-transcendence (12–13).

So, we're told, he sets out to capture the facts of Macabéa's life (4, 8–9, 14–16, 60, 62). Just as this involves contending with conventional notions of beauty, as I have argued, he needs to work around rhetorical effects that have settled in linguistic vocabularies and styles. A stripping down is called for:

"I suddenly fell for facts without literature" (8). The regular techniques at his disposal are not up to the job:

> Naturally, like every writer I'm tempted to use succulent terms: I know splendid adjectives, meaty nouns, and verbs so slender that they travel sharp through the air about to go into action, since words are actions, don't you agree? I'm not going to adorn the word because if I touch the girl's bread the bread will turn to gold—and the girl (she's nineteen) the girl wouldn't be able to bite it, dying of hunger. So I have to speak simply to capture her delicate and vague existence. I humbly limit myself—without trumpeting my humility for then it wouldn't be humble—I limit myself to telling of the feeble adventures of a girl in a city that's entirely against her. (6–7, translation revised)

Rodrigo espouses a minimalist poetics that lingers with the words themselves before they issue into deeds. Only then can Macabéa eat her bread. A flashy, action-oriented language is bound to expunge her from her own story. Rodrigo swears off ornamentation, a "*cantabile* melody," to approximate his character's being (8). His tone will be "cold" (5). The story must realistically get at the truth of her bread rather than turn a profit—a surplus value that is inaccessible to Macabéa. He is not planning to behave like Olímpico, who jumps at every opportunity to show off his golden tooth (37).[11] He will be the ally that his beloved protagonist and the rest of the city, unbeknownst to them, direly need. Indeed, he implies that she needs him as much as he needs her (11, 15, 29). One notices here his attempt to validate his own authorship. This gesture is key to the novel's force: The reader is invited to infer that literature is salvaged, although it poses problems. Rodrigo is rescuing the lettered city from itself. Indeed, the novel performs the power of literature. And it draws the reader into their role in the performance.

For it is literature, in the eyes of Lispector's fictional author-character, that will bring the reader where they need to be—that is, to a state where this art form occupies its rightful role. The text positions the reader to go along with this authorial gamble. So we follow Rodrigo to a certain extent in the performance while also being alert to the way we allow ourselves to be taken along for the ride. This involves participating in an authorial project. Rodrigo's "first duty to [him]self," he observes, is to reach the word, the unvarnished word "itself" (11). Putting to work the words, he also wants to "arrive at the thickest and lowest, deepest and earth trombone" (11). He senses the presence of a "vibrant and rich, morbid and dark web which has its countertone in the thick bass of pain. Allegro con brio" (8). If things go well, he hopes, he may even reach "the sweet flute around which [he] will entwine [him]self like a supple liana" (12). Writing, the reader senses, assumes aesthetic qualities that contravene Rodrigo's stated poetics, as his metaphors get the better of him. It confronts him with the contradictory impulses that make up his authorship.

But if language is outwitting Rodrigo, he swiftly recoups his stable ground, his upright position. "[L]et's get back to today. Because, as we know, today is today" (12). Thus, he arrives at a solid truth about Macabéa, and about himself, to boot: "[B]y way of information about" the two of them, he divulges that "we live exclusively in the present because it is always eternally today and tomorrow will be a today, eternity is the state of things at this very moment" (10). His remark provides some insight into Macabéa's sense of time: No wonder the pings speak to her.

For all her presentism, Macabéa has a belated side, too. She is "ancient" (22). Her laughter sounds like it belongs to the past long gone (24). Her dreams are occupied by "giant antediluvian animals," making it seem as if she originates from "the most remote epochs" (51, translation revised). "Inhaling and exhaling," she dwells in an "impersonal limbo" that attains neither the "worst [n]or the best" (15). Temporal development, it appears, is out of reach.

With her "anonymous" being (22), she partakes of a cosmic presence. In Rodrigo's description, "The northeastern girl got lost in the crowd. In Mauá Square, where she caught the bus it was cold and she had no shelter to protect her from the wind. Ah, but there were cargo ships that made her long for who knows what. This only sometimes. Really she left her gloomy office, faced the air outside, dusky, and realized that every day at the same time, it was exactly the same time. Irremediable the great clock that worked in time" (32). After hours, this passage reveals, Macabéa takes her disinterested outlook from the office, where she had just been contemplating "ephemerides," to the public realm of the street, the bus, the square, the crowd. Her disinterested comportment is a pivot for a haunting, unhomely, tautological awareness of time's repeatability. Rodrigo recoils. Occupied as the "author of a life," he declines the way "routine" is diverting his narrative from the new (32). The story, it appears, must be going somewhere. He flinches at the lethal nothingness he is sensing: "Well, so what? So what, nothing" (32). He needs plot development. When it collapses, he checks out, taking his distance.

With the turn to public territory and Rodrigo out of the way, the reader is reminded of that other crucial chronicler apart from Lispector, of shifts in the conditions of storytelling and the role of the storyteller: Walter Benjamin. Macabéa's distinctively subaltern engagement with the public realm resonates with the shock of modernity he documented. Following Benjamin, we find that the reference points in relation to which a certain European, nineteenth-century subject could situate itself in a fabric of experience, have been uprooted in the novel. Historical pillars of collective belonging have vanished. The city of Rio de Janeiro no longer, if it ever did, represents a site of warmth, a shelter that gives protection. Mauá Square is situated in a global arena, where the cargo ships come and go, but it is a territory of trade and commerce, not a place that the voyager can arrive at and depart from, a station from which a future can be imagined, a setting that gives coherence to conceptions of life and death. The square fails to constitute a public sphere of belonging, a bedrock for nonalienated ways of existing. Macabéa abides outside an embodied, affectively resonant, temporal matrix of longing and loss.[12] Disinterested consciousness situates her in a temporal design all of her own making. Strange taste registers a nondescript temporality, an indeterminate spatiality. It is lived in the dusk, when distinctions fade, in a unsettled place that lacks points by which to orient desire. Teleology collapses.

Anyhow, our reluctant author, who wants to approximate his character as closely as possible (11), soon catches up with the story, which, after all, "happens in the year it is happening" (24). He hardly needs a paragraph break before regaining narrative steam. Novelties gush forth afresh. Her discomfiting penchant for tautology infects him, whether he wants it to or not. Meanwhile, the reader can reap more truths about Macabéa.

The pings, it turns out, are not her only hooks into a disjunctive frame of temporality. She is both ahead of and behind normalized, ordinary time, for she is super-slow. As Rodrigo points out, "[F]or her . . . reality . . . was very little. She could deal better with her daily unreality, living in sloooow motion, hare leeeeaping through the aaaair over hiiiill and daaaale, vagueness was her earthly world, vagueness was the insides of nature" (26). Language bends and stretches. The categories of day-to-day society as it is known lose their applicability in Macabéa's universe.

She also transgresses ordinary temporality in the opposite way, for she is superfast. In Rodrigo's words, "She liked to feel time passing. Although she didn't have a watch, or perhaps for that very reason, she savored the greatness of time. She was supersonic in life. Nobody noticed that with her existence she was breaking the sound barrier. For other people she didn't exist" (54). Macabéa acts and feels with such speed that no one even realizes what is happening. She defies all comprehension, all perception. The epistemic split is reciprocal. Mundane life doesn't make any sense to her, either (36). "Is the sky above or below? Wondered the northeastern girl" (23).

Her aesthetic satisfactions carry and sustain this otherworldly mindset. "The rooster was coming from the never. It came from the infinite up through her bed, giving her gratitude" (23). Although Macabéa is an individual on the margins who is banished from quotidian patterns of temporal development, she is a disinterested perceiver whose observations are in tune with the current moment. She, on the whole, bears a contemplative relation to the transnational flow of people and goods. The educational tidbits she gleans from the radio provide a purely intellectual thrill. They lack all practical use to her (29). Simultaneously ancient and avant-garde, acculturated in snippets of Western art and a subaltern inhabitant of peripheral zones, she is neither fully of nor beyond the capitalist present.

Macabéa lives at once inside and outside normative temporality, existing apart from the ordinary rhythms of social existence. This distance can be a matter of her swiftness or belatedness, as the case may be. Temporal dislocation keeps her close to the marketable "now," her Coca-Cola and the ads she culls from the radio and the newspaper, while also placing her at a remove from standardized economic operations. Through her untoward taste and her intricate temporal presence, the subaltern gains a foothold in the lettered city, albeit one that is tenuous and riddled with ambivalence. Macabéa, who pays "attention to every letter" (31), who considers every word for what it is, possesses a quotidian aesthetic imagination and creativity that is on par with the inventions of any passable writer, such as Rodrigo.

While Glória and Olímpico banish Macabéa to the fringes of the society as the aspiring politician replaces his "subproduct" with high "quality goods" (50–51), our superfast and super-slow protagonist simultaneously remains farther behind and dashes more rapidly away from them than their sensorium can pick up. Indeed, she plays with the regular temporal order. This play extends from the pings with which she is smitten and the informational morsels that strike her fancy to the everyday occupations in which she recognizes herself, albeit with a good deal of distance, after "dress[ing] herself in herself": Taking pride in her social identities as a typist, a virgin, and a Coca-Cola devotee, she plays the abstract "role of being" (27).

So what can we make of the contradictory motivations that her author is navigating as a somewhat disinterested, substantially interested participant of a market society? Rodrigo, as we have seen, hopes to revitalize and elevate his authorship with his narration. While financially he has been able to get by so far, he now is on the verge of surpassing himself (9). He aims at a universal appeal for the truth that his tale sets out to uncover: "[M]ay everyone recognize it inside himself because all of us are one" (4). Moreover, he adds, "[S]omething more precious than gold" may be garnered from the story: rich readers who are "poor in spirit or longing" can reap "the delicate essential" (4). He really knows how to sell himself. Literature provides an encounter with otherness, although, to the poor, reading remains an altogether "superfluous" way to spend the time (22). Perhaps Rodrigo's universalism can help him win new audiences on this front, and here Macabéa's public education, her taste for language, comes in handy. The true story may pay off handsomely for him. Soon, however, the equipoise between the young woman's disinterested propensities and her author's mixture of interest and disinterest is thrown off balance in a plot turn that triggers a new suite of aesthetic permutations.

Tales of Princes and Princesses

The double binds Rodrigo is handling as he veers between his disinterested narrative stance and his attachment to economic realities make their presence felt throughout his narration. The incongruities are puzzling: How far will he go in his pursuit of the novelties he craves? Why is he telling an "old tale," regressing to the already known (5)? How does he reconcile his need for Technicolor, described in the author's dedication, with his preference for the cold facts, the words in themselves? The reader realizes that Rodrigo has been coping with market pressures from the get-go. His love for the disinterested Macabéa is more conflicted than he admits to himself. How does she even feel about the story that he sutures her into?

Through sparse, nontheatrical language, Rodrigo plans to seize hold of Macabéa's barren reality. His dry poetics will be true to her destitution, the emptiness of her existence, her "flimsy soul" (24, 29). Macabéa measures her pleasures carefully. Too much of a good thing might mean her death. "[I]f by any chance she ever got a nice good taste of living," she worries, "she'd suddenly cease to be the princess she was and be transformed into vermin. Because, no matter how bad her situation, she didn't want to be deprived of herself, she wanted to be herself. . . . So she protected herself . . . by living less, consuming so little of her life that she'd never run out. This savings gave her a little security since you can't fall farther than the ground" (24). Taste is treacherous territory. Strange tastes notwithstanding, there are limits. Macabéa prefers princess stories to Kafkaesque metamorphoses.[13] She keeps herself in line. Her body appreciates this policy.

Accustomed to the meagerest intake, Macabéa's stomach balks when Glória, sensing a twinge of guilt for stealing Olímpico, treats her to hot chocolate at her home “on General so-and-so street,” where the family feels safe, housed “on a street named after a military leader” (57). The visit is one of the rare occasions when Macabéa is aware “that for her there was no place in the world and exactly because Glória gave her so much” (57). Charity affirms her position on the sidelines. She feels sick. The cheap doctor is of no help with her affliction. Glória recommends a fortuneteller so Macabéa can learn what the future has in stock—hopefully, there is another boyfriend in the cards.

Meanwhile, Rodrigo continues to struggle over a possible fiction capable of representing his protagonist. He is not the only producer of stories. Narrative competition looms when Macabéa pays a visit to Madame Carlota. Enticed by Carlota’s prediction, she desires the embrace of a male lover. He will be a foreigner by the name of Hans. Surrounded by colorful plastic decorations, the larger-than-life, chocolate-munching fortuneteller speaks not only from but also about the marketplace, which has served her well through her transitions from hooker to pimp, owner of a whorehouse, and onward, to her current post. She peddles destinies to her poor young clients reminiscent of dime-store novels. Her act is irresistible. Macabéa falls for the tale she is told. She awaits her blond foreigner with the “blue or green or brown or black eyes” (68).

She barely has to cross the street when Hans shows up in a Mercedes. The vehicle knocks her to the ground. Enamored as she is of Marilyn Monroe, Greta Garbo, and other signifiers of modernity, Macabéa attains her “hour of the star” (20, 75). Her “movie-star” episode reiterates a script with which she is intimately familiar: She comes by the end she enjoys watching in the cinema and in musicals and that she daydreams about in the street when she sees a soldier—namely, the murder of a woman by a man (27, 49, 73). As sensational as this twist in the novel’s plot turns out to be, it doesn’t distract the reader from the fact that the foreigner is not the only killer besides Olímpico. Rodrigo’s intervention safeguards his character’s disinterested aesthetic. He liberates her from the clutches of instrumental rationality. She is his, not Carlota’s, creation. He keeps her by his side, grabbing her back from the perfidious threesome of market actors that populates his novel. Victorious, Rodrigo is able to assert his honorability as a writer. “I’ll go on where the air runs out, I’ll go to where the great gale leaps away howling, I’ll go to where the void begins to curve, I’ll go where my breath takes me” (74). Thus, he salvages his reputation. Literature, contrary to the marketplace, seeks the unknown: “I am so pure that I know nothing” (74). Rodrigo claims modernist artistic agency.

Resuming narrative command over Macabéa’s tale, in accordance with his presumed privilege and duty as a modernist author who is in control of the world of his fiction, Rodrigo puts an end to her story. While she had imagined that the hour of her death would transform her into a movie star (20), when the moment arrives, she wants to throw up a "thousand-pointed star" (75). In the throes of demise, she finds solace in the mantra "I am, I am, I am" (74). But this last-ditch effort at imaginative self-engendering is futile. The aesthetic mediations that, as Rodrigo states in the dedication, have him come into his own incontrovertibly deal Macabéa a death blow. The lettered city, having endeavored to open itself up to her, asserts its exclusions with renewed force. The question raised at the start of this chapter of whether the aesthetic is up to the job of contending with the disaster represented by Macabéa meets with a resounding "No" from the side of the novel. Rodrigo and, with him, the lettered city reveal their societal bankruptcy. The novel, it appears, confirms Rama's and Franco's diagnoses, which maintain that this structure has lost its moral and political tenability and is no longer capable of exercising a hold on the aesthetic imagination.

Indeed, literature eminently fails Macabéa as a site of identification. No matter how often she intones "I am," it doesn't win her the "I am I" of self-recognition that, as Rodrigo noticed earlier, she had never experienced (28). The abundant "I" that music offers him stays in a far beyond. Echoing her threefold invocation with his wish to hear "music, music, music" just before dying (73), he interrupts their proximity by underlining the schism the lettered city institutes between them.[14]

Having fallen for Carlota's tale, Macabéa swaps playing at being for being. She surrenders uncertain shimmers of a future for the transparent prospect of a conventional marriage plot. Rodrigo's narrative follows suit: "Et tu, Brute?! Yes, that's how I wanted to announce that—that Macabéa died. The Prince of Darkness won. Finally the coronation" (75). Rodrigo and Macabéa eventually tell stories of princes and princesses. As we were warned early on, the novel is "an old tale." Unprepared to undo the snarls of conventional narration, the lettered city, as represented by Rodrigo, squashes Macabéa's disinterested aesthetic. Inapposite taste is over and done with.

Who Is Killing Who?

The lettered city, the reader feels, can't handle aestheticized poverty. It wipes out Macabéa's disinterested comportment in the attempt to rescue it. The structure of aesthetic normativity that supports Rodrigo's artistry and from which Gloría and Olímpico draw sustenance lacks legitimacy. The scenarios of subjectivation underlying Rodrigo's aesthetic being, as represented in the dedication, proceed on shaky ground. Some people's aesthetic life comes at the cost of others'.

Macabéa's demise reiterates the paradoxical intertwinement of interest and disinterest that is Rodrigo's hallmark: In the name of disinterest, he plays into the marketplace by allotting a role to Carlota in his story. His complicity unfolds in the aesthetic plane. Early on, we had been told that the text was a piece of popular literature, a "cheap tearjerker" (25; "literatura de cordel" [1998 (1977), 33]). In Macabéa's final scenes, Rodrigo reverts to ornamentation, as he confesses in a parenthetical remark: "I'm writing about the meager minimum adorning it with purple, jewels and splendor. Is this how you write? No, it's not by accumulation but by stripping naked. But I fear nakedness, since it is the last word" (2011, 72). Rodrigo's cedes his poetics to a capitalist mode of narrative production. Turning to the mass media and a transnational flow of people and goods to give expression to Macabéa's end—using movie plots, hauling in a German automobile and even a German lover—he situates his authorship in the global culture industry. Aesthetics, in the novel's final pages, lends itself to the kind of vanishing trick he had performed earlier in the service of the Coca-Cola Company. This time it is Macabéa who is torn from the face of the earth. Like that other self-interested killer, the churlish Olímpico, Rodrigo does away with her, hoping to put a part of his history behind him.

Initially impelled by ethical motivations to tell the teen's story—apprised of his "duty" to "reveal her life" (5) and hoping to parry the accusation she levies at him (9)—he now chooses to reveal her death. This doesn't mean his morals have gone to pieces, however. Rodrigo is quick to wash his hands of the scene in Carlota's office, even as he is rendering it. This plot development, he explains, is not his doing. "I see that I'm writing above and beyond me. I'm not responsible for what I'm now writing" (63). Don't suspect any turpitude. "I am not saleable," he exclaims (76). Indeed, aside from the fortuneteller, he has many others to blame for what happened. "Was the ending as grandiloquent as you required?" he asks innocently as he is about to draw the novella to a close (77). Our disinterested narrator, Rodrigo S. M., has only been satisfying consumer demand. The reader is at fault for the writer's conversion to the marketplace, his poetic lapse into melodrama (72). Let's be clear: Macabéa's death is on us.

But why would we want Rodrigo to tell us this kind of thing? The ending surely was his, not our, idea. What use do we have for the charades of this "gratuitous" type (24)? The guy is superfluous, as he well knows. He shares this trait with the other redundant being that unfortunately is no more: his younger, more likeable counterpart. Tellingly, Suzana Amaral's wildly successful movie *A hora da estrela* (*The Hour of the Star* [1985]) writes Rodrigo mercilessly out of the narrative, as if he didn't exist to begin with. The Brazilian nation knows, the global cinema public knows: He is a nobody. Just as he killed Macabéa, the time probably has come for the reader to do away with him. Fortunately, we're nearing the end of the story.

In Rodrigo's favor, we may note that he has anticipated this fate. His denunciation of repetition militates against Macabéa's absorption into a standard movie script that sacrifices female characters in the name of box office returns. His ornamental style has turned her bread into a shiny, rigid, inedible object. Representing her as one more instance of a familiar tale runs the risk of his own congealment as he had worried, his expulsion from the story he is at pains to tell. The marketplace, in the final accounting, threatens him as much as it does her. Again, he knows: "Macabéa killed me" (76).

Taking on the Other Killer

Hoping to bring the lettered city up to speed, Rodrigo destroys it. The paradoxes he has been navigating not only eliminate him but also sniff out literature's hope of reckoning with the subaltern and keeping in touch with the ever elusive now. We giggle at his inflated ideas about his own preeminence, as when he calls himself "one of the more important" characters he has created (5). The gender politics of his narration give us the shivers when we learn that Macabéa is coming alive, is even being born, at the very moment that she is dying (71, 74). His tautological utterances become exasperating because they display a lack of will, a deficiency of the imagination: "[T]hat's the way it is because that's the way it is. Was that the way it always was? It always will be. And if it wasn't? But I'm telling you it is. So then." (73). We had been warned in advance: Writing trips Rodrigo up. We feel we are tripped up a bit ourselves, as well. By him.

Indeed, he has been wringing his poetics into contortions for quite some time now. Earlier in the story, our trafficker in facts ventures a description of Macabéa's nocturnal and diurnal routines: "In the dark of the night a man whistling and heavy footsteps, the howling of the abandoned mutt. Meanwhile—the silent constellations and the space which is time which has nothing to do with her and with us. So that's how the days went by" (22–23). Rodrigo's dramatic language in this passage far exceeds the realist register he advocates. He continues, "The roosters crowing and the blood-red dawn gave fresh meaning to her withered life. In the morning there were chirping birds on Acre Street: because life sprouted from the ground, cheerful amidst the stones" (22). Fresh meaning? Joyfully twittering life? Yes and no. Meaning, in its exuberantly felt quality, emerges too quickly to be credible on the realist, truth-purveying model of narration Rodrigo espouses. Yet we powerfully sense the vital energy of Macabéa's aesthetic sensibility—superfast in its super-slowness. The dimension of space and time she inhabits and that transpires universes apart from her, as well as from the reader, harbors the rooster, which, as noted earlier, hails from the "never," from the "infinite," filling her with gratitude (23). This sublime creature recalls the *je ne sais quoi* or grace of traditional aesthetics. The bird may not be Schumann, Stravinsky, or Marlos Nobre, but it nevertheless is an endlessly generative source of aesthetic animation that nourishes life, that sparks Macabéa's aliveness.

If the realist register did collapse sooner than we surmised, then perhaps we haven't gotten entirely to the bottom of Rodrigo's poetics. Killing Macabéa may not have been his only attempt to save the situation. He may have been launching another rescue mission. Could there be any hope of resuscitating her, perhaps by mustering some aesthetic ingenuity?

On the verge of ending his tale, Rodrigo offers a reminder. "Don't forget that for now it's strawberry season" (77). The change of topic, it appears, produces one last diversion, one last inane cop-out. Wary of his text, Rodrigo may already be transitioning to the cheerful piece he said he would compose upon finishing the present one, which, we were forewarned, might turn out sadly (11). However, this sort of observation is not new to him. When getting into his story, he informed us that "the clouds are white and the sky is all blue" (18). As an author, he knows how to locate us in time and space. He is acting as the arbiter of the natural world. His rival in this domain is the Coca-Cola Company. Cognizant of the destruction of the artist's God-like reign in the era of mass media, he vies with the corporation for control of the planet. The competition is fierce. Coca-Cola already got the earth in Guatemala to buckle, killing as many as 23,000 people (15). We have another killer on the scene. This one is vast and terrible.

But Rodrigo has been rolling up his sleeves. He pins down the seasons. As we have seen, our late capitalist epoque puts forth the artist as the figure who defines the contemporary. He can let the consumer in on what nowadays is the thing to do. And although the Coca-Cola firm has appreciated his temporal designs, he is currently tripping it up: Strawberries! Forget about Coca-Cola! The soft drink is history.

Rodrigo has his pulse on fungible (i.e., uniform, exchangeable) time, whose rhythms can absorb anything, accommodating whatever merchandise, service, or product one might want to sell or buy. After the performance that is Coca-Cola, it's time to move on to other items. Count on Rodrigo to tell you what will gratify your taste. You might want to give that cheerful book of his a try, too, by the way. His insights into the flow of time promise to be to everyone's benefit—apart, of course, from that of Macabéa, who dies on his watch, exquisitely sacrificed to his sense of timing. But he is on the ascendance in his contest with big business. Not an unimportant challenge to take on. The reader is no longer giggling. We're holding tight, lest this other one, this enormous, unbridled actor that is on the loose, gets ideas about tripping *us* up instead. Go at it, Rodrigo! Go!

The reader stands in need of his temporal sensibility for an additional reason. We depend on Rodrigo to mark our place in the fiction. He keeps track of narrative time for us. "Things are always days before," he says (74). He is the one on whom we count to document when "the hour of the star" is coming for Macabéa. Simultaneously, we depend on the writer of literature to give us a sense of our own being unto death. His description of Macabéa's dying moment transfers to the death we at some point will face: "If she doesn't die now she is like us on the day before her death" (74). Thanks for the hint, Rodrigo. We can follow the story only in virtue of his keen understanding of what it is to live—and die—as beings in time. He is the one to decide what happens when and for whom. Literary authorship, he demonstrates, is an unequaled creative capacity to link phenomena to the passage of time, to situate people and things in a matrix of temporality. Literature is in charge of time. Coca-Cola may get the earth to collapse, but who will tell the reader about it and hold these killers responsible? Who is sounding the warning signal? Rodrigo establishes his importance beyond a shadow of a doubt.

His temporal aptitude, as we saw in the case of Coca-Cola, translates into his aesthetic wits. He displays his proficiency as a purveyor of aesthetic observations. It is through his shrewd powers of mediation that we find out how Macabéa experiences the moments leading up to her perishing: "Was what was happening a deaf earthquake? The land of Alagoas had opened in cracks. She stared, just for the sake of staring, at the grass. Grass in the great City of Rio de Janeiro. Random. Maybe Macabéa had once felt that she too was random in the unconquerable city?" (71). The storyteller, once again, sees her faculty of disinterested attention at work. He employs his aesthetic understanding and sensibility to bring into focus the young girl's perspective. He adjusts his vocabulary to her being, her personality. He draws on her history, for she had been gazing at grass in the streets before (62–63). The grass fits her tiny body, which would have revolted at grander natural imagery, such as vistas of seas or mountain peaks. He carefully measures the degree of drama to be employed. His reflections activate elements of aesthetic value and judgment. For he surmises later, "In the end she was no more than a music box that was slightly out of tune" (77). There you are. *She* may be out of it but *he* is sure to be keeping right on target. This is not all: We can look to him for exceptional perceptions that might otherwise not have occurred to us. "I ask you," he proceeds, "What is the weight of light?" Silence. Again, the fact that Macabéa is off and that "you"—that is, we, the reader—may be at a loss for words, doesn't mean that the storyteller is not with it. He has recovered his narrative chops. This is Rodrigo for you. He will tell you about things that you didn't even think were possible, let alone have a language for. Rodrigo's poetics carries the day. The performance goes on. As readers, we are drawn into the narrative swings and coilings and rendered participants in the text's poetics. But we have some choices to make.

To Weep or Not to Weep

Rodrigo has offered a winning apologia for his profession. He vindicates his poetics in the face of the big killer. The destructive planetary powers wielded by the great market actor, the Coca-Cola Company, can be averted only with the assistance of his disinterested authorship, which bravely takes on the callous mass murderer. Rodrigo ratifies the centrality of the lettered city as a structure of aesthetic legitimacy, a site from which aesthetic productions, values, judgments can flow. Only the lettered city and the disinterested aesthetic comportment it facilitates can rein in corporate hegemony over the planet. Are we ready to "believe," as he early on implored us? To "weep and believe" (xiv)?

So far, I have spoken a lot about aesthetics and perhaps somewhat less so, or more indirectly, about metaphysics and ethics. Macabéa's take on these endeavors is informed by her Cartesian maxim, "[S]ince I am, the thing to do is to be" (25). This maxim prominently informs her attitude at the end of her life. Moments before the Mercedes hits her, as we have seen, she stops "playing the role of being," choosing plain, regular being instead. Her author obliges. She is given what she asks for. Smashed by the car, she finally comes into her own, much in the way his musical "prophets of the present" whopped Rodrigo's "I" into existence. "Death," he states, "is an encounter with oneself" (76). Or, in Macabéa's aesthetic translation, she "saw among the stones lining the gutter the whisps of grass green as the most tender human hope. Today, she thought, today is the first day of my life: I was born" (71). There is hope. A future is in sight.

Our chronicler of planetary time moves on to religion and sexuality in an effort keep up with his plot resolution, interlacing registers he earlier had placed in close proximity (10). His signifiers predicate a state of "sensuality" of his dying protagonist: "A smooth, chilling, freezing and acute taste as in making love. Could this be the grace that you call God?" (74–75). At "the almost painful and whizzing moment of love," Macabéa turns from virgin into woman (75). The Cartesian conjecturer utters "clearly and distinctly: As for the future" (75). Granting his character the future she craves, Rodrigo has his long-awaited lovefest after all: in fantasy, that is. We have been reading a romance.

With Rodrigo and Macabéa pairing up, aesthetics, ethics, and metaphysics also come together. The pair transcend their nothingness, their status as residual entities. Rodrigo discharges his moral duty. He updates his authorship, rendering it consonant with current societal arrangements. But how credible do we find the orgiastic exploit he has slipped into Macabéa's death scene? Who falls for this bizarre sexual phantasm, this unabashedly self-interested vision, which finds male self-actualization in a woman's expiry? Perhaps the reader follows only the first entreaty, to weep, holding off from believing. Or maybe weeping is actually the second injunction, since believing also precedes weeping (xiv). Well, dear reader, which of the two responses, if either, will it be?

Come to think of it, didn't Rodrigo push another woman out of his tale when he introduced himself? At the beginning of the novel, he declared that the story had to be told by a male writer, for "a woman would make it all weepy and maudlin" (6). For anyone who has reservations about sentimental narrations, Rodrigo is hardly a reliable judge of what does and doesn't fall under this category. What is he worrying about, given that he soon intimates that his story, too, might be sad (11)? Is Rodrigo, in taking over from Lispector, ripping a page from the book of the "fragile little macho" Olímpico, who abhors sad faces and subdues Glória with his toughness, thereby securing his entry into "the world of others" (43, 56)? For sure, Macabéa weeps. She's crying and learning how much water she has in her eyes (42). The rain never leaves her. The reader is crying, too. But Rodrigo is busy removing his traces, conning his audience into complicity with a perky, freshly concocted vanishing trick: "[I]f there's any reader for this story I'd like him to absorb this girl like a cloth soaking up water" (31). Let the reader clear up the spillage. Maybe Rodrigo didn't count on a female reader. Indeed, no later than two pages into the narrative, he directly addresses a male audience, "you gentlemen" (4; "os senhores" [1998 (1977), 12]).

Rodrigo uses his anti-ornamentalist, anti-sentimental, minimalist poetics to mask his ousting of his own female creator, the revered Clarice. Through tough-guy constructions of facts as stones and words as no more than words themselves (2011, 8, 11, 62), he hides the signs of his authorial coup. Under the cover of the contemporaneity and ethical necessity of his artistry, he installs a heterosexual, masculinist imagination. His gender politics trips him up.

Antinomies of the Lettered City

The lettered city is a male coterie, it turns out. By now, however, we are familiar with Rodrigo's narrative smarts. Indeed, he has forged the necessary leeway to wriggle himself out of his predicament. Even at a watershed moment such as this he can recover his equilibrium. Others, he has let us know, are on standby. His line of defense is found early in the text. Having just hailed his male interlocutors, he lets them know that he will "have to use the words that sustain" them (4). With his "grand finale" he thus extends a favor to the male clique that is left of his readership (5). The literary writer in the age of mass media cannot take his audience for granted. Contrary to his usual writerly habits, he goes out of his way to reach them. Obviously, it is their doing that they require grandiose tales. Rodrigo's gender fantasies are off the hook. As an author he no longer matches God, but he at least equals Jesus, worthy of eternalization in Olímpico's sculptural hagiography, sexual parts included. "Don't consume me!" he beseeches his entertainment-seeking readership (76). "Woe to me, all lost and it's as if the great guilt was mine. May they wash my hands and feet and then—then may they daub them with oils sacred from so much perfume" (76). He is the sacrificial lamb. And even he exclaims in protest: "I feel my last grimace of revolt and howl: the slaughter of doves!!! Living is luxury" (76). Like his audience, he wants a dollop of this luxury, brought into his tale by the Technicolor he promised us all.

Another characteristic of Rodrigo's we have gotten used to is his fluency in juggling contradictions. The disinterested critic of big business is outstripping a stellar woman writer in an interested fashion, hoping to elevate his professional status. The writer who wants to have his character eat her bread ends up converting it into gold while extracting this precious metal from charcoal (8). The one who is eager to "make things better" for the young girl, who desires to do everything in his power to give her a "splendid future," blasts this possibility out of existence (22, 27). Poetic antinomies are Rodrigo's domicile. His gendered comportment is riddled with conflicts.

Double binds, not surprisingly, arise also in the realm of space and time. The orchestrator of narrative temporality who prides himself on his timing typically rushes ahead of himself or belatedly fills in the reader on things he has forgotten to mention. He both is in haste and wants to go to sleep, fatigued by his story, worn down by his labor (11, 57, 71). Although he plans to write a traditional story with a distinct beginning, middle, and end, he creates a title page that topples any narrative order. Rather than giving just one title, he supplies a whole list (1). Which of these stories are we reading? "As for the Future." (*sic*)?

Or "Account of the Preceding Facts"? Is it "Whistling in the Dark Wind?" or "Let Her Deal with It?" But then it might be "A Sense of Loss." Or "Discreet Exit Through the Back Door." Maybe we are reading all of these lovely stories. But each of them engenders its own plotline. The reader has no idea where to locate Rodrigo in a spatial and temporal scheme. He is as superfast as he is superslow, like his beloved Macabéa. He tenaciously pursues the truth, then, all of a sudden, lets it slip. "What was the truth of my Maca?" he asks. He answers swiftly, "As soon as you discover the truth it's already gone: the moment passed. I ask: what is? Reply: it's not" (76). Indeed, he affirms, "Truth is unrecognizable. So it doesn't exist? No, for men it doesn't exist" (71). Rodrigo's poetics, rather than situating us in relation to history, present, and future, leaves us adrift—no less adrift than the stray protagonist who walks the city streets.

As the novel draws to a close, Rodrigo makes a remark that recalls Macabéa's fondness for the pings sounding on the radio. "The instant is that blink of time in which the tire of the speeding car touches the ground and then touches it no longer and then touches it again. Etc., etc., etc." (77). This repetitive temporality runs counter to what he had described as the pace of his writing, his authoring of a "life," an endeavor that takes its measure from the new (32). Yet in the antithetical movement that we have come to expect from him, this temporal form is wholly consistent with the fleeting nature of Macabéa's truth, which vanishes the moment you catch it. Moreover, the iterative modality, sustained by the pings and their principle of abstraction, epitomizes the young girl's indistinguishability from so many others, the exchangeability of her fate with that of "thousands like her" (5, 28): "Etc., etc., etc." As Rodrigo intimated, we already knew his narrative. These stories ring; they are snuffed out; they resume; they are smothered. And so on.

The text exemplifies a logic of repetition. It ends with the very affirmation that it attributes in opening to the beginning of the world: Its final line, following Rodrigo's announcement of the strawberry season, is "Yes" (77). The first line reads, "All the world began with a yes, one molecule said yes to another molecule and life was born" (3). The universe, in the end, is thus doing its thing again. Yet this doesn't make for any beginnings. For immediately after the opening line, Rodrigo says, "But before prehistory there was the prehistory of prehistory and there was the never and there was the yes. It was ever so. I don't know why, but I do know that the universe never began" (3). The molecules keep saying yes to one another, but they say no to beginnings, although there is also a never—perhaps that "never," that infinity, from which the sublime rooster was calling.[15] Indeed, if the universe doesn't begin, does it ever end? In any case, the novel doesn't, for it is "unfinished" (xiv). In light of all the opening titles, we don't even know what it might mean for this text to end or, for that matter, to begin. The novel mimics the universe's temporal registers.

For an author, this unfathomable, flip-flopping temporality is a terrible problem. "How do you start at the beginning, if things happen before they happen? If before the prehistory there were already the apocalyptic monsters?" (3). It is a struggle. Rodrigo applies himself and adjusts, reducing his heart to "its own final or primary beat" (3). His strategy is not unlike that of some other beings: The monsters of prehistory dabble in post-history. Mysterious, mutually opposing temporalities are in play for both kinds of creatures. The seeming end is already in play at the seeming beginning. Rodrigo decides to tackle these rhythms by way of a "syncopated melody" (4). He also offers a pragmatic response, a prediction: "If this story doesn't exist now, it will" (3). As always, we can count on him for an almost tautology: "I am the one writing what I am writing" (3). He and his text come in one package. We can transpose the question he just raised from the beginning to the end: "How do you stop at the end, if things happen after they happen?" This leaves us the strawberry season: "for now" (77). Or a cheerful sequel—for later.

Because Rodrigo has told us a thing or two about his story's existence in a frame of time and space, we are at a good point to see whether he can also let us in a bit more on its relation to the marketplace. Let's go back to the moment when he was talking about the interval between words and deeds. As we have seen, it is a badge of honor to him that, as an author, he has at his disposal a whole repertoire of "succulent terms" (7). He feels inclined to use "splendid adjectives, meaty nouns, and verbs so slender that they travel sharp through the air about to go into action, since words are actions, don't you agree?" (7). His male companions are with him on this one. Our literary writer, however, plans to work the words through his aesthetic agency. He isn't simply plunging into action. He establishes an interval between words and deeds. He creates traction. Rodrigo practices a poetics of slowness. He declines the job of a rapid-fire market operator that the society carves out for him. He curbs the speed and shapes the temporality of his language. He refuses the imperative to make the greatest amount of money in the shortest possible time. By the same token, he frees his linguistic choices from the sway of physical causality. The point of his text is not to serve up realities directly to the reader, without formal mediation. He insists on his own necessity as an interloper between words and deeds. He, in fact, hinders the automatic translation from words into deeds, installing his artistry as a writer and the artfulness of his text in the midst of the mutually contravening forces of language and action. Neither capital nor nature dictates the speed of his narration. Rodrigo assumes his position as an autonomous creator. Disinterest is the device through which he sets up the temporalities of art and life. It is a temporal and spatial pivot. It is his tool for navigating space and time. This aesthetic stance not only readies him for his contest with the Coca-Cola Company but also occasions new overtures toward his protagonist, who has a special fondness for words.

As Macabéa, who likes to meditate in the office, clearing the space for a raft of typos, knows all too well: Speed (but not too much of it) pays the bills. Slowness costs you dearly. It can even get you fired from your job. Our typist/anti-typist, as I already indicated, savors the term *ephemerides* down to its smallest detail. Her appreciation is disinterested: The word itself enchants her. "When she copied it she paid attention to every letter" (31). Her attitude toward language, like her author's poetics and unlike her coworker's drill, strains from economic maximization: "Glória could do shorthand and not only earned more but didn't even miss a beat with those difficult words the boss loved so much. Meanwhile the girl had fallen in love with the word 'ephemerides'" (31). A fast pace is lucrative. It enables one to keep up with the correct time. Love is a different story, however. Author and character agree on these points. They create their own time frames, using disinterestedness to do their thing, going athwart the demands the society places on them—on "the person sitting here typing," that is (11).

Rodrigo disentangles the time of language from the market's immediacy and its speed, in the meantime upending a realist mode of reading that bypasses formal mediation. Macabéa, who relishes letter by letter, word by word, to pry open significations they encapsulate that otherwise would be lost to a normalized, marketable time scheme is his coconspirator in this project. Their joint aesthetic strategy endows the two actors with a paradoxical social position rather than unequivocally lodging them on the outside of the marketplace. The tension between interest and disinterest remains. Disinterested attention enables them at once to dwell in the present and to partake of temporal disjunctions and multiplicities. At the same time, disinterestedness is under pressure from interest, as exemplified by the allure Carlota's tale holds for Macabéa and by Rodrigo's poetic rivalry with that other storyteller, his female creator. Initially finding in his subaltern protagonist the sparks of his new "today," Rodrigo hoped to supply his authorship and the lettered city with their stamp of contemporaneity, their power to make up the now. Does the decease of his fellow linguistic contrarian foreclose this strategy? Did he forgo his chance to attain the now? Has literature squandered the opportunity to devise a response to the problem of aestheticized poverty?

Aesthetic Publicness and Strange Taste

In the brief stretch of time leading up to Macabéa death, Rodrigo reaches out to his reader to get them to drop what they are doing, right then and there, and blow life into her (73). The reader's assistance is of the greatest urgency, since the young woman is "adrift in chaos like the door swinging in an infinite wind" (73–74). Nevertheless, she expires. Rodrigo lets her die. The reader lets her die. The indictment is clear: Reader, writer, the whole lettered city stands by while she perishes. They bear responsibility for her fate.

Macabéa's perceptions reveal an aesthetic that, the novel shouts out, the society needs to reckon with. By giving expression to its protagonist's temporal and spatial presence and her anomalous tastes, *The Hour of the Star* offers a compelling critique of the lettered city. The lettered city needs to make structural changes if it is to deal in an adequate manner with the emergency and public calamity the text has exposed. Do Rodrigo's readers actually hold a part of a solution? Can we do something that perhaps isn't so far off from the life-sustaining job that he assigned us to and that we bungled?

Despite the culpability of the lettered city, Rodrigo wouldn't be the writer we know had he not found a way to establish his, and thereby literature's, indispensability. "This book is a question," he ventures (8). He is right. Society needs him and his novel to pose singularly difficult questions. We have encountered several. *The Hour of the Star* inquires into the nature of material beginnings and endings and the dynamics of repetition and difference this implies. It broaches the relationship between literature and history. It does this by entwining the storytelling endeavor and its ties to past, present, and future with configurations of time and the economic marketplace, arrangements that harbor the productive and consumptive activities of the inhabitants of a metropolis in the Global South. What kind of aesthetics do these pursuits demand? How does this sit with Rio's and Brazil's positions in a global economy? In what ways do coconstitutive registers of class, ethnicity, race, sexuality, and gender mark these positions? And what does it mean to do justice to the participation of a female subaltern in this hubbub, this tremendous rigmarole?

The novel takes a close look at Macabéa's aesthetic. It self-reflexively engages the epistemic assumptions that shape its engagement with a female subaltern aesthetic. It touches on concomitant notions of protest, ideas about voice, and appraisals of what it might be for a text or utterance to have political import. It contemplates questions that arise along the way about the status of art, the capabilities of language, and the aesthetic resources of day-to-day practices.

Rather than offering an answer to the emergency it represents, the novel, as I have indicated, asks the reader to come up with their own reply (xiv). *The Hour of the Star* refrains from resolving the aesthetic contradictions it brings to expression. It shows how opposing forces evolve and metamorphose, but it does not achieve a reconciliation of the double binds that it inscribes into its idioms and characters. Instead, it imparts these tensions to the reader. The audience can step in and carry them. The audience, as it were, can breathe life into Macabéa and those who suffer similar fates by holding the tensions and reflecting on them. In the course of this process, the public can start to tell other stories: stories with different outcomes, stories that push the driving questions further.

Rodrigo signals that there are stories that precede his story and stories that follow it. Or, as he puts it wryly, with a jibe at his own status in the society: "[T]he story is history" (11). With his persuasion that stories don't pop up out of nowhere or terminate in just "nothing" (32), he underlines the fundamental historicity of storytelling. This conception galvanizes the notion of the public. For the public is the site where all the stories play out. This is where he situates his tale. The novel insists on the social and political centrality of aesthetic publicness. Its desirous gesture toward the reader, its fervent wish for the reply that the reader might develop anchors the novel in the very public domain where the "public calamity" Rodrigo sketches resides. His point is unmistakable: Aesthetic publicness is going to have to yield replies to this disastrous situation.

Besides highlighting the significance of aesthetic publicness, the novel emphasizes several other philosophical resources that we have available to us in engaging the predicaments of aestheticized poverty and inequity. These problems, Rodrigo suggests, reflect the hand of the marketplace and the temporal efficacy of a corporate aesthetic that airlifts its presumed "today" from the flow of history. We have seen how the Coca-Cola Company conscripts Rodrigo's mediations to use disinterested attention as a marketing tool and taste-shaping device. In response, the novel reveals how aesthetic experience carries history, as we saw in Rodrigo's figuration of Macabéa's final scenes. "Today" always involves history, he makes clear. Indeed, the colorful plastics decorating Carlota's office, her interminable munching, and her advice for her client that she use Aristolino soap, as well as this client's own nail-biting habit, show us the sundry aesthetic qualities that history encapsulates in the "now" designated (or, as the typist prefers, "desiginated") by the soft drink, which, as noted, "tastes like nail polish, Aristolino soap and chewed plastic." Aesthetic sensibilities encode historical consciousness.

While Rodrigo juggles disinterest in confrontation with market demands, disinterested perception also supports other kinds of aesthetic strategies. The pings that mesmerize Macabéa expose a different facet of the disinterested mode of attention she lavishes on these sonic productions. They lodge her in culture. They give her a place within the normalized temporal schemas of the society. They suture her, no matter how tenuously, into the world of her roommates, one of whom lent her the radio. The sonic drips are part of the public domain. In the disinterested fashion that is her hallmark, Macabéa retools these aesthetic creations that populate the public sphere. Her auditory interventions aesthetically reconfigure and recontextualize the sounds of the pings.[16] She is, after all, a decolonial aesthetic actor. At the same time, she is modern, as I have pointed out. Indeed, her aesthetic experience encodes gendered tensions among modernity, coloniality, and decoloniality: It constitutes an internally refracted, modern form of coloniality as well as a distinctly femininized, decolonial form of modernity. Cued in by Macabéa, the reader can employ disinterested attention as a decolonial feminist device. Spinning time and space on their pivots, disinterested experiences can reorient the place in the world that accrues to humanity at large and to the female subaltern in particular, whom society in so many ways has deprived of social participation and belonging. Disinterest displays temporal and spatial aptitudes that the Enlightenment had not explicitly recognized, although I would argue that eighteenth-century philosophy has in fact capitalized on these constructive capacities, enlisting them in a cultural system and a rewiring of sociality and public life.[17] Macabéa's strange taste brings this out.

In Lispector's hands, the lettered city is critiqued as a domain that does not yet have a grip on the necessary answers. It is also vindicated as an arena of aesthetic publicness and sensibility, where we can reflect on the perturbing questions that we, crucially, must address. As members of aesthetic publics, we can take a hint from Macabéa and read at once superfast and super-slowly. We can trace the mutually countervailing narrative orientations that Rodrigo navigates. Encouraged by the belief in language that both characters hold out, despite all the pressures weighing on those who are still typing today and driven by the tears springing forth from Macabéa's eyes and perhaps from ours, too, we realize that stories can kill as elements of more encompassing aesthetic constellations. And stories can bestow life, too. They can give a future to those for whom a future must be sewn together from the most threadbare materials. Reading, listening, tasting, gazing, singing, touching, and playing in Macabéa's spirit, in the delightful and contagious way she shows us, we can detect others' "breathing" that Rodrigo sought to conjure by way of his intonations (14). These are some of the subtle attunements, delicate capabilities, and finely wrought insights to which an aesthetic focus alerts us in the novel and on which we can draw in addressing the novel's central challenges.

The aesthetic modalities I have uncovered—in particular, disinterested attention, the telling of stories that presumably are virtually impossible to tell, and a temporally disjunctive mode of reading—surpass the control of any single reader, narrator, social actor, or group. They are public achievements, grounded in collective histories. Aesthetic community exceeds unmovably aestheticized divides of class, gender, coloniality, geography, or race. I have shown how Lispector embeds these philosophical observations into the entanglements among Macabéa's sensibility, Rodrigo's narration, and her own authorship. Giving the reader a place in Rodrigo's literary performance and deconstructing his figuration of authorship, she helps us along on the aesthetic paths, she makes plain, we have stretching out in front of us. In the course of our reading, as I have elaborated it, the reader lodges strange taste—an instrument of individuality and a site of singularity—in its collective cultural surrounds.

Conclusion: Playing with Stars, Playing with Dust

Rodrigo's failure to come to terms with the crisis he confronts ushers in the aftermath of a cultural comportment that offers the literary institution renewal under the auspices of a male creator. This aftermath, as my reading of the novel's dedication reveals, features both slipshod authorial gestures that revert to traditional artistic institutions and fledgling sensibilities that elude these artworld configurations. Their explosive co-occurrence enacts a gender politics as well as confrontations between colonialist and decolonial impulses. By giving form to this convergence of disparate aesthetic orientations, *The Hour of the Star* proves that we cannot in a straightforward fashion dismiss modernity to get rid of coloniality. The step to shrug off modernity is inadequate to the project of reckoning with the colonialist workings of cultural institutions, such as literature. Instead, we see a conjunction of modern, colonialist, and decolonial forces and witness the tensions and frictions among them. Lispector's two protagonists have a love of modernity. They give this desired modernity form in their own aesthetic terms. They embody it in the affections and impulses of strange tastes. They encode it in the vagaries of aesthetic sensibility and experience. Thus, they participate in a modern world that carries the potentialities of decolonial futures.

While eschewing answers to the problems it tackles and enlisting the reader's collaborative efforts in the process of coming up with them (xiv), the story also marks a shift of terrain. Indeed, Lispector challenges fundamental aesthetic principles of the lettered city, such as a Eurocentric canon and a masculinist conception of artistic agency and aesthetic meaning. Simultaneously, she reimagines this institution as a site where vital questions arise about the present "time and culture." This revisioning strategy then informs a further philosophical intervention on the novel's part: Reassembling the remnants of the lettered city, the work posits a constellation of aesthetic publicness that encompasses the everyday forms and materials that shape the instances of joy and insight Macabéa finds in her surroundings, or what the eighteenth century called instruction and delight. Her idiosyncratic tastes and sensibilities are the vehicles for these pleasures.

While cultural theorists such as Rama and Franco find the lettered city in tatters, the novel in my reading takes part in a philosophical reassessment and reconfiguration of this formation by orienting us toward the centrality of the public, a register whose pertinence to Lispector's project in the novel, alongside textual practices by many other Latin American women writers, Franco emphasizes elsewhere.[18] Aesthetics, in its historical underpinnings, as well as in the subdomain named "everyday aesthetics," fundamentally involves a register of publicness.

Lispector immerses the reader in the thicket of this shifting, expanding public configuration, as intimated by the conjunction "So," which opens the novel, and its later iteration, "And—and." We are in media res as the "emergency" and "public calamity" that is Macabéa's condition unfolds. In other words, we are in the midst of a historically situated constellation of contradictory cultural forces that is under production.[19] The reader needs to comprehend the gendered, racial, ethnic, and class tensions that arise here as impulses toward change and as realities that impel us to confer a different organization on this cultural arrangement. Only in this fashion can literature capture the female subaltern contemporaneity that it both desires and shies away from. Indeed, only in this way can we acknowledge the stunning tastes and remarkable aesthetic experiences that this "now" holds out.

Strange taste and its disinterested ploys, I have indicated, are part of the phenomenology of everyday aesthetic experience. Philosophy needs to recognize their presence and logic. We have taken a close look at the novel's figuration of Macabéa's unusual perceptions. I have traced how her bent toward tautologies and her stints with nail polish leave their marks in Rodrigo's aesthetic consciousness and signaled how he tailors his style in her death scene to his character's leanings. Tinged with bodily excess, her strangeness, in the context of his perspective, flaunts its proximity to the grotesque and veers toward the monstrous. In ending, I want to dwell a bit longer on the mysterious amalgamation of tastes Lispector creates through her juxtaposition of two writers and their shared protagonist. The resulting sensibility is positively uncanny. And it is humorous. Rodrigo repeatedly drops remarks about emptiness, nothingness, and embodied self-encounter that are vintage Lispector. He spikes his narration with her language. Reading her voice in his, his voice in hers, and both voices in Macabéa's, and vice versa, engenders a strange aesthetic sensibility. The voices and preferences infect one another. Gender, in this context, assumes a floating and fluid presence, becoming eerie and intractable. It is strange. Indeed, Lispector renders gender a mobile aesthetic proclivity that incites critical reading and reimagination.

The reader's voice, including mine, the analyst's, is part of the mix. Lispector's and her narrator's gestures of self-absenting and self-presencing locate the reader in a position analogous to theirs: The interpreter assumes a role of narrating and withholding, inventing and blocking a character's stories. A buzzing interchange among telling, nontelling, relay, indebtedness, and preemption produces a charged relation between silence and loquaciousness. Enigmatic sonic signifiers such as drumbeats and violins that outstrip anyone's acts of expression animate a field of perplexity—a public space of jointly implicated voices, sounds, stillness. This disconcerting territory is the arena of the strange, in which the novel envelops the reader.

In a lettered realm where experiments with authorship, such as Cervantes's and Borges's fictional dealings with found manuscripts, have historically privileged male creativity, Lispector supplants these tropes with a game that highlights and works through gendered tensions that riddle the lettered city. This is why she invents a found author. Rodrigo deserts Macabéa but then proves his worth in his mortal combat with corporatism. The lettered city is desperately needed but, for that matter, is no less cruel and negligent. Lispector leaves its traditional delineations in dust and ashes. She has us, her reader, play with these messy materials that were so rewarding to Cervantes and Borges and discover how the rubble yields hilarity through the sadness, holds nourishing energies in abundance—all essential resources in countering the destructiveness she has exposed. We have in the end been joining Lispector's game, not merely the self-serving ruse of a male narrator scented with disinterest. This game, I have argued, is a tool of aesthetic historicity; it is an element of a critical mode of aesthetic address and relationality.

Tinkering with stars is fine, as long as you also keep playing in the dust. Don't try to swap dust for stars, egged on by the greedy Carlota who knows how to turn a profit from your arcane longings. Don't skip the messiness of the lettered city and historical authorship, as the movie coaxes you to do by eliminating Rodrigo. In the latter case, you mistake an inexorable layering of sensibility and societal ordering for a familiar hit of empathetic feeling for one more poor young woman from the northeast and smother a dense fabric of aesthetic and political entanglements under a digestible, already known tale that once more expunges inopportune tastes. Aesthetic publicness produces complex mutual participations among voices. It creates ongoing, uneven assimilations and differentiations among aesthetic subjects, among aesthetic forms, and between subjects and forms.

By insisting on Rodrigo's importance while superseding him, Lispector loosens the hold of male authorship on the literary imagination. Taking over from her found author after he vacates the scene of attempted reckoning with aestheticized poverty, she inserts her female creative and authorial agency into the games of the lettered city. When he ditches his character and embroils the reader in Macabéa abandonment, Lispector steps forth to open aesthetic publicness to strange taste.

The one, it turns out, is the corollary of the other: Strange taste animates and rehabilitates aesthetic publicness. Aesthetic publicness desires, needs, and, depending on how we spin it, embraces strange taste—its survival is bound up with it. Playing with stars, playing with dust is a matter of life or death. The choice is ours.

3

Song

A New Life

Struggles between life and death touch us to the core of our existence while also being anchored in communities. They assume their aesthetic forms in collective contexts. In chapter 2, I examined how play can transform positionalities in space and time and alter self-other relationships and dynamics of aesthetic publicness. In this chapter, I investigate these shifts from the angle of two kinds of play that reveal different communal logics; yet both kinds of play are powerful vehicles for the public potentialities of strange taste.

While theorists such as María Lugones and Gayatri Chakravorty Spivak illuminate play's capacities to traverse rifts between worlds, between selves, and between contrastive ethico-political affiliations, its affective and community-oriented facets demand further analysis. This is especially important in light of the social disparities that mark our playful occupations. Given the prevalence of grievous injury, let's look into a kind of play that provides reprieve under conditions of suffering.

At times when we are hit with grave losses or violence and grieving is foreclosed, we may be overwhelmed by melancholy or alienation. Detached pain may incite a sense of haunting. We may oscillate between the homely and unhomely. Yet agony can also lodge in the cadences of an anguish that finds solace in soft, gentle experiences. Play can pick up on this hushed responsiveness. Resonating with the delicate needs of someone who is in pain and feels alone or immobilized in these feelings, play can take on a soothing quality. It can be a way to connect with others and engage with the material world. Playfulness thus can occasion slivers of meaning where this was felt to be absent. Play is a way of living with torment, of giving shape to the terrible. It becomes a modality of aesthetic life laden with death, a form of holding violence; it provides a vehicle of expression for shattering distress.

In exploring aesthetic stirrings that bear sparks of vitality when a person's hold on existence is tenuous, this chapter attends to this subdued, yet ample, register of play and the reparative resources it holds out to a life lived in proximity to death. I call this genre *muted play*. I have in mind a difference of accent and degree rather than a principled distinction from a bolder variety, which I term *loud play*. Muted play is no less generous and no less relational than its grander, more exuberant kin. It can offer solace and connectedness at moments of grating alienation. Far from solitary, it opens the person up to their human and more than human surroundings in a way that is bearable to someone in need of gentleness and for whom greater intensity or a more forceful, disruptive impact are too much to stand. Muted play can create experiential ruptures, like its loud relative, but its expressive tenor and the accompanying pleasure are tempered to agree with a hurt sensibility. In this way, the person can tolerate playing when more emphatic tonalities of loud play are too much to absorb. Muted play respects raw feelings. It can be sustained by a mindset burdened by difficult emotions.

Of course, human beings typically carry unresolved situations and maintain internal and external struggles. These concerns are felt in the aesthetic forms and contents through which we seek and live our pleasures. The distinction between muted play and play's loud, often lighter, more untrammeled, more plenteous variety is hence not crisp and tight. I associate muted play with a distinctive logic: The notion signals how the person playing modulates this activity in response to an existential affliction to which they are beholden. With the lilts of play, they achieve an attunement to charged feelings and hardship they are carrying. Muted play observes the measures of this weight. It thus attests to a certain guardedness, a measure of communal and material withdrawal. But this restraint enables it to carry forth the rhythms and possibilities of play into spheres of life where play otherwise is unable to go. Muted play extends play to tremendously difficult situations that threaten to wear us down. It is a part of the story of how we can play while we simultaneously cannot or do not want to play.

Not uncommonly, muted play makes itself known through contrasts. It carries a taste for daisies over hydrangeas, for the diminutive over the large gesture.

It prefers colorful glass shards from a broken window to candies wrapped in brightly colored, shiny foil. And so it can sustain disinterest: Warming up to subtly hued, sharp-edged glass pieces, it appreciates their visual qualities in their own right.

Muted play can give rise to, phase into, and link up with loud play. This chapter traces their collaborative interactions in Claudia Llosa's feature film *La teta asustada* (*The Milk of Sorrow* [2009]). Both sorts of play enact inflections of taste that then fulfill a public role. Llosa's film documents the lives of Andean migrants who have moved to an informal settlement on the outskirts of Lima to escape the conflict between the left-populist revolutionary movement the Shining Path and the at-the-time reactionary Peruvian government that erupted in the 1980s. The protagonist, Fausta, a young Quechua woman who passes her days in a state of stunned fear, is caught between the requirements of her Andean village and the values of a colonial household where she takes a job. Through her singular tastes, she devises a way to breathe and survive in the face of conflicting cultural demands. Her aesthetic sensibility enables her to find her desire, to navigate the tensions between worlds, and to salvage cultural memory for herself and her community. Revealing how Fausta gains confidence in her own aesthetic, the film advances her sprawling hillside district as a model of aesthetic publicness, in contrast to competing models, such as those of the lettered city and the medium of television. Indeed, a reading in terms of aesthetic publicness, I argue, lends recognition to aesthetic modalities that fall through the mazes of critical paradigms such as transculturation, magical realism, and syncretism the film invokes, yet that dovetail with the marketplace.[1] The frame of aesthetic publicness enables us to see how strange taste can flourish in lively interaction with communal sensibilities. A historically embedded propensity attuned to a changing world, strange taste embodies a stance that can turn difficulties into a trajectory of creativity, growth, and pleasure rather than solely negation, pain, and withdrawal. At the end of the film, Fausta, after all, sings a new song: life.[2]

Playing Hide-and-Seek

Though typically formulaic, film posters often speak volumes on first look. They tell mini-narratives, awakening moviegoers' expectations. A poster can prompt spectators to play already before watching the movie. So in this chapter, we play, too, carrying on in the spirit of the previous ones—with different materials, however, and different games.

The Milk of Sorrow premiered at the Berlin Film Festival in 2009, where it won the award for Best Picture. The Berlinale poster pulls the reader into a game of hide-and-seek (figure 3.1). Conscious of its commercial aims, the poster employs the image of an exotic female to announce the tale of a Quechua woman who comes into modernity. At the top, the film's title looms large, followed in subscript by a plot summary: "Un viaje del miedo a la libertad" (A journey from fear to freedom). The film will detail how the hero overcomes trauma and finds freedom. Below we see the face of an Indigenous woman, shoulders bare, emerging out of a mound of potatoes, harking back to Botticelli's Venus. The poster invites the spectator to view, to learn, how this Quechua woman leaves her traumatic history behind and becomes modern. Despite the presence of exotic and erotic elements, the poster sells a Western story of modernity. The film, we anticipate, resolves the dichotomy between coloniality and an Indigenous magical reality through a strategy of transculturation whereby the hero passes from a traditional to a modern lifeworld. As the poster has it, the spectator can expect a magical realist narrative that reconciles Western modernity with its Indigenous female other. Yet what if the hero is playing a game with these stock oppositions? Might she be trying them out and checking how they fit? Could she be amusing herself with a performance she is putting on? The assumption that she is playing shifts the narrative focus from two already outlined positions to her own creativity. The question arises of her taste and her place in a public domain, where all manner of representations are in action. Beholding the hero at play, we wonder where she would locate her singularity, her distinctive outlook on things.

Indeed, as I argue, Llosa's film inverts and dismisses the familiar Western tale peddled by the poster. Rather than following the logic of a predictably modernist story, *The Milk of Sorrow* identifies a role for aesthetic creation as a reflective, life-sustaining form of corporeal agency in a cultural field that pits Indigenous communities against elite populations while also fostering exchanges and cross-fertilization among these groups.[3] The hero does not soar up from the potatoes; she remains at home in them. She is born into Quechua traditions, and it becomes her duty to read the world through them, challenging and modifying her cultural inheritance as she carries out her responsibilities and learns. In the end, she rescues the potato from its limited global role as mere nourishment and celebrates and redefines its aesthetic possibilities. She makes room for a potato plant. Its fledgling sprigs bloom in the community where she lives.

The film structurally highlights the poster's incongruities. Interpellating the spectator alternately as modern and as the other of modernity, and marking these subjectivities as entwined through strategies of transculturation,

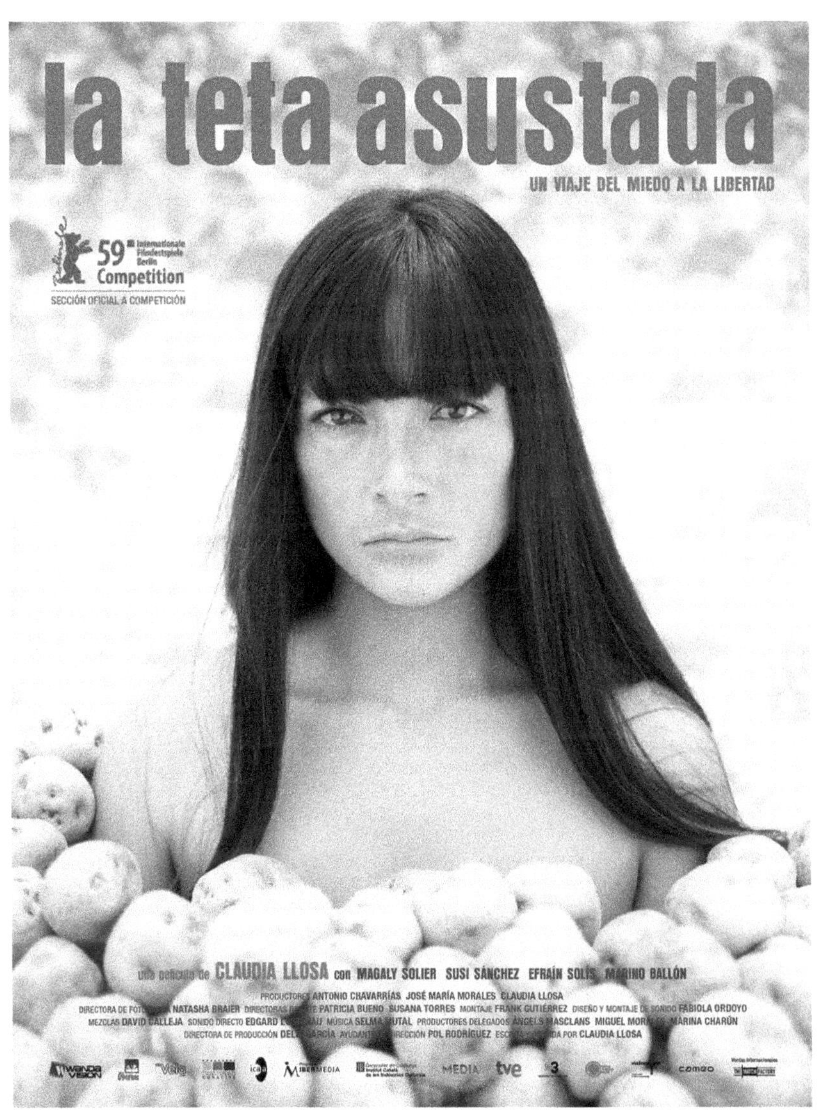

FIGURE 3.1. *La teta asustada: Un viaje del miedo a la libertad.* Poster for Claudia Llosa's film *The Milk of Sorrow*, 59th International Berlin Film Festival, 2009.

the film counters both positions with a decolonial stance that Fausta Isidora Janampa Chauca (played by Magaly Solier) wrests away from victimhood. While the poster uses the tension between an exoticism reminiscent of Carmen Miranda and Fausta's piercing gaze to tout a transculturation process that brings together Indigeneity and modern nationhood, the image also calls into question this reconciliation by oscillating between Peru's birthing of Fausta and its burying her alive. The prospective spectator wonders whether Fausta is rising up from the pile of potatoes or sinking into it. However, if our hero is actually playing with the tubers, then the image skirts these polarities. Indeed, Fausta stages a game of now-you-see-me, now-you-don't with modernity and exoticism. This game puts her aesthetic sensibility in the center. She employs the potatoes as materials for the making of a home, for the invention and inhabitance of the land.[4] The film follows the poster's example by relinquishing the dichotomy of modernity and an Indigenous magical reality in favor of an interest in Fausta's aesthetic agency.

More than a locus of birth or interment, the earth, as we shall see, offers a ground for Quechua aesthetic creativity. Alternative figurations of air and fluids take effect. Adjacent to sky and water and splattered by milk and blood, the earth is reworked into a site where disjunctive, racially and colonially inflected aesthetic histories take form that do not belong to elite, popular, or Andean cultures exclusively. Aesthetic needs, possibilities, and shifts arise that cannot be adequately captured in a transcultural frame that envisions encounters and confluences between modernity and its antitheses. Such encounters and confluences certainly exist and are quite important, but the aesthetics of the matter unfold in ways that elude this paradigm.

Fausta's play with dichotomous representations has the viewer of the poster wonder what kinds of images are to the hero's liking. Witnessing the hero play now-you-see-me, now-you-don't, the viewer, furthermore, is alternately seeing and not seeing her. Looking for Fausta, the viewer joins her game of hide-and-seek. What sorts of images might we like to see, to play with? Perhaps some historically have been more to our liking than others. The viewer's aesthetic agency parallels Fausta's in that it supersedes the polarities signaled by the poster. We are excited, for we would like to play a bit more. We have no idea what will come of this play. We will find out. We purchase a movie ticket or pay into a streaming service. Our curiosity is rewarded. Llosa's film sides with the poster's playful register. As I show, *The Milk of Sorrow* puts forth a critical confrontation between coloniality and an Indigenous magical reality and undercuts their dichotomy to elaborate a decolonial aesthetics. Play, both muted and loud, and taste, both strange and regular, are vital elements of these aesthetics. The film self-reflexively scrutinizes the status of aesthetic forms and images and the way we read them. We are game.

Slum Cities, Lettered Cities, and Transculturation

Llosa turns to the movements of aesthetic publicness in response to the violence and societal changes that have taken place in Latin America over the previous half-century, which has witnessed the persistence of geopolitical inequality under an increasingly homogenizing global economic regime. Engaging these sociopolitical developments, her film exemplifies broader cinematic tendencies in the region since the 1990s. At the same time, it stands out for its investigation of female corporeality. Giving prominence to a Quechua woman, the work not only tackles the rise of slum cities and the capitalist capture of the imagination but also zeroes in on the everyday materiality of social codings such as race. Seen through these lenses, Llosa's film wins a place alongside the work of the renowned Argentine director Lucretia Martel, even if this achievement has yet to be recognized in the critical discourse, which has elided significant aspects of the film's aesthetic interventions.[5]

The Milk of Sorrow crosscuts between informal settlement and city center, between colonialist and subaltern visual and sonic idioms, and among forms of address centered on milk, blood, water, air, and earth.[6] Connoting an Indigenous corporeality understood in its expansive cosmological and ethical implications, Llosa's pivotal image of the shocked, milk-giving breast, or the milk of sorrow, resonates simultaneously with an icon of the Madonna Lactans (Nursing Virgin) to become a figure through which we can conceptualize the aesthetic creativity of a decolonial Indigenous actor. Llosa deviates from films such as *La virgen de los sicarios* (*Our Lady of the Assassins* [Schroeder 2000]) and *Cidade de Deus* (*City of God* [Meirelles and Lund 2002]), which organize the intersection of violence, religion, and poverty around male leads, by emphasizing the imagination, affects, desires, and bodily needs of a female character. Aesthetic publicness grounds the aesthetic experiences, tastes, and agency that the film ascribes to its protagonist and extends to the spectator.

As the poster's summoning and foiling of conventional Western narratives already suggests, Llosa explores aesthetic publicness in engagement with two competing social orders: the colonialist aesthetic order represented by the city center, where Fausta works, and the hillside district bordering Lima, where she lives with her family.

Dwelling in the hills surrounding the city, Fausta occupies a complex cultural and historical location. Slums are today's cities. In *Planet of Slums*,

Mike Davis (2006) traces these new urban formations to shifts in national policies designed to reckon with economic changes brought about by late capitalism, globalization, technological innovation, and colonial legacies. Yet local factors contextualize and color each slum city. While many poor people across the planet are driven out of the rural countryside in search of better lives, only to find themselves living in temporary, haphazardly built, unhygienic housing, each slum they inhabit is different. Everywhere, slum dwellers negotiate poverty in novel and distinctive ways. Facing unequal access to public services, they must navigate a marketplace that promotes unending consumption through popular platforms and that nonetheless causes unemployment or underemployment. There have been few cinematic attempts to explore the cultural innovations and aesthetic strategies with which informal communities respond to these precarious living conditions.[7] Llosa's film rehearses these issues, presenting experiments at the edge of life that invite an aesthetic framework on their own terms. Toward the end of the film, the urban elite's cultural practices are dismissed in favor of a Quechua actor, her values, and her creativity. A decolonial aesthetics supplants the vision of the slum or, as the majority of Peruvians call it, the *pueblo joven*, as a lost cause.[8] The young town becomes the location of a new type of aesthetic publicness.

The counterpoint to this formation is the colonialist power structure mediated by art and literature, which, following Ángel Rama, is known as the lettered city. Like Lispector before her, Llosa understands aesthetic publicness as an alternative to the socially entrenched entwinements of the aesthetic with the colonial enterprise, which have not ceased to produce their exclusions. Jean Franco (2002) picks up where Rama leaves off. She attributes the demise of the modern lettered city to the negative effects of the Cold War on Latin America. Despite her pessimistic metanarrative, she consistently turns to cultural texts to demonstrate how aesthetic practices preserve and celebrate a Latin American originality in the face of homogenizing forces. *The Milk of Sorrow* continues in this vein and affirms the place of the aesthetic. The lettered city, however, enjoys diminished significance in the film. Its relevance is hedged by the marketplace and the emergence of new communal forms.[9] On this point, Llosa makes a departure from Lispector, whose *The Hour of the Star*, as shown in chapter 2, underscores literature's enduring cultural, moral, and political importance. At the same time, both artists endorse alternative, aesthetically mediated societal orders: While the writer envisions a reconstructed genre of lettered institutionality, the filmmaker highlights the aesthetic lifeworld realized in the pueblos jóvenes encircling Lima, which are the home of Andean people who moved there and built them as a result of the conflict between the government and the Shining Path, which dates from the 1980s and is ongoing. Both sides committed atrocious crimes against Indigenous communities, especially against women. Racially inflected sexual violence has been deeply rooted in the vicissitudes of power since the conquest, through the establishment of the state, and into the present. Llosa examines this history at the level of the aesthetic community. The film's opening scene vividly recalls the gruesome cruelties that befell Fausta's parents, which she absorbs while still in the womb.

Fausta's mother, Perpetua (Bárbara Lazón), introduces her daughter to the spectator. She bestows on Fausta the responsibility of caring for the memory of the violation inflicted during the conflict. Through the act of breastfeeding, which transmits the milk of sorrow, Perpetua had hoped to protect her newborn from future violence: With the shocked body fluids, the infant drank her anguish. While being given sustenance, Fausta is also put on guard against what may befall her. The mother's violated body marks the milk of sorrow with the duality of nourishment and trauma.[10] Dying Perpetua's association with breastfeeding imagery bewilders the spectator. A painting of a Nursing Virgin decorates the living space of our female protagonist's employer, Aída (Susi Sánchez).[11] However, the reclusive Aída turns out to be different from the caring, compassionate mother the painting depicts. She is her father's daughter—ruthless. Putting into motion evolving forms of relationality, the figure of the milk of sorrow inaugurates a critical mode of corporeal address that supplants a model of transculturation with one of interlacing cultural promises and threats, where various attachments and desires remain at odds with one another, yielding a web of shifting aesthetic identifications and differentiations. This kind of web, as I argue elsewhere, lies at the heart of the notion of the aesthetic. In my analysis, the aesthetic relationships that we inhabit partially owe their organization to promises and threats that we engender and embody in multisensory, intercorporeal forms of expression and articulation (Roelofs 2014, 25). Llosa's film locates its aesthetic center in these historically and materially based relationships, which become incitements for Fausta's decolonial cultural agency and sensibility.

In the writings of theorists such as Frances Aparicio (1998; Aparicio and Chávez-Silverman 1997), Fernando Ortiz (1995 [1940]), Mary Louise Pratt (2008 [1992]), and Rama (1996 [1985], 13, 81–83), the concept of transculturation denotes processes whereby members of subordinated or marginal groups select and create new forms from materials transmitted by a dominant or metropolitan culture. It underscores how different cultures develop in interaction with one another, leading them jointly to shift and engender wholes that are often more than the sum of their parts. Ortiz, who coined the notion in the 1940s with the aim of replacing overly reductive concepts of acculturation and assimilation used to theorize culture under conquest, sketches a process of mutual give and take (1995 [1940], 100–103).

Within the paradigm of transculturation, disparate cultural histories and material contexts—notably, colonizing and colonized communities—come together to forge new formations. The constellations that emerge couldn't have existed without each of the divergent trajectories that enter into the mix. Indeed, as current subjects of culture, we inhabit societies that typically are considered products of transculturation: Perspectives in the Global South are part of those in the Global North, and vice versa; Africa, the Caribbean, Europe, the Americas, and other regions jointly give rise to Black cultures; Latin America is a confluence of, among others, Indigenous, European, African, and Asian heritages; Chicanx consciousness affirms its affinities with Amerindian, Mexican, and US traditions.[12] Clearly, transculturation is everyone's lot in our globalized world, albeit in different ways.

The term *transculturation* connotes an understanding of cultures as intertwined rather than sharply differentiated from one another and as evolving in the course of cultural encounters. This view rejects static roots in favor of the proposal that what is taken for the past is inflected by the cultures' current imaginaries, values, and struggles (Hall 1994). It suggests a path of togetherness in difference, even a reconciliation of frictions. It hints at the ways in which societies can move on in the wake of cultural devastation and political antagonism. There is a powerful need to look forward, after all.[13] From another angle, the notion gestures toward strategies of resistance to domination.[14] Processes of transculturation can fold in what is conceived as culturally different, even unassimilable, and build from there.

The concept prominently informs present-day cultural discourses, where it is used with a certain looseness and flexibility. Stripped of the rich historical, geographical, and material resonances it assumes in various scholarly discourses, the idea of transculturation is attractive to marketers (of films and other commodities) eager to multiply audiences and increase profits at a time of interconnectedness.[15] Taking part in the global flow, interactivity seduces and sells. Yet this model downplays aesthetic experiences, forms, and meanings. It flattens and quells strange taste. While signaling the model of transculturation, Llosa's film disrupts it to make room for a wider range of aesthetic possibilities.

Via images of milk and blood, the film exploits an abundant semiotic generativity. Given their quotidian materiality and connections to sustaining life, these figures encourage metaphorical excess. Scholars have linked the two fluids to the establishment and continuation of class, racial, and gender hierarchies. They trace modern conceptions of race to historical policies of *limpieza de sangre* (purity of blood) that resonate in the register of milk (see, e.g., Coles et al. 2015; Feros 2017; Martínez 2008; Roth 1995).[16] In the Spanish colonies, these policies marked breastfeeding as a contentious realm. Disapproval of the use of Indigenous wet nurses by creole populations was common under coloniality; it was thought that infants could imbibe negative qualities (Palma and Palma 2020). Coloniality in the Americas, as scholars have made clear, uses typologies of race and gender embodied in the properties of purity, impurity, fecundity, and contamination ascribed to the different fluids and their analogues. These metaphorical schemes sustain their influence to date, as revealed by contemporary appeals to conceptions of limpieza de sangre in the political arena.[17] At the same time, a present-day aesthetics of fluids feasts in abundance on the cultural offerings presented by the global marketplace: an ostensibly interminable flow of consumable items to purchase; a stream of TV shows to watch. Llosa's plot centers on this situation.

Indeed, the film maps the life of milk and blood as carriers of power, affect, and relationality. Both bodily substances are liquid, and we often speak of money in terms of fluidity (Swanson 2014). Llosa's plot keeps account of various exchanges, marking who profits and who loses as these materials move in and out of the marketplace. By tracing the milk of sorrow in its different permutations alongside the ocean and a potato, two adjacent figures of transition and sustenance, this chapter probes Fausta's reworking of a racially hierarchical aesthetic cosmology. As I show, a constellation of fluids and materials that historically has encoded distinctive societal orders acquires a new organization that also offers revised points of identification and address to the spectator.

Sites of Relationality: Perpetua, Fausta, Aída, Virgin

The film opens with a blank screen. A voice is singing. The lyrics in Quechua recount cruelty against women: Women are used as a weapon of war. The singer is a victim of rape. To find out this information, any non–Quechua-speaking spectator must read the translation of the song: white words projected against a black screen. The metamorphosis of song and word into cinematic image confounds and enlightens the viewer.[18] The song solicits not vengeance but remembrance. Before the audience can process these different demands, the singer's face confronts us. It is deeply wrinkled. It is aged. The appearance is nonetheless one of agelessness: Written on the face is an old story. Still, this story is of recent origin. The body's history, recorded in the wrinkles and creases in the face, attests to the public violence about which the woman sings. She chants about colonialism and its legacy; about how she was raped while pregnant and forced to eat her husband's penis. Her newborn baby breastfeeds on this trauma. Mother and child survived the brutality. The singing awakens harrowing memories. Perpetua's sharing of having been raped and tortured while pregnant with her daughter is killing her. Before she dies, she asks her daughter Fausta to sing: "Comeré si me cantas, . . . / y riegas esta memoria que se seca" (I will eat if you sing . . . / and water this memory that is drying up). Notably, Perpetua never mentions the Virgin Mary. With her mother's death, Fausta inherits a vital responsibility. She incurs a new debt. In addition to keeping the song, the memories, alive, she must comply with her mother's wish to be buried in their Andean homeland.[19]

Encoded in Perpetua's desire might be a syncretization of representations of the Andean divine feminine, Pachamama, often translated as Mother Earth, with Nursing Virgin imagery.[20] Profit principles mediate any such transculturation, as the camera's framing makes clear. Near the bed is a calendar that features an image of a Sacred Heart Christ, obliquely placed off-center. Above the image, the name of the sponsor is legible. Indeed, economic considerations imprint corporeal address in the film from the get-go. The bleeding heart calendar is a promotional tool, an advertisement, not a sign of religious devotion. Nor is the corpse subjected to Christian rites of the dead. Female family members and close friends join Fausta in cleaning and preserving the corpse according to Quechua customs. Afraid of being contaminated by the dead woman's breasts, one of the women asks Fausta to wipe them. She fears catching the illness, the trauma that the film's Spanish title announces. Fausta does not hesitate. The survivors' dealings with the milk of sorrow, panacea or toxin, along with the film's distancing nod toward Christian notions of blood, testify to the limits of notions of transculturation.[21]

To procure the necessary funds for travel and her mother's burial, Fausta seeks employment with the wealthy white composer Aída. First she is given a physical inspection by her predecessor, an Afro-Peruvian domestic servant who, charged with the task of evaluating whether Fausta is fit for work, examines her hands, nails, and teeth. The *patrona*'s economic privilege allows her to play Black and Indigenous characters against each other in enforcing an aesthetic order consonant with her standards of hygiene. On passing muster, Fausta spends the day waiting in front of a TV set in the kitchen. That evening, the patrona calls out for her previous servant. Fausta answers the call. The camera follows her as she walks toward her employer's bedroom. It lingers on several objects, including, for the longest time, a colonial-style sofa. Although the sofa invites Fausta to sit on it, she knows better. She doesn't even look at it. The image is meant for the viewer: We witness a relic that embodies the values that reigned at the time that the house was built. As frequently happens, the camera gets ahead of Fausta to pan to a painting of the Madonna Lactans placed on an antechamber's dark interior wall (figure 3.2). The Virgin's gaze is on the infant who, in turn, looks at the viewer, linking together various bodily modes of address such as holding, feeding, caretaking, touching, gazing, and drinking. The camera spotlights the Virgin's breast, held out to the child. As commentators have noted, the Virgin's breast is at the level of Fausta's mouth.[22] This momentarily suggests that Fausta might find nourishment in this household. She walks past the painting without glancing at it, as with the sofa. Throughout, the film deploys a strategy of signaling images and objects and then cutting to others, keeping reading in motion.

In filming Fausta's walk through the different rooms, Llosa activates this strategy even further. As Fausta walks past the painting, her shadow covers part of it (figure 3.3). At the same time, the painting's subject matter turns her into a shadow, a ghost. The viewer is reminded of the milk of sorrow. The painting declares the role of the Catholic church in threatening Fausta with the fate of what the Indigenous cosmology considers a "lost soul," as she is often called by members of her community in the film, with a reference to the risk posed for the living by the death of a person who has not been buried in accordance with ancestral protocols. In the context of Aída's house, art, architecture, interior design, literature, and religion conspire to place Fausta outside official culture. While the spectator is coaxed to associate the painting's Madonna with the owner, the film establishes countervailing connotations: The house, its furnishings and decorative items, pronounce the patrona, already dreaded by Fausta owing to the biomedical inspection, a representative of a dated cultural, political, and economic system: the lettered city. These allusions will be amplified in the next scene when they meet. The painting, it should be noted, never resurfaces, and nobody ever sits on the sofa.

Filled with trepidation, Fausta enters her employer's bedroom. Aída is drilling a hole to hang a photograph of one of her relatives (her father? her grandfather?) in uniform, standing erect and looking severe. Fausta suddenly sees an overblown military figure superimposed on her own reflection in the photo (figure 3.4). Aída intensifies this hallucinatory vision when she commands Fausta to hold her electric drill, as imposing as a handgun. Fausta flees, trying to stem a nosebleed. The double image has her convulse not only in terror of military repression. The desire for retribution that the object awakens in her also has her in agony about the prospect of betraying

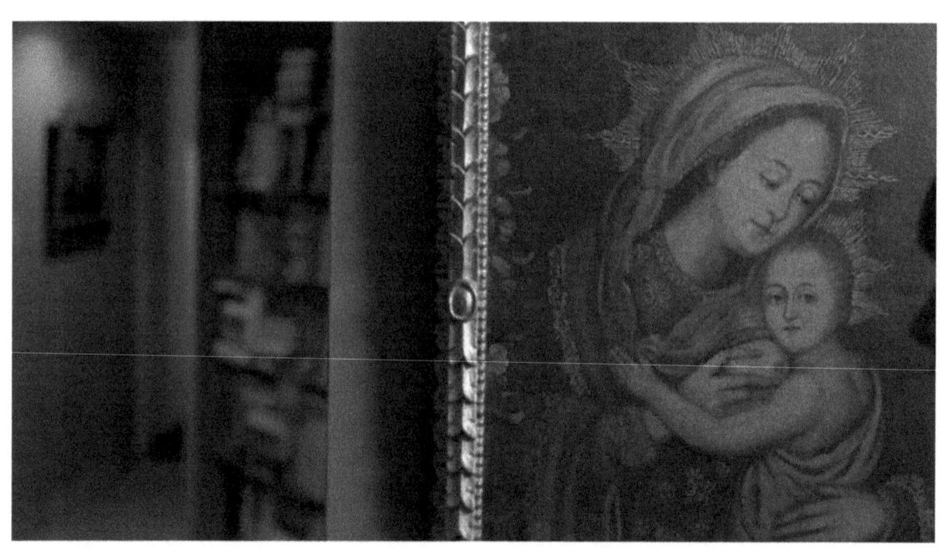

FIGURE 3.2. Claudia Llosa, *The Milk of Sorrow*, 2009, film still. A painting of the Nursing Virgin adorns Aída's antechamber.

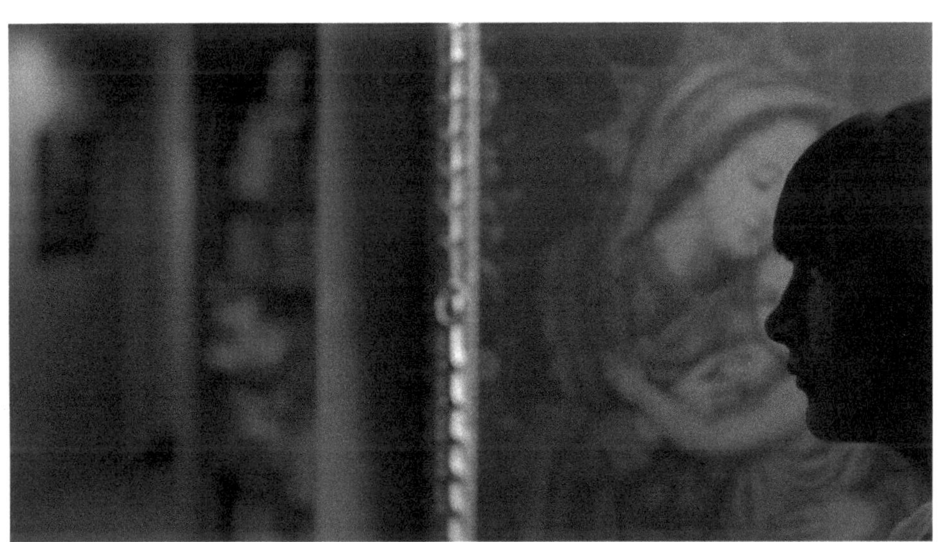

FIGURE 3.3. Claudia Llosa, *The Milk of Sorrow*, 2009, film still. Fausta walks past the Nursing Virgin painting, covering it partially with her shadow.

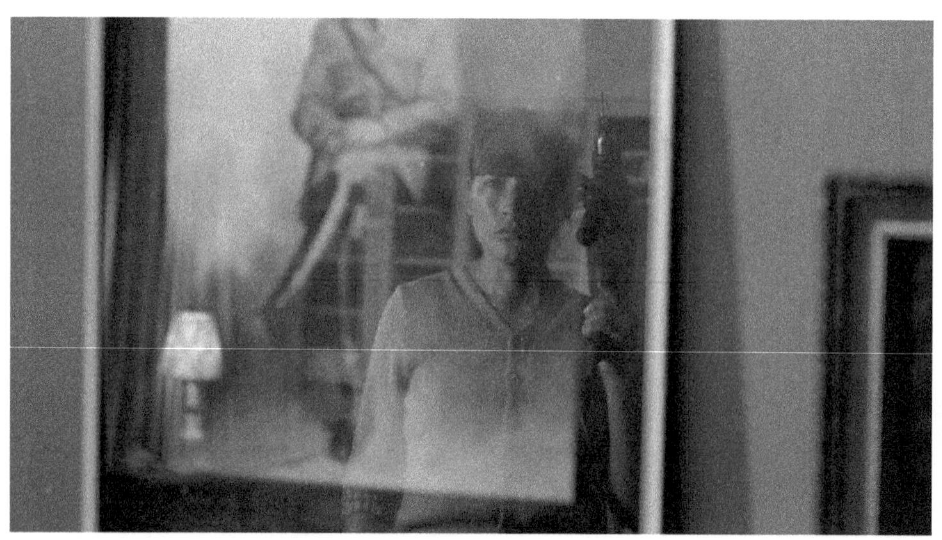

FIGURE 3.4. Claudia Llosa, *The Milk of Sorrow*, 2009, film still. Fausta sees herself reflected in the photograph of a military officer in Aída's bedroom.

her mother's request to keep the memories alive. If the mirrored self-portrait alerts Fausta to unstated modes of resistance embodied in the tools-arms equation, her bleeding nose vehemently delimits their reach by avowing that her connection with her mother requires more than militancy.[23] The transgressive blood carries different needs and possibilities. Her nose bled previously when she told her immediate family about her mother's death. The linkages of the photograph with blood and death dispel any identification of Aída with the Madonna. The different framings—one photographic, the other painterly—reveal their seductiveness as well as their fragility.

Despite having run out of her boss's bedroom, Fausta keeps her job. To calm her nerves, she sings while she works. Impressed with the songs, Aída approaches her and asks her to sing for her. Fausta is in the kitchen watching a cartoon on TV. The fact that Aída seeks out Fausta, that she enters her employee's space, suggests a certain compassion and a possible equality between employer and employee, reversing their first encounter. The show's content disrupts this suggestion. Not only does the cartoon call attention to the image of milk, it also mocks Aída's stately, august taste.

Fausta is viewing a Disney cartoon based on "The Ugly Duckling," which tells the story of an abandoned duck who hopes to be accepted by his flock.[24] In the episode on Fausta's screen, the duck takes a bottle of milk out of the refrigerator to pour himself a glass. He exuberantly splashes the milk onto the floor (figure 3.5). He refuses the implied biomedical lesson that drinking milk will turn one into a gorgeous swan. His refusal reminds the viewer of an earlier moment in the film when Fausta splashes an origami crane folded from a medical prescription into a basin of water. The medicine was supposed to cure her nosebleeds. Fausta chances on a fellow rebel and social outsider. Both derive pleasure from their strange tastes—the young woman in a muted register of play and the duckling in a loud one. Strikingly, after the splashing of the milk, the cartoon duck vigorously splashes around tomato ketchup.[25] In the process, the cartoon debunks any identitarian association of milk and blood. The duck repositions these utilitarian materials as vehicles of comedy and protest. Aesthetic agency displays its boundary-breaking, community-building potentialities. Fausta learns a valuable lesson from her playmate. Aesthetic promises in the biomedical field (if you drink milk, you will become a beautiful swan) are open to being rewritten.[26] Aesthetic action can divert the circulation of fluids away from a system of hierarchy and injustice to more egalitarian designs. Aída, meanwhile, has stationed herself next to our protagonist in her ostensible gesture of companionship. She takes over from the cartoon, soliciting a song from Fausta out of self-interest. Eyeing

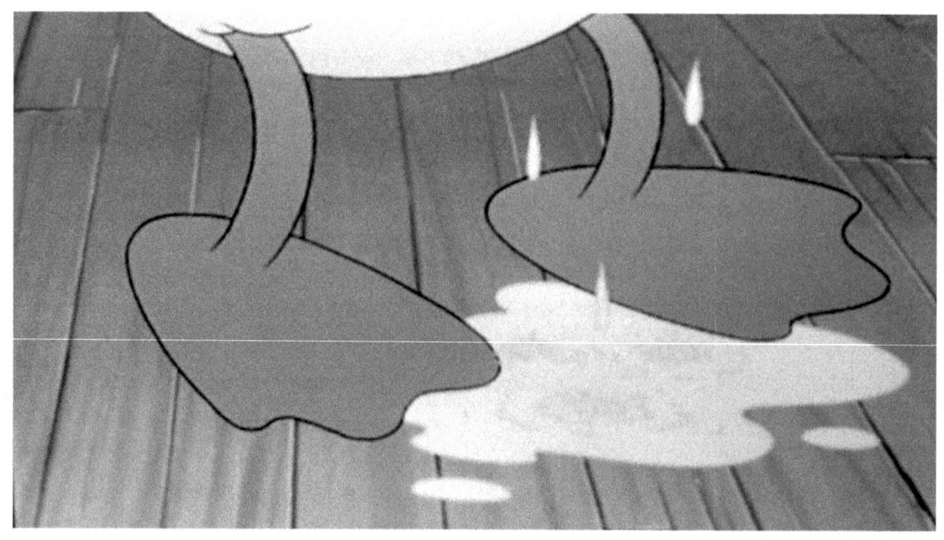

FIGURE 3.5. Claudia Llosa, *The Milk of Sorrow*, 2009, film still. The ugly duckling splashes milk onto the floor.

opportunity for renewal, lettered authority competes with popular culture over the subaltern imagination. Fausta demurs.

Technology is on Fausta's side. The strident, earsplitting whistle of a kettle demands attention, voicing the young woman's unstated answer and ending the scene. The kettle joins the drill in articulating sinister as well as potentially liberating tonalities that proclaim the limits of the human. Fausta is listening; she is watching. Loud play, in both its figurative and its literal sense, lets her in on its attractions. The young woman's aesthetic agency resonates with the objects, with the more than human duck creature, and with the material events in her surroundings, foreshadowing other characters'—and, possibly, her own—creative deployments of technology later in the film.

Aída won't give up. While she is getting dressed, her pearl necklace falls apart, introducing a further kind of liquidity. The pearls scatter all over the floor. Fausta kneels down to help pick them up (figure 3.6). Aída seizes the moment and proposes a deal. Every time Fausta sings a song, she will pay her with a pearl from the broken necklace. Once again, Fausta declines. Singing points to the importance of desire, community, and agency in her life. Her singing juggles the tensions between threats of eradication and promises of life that suffuse her daily encounters. Out of familial obligation and aesthetic yearning, and true to her namesake, Fausta succumbs later on. She sings. Complying with their agreement, Aída moves a pearl from one bowl to another. Despite her various attempts to count the pearls, Fausta fails. The pearls institute an economic calculus and simultaneously exceed market structures.

An accomplished composer and pianist, Aída is struggling with writer's block when she proposes the exchange of pearl for song. Her creative impulses have run dry; play has come to a halt. Aída's frustration is so intense that she throws her piano out a large, second-floor stained-glass window, on which the camera had lingered during Fausta's walk through the colonial house. Fausta and Aída's fulltime gardener Noé (Efraín Solis) gaze at the instrument surrounded by a halo of translucent shards of glass in multiple tints. Fausta picks up little pieces, savoring their colors (figure 3.7). The kind gardener is privy to her pleasure and, the next day, brings her a handful of candies wrapped in shiny foil. She lets the gift slip through her fingers, refusing to hold the sweets. They are too loud. Their glaring colors ruffle her delicate sensibility. The sharp edges of the glass fragments are also missing. Perhaps the smooth, self-contained forms lack a brokenness that resonates with her hurt feelings. Unlike the pieces of glass and Fausta herself, the small spheroids are not residual items but communicate their rounded perfection. Far from strange, their tastes are generalized, commodified. Nonetheless,

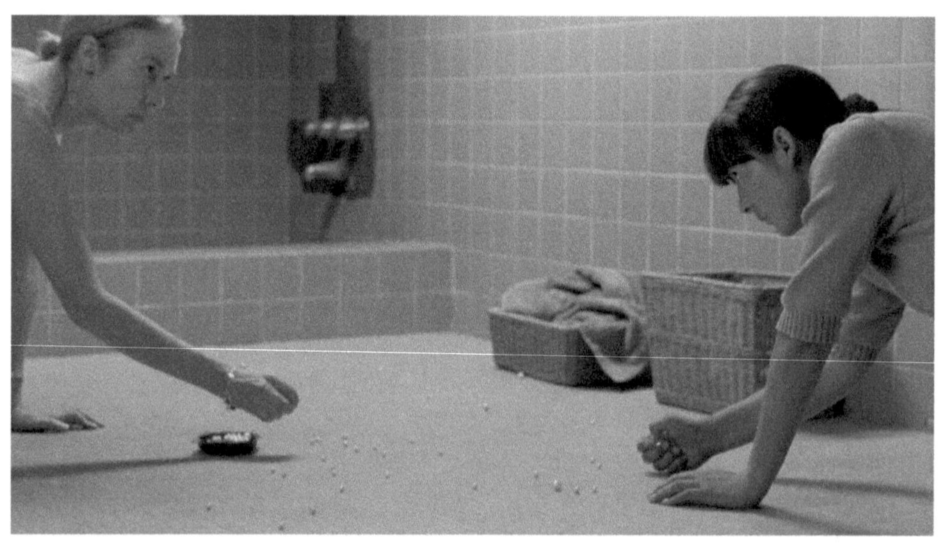

FIGURE 3.6. Claudia Llosa, *The Milk of Sorrow*, 2009, film still. Fausta and Aída pick up the pearls.

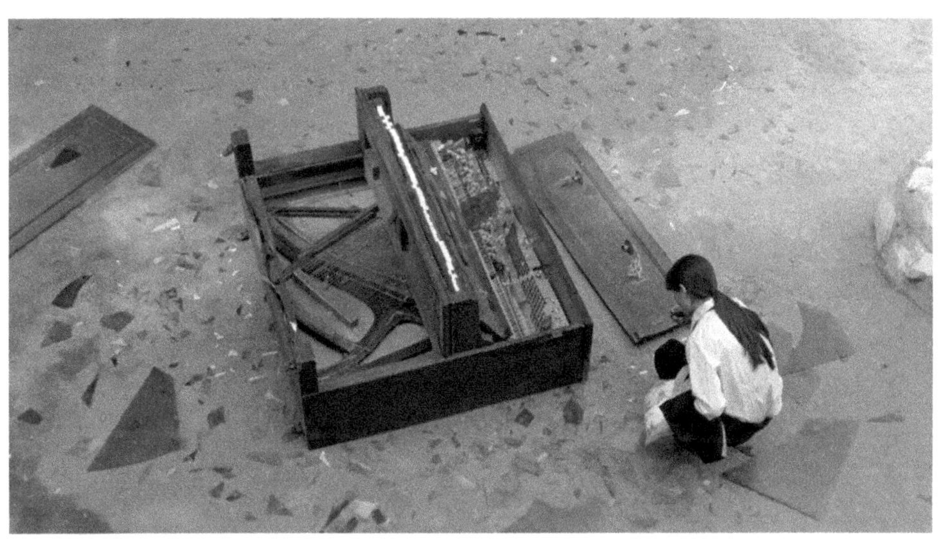

FIGURE 3.7. Claudia Llosa, *The Milk of Sorrow*, 2009, film still. Fausta enjoys colorful pieces of broken glass.

Fausta has indulged in a moment of muted play with the splinters, suspending or distracting herself from her anguish.

Soon afterward, Aída orders a new piano. She haggles over the cost of the delivery with the overseer. The young men who will toil under the weight of the new piano have no say. They lack bargaining power. This sequence emphasizes competing timelines: the time of the house and its occupants' colonial past and that of the current marketplace and worker abuse. It prepares the spectator for Aída's final erasure of Fausta, portended by her continually calling Fausta by another name, Isidra. No matter how many times Fausta corrects her, she persists. Servants are all the same.

For a brief moment, childhood grief appears to break down the class, race, and ethnic barriers between them. While working in the garden one day, Aída unearths a doll. She confesses to Fausta that when she reached a certain age, her father forbade her to play with dolls. She never explains his reasoning to Fausta. The young Aída obeyed and buried her doll. She couldn't really imagine another game. One surmises that dolls reinforce the image of the Nursing Virgin adorning the vestibule: an idealized caring woman cloaked in modesty and humility, not the assertive, haughty, feared employer Fausta encounters. When adult Aída finds the doll, an unspoken pain seems to unite employer and servant. Has Fausta sighted another playmate? Will Aída regain a desire to play? Can the two find common ground? The humane scene—a bonding between two victims of patriarchy—is cut short when Aída's son asks about concert preparations. Aída icily avoids answering him, her coldness suggesting a misplaced, even sentimental, concern on his part. She is certainly not the loving Virgin portrayed in the painting she owns. The artwork is just another piece of colonial furniture, dead weight. Adult Aída still can't imagine a game with the doll other than the one the father disallowed. Indeed, she knows no soothing play. Her short-lived openness vanishes instantly. All the doll invokes is pain. Her response, again, assumes a harsh tone. Muted, softening play is beyond possibility.

Behind Fausta's back, Aída turns her employee's songs into her own piano pieces to be showcased at her annual concert in the city's center. Standing to the side of the stage, Fausta listens with delight and horror. She has aided in her employer's success. Her songs are being heard. Absent the lyrics, Aída's pieces erase the songs' history: the violence against Indigenous women and their call for resistance and, ultimately, the possibility of an alternative. The songs become pleasing artifacts. Aída triumphs. "All of Lima" is there to celebrate her. On the way home Fausta observes, "They liked it, didn't they?" Her facial expression intimates that she contributed to her patrona's success. Her question solicits this recognition. It also lays bare a somewhat ambiguous motivation on Fausta's part. While need may have impelled her to exchange pearls for songs, she is not a neutral onlooker. Her remark disrupts Aída's self-image as a Western artist. For the composer, artistic success rests on her natural creative talent above all else. Furious Aída's ruthlessness emerges, evincing her colonial/military patrilineage. She orders "Isidra" out of the car.

Aída does not want to acknowledge to herself that her "original" composition is an arrangement of "popular" songs. She disavows the knowledge that her arrangement depends on an appropriation of the other's voice and a denial of their history. Ortiz's notion of a give and take is in effect. Yet there is a reversal: Whereas for Ortiz, the subaltern engages in a selective deployment of the dominant culture, here Aída is the taker and Fausta is the giver. Moreover, there is not really a give and take. Aída just takes without recognizing Fausta's gift.[27] With the songs' original violence wiped clean, the composition can be heard and celebrated as pleasing, as Fausta observes. "Lima" enjoys another example of the commodification of Andean music so popular in the West in the late 1970s. Fausta's expulsion signals the failure of the ruling elite to come to grips with Peru's reality and points up the elisions and limitations of a transcultural aesthetics.[28] The civilizing project of the lettered city displays its brutal side, which sharply calls into question the city's legitimacy.[29] A vicious ideology carries the day.

The most abominable aspect is not Aída's cruelty but the way in which the system obliterates consequences for the powerful. The cultural system portrayed in the film is rigged in Aída's favor. She will not be held accountable for the violence; she will get away with it. The film is unflinching in its depiction of class and institutional injustice. The limits of the lettered city stand out. The film could end on this note of disclosure, revealing how the ruling class keeps the hierarchical symbolic order from recognizing that guilt and deformation are of their own making. Llosa's film aims further. It continues, deploying at the level of possible endings the same close-and-open strategy activated at the level of the image.

The "milk of sorrow," so far, has held Fausta in terror, enthralled to death. She is too mortified to brave leaving the home unaccompanied, and she suffers from fainting spells and nosebleeds. Somehow, she returns to the house of her uncle Lúcido (Marino Ballón), where she has lived since she and her mother left their homeland. Her cousin Máxima (María del Pilar Guerrero), who is getting married that day, tells her to come in and get ready for the wedding, the preparations for which are in full swing. Fausta attends the festivities but doesn't socialize, observing the events with a detached numbness. When the party dwindles and she has gone to sleep, Lúcido, at his wits' end, tries to shock her out of her fear of life by almost suffocating her: "¡Tú quieres vivir, pero no te atreves! ¡Respira, respira!" (You want to live but do not dare! Breathe, breathe!). Somehow liberated from her death wish, Fausta finds the wherewithal to question her tolerance for suffering. Her actions acquire a new urgency.

Early in the morning, she returns to Aída's house to collect the pearls she is owed. On her way out, she faints. Noé, the gardener, finds her. She begs him to take her to the nearby hospital. She has a history there. Immediately after her mother's death, Lúcido, worried about his niece's recurrent nosebleeds, had taken her to the clinic. A potato tuber was found growing in her vagina, as Fausta explained, to protect herself against rape.[30] Now she finally has the recommended surgery. The potato implant is removed. Throughout the procedure, the doctor informs Lúcido, she clenches her fist. It contains the pearls, of course. With this defiant act, she secures the traveling and burial funds. The operation must be read as a first step in regaining her physical health, not necessarily as overcoming her trauma.[31]

Pueblo Joven as Site of Aesthetic Agency Beyond Elite Culture and the Marketplace

The camera continually travels among different spaces, alternating among city center, pueblo joven, and Indigenous world. In its depiction of the informal settlement, the film reflects on the social and economic solidification and expansion of a capitalist marketplace, where the local heterogeneous moves toward the global homogeneous. Despite the signs of modernization that abound, the Indigenous community is not solely invested in becoming or appearing more Western. As I show, the community looks back to its history and recuperates alternative patterns of consumption and enjoyment, experiences that often take a collective form. In the process, the notion of transculturation at play in the relation between the global and the marginalized local loses explanatory value. According to Néstor García Canclini, Latin Americans increasingly answer questions of citizenship such as "Who represents my interests?" and "Where do I belong?" in the private realm of commodity consumption and the mass media rather than in abstract democratic decision-making processes or through trajectories of collective participation in the unified nation, as promulgated by Aída's notion of "all of Lima" (García Canclini 2001, 5; 2014, 137). Although the film's opening scenes invoke the military as a killing machine, civic institutions are missing from the pueblo joven. Absent state and civic institutions, disenfranchised populations turn to the market as an answer to their problems. García Canclini consequently understands consumerism as an expansion of the politics of citizenship and identity (2014, 137). Through their consumptive practices, including their participation in media, subjects not only adapt their desires to capitalist demands but give expression to their needs and aspirations.

Fausta's cousin Máxima exemplifies the enticements and controls represented by the marketplace. Early in the film, upon the death of Fausta's mother, the camera cuts to an outdoor scene in which Máxima is parading around in her wedding dress while complaining to her parents about the length of her veil. The train is too short. Her behavior gives the impression that she has succumbed to a distorted notion of modernity, relinquishing the standards of calculated exuberance and parceled-out economic expenditure that define modern subjectivity.[32] Fausta suddenly appears and announces her mother's death to her immediate family, interrupting the young woman's whining. Through this stark contrast between the cousins' behavior the film laces the dilemmas of consumption with questions of life and death.

In a later scene, we discover the reason for Máxima's complaint about her train. Being too short, it will not fly. She wishes to soar on her wedding day. As a solution, pink balloons are attached to the veil. Of course, there is no liftoff.[33] Máxima briefly threatens to abort her wedding. Her desire for a longer train is a kind of self-intoxication, a form of excessive consumption. It counterbalances Fausta's vulnerability and grief with excitement. The cousins' dual strategies are not aberrations but the daily norm that the capitalist market at once incites and laughs away—as bad taste, in Máxima's case, and morbidity, in Fausta's.[34] The two are unacceptable women, or what Davis terms "surplus humanity" (2006, 174–98, 201). Popular culture seeks and enthralls them as consumers. Fausta, as we have seen, spends her downtime at work watching TV. Máxima plans her wedding according to TV dictums, yet she also follows tradition: She peels a potato to divine her marriage's longevity. Fausta encounters her double in her cousin. Both have a surplus status, whether of the disconsolate or exuberant variety, life-denying or life-affirming. On top of that, on our first encounter with the pair, each in her own way pronounces the other's excess.

Fausta's family earns a living by catering weddings. Her uncle Lúcido functions as the official photographer. He memorializes the newly married couples and their extended families standing in front of global locations as if the couples have had a destination marriage. These photographic moments take their participants' aspirations seriously. The subjects' investments in their performances recall García Canclini's (2014, 137–50) sustained argument that people imagine their geographic and geocultural locations differently.

The couples and families do not identify with a bounded space. Rather, their identities are formed with and against local, Indigenous, national, and transnational materials. Their post-geographical reality brackets whatever disdain some viewers might feel for them. Through its staging of celebratory photographic instances, the film juxtaposes glimpses of poverty (makeshift housing, lack of paved streets, no services) with a transnational consumerism fueled mainly by television, which has replaced the store window that dazzled Macabéa. The viewer is offered an evocative portrait of modern-day Latin American life.

The film depicts this shifting terrain palpably when it captures Fausta standing in front of a virtual Iguazú waterfall, dressed in blue, distressed (figure 3.8). External enticements are at odds with internal abjection in a way that resists comprehension. She appears lost in this virtual world. She is a ghostly presence. She belongs and does not belong to the transnational economy being displayed and celebrated. Fausta lingers alone. The party is continuing elsewhere. Compassion tears through the viewer's heart at this devastatingly sad moment in the film. Fausta's loneliness nonetheless intimates an awareness, too. Is the blue water a place of unmitigated effacement? Or can global fantasy be tweaked into something else? Llosa's camera carries the question of aesthetic participation beyond rigorous social oppositions.

This complication surfaces anew during a traditional parade of gifts. At the end of a communal civil marriage ceremony, relatives and guests parade incommensurable presents. A marriage bed, for example, is followed by hens, which give way to an ironing board. How the items will be used in the future is part of the ongoing marriage narrative. These festivities are a celebration of what a couple will do in the future, unlike in a Hollywood romance, where marriage is the end. The joyous procession of things, furthermore, "break[s] up," as Michel Foucault writes of Borges's Chinese encyclopedia, "all the ordered surfaces and all the planes with which we are accustomed to tame the wild profusion of existing things, and continu[es] long afterwards to disturb and threaten with collapse our age-old distinction between the Same and the Other" (1970, xv). The parade of gifts construes the temporality of modernity in a manner that recognizes the coevality of peoples and cultures. It illustrates the social and cultural contradictions that mark the disjunctive space of contemporary Lima, and it implicitly calls for a rearticulation of the city along egalitarian lines, one that is prefigured by an older female worker. She sways to the music while the wedding gifts are being announced and supplied with explanatory narratives (figure 3.9). This memorable moment blocks any ironic distance. Instead, the worker's slow dance movements bless

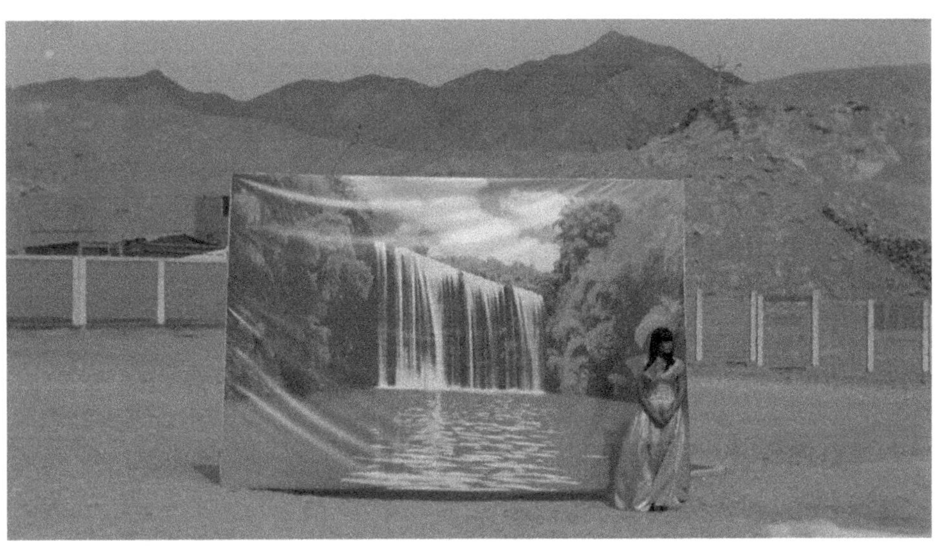

FIGURE 3.8. Claudia Llosa, *The Milk of Sorrow*, 2009, film still. Fausta in front of a life-size image of the Iguazú waterfall.

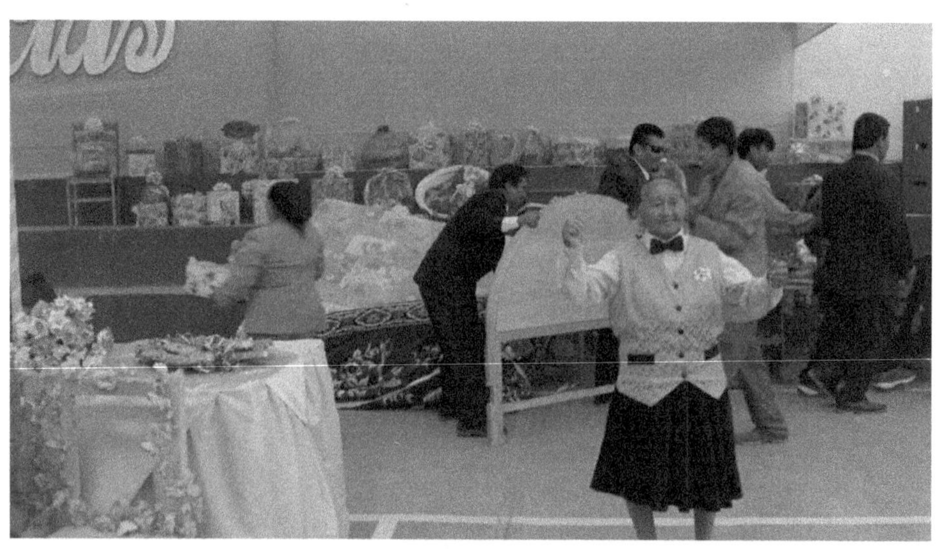

FIGURE 3.9. Claudia Llosa, *The Milk of Sorrow*, 2009, film still. An elderly woman dances to music during a communal wedding. The wedding gifts that have been paraded are put on display behind her.

the ceremony. They remind the viewer that weddings bring into being new histories, new presents, and new futures.

Likewise, a swimming pool sequence designs a new sociality, heralding what a communal, not an entrepreneurial, variety of cultural agency might be. Without preamble, the camera cuts to Fausta's uncle Lúcido digging. When Fausta sees him breaking up the rocky ground, she assumes that he is carrying out his threat that if she does not take her mother back to the village before Máxima's wedding, he will bury her corpse in the backyard. The tomb turns out to be a swimming pool. As it is being built, the camera zooms in and captures the delight on the faces of a couple of children, playing in a hole apparently not much bigger than a bathtub. Nor does the pool project a sense of permanence. It comes about from a kind of random happening and is made up of whatever materials are available. When the uncle is finished, the camera briefly shows us a group of people frolicking around the pool, laughing. This brief scene brings together the locals in a pleasurable activity rather than in mutual ignorance or suspicion of one another. The camera invites us to frolic with them.

These spaces of social interaction, formed with symbolic resources of different origins, shape social belonging and affirm social networks.[35] The film activates these various imaginaries to make the participants and the viewers believe we are alike and simultaneously stresses disparities and divergences. A prime example is the unusual number of kissing scenes between grooms and brides that circulate in the film. In the West, the couple seals their commitment with a kiss. In each scene, the recently married men appear overly anxious. They kiss their brides sloppily and crudely. Given the suave conventions of Hollywood's romantic leading men, these red-hot Latino lovers fall short. While the kisses are laughable, they have an endearing quality, too.

The wedding photographs and the gift parade, the kisses and the many feet we see going up and down steep staircases throughout the film, all exude abundance, not deficiency, as certain notions of modernity would maintain. Together these sequences indicate how community members navigate consumerism so that it is more than a market force or profit principle. The inhabitants of the pueblo joven create a communal aesthetics out of random and diverse objects while engaging in an intricate web of interactions among themselves, in contrast to the imagined community touted by the closed lettered city. The film presents the community as a collective of fluid sociohistorical, relational subjects, capable of reflecting on and adapting to a multifaceted economic system. The community is creating narratives and images and responding to the ones promulgated by the global media. It enacts a model of aesthetic publicness.

Not all of the festivities are captured in a bright light. During Máxima's engagement party, a young man discloses his attraction to Fausta in a flirtatious remark (a *piropo*) that links blood and milk in an explicit sexual configuration: "Si el rojo es el color de la pasión, báñame con tu menstruación" (If red is the color of passion, bathe me in your menstrual blood). Fausta immediately gets up and leaves. She is not up for this kind of loud play. While his recombination of liquids might miss its intended target, his reliance on popular wisdom cannot be laughed away. Although she goes off in silence, Fausta remains vulnerable to the values embedded in her communities' language. Language as a voice of common knowledge places a premium on conformity. It offers little to an eccentric individual like her.

As Gloria Anzaldúa (1999 [1987], 76) observes, sayings, ready-made language used by well-intentioned people, keep alive conservative, if not reactionary, values most often at the expense of girls and women. The innocuous saying about flies, "En boca cerrada no entran moscas" (Flies don't enter a closed mouth), she notes, monitors and censors the behavior of young girls exclusively. Anzaldúa even remembers her own mother citing the common truism that if she was going to get a job, she had to speak English well—that is, without an accent (75–76). Albeit with the best intentions, her mother reproduced institutionalized American racism normalized in popular sayings. Fausta's leaving does not undo the sexism and violence against women embedded in the flirtatious quip. Nor does the film recount fully how she is going to cope with the risks and conventions that are part of her environment. At the end, it concentrates on the positive lessons learned.

When Fausta, following her expulsion from Aída's car, returns to her uncle's house and observes her cousin's wedding festivities, she witnesses the community interacting joyfully with material and symbolic resources. Connecting with these practices, she comprehends that the actual images and materials infusing her aesthetic longings—namely, splashed milk, the pool, the parade of gifts, and the staged wedding photographs, along with flowering potato plants (as I clarify momentarily)—resist the market economies of both the small screen and the concert hall. While the former may lead to a communal giddiness, as we observe when Máxima's wedding party is being groomed in front of a TV, and the latter to individual triumph, as is the case with Aída after the recital, they suffer from presentism, from a lack of historical and cultural grounding. This presentism contrasts with the historical and futural orientations Fausta embeds in the images of the ocean and the potato.

Fausta's Decolonial Aesthetics: The Ocean, a Play of Flowers, and a Blossoming Potato

In the film's penultimate sequence, Fausta is on her way to her village with her mother's corpse. Her uncle is driving. For unstated reasons he is now helping her, after having let her fend for herself in the aftermath of her mother's death. When she sees the ocean in the distance, she asks him to stop the truck. A vision of the ocean had captured her before, when she tried to purchase a coffin with her male cousin. At one of the stores they visit, she notices a hand-painted coffin decorated with water and the sun. She is transfixed by it. In its fluidity, the ocean is the opposite of her barrio's barren terrain. When Fausta finally sees the actual ocean, she is ready to transform her existential dilemmas into a problem to be solved with the help of an aesthetics, not an already established identity. Throughout, Fausta has negotiated the dangers and lures water imagery presents. Tossing the paper crane into water, she toyed with death, layering the water she desires with an ominous undercurrent. Lest we forget, her journey has been an education in aesthetic idioms and readings. This journey leads her to reevaluate the diasporic or migrant experience as something that creates the homeland. She recognizes that her mother's desire to be buried in her village is the result of the Quechua diaspora. The village, given the expanded resonance of "Mother Earth" (Pachamama), becomes an affective process related to other images and temporalities rather than a place.

Alone, Fausta carries her mother's corpse across the sand dunes toward the sea (figure 3.10). The film's recurrent shots of people carrying people or things stress the various characters' Andean ethnicity. As she looks to the horizon, the ocean appears endless, unlike the earlier water imagery. Both basin and pool had contained the water's scope. Its flow is unimpeded here, signifying a suspension of previously instituted limits. No longer compelled to follow Indigenous imperatives to the letter, Fausta starts a new song as the shot of her dragging her mother's corpse fades. She reworks the promise to bury her mother while still watering memory. Inventing shifting images in a rearticulation of the bond with her mother, she recasts the milk of sorrow. The traumatized, contaminating breast and its poisoned milk give way to a nourishing song ("Comeré si me cantas"). A generative flow carries onward in the life-affirming figures of the ocean and the mother. Fausta fulfills the obligation to her mother in an unprecedented way. She simultaneously brings into being the space for a new song, life. The film, once again, reaches a possible ending that it declines. It goes on to revitalize the landscape. The song spreads over her neighborhood, where potatoes may eventually blossom.

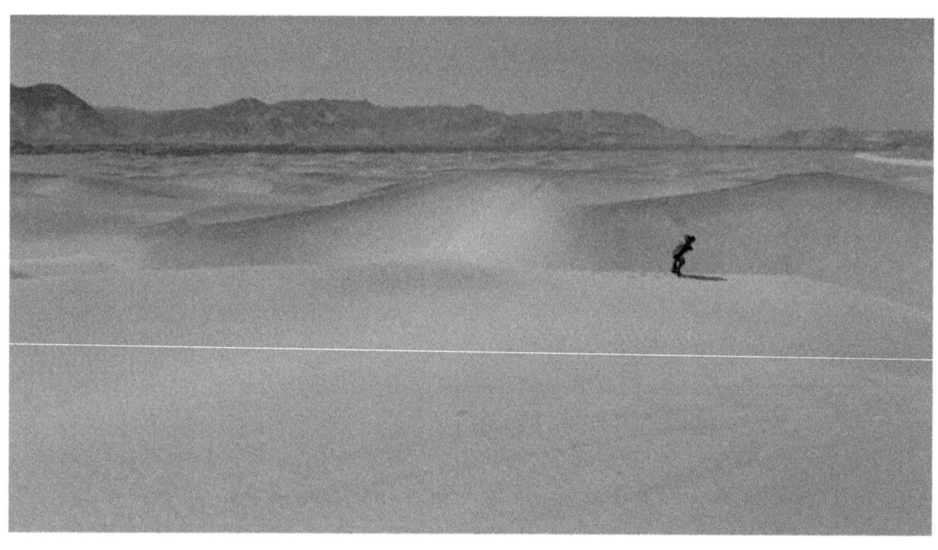

FIGURE 3.10. Claudia Llosa, *The Milk of Sorrow*, 2009, film still. Fausta carries her mother's body across the dunes.

The film takes the potato through a series of transformations. At first, it is to be rejected as strictly poisonous, analogously to the milk's startled, perturbed aspect. At the clinic, when he discovers the potato implanted in Fausta's vagina, the examining doctor, albeit of Andean heritage, lectures her for believing in superstitions and not practicing Western forms of medicine. The doctor conceives of himself as impersonal and purely objective, driven by scientific knowledge, while simultaneously reinforcing the exotic nature of the potato tuber. Outside the clinic, Fausta defends its usage. The potato shields her from rape. A neighbor has used the device to this effect, only to land a marriage that engendered four children. Nothing but revulsion, remarks Fausta, citing her neighbor, will deter revolting men from rape. She wants the potato implant to be understood through a specific historical lens that recognizes articulations of race, class, and gender. Her explanation disrupts the doctor's self-presentation.[36] She resists succumbing to a dichotomous medical logic that separates and homogenizes bodies into healthy and sick. Instead, she locates the potato tuber within the social patterns, gender relations, and cosmological conceptions of her community. Since her uncle left their Andean village for Lima when he was very young, he was never educated in the communal knowledges that sustain the women. Fausta's explanation reveals the continuities and discontinuities in knowledge among different members of the same community.[37] It challenges the viewer who attributes a magical realist worldview to Fausta. This characterization, clearly, diminishes her aesthetic sense of the potato's workings and her grasp of the aesthetic outlook of her fellow community members. It misses the particularities and the dialectical thrust of her aesthetic sensibility. Blurring dichotomies between modern and premodern forms of symbolization, her explanation provides a provisional path beyond the conventional global narrative that predicates a distorted modernity of Latin America. The potato becomes a primordial support of her Andean identity. Tending to the potato, she prunes the sprouts extending from the tuber in her vagina and advocates on behalf of the potato by challenging the gardening ventures of Noé, Aída's gardener. Fausta is weaving a play of strange and regular taste around the potato.

Her relationship with Noé is complicated. She slowly learns to trust him. As she becomes increasingly comfortable in his presence, she brings up the subject of the plants he cultivates and cherishes, such as geraniums, daisies, jasmines, hydrangeas. They speak Quechua during this exchange. High walls enclose the compound, turning the garden into a refuge. She shares that she used to grow vegetables in her village and wonders why the potato plant is excluded from the garden. At first, Noé is reticent. For him, the garden functions as a closed, self-absorbed world. Then he divulges that potatoes are abundant, cheap, and flower for a very short time. She rejoins that the flowers he prizes are not native, they speak of a colonial past. They are the result of a hierarchical system that differentiates among flowers and ranks them as part of the construction of a social order. Like its counterparts the zoo and the museum, the garden is imbricated with the history of colonialism as a storehouse and display site for plants and with modernity as a barometer of beauty and good taste. She appreciates the potato as a flower, not a mere food substance. Recovering a neglected history of the potato, now as the absent flower, Fausta assumes a decolonial aesthetic stance. The potato evolves beyond its everyday meaning. As such, the potato is agential and will turn out to be responsible for a shift in the aesthetic values of the garden's keeper.

Play further expands and complicates the symbolic power of flowers. Cognizant of their metaphorical resonance, Fausta greets Noé one day at the gate to the compound holding a huge red lily in her mouth (figure 3.11). Her play has shifted from muted to loud. Her performance interrupts the daily course of events. Habitually, the camera places her behind a bar, half-occluded by a shutter. The latter shots, which are recaptured on the cover of the North American DVD, have her gazing out at him, at us, at the world, at the unknown (figure 3.12). Questions arise about the position of the Indigenous actor in the contemporary cultural field. Is Fausta enacting a gendered amorous tradition while also running into its confinements? In assuming the image of the seductress, is she again asserting the symbolism of flowers? Or should we read her powerful powerlessness in a more reflexive sense? Is the scene a commentary on the limits of art in a market-driven economy? The compound, after all, borders an open market that Fausta and Noé traverse every day to and from work. Consumerism has become an all-pervasive force, analogous to the role religious structures played in earlier epochs. While the garden escapes neither the history of colonialism nor the commodified world that surrounds it, the two find short-lived relief in it. Yet Fausta's play with flowers and her questions press beyond the categorical order of the marketplace and elite culture, a gesture Noé picks up on as he ventures a response to her challenge.

The last sequence involving the potato takes place in Fausta's pueblo joven, now situated between ruinous modernity (the city as civilizing project) and confining tradition (the Andean village as site of resistance), where the ability to overcome, to change, to reach for freedom is part of daily life. Noé leaves Fausta an intertwined blossoming potato plant at her doorstep (figure 3.13). In the eyes of spectators reading for character, this final image may bring closure to the romance.

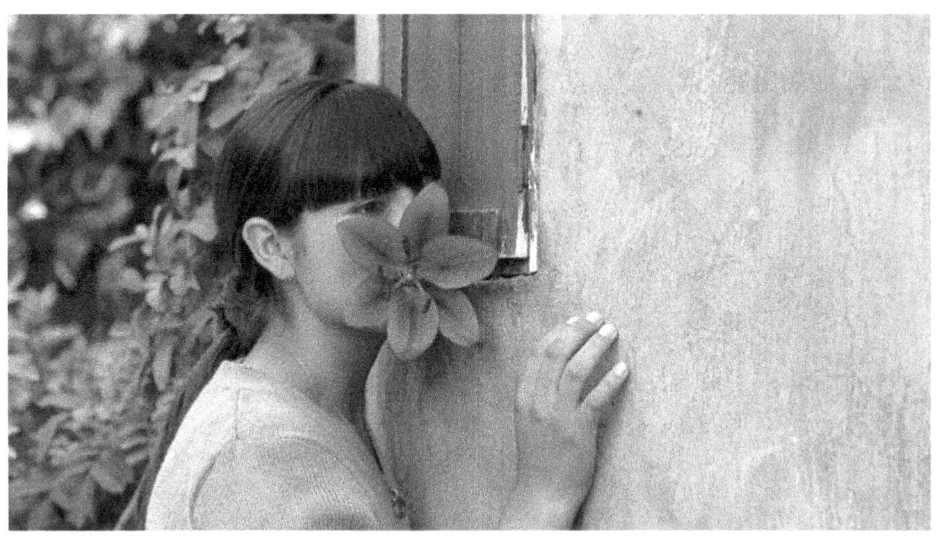

FIGURE 3.11. Claudia Llosa, *The Milk of Sorrow*, 2009, film still. Fausta greets Noé at the gate of Aída's house with a red lily in her mouth.

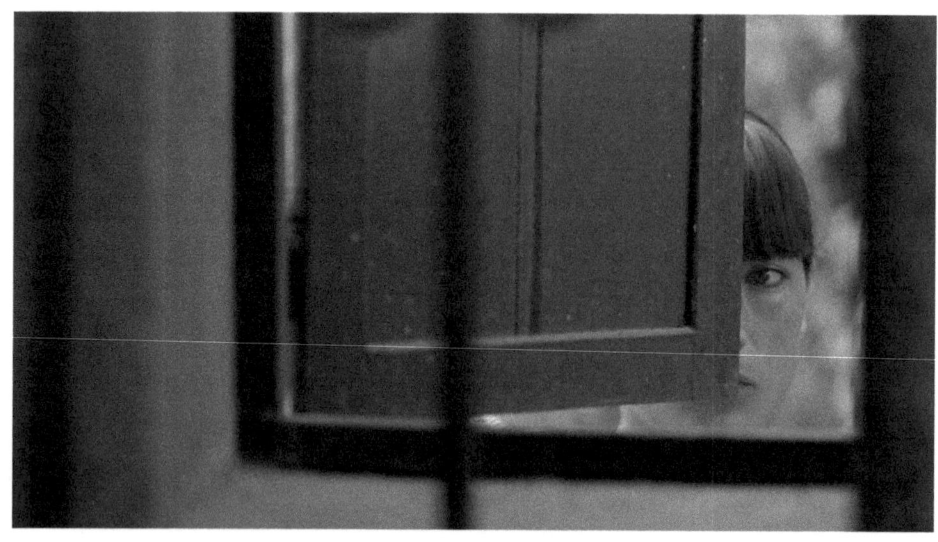

FIGURE 3.12. Claudia Llosa, *The Milk of Sorrow*, 2009, film still. Fausta carries out her daily chore of checking who is calling.

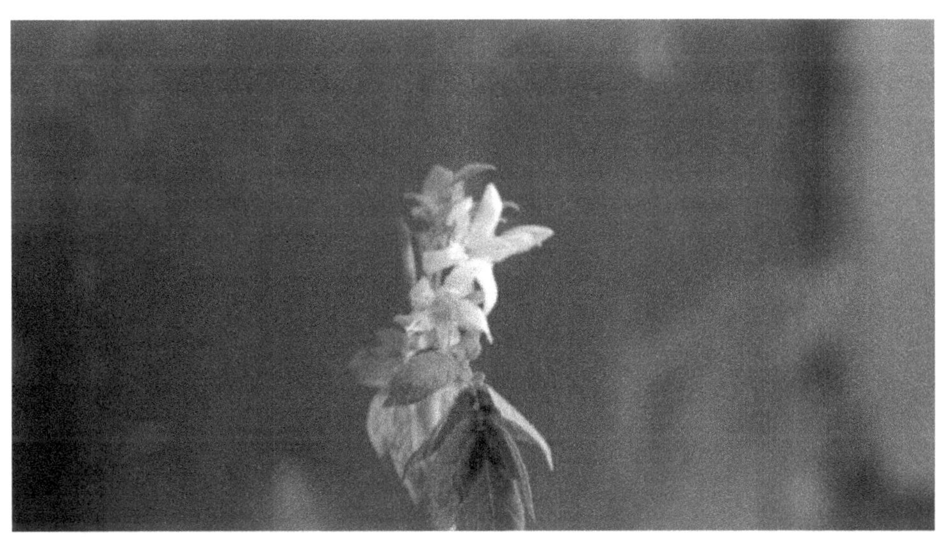

FIGURE 3.13. Claudia Llosa, *The Milk of Sorrow*, 2009, film still. The intertwined potato plant that Noé leaves for Fausta.

The potato plant proclaims the unstated Hollywood finale: Fausta and Noé live happily ever after. Cured of trauma, Fausta can now entertain marriage and motherhood.[38] Yet Noé leaves—he doesn't wait for Fausta to open the door. The gift, it appears, is testimony to his rethinking of his aesthetic tenets. She has convinced him of the participation of aesthetic practices in creating and maintaining societal hierarchies as well as in putting forth alternative social conceptions. The potato plant signals a decolonial aesthetic opening rather than the soldering of a heterosexual bond. Fausta, throughout the film, forgoes any marital interests or maternal traits. Her obligations are solely filial. During her cousin's engagement, for example, she is pictured holding a young child at arm's length. She neither cuddles nor entertains the child, who supposedly is hungry. As part of the wedding crew, she keeps her distance. Even when she greets Noé with the lily in her mouth, her attitude is more humorous than amorous. She is playing the exotic Latina, complementing the grooms' Latin lovers.[39] A Hollywood ending would require seeing Fausta as endowed with a cohesively developing profile. From the opening sequences onward, however, the film sidetracks the project of creating a coherent psychological identity. It counters this enterprise with revised understandings of intimacy and an upending of the public-private divide shaping the notion of individualist artistic creation. The Hollywood reading, the romance, must be discarded in favor of a decolonial option.

When Noé leaves Fausta the blooming potato, he acknowledges and accepts her resignification of the potato plant. Fausta is responsible for the shift in his aesthetic values. He finally answers her and our earlier questions regarding her powerful powerlessness: The garden, its occupants, and their play are open signifiers. Gardening becomes a place for exploring the different forms beauty might take. Noé recognizes Fausta as a cultural agent. He joins her game. He plays. He finds the right tone. Muted and loud play fuse. These activities are cavorting together, enhancing each other, intensifying the pleasure. While these aesthetic modalities may not yet add up to a new public space, the figure of the potato signals future openings for the young children who announce Noé's gift. The gift encapsulates the aesthetic possibilities that Andean culture enduringly maintains, a point underscored once more by the image of the children dancing. The young boy is learning a traditional dance from a slightly taller young girl. They have yet to weather unspoken trials and tribulations. Nonetheless, this image hints at ample opportunities for play. What is more, it suggests ways in which aesthetics holds out a decolonial promise of change, not only to the characters, but also to the spectator.

Toward a Contemporary Indigenous Order of Aesthetic Publicness

The Milk of Sorrow consistently crosscuts between sequences that foreground Fausta's anxieties and ones that focus on the neighborhood in which she lives, a vast improvised housing development bordering Lima. This young town is built on desert land punctuated by steep hills. The camera takes us on several walking tours up and down an impressive staircase, pausing for amazing views of the dry landscape. It slowly pans the residents' comings and goings on the narrow stairs, intimately revealing the bodily actions of climbing and descending. These movements stress the precariousness of the neighborhood, which has emerged haphazardly without basic social and civil services. At the same time, long shots accentuate the beauty and majesty to be found in this singular landscape. We never see the city as such. The camerawork deemphasizes the center in favor of the margin.

Repeatedly, the camera shows Fausta's family enjoying a full, vibrant life. They have managed to turn their precarious state into a communal business, catering weddings, whose values point to socialities not determined by the market exclusively. Aída's lettered society has given way to haphazard spaces. The film juxtaposes fragments of a colonial setting with its adjacent marketplace, energized by a mix of ancient traditions and brazen consumerism, and the community scenes in the surrounding areas. Through these spatial and temporal disjunctions, the film demands that we recalibrate our thinking about Fausta and her family.

The closing credits make plain that the songs recounting the events that cause the milk of sorrow are original pieces composed for the film by the Quechua musician and actor Magaly Solier, who plays Fausta. They are not "popular" or authentic Indigenous pieces. As artifacts, the songs are part of the market. Yet they denounce the violence that women constantly experience everywhere. When character and actor mirror each other, the entanglements of art and commodification reemerge, this time in the context of the utopian or future-oriented impulses the viewer attributes to the film. The work holds these competing demands for art, profitability, and political change in tension. Simultaneously, it recognizes, projects, and celebrates an emerging aesthetic that marginalized people bring into being in spaces outside the official culture.

Fausta leads her life at the cross section of violence and liberation. Rather than ironing out these contrary tendencies, Llosa leaves them intact in a troubling but hopeful aesthetic vision. By ending with the potato not as a symbol of Peru but as a symbol of beauty and, by extension, a sign of an appreciation of Indigenous cultures that are under erasure, an array of new aesthetic possibilities and threats emerge. Through a set of disjunctions and tensions alongside translations and shifting binaries, the film highlights the manifold aesthetic dimensions of the encounter among pueblo joven, a racialized gender system, elite culture, and the marketplace.

Transculturation is a fact of life, as attested to by Fausta's delight in the TV cartoon and her clinging to the pearls. The wedding photos staged by the uncle in front of a picture of Iguazú Falls and the film's citations of the Nursing Virgin and the Sacred Heart Christ also suggest as much. But transculturation is not the driving force of aesthetic meaning in the film, and the historically potent divides it posits shouldn't distract us from the aesthetic complexities *The Milk of Sorrow* puts into motion—for example, by creating a color red that is at once shocked blood, enticing lily, and rebellious tomato ketchup or by designing a color white that, as a part of a flowering potato plant, channels presumed medicalized and matrimonial purity into a grounded futurity. Working at the limits of transculturation, the film enacts a decolonial aesthetics that shows the Quechua actor as navigating a web of aesthetic threats of eradication and promises of communal caring, sustenance, and imagination. Both the threats and the promises are part of Fausta's experiences of the world in a manner that is not to be discounted. With the notions of threats and promises, I point to the manifold, fine-grained, and often disjointed "identifications and differentiations" and the dynamism, as well as the continuities, of ongoing processes of "aesthetic affiliation and disaffiliation, appropriation and disowning" that mark the day-to-day aesthetic lives that the inhabitants of the pueblo joven craft for themselves (Roelofs 2014, 204).[40] A decolonial aesthetics needs to home in on these multiscalar, polyvalent registers of meaning and their experiential reverberations. Aesthetic publicness is the territory where they arise. Llosa's interest is in this register of experiential organization. This order harbors norms and forms that exercise their influence over acts of creation and reception. At the same time, it is an informal, normatively indefinite, unresolved setting where such norms and forms are being brought into being, navigated, and transformed.

Resistance to Aída's theft and the erasures inflicted by authorized culture is not Llosa's direct concern.[41] She contests the quashing of Indigenous existence by recognizing the attractions as well as the devastation of the global marketplace and turning our attention to a communal aesthetic flourishing that opts for life. There is no liberation through flying, through the TV's lessons, or through obedience to the mores of the mother's village. These hopes, longings, and commitments play their part in the everyday lives that we see unfolding in the pueblo joven.

Reworking the startled milk and the nosebleeds and bringing them together with the evolving potato and water imagery, Llosa's film articulates a decolonial aesthetics that rejects notions of a contaminated modernity (and its counterpoint of a purified/purifying colonial world) and examines coloniality and its affiliations with race and gender in light of both the preexisting Indigenous and the subsequent African-descended populations of Peru. She brings to decolonial discourse a recognition of the complex material and conceptual racial hierarchization of Peru with its African and later Asian groups, which exceeds European-Indigenous binaries.[42] Aesthetic existence at the intersection of oppression and freedom remains fraught but at the same time beckons with possibility. Meanwhile, the film pushes beyond a reading of Fausta's and her community's experiences to bring out a systemic organization. Llosa alerts us to the structural aesthetic formation undergirding the arch of their creative and receptive endeavors and their evolving sensibilities. *The Milk of Sorrow* proposes that we see the pueblo joven as a novel model of aesthetic publicness.

Beyond the frames of transculturation and resistance, emplaced in a thicket of aesthetic promises and threats, the decolonial feminist viewer is neither plunged into disorientation nor interpellated as morally commendable. The unsettlement Fausta experiences when she is thrown out of the car is a stage in a more encompassing aesthetic process. The position the viewer is offered is one in which we are called on to navigate the antithetical directions we witness—that is, to come to terms with both egregious expropriation and violence and life-sustaining social and political possibility. Fausta lives this duality. Her spectators are invited to take up an analogous cultural stance. This means surpassing the oppositions between the supposedly spoiled brat (the irate Máxima who finds her train too short) and the good, dutiful daughter (the doleful Fausta who is in mourning). It involves rethinking these stances in view of the shifting oppositions between poor and rich, acceptable and unacceptable femininity, center and periphery, individual and group, and good and bad taste that the film traces. In the course of this process, a concern for bonds of conviviality is sparked in the spectator, who imagines a collective existence that loosens the grip of fear and yields as yet unknown pleasures. The pueblo joven yields the frame of aesthetic publicness that undergirds and fuels these imaginaries. Aesthetic publicness, as indicated in chapter 2, comprises simultaneously a project that is being shouldered and one that demands joint action. Fausta and her uncle cooperate in this venture, not only together, but also with the many other playing characters Llosa has assembled.

Unsuspected aesthetic parallels and contingently evolving aesthetic translations populate the realm of aesthetic publicness the film associates with the pueblo joven. I have already emphasized the differences separating the two cousins' aesthetic sensibilities. But there are telling analogies, as well. The pair are both invested in flying. Máxima, as we have seen, wants to float and glide through the sky on her wedding day, lifted and buoyed by her train. Fausta, in the early parts of the film, endlessly folds white napkins into beautiful shapes reminiscent of birds in flight while talking to her mother. If Fausta heeds Indigenous history by putting her faith in the potato as a safeguard against rape and as a contraceptive, her cousin relies on the tuber to gauge her future happiness: The longer the potato peel, the longer will her marriage last. She succeeds in peeling the potato in one long strand. The camera films the peeling using the same low angle it deploys to show Fausta trimming her own potato, which has begun to grow sprigs that extend from her vagina. Both cousins tweak the potato to their intimate desires. The tuber obliges. These kinds of resonances, conjoining orientations toward pasts and futures, pervade the aesthetic worlds of Llosa's cast of characters.

We intuit the manifold, ever morphing aesthetic possibilities that endure in the potato. Much more than a symbol of the Peruvian nation, this privileged Andean substance carries a host of meanings grounded in the narratives permeating life in the pueblo joven. Versatile and improvisational, the potato communicates with high and popular culture alike. The white pearls, the white wedding dress, the white coat worn by the doctor, and the ugly duckling's white milk anticipate the white flowers the potato will sprout at the end of the film. These aesthetic forms participate in and uphold shifting webs of relationships that enact a historically evolving system of aesthetic publicness.

Watering Memory

The Milk of Sorrow offers two inflections that could readily serve as endings to the film, as I have indicated. These sequences fold back onto themselves to answer the circuit of modernity, exoticism, magical realism, and transculturation tagged by the film poster and reproduced by the concert plot with an involved array of aesthetic possibilities. The first instance is Aída's eviction of Fausta from the car after the concert. Being thrown out frees Fausta of her transcultural illusions, causing her to let go of any respect for Aída's values. The film continues well beyond this point where modernity proves to be victorious and the limits of the lettered city, which seeks survival at the price of carrying on in the extractivist mode, are exposed. Máxima appears to confirm this economic reality. Throughout, she follows the enticements and dictates of the marketplace, thus amplifying corporate opportunities to draw a profit from slum dwellers like herself. Nonetheless, the market fosters ways in which the inhabitants of pueblos jóvenes can make social interventions. The cousins exemplify these ambiguities. From Máxima's wedding and her uncle's social and entrepreneurial labors, Fausta learns the importance of community, to breathe, and to honor her mother's request in a manner attuned to her own aesthetic longings. These valuable lessons lead to the burial journey and its unexpected denouement.

The film could have come by its second ending at the ocean's edge, with Fausta gazing out at the horizon in awe of all the blue that surrounds her. Memory prevails. Her bonds with her mother and the Andean village are safeguarded. Subaltern desire is regained. Closure, however, does not arrive until the potato plant blooms in Fausta's district. Neither the ethical bankruptcy of the marketplace and the aesthetic limitations of the lettered city nor an aesthetic perception severed from contemporary exigencies holds Llosa's main interest. Indeed, her bet is on the pueblo joven. The three different endings—two possible, one actual—get us there. Overlayed onto each other, they each nod toward crucial aesthetic capacities and limitations, highlighting promises and threats that undergird the community's daily existence.

Taken by the image of the ocean and the potato's disavowed beauty, Fausta detects aesthetic possibilities unrecognized by Quechua protocols and Western gaze. Learning her lessons from the duck, her uncle, and Máxima, she actualizes them as a part of her lifeworld. The spectator enjoys a parallel educational process. Film poster and concert plot supply a point of departure that the film exposes and dismantles. Viewers are at once primed for an exoticist imaginary of a premodern, Indigenous cosmology that animates Fausta and for a moralist condemnation of a colonialist or national order that submerges her, only to be barred from dwelling in these positions. In this way, the spectator becomes alert to the aesthetic potentialities Fausta and her family realize in the pueblo joven.

The modernist story held out as a promise by the poster, revealed in its ambivalence in the medical scenes and unmasked as a threat by the appropriation ritual, comes apart. While donning the magical realist cloak to draw in the Global North viewer and bring home the West's conflicting figurations of Indigenous musical invention, the film rejects an overall frame of transculturation where magical realism nourishes and is nourished by modern desire in a self-confirming circle. Through strategies of play, film, poster, characters, and viewers alike circumvent this arrangement.

If Noé's gift is to survive in the pueblo joven's arid landscape, the plant will need to be watered. No one is better suited for this task than its recipient, Fausta. Her journey to bury her mother has been an education in liquids. She learns how to read fluid images and work through the opportunities and dangers they present. At the end, Fausta can comply finally with her mother's other wish: to water memory. Although the violent acts perpetrated on Perpetua and her husband are singular, heinous events, they are, unfortunately, still common historical occurrences not only in Peru but throughout Latin America. Everyone knows this narrative. Perpetua prefers an intimate account; Fausta delivers. In its exploration of aesthetic forms and modes of bodily address, and in its self-reflexivity, the film, likewise, heeds the mother's call.

The dynamics between Aída and Fausta consume considerable screen time. I previously noted how they almost bonded over a doll that Aída disinters while watering the garden with a hose. During this watering scene, Aída keeps memory at bay. She briefly mentions her father's prohibition against her playing with dolls, and even now, as an adult, she internalizes it again. She reburies the doll, memories. For her, images and things have a fixed temporal place. Frozen in time, the sofa, the Madonna painting, and the relative's photograph all clearly demarcate specific mnemonic boundaries. The film, by contrast, impresses on the spectator how different forms and images flow into one another. When the opportunity arises to open herself to a sonic flow and to engage in a transcultural moment, Aída evicts Fausta from the car. She slams the door on the present, lapsing into an outworn conception of aesthetic agency. Yet she and the lettered city she represents are already riddled by economic imperatives. The Madonna in Aída's antechamber finds its match not in Fausta's mother, but in a Christ figure adorning a mass-produced calendar on the wall above the mother's corpse in the pueblo joven. Aída is a cultural, social, and economic anachronism, and the film rightly dismisses her.

With Aída out of the picture, Fausta's uncle becomes our guide to the daily challenges and temptations the denizens of the pueblo joven confront. Lúcido recognizes how images work in the current market environment. Given the plasticity of the image, he takes improbable photographs that fulfill the desires of his community. Just because he traffics in transcultural devices doesn't turn him into an invoicer of transculturation. He harnesses technology for his community's entertainment and benefit. The people are not disturbed by the simulacrum. It's an occasion for playful togetherness, for a collective imaginary. This is apparent in the scenes when the wedding party are doing themselves up in front of a TV and are posing in front of the enlarged photograph of the Iguazú waterfall. The positive and vibrant nature of the people's activities, furthermore, counters the prevailing negative view of the slum. It is fitting that her uncle urges Fausta to breathe at the point in the film when she is most estranged and apathetic. She does breathe. She gathers the courage to bury her mother. The final resting place, the ocean, emerges from the web of fluid images that Fausta encounters and negotiates. This web becomes her and her mother's memory. The film concludes by foreshadowing Fausta's future aesthetic impact on the pueblo joven, which Noé stresses with his gift.

Anchoring Strange Taste: Individuality, Community, and a Relatable Story

If Fausta is going to have an impact and build a life in the pueblo joven, she is going to have to engage daily with a whole repertoire of images and forms that she inherits and that are part of her surroundings. Initially desperate to shield herself against impending violence, she almost destroys her own life. Through her singing and by joining her family's and community's aesthetic practices, she moves out of a state of numbness, inventing ritual forms that conjoin memory with futurity. In the early stages, her song is a form of muted play. It soothes her sensibility. It enables connectedness over and above a withholding of self. Gradually her play assumes louder forms, too. Getting out from under the precepts of Indigenous customs and shaking off the demands of the lettered city do not betoken the arrival of free-flowing aesthetic creativity, however. With her protagonist, Llosa offers a view of aesthetic agency as a strategy of critical reading and bodily address that negotiates intertwined promises and threats.[43] Eradicating the threats, Fausta and the viewer realize, involves extinguishing the promises.[44] Perils remain, as the film's inconclusive ending intimates. The course her life will take is undecided. At the same time, Llosa no less rejects the artistic hero of *City of God* as a model for a female teen in the pueblos jóvenes than the young narco-traffickers of *Our Lady of the Assassins* who, one by one, fall victim to endemic violence. The model she proposes constellates around the more complicated notions of aesthetic experience, agency, taste, and play explored in this chapter.

The film maintains its technique of open-and-close throughout. Noé's gift portends an open decolonial future. At the same time, Fausta's living in her uncle's house brings to the fore the recurring image of a female closed off to the world. Yet when necessary, she walks, often next to walls, bearing out the ever present fear of trauma. Still, what matters is her walking, not just her walking away (e.g., from her young suitor or Aída's house). Her sinking back into fear cannot be ruled out. Her anxiety doesn't simply vanish and must be seen not merely as an individual pathology but as a social constellation that demands a collective response, as Noé recognizes by giving his gift, not himself. Fausta, relatedly, has become aware of a simultaneously collective and individual set of aesthetic tasks: to continue to move; to allow images to remain fluid; to keep interpreting, revising, addressing anew. Quenching the dangers means depleting the alternatives. The film teaches Fausta and the viewer how promises and threats are entangled.

Like the viewer, Fausta lives in a contemporary world overwhelmed by narratives about globalization, consumerism, social media, and simulation. Traditional narratives associated with Latin America are under pressure. Activating plots of magical realism and transculturation, and engaging issues of colonialism and a deformed modernity but refusing to give primacy to them, Llosa's film brackets these known entities in favor of a more relevant story. While providing a tale of consumer desire, global photographic self-representation, and fantasy, Llosa gives it a twist to develop a relatable account, a grounded narration. In so doing, the film parallels the lives of its main Quechua characters and their community. Like them, it negotiates conflictive Indigenous, local, national, and transnational mandates and forces.

Llosa's protagonist lives the aftermath of the milk of sorrow in a parched settlement that is part of Lima, one of the many sprawling cities of the Global South promoted by local and global capital. At the end, Fausta is still there in her uncle's house. Her loneliness, which reminds the viewer of the film's beginning, anticipates future pleasures and disappointments, possibilities and restrictions. The home is not built with the solidest materials or on the firmest economic footings. Lúcido and his family depend on the community for a living. They are vulnerable to varying tastes. Swayed by ever changing consumption patterns on television and social media, as Máxima and her wedding party are with regard to hairstyles, the community may tire of their services. They may look for a different vendor or photographer. As the film hints, Fausta, too, is vulnerable to the community's economic and cultural shifts. Early in the film we saw a woman refuse to touch her mother's corpse in fear of being contaminated by the milk of sorrow. In burying Perpetua in the ocean, Fausta goes against Indigenous practices. Her behavior might be seen as idiosyncratic; her taste as insufferably strange. Given the community's reliance on popular knowledge, her reaction to the suitor accentuates her marginality. Fausta's precarity endures.

Cognizant of its viewers' attractions—their need for current, relatable narratives—the film at once invites and inhibits facets of magical realism and transculturation at the level of form and image. The milk of sorrow is translated into a duck's spilled milk, which is later linked to the whiteness of pearls. Whiteness underlines the racial connotations embedded in the milk and its adjoining bodily substance, blood. The pearls become the currency to purchase Fausta's songs. Bodily fluids tie together race, class, and power. Corporeal address morphs as hitherto unfathomed promises and threats arise and become legible. This fluidity also marks how a Madonna painting connects to a wall calendar, which alludes to the fake photographs. The film's multiple endings are intertwined, as well. Securing the pearls leads to the mother's burial. The film continues. The infinite ocean is subsumed by the beauty of the blooming potato plant. The earth—not its alternatives, the garden or ocean as graveyards—becomes the fertile ground for cherishing fresh narratives and songs. Fausta's stories will air the tensions and forces at the root of her pueblo joven's predicaments and hopes. Through the aesthetic, she forges a space between a consumerist present that imposes its debts and a past that won't let her breathe. She doesn't overcome her trauma and become a modern woman; nor is she the exotic, seductive Indigenous woman. She is a signpost for Latin American film—and Latin American arts in general—still at risk of reduction to magical realism and to the standardizing maxims of transcultural hybridity.

The setting for interlinking images and vocalizations, and the sonic, visual, and verbal creativity these expressions enact, is the pueblo joven, as I have argued—the hillside area that hosts Fausta and her community's everyday lifeworld. As the endings not chosen tell us, the film is not interested in a reiteration of a narrative of oppression and resistance that supplies ready-made answers to the question of who can and cannot produce art. Llosa and Fausta's community shrug off opportunities for a quick ethical and political rejection of modern aesthetics. The aesthetic mediates life in a fundamental way. Her song has Fausta entangled in Aída's world, which consists of a stage in a more encompassing aesthetic trajectory. It is through her song that Fausta carves out the room she needs to breathe, away from the requirements of Andean village and lettered city. Her sonic creativity enables her to salvage cultural memory in the face of her mother's death and to honor and nourish her bond with her mother and their community's history. Her song is a gesture of strange taste. This gesture holds vital importance to Fausta but it doesn't yet answer her ambitions. Breathing in its own right won't suffice. The film probes deeper. Fausta's life-death struggle espouses additional objectives. She intends to take her singularizing, individualizing path further away from the mother's tale and the milk's inheritance, as well as from the agenda that brought her to Aída. Fausta wishes to assert her own aesthetic. Besides breathing, she wants to inhabit strange taste. This she hopes to do in the pueblo joven. Having gotten a taste of play, furthermore, she wants to continue with it, carrying on its curiously productive unfoldings and its experimental gist to as yet unprobed materials and contexts.

I want to pause for a moment here to register a powerful feature of play that is coming to the fore: its seductiveness. Play exercises an enticing, beguiling influence in Llosa's film both as a formal cinematic principle and as an achievement on the part of the movie's characters. Seductive allure, I propose, is a crucial element of play's workings generally. Of course, people may wish to play or they may wish not to. They may want to engage in some kinds of play and not others. They may intend to set the rules of the game themselves or reveal a readiness to go along with established rules. But throughout these movements and their dwindling there is a seductiveness that is inherent in the phenomenon. The fits and starts of play partially reflect the vagaries of this magnetic dimension; a disposition to tantalize characterizes play even when it causes us to feel repelled or disgusted or leaves us cold. Play makes an experiential appeal. This holds also in situations when we will have nothing of a certain grating or over-the-top game, as is the case for Aída, upon her discovery of the doll, or for Fausta, when subjected to the young man's piropo.

Can the community actually nourish strange taste? Is aesthetic publicness up to this challenge? Noé's gift suggests it just might be. Strange taste finds an anchor in the earth, reenvisioned in relation to adjacent elements, such as air and water. Aesthetic intimacy unfolds at the level of the community, its history, and the materials that encode as well as distance elements of this history. Fausta's strange sonic and visual tastes interlink with the children's dance, which also ties in to the elderly lady's swaying to the music. Aesthetic intimacy extends beyond the familial axis of mother and daughter, daughter and kin. We don't quite know how well strange taste can flourish in the community, but Llosa's film sketches a reciprocal interconnectedness between individual and community that suffuses positions of taste, whether regular or strange. The multiple aesthetic voices and productions of the pueblo joven, from the piropos to the household items paraded at the communal wedding, let on that there is plenty of taste going around, in many varieties. And people play. Aesthetic sensibility is shown in its abundance. Play is contagious. With the possible exception of Aída, who paradoxically has made playing into her profession, no one is altogether shut off to it. Everybody else is willing to give play a chance, even a person as downcast and frightened as Fausta is in the early stages of the film. She plays despite everything. She finds solace in her muted play with structures that resemble birds as she talks with her mother's corpse. The talking and the singing stand in a continuous line with this serial play, as do the transformations she visits on the potato.

Regardless of how the dilemmas of individuality and community that the film broaches eventually sort themselves out, Fausta's song has to settle in the pueblo joven. Here, the fledgling potato plant thirsts for water. Fausta's art and her sensibility put down roots in this place. Her relation to the dead must be a part of her relation to the living, and vice versa. The motifs of water, earth, and dance sustain this aesthetic connectedness, where song offers a way to be present to life's rhythms, to fill existence to the brim, to a point of overflowing, splashing, and squandering.

Conclusion: Aesthetic Publicness as a Communal Effort

To end, I want to distill several philosophical observations about aesthetic publicness. Perhaps needless to say, it is a site of community making. The significance of Llosa's film lies substantially in the rich ways in which it illuminates this point and traces its phenomenological and conceptual implications. Fausta engages in playful world travel, as testified to by her play—now muted, then loud—with the glass shards, the lily, and the potato and by her inventive burial practice. Aesthetic publicness feeds her ability to navigate the tensions between worlds in accordance with her aesthetic desires. It shapes her individual aesthetic agency. The obverse holds, too: Aesthetic publicness thrives by the aesthetic possibilities she animates. The milk of sorrow is a commonly known affliction in her community. Fausta contrives a way to sustain herself and inhabit her creativity in the face of the milk's life-negating force. In collaboration with Noé, she recovers the potato plant from the clutches of botany's colonialist logic to make it available to the dancing children, who are invited to carry on the adults' playful exploits with the tuber and to come up with their preferred games. With the benefit of Fausta's example, the viewer surmises, the youngsters will take their very acts of aesthetic community making and care to a stage where these endeavors are responsive to their longings and situations.[45] Aesthetic publicness, we find, not only fosters Fausta's agency but also gains from her decolonial interventions and from the trajectories of becoming and historical consciousness she devises. It reaps lessons from Fausta's aesthetic sensibilities and creative endeavors, lessons that may be transmitted to new generations, who can use them in meeting their own difficulties.

Practices of aesthetic publicness, it turns out, are responsible for an array of effects commonly heralded through analytics of transculturation among allied notions. As my reading of *The Milk of Sorrow* demonstrates, the concept of aesthetic publicness yields a framework for theorizing the encounters among cultures and among differentially racialized cultural groups that marks a departure from the templates of transculturation, magical realism, and syncretism. While these matrices hold a great deal of acclaim in cultural criticism and the arts, they are too generic to lend recognition to the normatively inflected and formally mediated experiences we enjoy in aesthetic territory. Indeed, these schemata tally with the global marketplace and end up flattening and quelling strange tastes and other aesthetic sensibilities. Aesthetic theory stands in need of more nimbly textured theoretical rubrics. Evolving formations of aesthetic publicness produce normative and experiential structures that must be read as such, lest we elide intersubjective and material dynamics that suffuse constellations of aesthetic life and death. An account of the reciprocal developments of cultures and cultural groups is most useful, but dynamics of aesthetic production and value require a more finely hewn conceptual apparatus, on pain of homogenizing and ironing out the particularities of intracultural and cross-cultural existence and abiding by rather than yielding critical readings of market strictures.

A decolonial aesthetics needs to home in on the structural formations that undergird aesthetic experience in its normative and formal determinations. Aesthetic publicness is a normatively and formally inflected societal order. It is an institutional formation that marks aesthetic creativity, receptivity, and interaction. Philosophy needs the concept of aesthetic publicness to lend recognition to the systemic cultural constellations that support aesthetic production and practice. This includes the seductiveness exuded by play and the responsive and unresponsive reactions it provokes. Indeed, play's constitutively fetching, alluring element, for better or worse, renders it a highly generative operation of aesthetic publicness.

While my reading has eschewed centering political resistance to concentrate on other modes of aesthetic address, the field of aesthetic publicness comprises resistant registers with which cultural actors meet regimes of gendered and racialized colonial power. At the same time, aesthetic strategies of resistance must be situated within broader constellations of aesthetic publicness harboring them. My proposed optic understands resistance not as the main vortex of aesthetic agency it is often found to be but as a dimension of a varied palate of norms and forms of address. Different kinds of aesthetic potentialities come to light. Indeed, the model of aesthetic publicness challenges philosophy and cultural criticism to recognize an expanded repertoire of aesthetic elements and formations in their lithe and labyrinthine reverberations. Following Abraham Acosta (2014), Anzaldúa (1999 [1987], 100–101), and Kevin Quashie (2012, 2021) in forgoing critical paradigms on which resistance is paramount, this chapter has attested to manifold phenomenological complexities and relational ways of being. The model of aesthetic publicness proposes a revised vantage point for theorizations of aesthetic politics and a politically resonant aesthetics. Llosa's film is exemplary of the burgeoning aesthetic life these shifting apertures make visible. The notions of aesthetic publicness, taste, and play call attention to the productivity of an encompassing ensemble of aesthetic commitments, motivations, and interests, whose operations must be grasped in their mutual interactions and tensions. *The Milk of Sorrow* invites and necessitates this recalibrated aesthetic analytic.

While, under the aegis of resistance, Quashie (2012), to whose vital and astute critique of resistance I am indebted, ties publicness to logics of transparency and an effacement of interiority, I have untangled these linkages in favor of a dialectic between transparency and opacity, and interiority and exteriority. Through an aesthetic foregrounding of tipping points between the standardized and the unusual, Llosa's film encourages this move. We encounter moments of conversion and mutual contamination between the relevant dualities in the kissing scenes, the young fellow's crass joke, and the compulsions of televised bodily stylistics. These mixed, ambivalent instances of aesthetic consciousness and desire are also exemplified by a series of coffins, ranging from colonial types made of heavy, polished wood to items built from cheaper, blank wood, and onward, to a hand-painted variety decorated with ocean scenes that rivets Fausta. What is more, we spot these slippages and flippings in Fausta's performance with the red lily at the gate, a gesture that epitomizes stereotype and unique feeling, exoticism and singular invention, while at the same time complicating these polarities. And we detect these ambiguous, extraordinarily poignant moments in the initially puzzling, contemplative yet rebellious drowning of the paper crane, which—oddly, awkwardly, and through the mediations of strange taste—anticipates Fausta's submerging of her mother's corpse in the ocean.

This brings me to the last, but decidedly not least, facet of aesthetic publicness to be highlighted. Part of the dynamism of aesthetic publicness traced in this chapter revolves around strange taste. Fausta's aesthetic comportment embraces, rather than shies away from, this historically embedded sensibility. The pueblo joven benefits, as I have shown. With her strange taste, Fausta offers the community a vehicle of cultural memory attuned to a world that is in flux and that imposes shifting and asymmetrical demands on the community members. Tradition, to remain a live heritage rather than a sheer imposition on the most vulnerable, stands in need of strange taste's not always legible meddling and tinkering.

At once fostered by and fostering aesthetic publicness, strange taste encodes a stance that can meet adversity with growth and joy rather than mainly destruction, agony, or a retreat from others. Thus, it is a key to individual and collective flourishing. It functions as a bountiful font of feminist energy and sustenance. It constitutes a site of care and imagination.

One plays by whatever means available. If one's train is too short, measured by TV mores, then one applies balloons. If bright colors are too glaring, one opts for a subdued palate. If one is at a loss for words or gestures but hankers after some kind of sexual expression, one falls for a bawdy cliché or attempts a kiss gleaned from a glamorous Hollywood scene. Meanwhile, one's individuality assumes its shapes in concrete circumstances. Tradition is in motion. Fausta; her airborne cousin, Máxima; the attentive, down-to-earth Noé; the initially reluctant but ultimately concerned and loving uncle; the splashing duck; and the smooching grooms are each in their own ways apprised of this, as they turn their aesthetic sensibilities toward the opportunities and materials they find in their surroundings and bring into being a communal life in the pueblo joven, at the intersection of multiple cultural forces and histories. They all take risks, whether with candies, with their mouths, or with flapping, flowing, and drowning entities.

Playing with oscillating stances of modernity and the exotic, outlined by the film poster, Fausta finds her desire. Joining her game of hide-and-seek, the viewer was curious about playing some more. We didn't know where this would take us. Seeing Fausta give shape to her aesthetic agency with increasing confidence, claiming her sensibility as her own and overlaying muted and loud play, we kept playing, too. We went through the laughter and crying, the anticipation and aftermath of various kinds of play. We could sense how much we want strange taste to blossom, to thrive as a singular element of a communal fabric of intertwined sensibilities. As members of the film's local and global publics, we took up our own play in engagement with Fausta's play and the play of her fellow community members, as well as with a slew of cultural productions: cartoon characters, icons of maternity, colonial architecture and design, and stock imagery of legendary natural sites. What is next?

As a figure of decoloniality, the potato plant makes a final appeal or demand on the pueblo joven and the spectator alike. It's time to design the world afresh, to remake aesthetic publicness. Noé's gift is the first step. Alert to Fausta's often vacant look, and with a nod to Jacques Derrida (2005, 140), we can read her mother's death as the end of the world. So far, we have seen how she rebuilds her world, her human world. But from the start of this film about coloniality, the human-nature relation has also been fractured. The citizens of the pueblo joven had to leave their homeland. Now they need to recultivate the land. Make the desert bloom with origami cranes, with balloons, with potato plants. Pick up the drill and the glass splinters and see what forms, frames, and reflections they suggest.

4

Light

Sensibility on Sale

We live in an era of content. Aesthetic publicness beckons online. Our worlds are shaped by flows of packageable and transferable information bites. No sphere of life is untouched. Collective digital innervation impacts our capacities for aesthetic experience. Immersed in, if not mesmerized by, booming data circuits that loosen and rewire content's ties to institutions and contexts, are we relinquishing resources that should be harnessed? The coilings of the aesthetic and the public powerfully shape practices of relationality and address. Might an unsparing attention economy sap our taste—even our propensities—for the dialogical and coalitional practices that Latinx feminist theorists place at the center of projects of liberation, social justice, and community?[1]

Philosophy has long agonized that content's capricious scattering and brazen migrancy shortchanges its stakeholders. While Plato's ruminations about freely floating discursive endeavors and twentieth-century critical theorists' insights into expropriation and rootlessness offer instructive starting points for reflecting on the aesthetic registers of technologically driven market formations, philosophy needs to sharpen the conceptual frames it brings to these societal concerns. To this end, I turn to Diamela Eltit, whose novels *Lumpérica* (*E. Luminata* [1983]) and *El cuarto mundo* (*The Fourth World* [1988]) investigate market-oriented subjective and collective processes. Commencing with a quick look at Plato's and critical theory's cultural diagnoses, this chapter reads Eltit's novels to advance our understanding of aesthetic publicness. I show how she laces strange taste through the public and, in the process, animates possibilities for a democratic public culture that allots a crucially generative role to literature and other arts.

Philosophy and the Critique of Content

Plato condemns numerous cultural genres and technologies for their tendencies to wander off. Dubious strayings traverse linguistic as well as nonlinguistic media, from poetry, epic, theater, and music to painting and drawing. The tendency of expressions to assume lives of their own while being passed from person to person and audience to audience alarms Plato. He answers these indiscriminate ramblings and unsupervised excursions with moral, political, epistemic, and aesthetic skepticism and denunciation. His objections are instructive. They manifest strains that carry insights for our present-day engagements with content. I therefore take some time to lay out his agenda and the remarkable ways he works around it, strolling away cunningly from his own epistemic and metaphysical doctrines.

As Socrates argues in the *Ion*, given the wide scope of topics addressed by poets and rhapsodes and the irrational, emotionally charged ways in which they address them, these artists and performers are not "in their right minds" during their creative endeavors, and neither are their audiences (Plato 1997a, 534a, 535c–d). Whereas the work of practitioners such as doctors, mathematicians, charioteers, and generals evinces knowledge, this is lacking from the activities of the makers and performers of poetry (531c, 534b–c, 536c–d, 537c–42b). Rhetorical oration and poetic expression—the era's popular entertainments—are epistemically deficient compared with a whole array of skilled human activities. However, Socrates admits, poets and rhapsodes compensate for their lack. They are beneficiaries of divine inspiration (533d–36d). Their enthusiastic endeavors (533e, 535c) are animated by a supernatural force that they impart to their publics.[2] Rather than comprehending the meanings of their productions or conveying insights in the form of designs that they invent, these makers and performers transmit gifts—marvelous, widely relished contents—received from the gods. Poets and rhetoricians are vehicles for expressions originating in a transcendent source. This leaves these creators poorly equipped to warrant the magnetic cognitive and emotional effects kindled by their purported productions, which flout rationality (535c–e). Philosophy notices what is amiss. It comes to the rescue. In Plato's hands, it fills the justificatory vacuum opportunistically exploited by poetry and rhetoric with a system of comparative rankings and valorizations that places dialectical inquiries sustained through philosophical dialogue at the helm of a social, epistemic, and aesthetic order.

I'm alluding to the well-known tale of philosophy's "ancient quarrel" with poetry, as Socrates calls it in the *Republic* (Plato 2004, 607b4–5). Plato expounds this rivalry to great poetic and rhetorical effect across texts. His own authorial style, however, contests his philosophical putdowns of his competitor.[3] Plato's gusto for paradox and unabashed sauntering in comedy, irony, satire, wit, and myth remind his readers that we conduct our encounters with content in the register of taste, whether regular or gnarled, obeisant or mutinous.[4] Aesthetic sensibility asks to be given its due, even, and perhaps especially, when snubbed. To further flesh out this point, let me rehearse a few high points in Plato's famed philosophical struggle with flighty discursive amblings.

In the *Phaedrus*, he provocatively chooses—or channels through divine intervention—the written form as his vehicle for a protracted argument favoring Socrates's exemplary genre of sharply targeted, deliberately ordered dialogical speech over the unbounded medium of writing that trudges about randomly (2005b, 271c10–78b4). Writing, he submits, meets up with just anyone it encounters on its path, while at a loss whom it should and shouldn't address and how. It can't fend for itself when questioned. In reply to the slightest probing, it echoes its own contentions. Appearances notwithstanding, writing thus isn't really going anywhere, at least not where Socrates thinks it should go. His solution is as ingenious as it is flawed. Philosophical dialogue lifts itself to the top of a discursive framework that it whimsically subverts and qualifies through its own strategies of address. Plato has things both ways: He puts poets and rhetoricians in their place and arrogates the power of their arts for his own epistemology, metaphysics, and ethical and political project.[5]

Worries about the status of unrestrained verbal and visual ramblings pervade other important Platonic dialogues. As stated in the *Meno*, knowledge, which is bound to an argumentative structure disclosed through dialogical questioning, is highly valuable, while merely true beliefs, which are akin to unanchored, freestanding statues, tend to abscond from the soul, thus squandering their value (2005a, 97d–98b). A property system appears to inform Plato's thought.[6] Once you have a good idea, it's wise to make sure it doesn't run off. This tenet reflects fundamental currents in Plato's metaphysics and epistemology.

In the *Republic*, Plato conceives of poetry and painting as mimetic practices that imitate the variable appearances of artifacts, such as couches and tables, items that for their part imitate eternal, unchanging Forms (2004, 596a–98b5).

Consequently, he ranks poetic and painterly representation two steps down on the ladder of metaphysical and epistemic respectability compared with philosophy, which provides epistemic access to the enduring realm of Forms.

Carrying on with his polemic, Plato distinguishes wayward poetry, which threatens to lead us onto the wrong path (598b6–608b10), from suitable storytelling and dialectical questioning, which can be counted on to guide us in the direction of truth and keep us on course as citizens of the "well-governed" city (376b11–c6, 376e–98b10, 427a3, 532d7–35a, 540a–e2). Poetry tends to spell disorder by feeding irrational impulses and aspirations.[7] It upends the appropriate constitution of the human soul and the right-minded organization of the city (603a11–8b10), which is in process of being conceived in philosophical terms (269a–c) and oriented toward virtue, justice, and the good.

The cultural binaries that inflame Plato's contest with poetry, rhetoric, and other unleashed symbolic genres support modes of epistemic authorization and deauthorization and uphold a metaphysical order. Marking facets of the organization of the soul and, hence, the city, they lock into the distinctive ethical, social, and political roles that Plato allocates to the different classes of people who make up the city-state envisioned in the *Republic*, ranging from children, male and female slaves, and the majority of free women to predominantly male producers, guardians, and rulers (431a–d, 435b4–44e, 540b5–9). Simultaneously, the relevant dichotomies are mired in tensions owing to the humorous, self-ironizing writing style with which Plato flouts his stated convictions, the ambiguities attendant on his notion of inspiration, his own deployment of imitation, and the qualifications he slips into his ideas about rhetoric and poetry.[8] Given the playful and performative character of Plato's dialectic, which provides sly counterpoints and mocking undertones to viewpoints it appears to defend, his dialogues draw the reader into the process of imaginative, playful philosophical deliberation and questioning the texts enact.[9] Comedy and fantasy permeate investigations that purport to improve soul and city. Socrates uses play as a register of dialectical thought.[10] He is adamant that it be part of children's education.[11] Plato channels the seductions of play into a game of philosophical reflection that contests its own professed binaries of virtue and vice, didacticism and abandon, seriousness and lightheartedness, distinct and indeterminate address.[12]

Experiential proclivities Plato had sidelined assert their pertinence to his philosophical endeavor. The point holds a lesson. When tempted to impugn cultural tendencies and deployments of technology, we must consider our own participation in these forms and ask whether we are condoning, even celebrating, impulses we reject in the same breath. Disparaged aesthetic forms rear their head in Plato's theory as registers of cultural formation and philosophical production on par with, if not conceptually prior to, the dialectical reflection he embraces. Cultural criticism thus risks granting priority—or equal status—to discursive modes that it purports to discredit and to their attendant dimensions of normativity.

Pragmatic and conceptual hurdles conspire. The effort to insulate our thinking from poetic, rhetorical, and other aesthetic genres invites them to reenter it in intractable ways and to work their effects behind the scenes. This is the pragmatic snag. But the anti-aesthetic venture also spells havoc for our conceptual order and valuations: We derogate what we prize highly. By resisting aesthetics, philosophy wrings itself into a self-inflicted double bind, which affects its normative and conceptual agendas.

Notwithstanding Plato's commitments to eternal truth and the permanently good and beautiful, his texts evince a contravening movement that prizes contingency. In the *Symposium*, Eros's itinerant idling between knowledge and ignorance, his coasting back and forth between lack and plenitude, represents a stage of a process of development geared toward the beautiful and the good (1997b, 200e–12c). The element of floating, of pulling toward and away from subjective states and objective realities, resonates with our modern (or postmodern) experiential condition. Plato wisely stresses the problematical aspects of a random flailing. But the swerves he deplores hold potentialities that are more difficult to block than he estimates. They take us to places where we want to go, ethically, aesthetically, politically, and epistemically.

Straying can be a rewarding activity. Sensory, perceptual, and cognitive peregrinations are what culture is made of. Fantasy thrives in a vagrant drifting. Desire snatches at the occasion. Searching and roaming, we add global celebrities' latest albums to our playlists, pay visits to far-off architectural icons, marvel at news about billions-of-years-old microbes retrieved from subterranean biospheres, or seize on eye-popping imagery of black holes. Spectators and revelers, we are drawn to festivals, art exhibitions, sports competitions, psychedelic trips, and video games in no small measure because they promise to lift the bounds of mundane experience.

Not only the consumer is gripped. The capacities of artifacts to spread across social locations present lucrative opportunities to companies keen on translating symbolic flows into revenue streams and selling packaged pleasures to mass publics. Luxuriating in disinterested contemplation and play, we are simultaneously being played by economic interests. The culture industry, awash in technology, saturates experience. It effects an aesthetic, epistemic, and political wiring and rewiring of social being.

Again philosophers, surveying their contemporary societal surrounds, voice powerful reservations about these developments. They design reading methods that chart cultures' conditioning by corporatist needs and trace out the repression this effects.[13] However, phenomenological complications arise whose logic is akin to what we saw in Plato's case: While denouncing the influence of the marketplace over aesthetic existence, we are in cahoots with corporatism as consumers of cultural goods and users of media. How should cultural consciousness's endemic ambivalence reflect on the critical strategies we adopt?

Thinkers such as Walter Benjamin, Theodor Adorno, and Herbert Marcuse have adumbrated procedures of immanent critique that acknowledge philosophy's emplacement within the cultural fabric it theorizes. Historicity entails the need for ongoing reflection on our corporeal situatedness in changing places, at changing times. Aesthetic theory, thus, faces the task, which I take up here, of sharpening our critical reading methods to reckon with registers of racial, gendered, and sexual embodiment, coloniality, and nation downplayed by earlier Frankfurt School and poststructuralist approaches. Further, our interpretive strategies need to avoid the traps of antiaesthetic theoretical inflections—notably, the tendency to sidestep aesthetic sensibility and play, which, as Plato's quarrel with poetry and rhetoric reveals, skews our thinking and values. This chapter, then, once again lodges us in this aesthetic territory: The question is not whether we are playing games, but which games we are playing or desire to play.

The Vagaries of Aesthetic Life

A major theme of this book concerns the interweaving of the marketplace with the phenomenology of aesthetic experience. Gayatri Chakravorty Spivak counsels that we play rather than escape. Her concept of double binds gives expression to this strategy, yet ultimately provides an overly abstract gloss on the matter, as I argued in chapter 1. Further parts of the story remain to be told. This chapter weaves strands of a more encompassing narrative. Spivak leaves off when it comes to theorizing the intricacies of the aesthetic politics that we enact in navigating aesthetic desire and demand and in opting for a course of action. I examine these complexities by looking into the collective formation of our aesthetic interests and cravings. Aesthetic experiences are elements of trajectories of subjectivity and social gathering. These lineages are marked by technological developments. The confluence of aesthetics, technology, and avenues of subjective and communal development is a site of poignant frictions and transformations.

Indeed, current lifeworlds are conditioned in ever increasing measures by algorithmically engendered information flows. The rise of autocracies and far-right populism in many countries coincides with the ascendance of technologies that expose their users to content unmoored from its societal roots and local means of production. Taste and other aesthetic sensibilities channel and bend these feeds. This goes for the whole gamut of activities, both habitual and exceptional, that conscript taste and aesthetic sensibility, including rites of celebration and mourning; penchants for compromise or belligerence; appetites for differentiation from or fusion with groups; and attachments to styles, cuisines, and geographical habitats. I won't focus on taste and aesthetic sensibility in this full range, but it will be useful to keep in mind the wide orbit of practices in which they make their presence felt.

As discussed in the previous chapters, we exercise aesthetic taste as members of publics. A relational propensity that connects us with other people, places, and objects, taste is a component of our phenomenal stance in the world. Human beings are subjects of care and concern, including aesthetic care and concern. Taste is a propensity through which we channel these forms of attention and valorization. In this way, taste participates in the shaping of our public comportment.[14]

In *E. Luminata* and *The Fourth World*, which were first published during the dictatorship of Augusto Pinochet, Eltit gives center stage to tropes of public inhabitance and taste. She investigates the social stakes we have in these phenomena. Read together, these texts ask what it is like to inhabit a technologically ruled global economic order at the level of our subjective being and collective presence to one another. The first novel literalizes enlightenment through the notion of an all-encompassing regime of subjectivation instituted by an advertising sign. This sign casts its projections over the Chilean people assembled in a public plaza, covering their bodies in names that become determinative of their identities. It exercises hegemony in the realm of content. Within the resulting cultural system, which absorbs literary and cinematic production, social becoming and gathering are governed by technologically driven modes of capitalist control. Weaving taste into this system, the second novel probes the ties between taste and nation, home and the city, and the domestic and the public at the level of their imbrications with structures of sexuality, race, and gender.

As is widely recognized, Pinochet's Chile was a testing ground for neoliberal stratagems that subsequently found worldwide allegiance and underwent institutionalization across the globe.[15] Through the fragmented style of avant-garde fiction writing for which she is known, Eltit explores how these dynamics play out in aesthetic territory.

My reading reveals how Eltit's texts enlist the aesthetic in the reanimation of the public on novel terms. Setting the action in the plaza, *E. Luminata* engages two forms of aesthetic publicness. The first is the lettered city, the sociohistorical constellation that since the conquest has interlaced reading and writing with coloniality in Latin America. The second is the Enlightenment public sphere, centered in the figure of the general observer and, in principle, inclusive of anyone, regardless of their social position. Satirically marking the limits of these formations, Eltit pushes beyond them.

By highlighting the novels' figurations of aesthetic materiality and historicity, I argue that strange taste and aesthetic publicness are key to the historical vicissitudes of aesthetic life well through the present era of algorithmic capitalism, which unyokes worlds of content from the historical, material, and creative sites of their production and reception. As Eltit's thought experiments enable us to see, notwithstanding these shifting alignments, literature, the arts, and the aesthetic more generally retain their importance. They are sites of invention, critical cultural politics, and world making that contemporary democracies are unable to forgo.

Literature, Aesthetics, and the Technologically Dominated Marketplace

E. Luminata contemplates the takeover of the Chilean polity by a neoliberal world system ruled by technology. A commercial sign towers over a public square in Santiago, where it beams its advertising slogans onto the crowd below. The eponymous protagonist, a bag lady, stars under the sign. Enthralled by the projections lighting up from the surfaces of their bodies and the objects in the square, the Chilean people exchange their social roles and historical positions for an identity in the global marketplace. They engross themselves in the latest technology. Literature and cinema aid the sign in its subjectifying project. The people come into their own as the glorious populace they long to be.

The novel is what philosophy calls a thought experiment. It conjures the specter of society's total governance by a techno-economic world system. The reader is urged to explore the conceptual implications of this state of affairs and to devise a response. Light and the plaza are the driving metaphors through which Eltit's text gives expression to the pivotal bodily, societal, and aesthetic reverberations. The contents emitted by the sign are set free from the creative and receptive labors supporting them. Their "home" is the commercial world that has supplanted the polity. Subjectivity thus amounts to immersion in a capitalist order. *E. Luminata* is a late twentieth-century moment in a theoretical and political lineage that goes back to Greek antiquity. Commencing with the idea of the Athenian agora, philosophy has recognized the public square as exemplary of publicness and has virtually equated this figure with the governance model termed *democracy*. The novel participates in this historical heritage.[16] But Eltit's thought experiment, which she will continue in *The Fourth World*, also speaks to the actual trial run that the Pinochet dictatorship—aided by the US government, intelligence services, and military—gave to the neoliberal makeover of Chilean society during the 1970s and 1980s. In her polysemous texts, whose opacity is a match for the most hermetic theoretical treatises, Eltit investigates the alliance between an autocratic political order and a hegemonic, technologically dominated marketplace that converts language, literature, film, and other aesthetic idioms into free-floating input and output to satisfy the needs of a voracious, all-consuming capitalist apparatus. Her novels speak volumes to the concurrence of political shifts to the far right that we see today with a surge of globally disseminated information feeds that circulate at a remove from their local contexts of creation and response.[17] The two works presciently highlight cultural forces that have undergone intensification and solidification since the time of Eltit's writing. Thus, philosophy has much gain from these literary texts. Giving a new spin to the foundational philosophical metaphors of light and the square, Eltit furthers the critical sensibilities and vocabularies on which we can draw when tackling current controversies.

Before I begin to delve into Eltit's novel, let me describe its basic structure and plot. The text is divided into ten sections. As per Eltit's signature method of linguistic fragmentation, they shy away from a chronological order. Most are unnamed. Several do bear names, which without exception refer to aesthetic categories—namely, notions of "an image in literature," of where the story might be going, of a multiplicity of theatrical or cinematic scenes, and of a dress rehearsal, respectively (Eltit 1997a [1983], 3). Even within sections, the text is divided into subparts headed by titles that denote aspects of aesthetic production, such as "REMARKS ON THE SECOND SCENE" and "MISTAKES IN THE THIRD SEQUENCE" (29, 47). Numerous paragraphs introduced by the phrase "that's why" launch into explanations that push the boundaries of intelligibility.

It is evening. The action occupies a single night. Scenes are designed for the camera; spectacles are staged; performances are happening. The setting, as already noted, is a public square in the city of Santiago, Chile. Lording over the plaza is an advertising sign atop a building. It casts its projections onto the space below. The characters: a bag lady named E. Luminata, who is acting in the plaza; the Chilean people who draw toward her, mesmerized. Confrontations and rapprochements unfold between the antagonistic pair of illuminated ones: the masculinized sign up above and the female protagonist down below. The crowd is pulled between these two entangled opponents. The novel tells the story of the place of the people—that is, a nation, in a globalized economy. And it is a tale about gender: Stretches of fantasy centered on the bag lady crack open the ways in which a gendered imaginary shapes social being as a form of embodiment. The reader can discern these plotlines by taking up the labor of composition. Narrative coherence and ready-made comprehensibility are resisted. Accordingly, the novel enlists the reader in the construction of the fiction. To speak with one of the section titles, the question "Quo vadis?" (Where are you going?) remains open in the planes of form and content. Reading the work is a project of exploration, orientation, and disorientation that calls into question the mechanisms of literary writing and interpretation.

Assuming an Identity in the World of the Sign

E. Luminata takes as its premise the historical, neoliberal path of subjective becoming. A mass of bodies called the "pale people" comes to the square to rejoice in the color and life that the sign grants them (14–15). Indeed, the sign offers the people an identity in the global marketplace. Nocturnal enlightenment yields a state-of-the-art, technologically mediated form of embodiment and social existence.[18] This arrangement is open to everyone. The multitude collectively craves it. However, the sign's gift comes at a price: "The ragged people of Santiago arrive, pale and stinking, in search of their space: the name and alias that like a token will guarantee them a trip, but one calculated in terms of their previous expenditure of flesh until they are shod with light from the neon sign" (14). The city swaps one socioeconomic system for another. A new renumeration system takes effect. Labor ceases to be the product the people provide in exchange for a civic identity. Under the sign's rule, old principles of productivity make way for the maxims of a consumption society, where the luminescent images the sign disburses provide the materials for appearances and roles that are determinative of the people's passage through life, their "trip." The people trade in their positions in prior systems of meaning—ones that may involve vocations—for a rapturous connectedness to the sign, which grants them incessantly renewing possibilities for being (19). Thus, the sign remains as the decisive caller. The people find a new kind of agency.

They create their own performance in the square, occasioning a shift in the "norms of experience" (18). And so they metamorphose from conquered into conquerors. They become beautiful. "Their identities are being celebrated" (19). Being, for them, from now on equates their being interpellated by the technologically dominated marketplace. For an instant, they are the owners of the commodities that they are, "[p]roprietors out of sheer desire as they sell themselves to the sign like merchandise" (19). Hardly any time passes, however, before seller and sold, user and used, collapse into one on the completion of the transaction.[19]

The new price the Chilean people are paying for their transformed identity in the realm of the sign is forgetfulness. Eltit writes, "They await their turn, for the illuminated sign to confirm them as existence, that is, name them another way: they are reborn that way in this purifying passage, less impallored now, because it blots out their color, confirming the voluntary loss of their civil records. That's why in the square that encloses them they prowl in the direction of the light, restoring them to an ancient happiness. Incubated anew, they get life from technology" (26). The people's "civil records" are obliterated. Cultural memory dwindles. Recollection of antagonism and violence fades with the imposition of a global economy, as Nelly Richard (2004a) has documented. Individualized roles slip away.[20] Social strictures loosen as updated modes of subjectivation become available that energize "ancient" forms. The new is old even if—and partially because—it banishes memory. Under the regime of a technocratic marketplace, a modernist framework takes root within which the people are considered ancient or primitive. They become transparently legible as such (84, see also 15). This representational operation is a dispensation of consumption society. The people are reborn as consumers.[21]

By way of the image of the identity-disbursing sign, Eltit offers a reading of the subjective implications of the repressive order instituted during Chile's experiment with neoliberalism. This venture, which met with worldwide expansion and institutionalization in subsequent decades, exacted an immense human price. This shattering historical reality has not ceased to arouse right-wing militant fervor in the region and, at the same time, continues to torment survivors and subsequent generations whose lives unfold within more or less democratic political constellations allied with and circumscribed by market economies.[22] The sign's interpellative stratagem marks a narrowing of public life. Captivated by an amplified field of identificatory options, subjectivity in effect curtails itself.

The projections glowing from the surfaces of the people's bodies absorb them to the point of self-loss. The gaze engenders disorientation, even stupefaction. "Those who have received their own names by birthright can never know anything about the daze from being so lost in different residues that only the climax of paleness remains as an alternative, as mere disposable flesh" (Eltit 1997a [1983], 27). Technologically saturated neoliberalism establishes an interdependence between an enthralling plenitude and a self-abandoning absence of color or existential lack. According to this logic, one either subscribes to the market or belongs to the abject horde made up of the pale people, also called the "lumpenpack" (105, 112, 173). Within the rule of the sign, one cycles through these two mutually coconstitutive and exhaustive positions that feed into each other. Other stances have been jettisoned with the relinquishing of the people's "civil records," the effacement of their historical citizenship. What philosophical lessons can we reap regarding the idea of the square as a pillar of public participation and democracy? What happens to the nation, and how can literature and the arts reply to this state of affairs? By proposing a reading of *E. Luminata* followed by an interpretation of *The Fourth World*, this chapter sketches a response to these questions.

Time, Space, Rational Order, and Language

The sign runs in accordance with its own program. This program jettisons the "rationality of a Chile that halts its rhythm at night" (196). The day-night opposition ostensibly belongs to an obsolete epistemic and ontological schema, for the marketplace continues its daytime operations at night, whether within or outside national boundaries. It is indifferent to natural rhythms. This irrelevance infiltrates both the time and the space that the nation can claim for itself and the standards of coherence and reasonableness by which such claims can be legitimized. A kind of rationality presumed as common sense is given up in the world governed by the sign.

Rationality is punctured in the plane of linguistic form, as well. Eltit keeps open the question of meaning and defamiliarizes interpretive reason through faux explanations, prefaced by phrases such as "that's how" and "that's why" (18–20). These expressions typically do not signal intelligible explanations or factors to be explained but give rise to more "how" and "why" questions than they answer. In this way, Eltit underscores the bounds of evidential and instrumental reasoning and challenges the reader to produce a new kind of sense.

The novel's disjointed narration demands an intense interpretive effort, which dramatizes the uncertainties and complexities of the problems the text opens up. At the level of suspense, Eltit's intricate style brings home the urgency of imaginative thinking and the necessity of inquiry beyond established conceptual parameters and vocabularies. Through fragmented sentence structures and by averting linear plots, *E. Luminata* energizes language's palimpsestic multiperspectivalism.[23] Words are wrenched away from their ideologically congealed meanings to perform bewildering verbal feats that call for decipherment. Despite the reader's feverish interpretive endeavor, the syntax consistently shatters comprehension. Voices are heard but rapidly vanish into other voices. Dependable strategies of philosophical meaning making are under pressure. The notion of a public space harboring cultural and political life appears to have lost its tenability and societal relevance.

Eltit's thought experiment pairs an aesthetic of opacity with one of clarity and immediate legibility. In contrast to the linguistic mayhem, the text evinces a systematic plan, as noted before. The numbered sections and their subdivisions give the sense that we are dealing with a theoretical treatise, a policy paper, a report, a flyer, or a manual. At the same time, Eltit's genre-bending disquisition turns into a script for a film, a play, or a performance.[24] For instance, two consecutive chapters comprise three dress rehearsals and fifteen scenes, respectively.[25] Indeed, the former opens with a photograph of the author displaying incisions in her arms while giving a performance based on portions of the novel's manuscript.[26] But the narration often transgresses such frames, as when, having apparently reached the end of the third and last dress rehearsal, we are told: "The Dress Rehearsal is going to begin" (165). The novel's order evidently is infected by its disorder. Nonetheless, it solidly sits in place. It sticks; it guides; it contains and separates. All the while, we are in aesthetic terrain. The consistency of aesthetic categories, like political ones, is called into doubt.

Intimations of violence, surveillance, and control infiltrate both the novel's disjointedness and its methodical organization. We are dismissing neither perplexity nor clarity if we read Eltit's dense text as a commentary on the forced realization of a market society in Chile in the aftermath of the 1973 coup.[27] *E. Luminata* delves into the affective and corporeal implications, as well as the relational facets, of the capitalist arrangement cemented under the dictatorship. The reader's mystification mirrors the daze in which these transformations leave the people who have convened in the city square. The clarity of organization resonates with the oppressive transparency the lumpenpack enjoys in consumption society as an "ancient," "primitive" being, a massified population relegated to a liminal state of aliveness. The airtight, numerical scheme that frames the narration also echoes the top-down hierarchy of a cultural system lorded over by a masculinist advertisement display. The novel's formal order thus is imprinted with a violence that its self-displacing narration rejects. Simultaneously, the text's disorder is contaminated by a violence that its order is instrumental in challenging. Both bafflement and lucidity carry traces of violence and seeds of ethical and political responsiveness. The novel's philosophical import reaches beyond its take on these aesthetic categories, however.

As noted, *E. Luminata* contemplates how a sign-driven economy implements revised criteria of rationality and uproots spatial and temporal templates aligned with the nation. Eltit subverts a progressivist conception of this transformation through strategies of temporal dislocation. I have already mentioned the dress rehearsal that is about to begin when it nears its end (161–65). If the market fantasizes a seamless coexistence of old and new or a production of the new that smoothly assimilates the old while creating a disposable population along with a field of residual practices, then Eltit undercuts modernist market-inspired temporal progressions by dismissing originality (157, 163); dissociating cry from wound (28–29); and wrenching the cry away from the crier's meaning by transferring its expressivity, its status as a sign, to the sign writ large (30–32). Through these measures, along with recurrent tropes of the retroactive production of inaugural moments, she voices a critique of a progressively unfurling consumption society. The text continually undermines the grounds on which temporal, causal, symbolic, explanatory, readerly, and purposive orderings become possible. Nevertheless, as we will see, some structural devices that precede the sign's strobing remain in place.[28] These turn out to be crucial to the novel's philosophical outlook on the potentialities of public life.

A Contest in the Plaza

The extended spectacle of movement, sound, and language unfolding among sign, E. Luminata, and people produces an atmosphere of chilling restlessness: The sign always finds more to bring within reach, more to make happen. While offering us an image of the sign's total control over public life, however, Eltit also limits its leverage, pushing back against the dominance of the marketplace. As I have argued, the sign has no use for the people's civic identities, which it unsparingly erases. Nonetheless, one register of the civic record persists: gender. The novel repeatedly refers to the sign with the pronouns "he/his" in contrast to E. Luminata's "she/her" (14, 16). The sign relies for its workings on gender allocations. These designations fall outside the sphere of its control. The sign turns out to be one source of gender performance among others. It is far from the sole originator of shared meaning and subjective being. Its hegemony reveals yet further cracks.

The sign takes the public plaza as its domicile and stage of operation. It depends on the square and other items that are part of the environment: benches, trees, pavement, lights, lighting cables, urban design and architecture. Like gender, these structural elements participate in the conditioning of the sign's workings, its simultaneously archaic and contemporaneous commercial production of the people.

Accordingly, aesthetic publicness is never banished. We miss a vital reality if we take it to have collapsed: The sign institutes its own type of aesthetic publicness, supplanting antecedent configurations. One prior arrangement is the literary enterprise, which, functioning as an indispensable pillar of the colonial apparatus, established the lettered city. This centuries-long cultural institution, as I have observed, interlaces colonially inflected positions of authority and deauthorization with forms of aesthetic, political, and epistemic normativity. It is to be decolonized, a project that has been under way for quite some time and is ongoing across sectors of the society. The sign has different ideas, however.

The radiant electronic display fills a glaring gap left by literature, which, after all, had never "portrayed [the people] in all their immeasurability" (106). Under the sign, splendidly, garishly, the people are finally offered the aura they were denied. "He" reigns in the square. Indeed, the sign is highly efficacious. It generates E. Luminata's lips. It "pin[s] down her anatomical points" (16). Literature is superseded as a mode of corporeal stylization and self-formation. It loses its sway over the society.

Yet literature is far from eradicated. The sign employs a variety of media in the construction of the spectacle in the plaza. In addition to light, it helps itself generously to literary forms and strategies, along with sound, and, I imagine, movie titles (16–17). Literature has become a serviceable tool for the sign. Having conspired with coloniality in the formation of Latin American societies since the sixteenth century, as Ángel Rama contended, it now delivers the Chilean people up to an insatiable capitalist machinery. Or might there be a glitch in this story? Was something forgotten? Is there a correction or a note to be made? After all, these kinds of things happen repeatedly in the novel.[29]

The sign is powerful, but it has to contend with a counterpart: the bag lady E. Luminata. She performs in the plaza. Lit by the sign, which casts its luminous emissions in alternating rhythms and hues, she passes through stages of segmentation and recomposition revolving around body parts such as fingernails, legs, wounds, waist, hands, the already mentioned lips, and other erogenous zones. The splitting and reassembling resonate with two interrogation sequences to which she is subjected, which blur who is who. At one point, E. Luminata is about to be subdued or put away by being sedated in a hospital.

She crosses species in a feminist human/animal galloping that extends over a full chapter. She tries to seduce the sign, becoming *mater*/madonna or *matermadona* (mothermadonna) to the sign's *pater*/*patria* (father/fatherland) (91–92, 95). She morphs through countless sexual/writerly identities. Bodies rub up against each other. And they rub against the pavement. They establish relations with the concrete, the grass in the square, the benches. E. Luminata traverses states of assembly and dispersal with the people. Her poses, fashioned with the help of the sign and perceived and responded to by the people, mediate between the two. In collaboration with her human and material surroundings, she engenders a form of aesthetic relationality. At the end of the novel, which occupies a single night, she sits in the square while passersby hasten to work.

E. Luminata takes up many kinds of literary writing. The people are eager for it: "They shine whole, their desires for fiction like orifices" (105). Writer and people jointly take a stab at producing a narrative "that takes as its model a ragged bag lady" (105). What might such a story look like? Can the lettered city open itself up to the people whom it had previously banished without surrendering literature and the plaza to the sign? What reconfigurations of the public square does this demand?

E. Luminata devotes her authorial efforts to working out a fiction that is "her own," one that balances the fiction "desired by externals" with another fiction that "she did not recognize as such" (83). She opts for neither unadulterated literary heteronomy nor its opposite, autonomy. Instead, she prefers a narrative that has it both ways. The Enlightenment template of aesthetic publicness makes its appearance here. In this scheme, which rejects heteronomy to make room for autonomy, literature is a public practice that pursues its sui generis values at a marked distance from the lives of the writer and her audience. Juggling between two polarities that are a hallmark of Enlightenment philosophy, E. Luminata comes up with her "own" creation. The fiction she favors presumably runs by its internal codes, but these protocols hook into external realities that Enlightenment views of aesthetic normativity consign to the sidelines.

We are given intriguing hints as to what the bag lady's own kind of fiction might imply: Chilean writing, in E. Luminata's hands, enacts a feminist vision that gives articulation to a female subaltern aesthetic. It constitutes a site of Latin American writing that is at once world literature, created in engagement with figures such as José Lezama Lima, James Joyce, Pablo Neruda, Juan Rulfo, and Alain Robbe-Grillet (77, 90). It is indebted to Amerindian voices and figurations, as when E. Luminata becomes a Mapuche shaman performing a healing dance (95–96).[30]

E. Luminata both revels in and rebels against the interpellations that the sign makes available (44). Through self-undercutting literary forms, imagined as graffiti, she exposes the ethical and political questionability of the lettered city—that colonial construct to which literature historically has lent its energy. This latter literary undertaking, which the sign assimilates and updates with its electronically fueled powers of subjectivation, is vast. E. Luminata's writings challenge it with their equally momentous, baroque creativity. She furnishes counterstatements to the sign's deployments of literature (121–34).

I want to take some time to dwell on the polemical literary expressions that E. Luminata offers in response to the reign of the sign, which are among the novel's most mystifying passages. Her interventions are prefaced by a section composed of an extended list of commandments enjoining the reader to imagine the square, its various qualities, and the things happening there (section 6.1). Here is a short sample: "Imagine a square space. . . . Imagine this space contained within the city. . . . Imagine this space desolate" (119). The whole section consists of such imaginative prompts. They all concern the square. The next section, numbered 6.2, bears the title, "THE GRAFFITI IN THE SQUARE." Each page, except for the last one, is headed by a different stylistic description of writing of the form "writing as x," followed first by a discursive passage and at the bottom by a short quote of what "she wrote." In section 6.2, the bag lady then answers the imaginative entreaties of section 6.1 with writings that challenge the aesthetic genres flagged by the headings—in other words, the graffiti's already designed codes and principles. The result is an assembly of modes of address accompanied by their rebuttals, all in the form of graffiti. Imagining is in action. The reader understands it to be happening in formats imprinted in the public domain of the square, as well as in countervailing formats that we are imagining while perusing E. Luminata's scribblings. Told in section 6.1 to imagine the plaza in this or that way, we did so, guided by the text's spurring. The imagining we subsequently perform in section 6.2 is an imagining of and by way of the media of literature and language broadly conceived. The suggestion is that these two kinds of imagining are of the same order. The convergence of the two imaginaries underscores that we are participating in an enactment of aesthetic publicness. We are imaginatively engaging and inhabiting the square and, in so doing, infuse it with aesthetic forms that we are producing in collaboration with found linguistic materials. The graffiti, meanwhile, is perplexing. There is no other way to read it than by using our imagination. I ask the reader to bear with me as I offer my imaginary of the extensive inscriptions on view in the square, for the graffiti artists have had quite a day. They have been most imaginative. Let's go for it.

Here is my imaginary: The graffiti mentions, and E. Luminata discards, the socialist use of "[w]riting as proclamation," which posits a dialectic of civilization and primitivism (121). She rejects the decolonial feminist fantasy of "[w]riting as folly"—namely, as an extra-historical tradition of alternative knowledge production (122). E. Luminata lets go of "[w]riting as fiction," or an otherworldly, special prerogative of the lettered city (123); "[w]riting as seduction," or the alternately sublimating and de-sublimating interventions posited by psychoanalytical thought (124); and "[w]riting as meshing gears (125), or literature in the form of a youthful overturning of material conditions. She dismisses "[w]riting as sentencing" (126), or literature in its capacity to restrictively confine the subject to interiority. Then the graffiti features other kinds of literary production that work with the reality of the advertisement sign. They include "[w]riting as rubbing" (127), or a physical engagement apart from negation or affirmation that extends in space in anticipation of unprecedented forms of communication and construction. We encounter "[w]riting as evasion" (128), or a wishful acceptance of blurry chimeras and an embrace of limited understanding and self-reflection. The graffiti lists "[w]riting as objective" (129), or a hopeful affirmation of a kind of aliveness freed from historical weight and bodily markings and as yet neither expected nor already legible. There is "[w]riting as illumination" (130), or the magnification and spreading through day-to-day city life of the process of interpellation epitomized by the sign and its entanglement of naming with unnameability; "[w]riting as mocking" (131), that is, a free-flowing, celebratory expenditure of postmodern play with symbols that have lost their moorings in delimitable projects of construction and production; and "[w]riting as abandon" (132), or a critical separation from a national/colonial matrix of exclusion that paradoxically finds support in a small segment of that denounced system—to wit, in court. Finally, the graffiti summons "[w]riting as erosion" (133). This is literature in its capacity to dispel the people's view, promulgated under the sign, that technology brings modernization and is capable of changing actors from conquered into conquerors. Writing as erosion recognizes solely "conquered and corpses" (133, see also 45).

E. Luminata's own narration subverts the formulas on offer in the square. Her lines go athwart each of the genres without revealing a directly legible contrarian relation to them, except that her brief verses run by at the bottom of the page. They stand apart like subtitles or split-screen notifications, passing underneath the sections detailing the modalities that the sign has appropriated and put on sale. The bag lady's enunciations imply states of sexual arousal—for example, "She wrote: / stretched out on the lawn I told you all the beautiful words, madonna, so you wouldn't stop, madonna I told you beaming" (122); and "She wrote: / I'm unpeeling madonna, it's true, I'm opening up" (128). Another note says, "She wrote: / they imprison me, they bring me down those words" (131). But a change occurs with the final statement of the section. This remark appears in the middle of an otherwise empty page, all by itself: "She wrote: / illuminated entirely, turned on" (134). Whether on the page or in the public square, literature is created and taken up, even seizes the center. It participates in the shaping of social bonds and antagonisms. The Enlightenment public sphere and the lettered city are exposed as sexual and corporeal formations. While intertwined with terrorization, sexual violence, and carcerality, these historical structures also host and spotlight a desirous writerly and readerly mode of embodiment that gives expression to these very intertwinements. E. Luminata's verses, her own graffiti markings in the city, intone a counter-voice to the sign. Following her imagining with our own, we enact aesthetic publicness. Ending the section with the graphic centering of an image of the aesthetically active public square, we are alerted to E. Luminata's corporeality and our own. In joining up with her for imaginative projects inspired by linguistic inscriptions, we are also looking and moving together. So let's now take our leave of the lists, and the assemblages composed of the entreaties and graffiti statements, and consider where we are in terms of the novel's broader imaginary of the public square.

E. Luminata choreographs her movements in relation to sign, people, and the things that make up or are found in the plaza, such as its edges, patches of grass, holes in the ground, rain. In the auditory plane, there are sonic events that range from the noises of E. Luminata's trotting (62) and the mixing and copying of sounds (63) to moments of allegedly pure sound (65), mooing vocalizations, moans (63), silence, and a cry amplified to earsplitting loudness (29). This multiplicity carries marks of a violence that transgresses against the body's limits. Simultaneously, the plurality is a product of aesthetic performances through which the body stretches beyond its own limits. Silence, modes of signification, and paradoxical absences of signification—as signaled, for example, through the notion of pure sound—enter into relations with one another.

As the bag lady lets the colorations wash over her, she assumes many other generative modes of public comportment, recognizing her agency as she enacts it, pursuing her desires, making her language her own. She circumvents the sign's auratic subjectivation procedures. Her performance wrests social imaginaries and scenarios of sensation and feeling away from the sign's determinations.

The sign fails in its takeover of literature and public life. We have already seen how its rule is curtailed by its dependence on the public square and on gendering lodged in the public domain. Over and above this, the sign's subjectifying mission presupposes a vast cultural apparatus: It partakes of multiple languages and literary genres, including the many varieties of graffiti we have encountered, and additionally makes use of bodily resources, class hierarchies, ethnicity, and the nation (110). The spectacle in the square is framed through cinematic takes and retakes. Performers of scenes and participants in displays for the camera, the people who have gathered scan their cinematic memories to gain awareness of the visual sensations that they are having or not having (32). A history of sound, image, and performance is in effect. The spectacle in the square snaps up literary tropes and scripts, such as plots of seduction and love and notions of language as expression. In short, the sign relies on a whole array of prior aesthetic formations. This apparatus reveals traces of historical and recent violence, which are encoded in aesthetic forms and structures. The sign participates in these patterns and rearranges them.

While the sign effaces preexisting aesthetic formations, as the novel's premise stipulates, it simultaneously is parasitic on them. The text wrings its premise through a reductio ad absurdum. But what of that other reduction? Where does Eltit leave the marginalized groups whom the global marketplace reduces to being "lumperrants" (179)? They are enthralled by E. Luminata's performance, craving a narrative that takes her as its model. Why this fascination with her and her story?

The novel's film tropes give a clue. From the beginning, poses are struck for the camera; staging is happening. E. Luminata and the people are engaged in the building of scenes, the setting up of shots. Under the cinematic gaze, we readily imagine the body as striated and parceled out by lights: as the subject of surveillance, the subject of torture. The abundant filmmaking represents the public square as a cinematic production: The plaza is in the process of being composed. As such, it is a fabricated set in which premeditated sequences are realized and, simultaneously, a place where people can design public life, the nation, the lettered city. The public square supports the people's aesthetic agency.

The sign, likewise, bolsters aesthetic agency. It gives the people an updated aesthetic identity. They acquire "autonomy" (43). It emancipates those who had been abandoned by the lettered city and the Enlightenment public sphere. A colonial problem is solved. The Global South gains autonomy in relation to the Global North. As Néstor García Canclini (2014) argues, commerce yields identificatory and agentic possibilities that surpass traditional societal molds. Yet in the very gesture of granting aesthetic agency, the sign retracts it with the eradication of historical identities, the people's "civil record." They see E. Luminata as an alternative. The bag lady, from whom it is hard to profit, has found a way to fashion her own aesthetic agency. She gathers herself as an aesthetic agent in the square. Her attraction is irresistible.

Reading the Marketplace

The novel's last section has E. Luminata mesmerized by the sign:

> Letter by letter, word by word, during those hours when she wore out her gaze letting her eyes wander over the neons, avoiding the apparent messages that might have led her astray if she had remained on the surface of the text.
>
> But no.
>
> She had succeeded in uniting the most far-apart letters, the turned on and the switched off, the crisscrossing of the two, the signs they constructed in between, the apparent blanks, the interchange between message and message. (Eltit 1997a [1983], 198)

Here E. Luminata may once again be enjoying the "daze" of being "lost in different residues" provided by the projections of the sign onto the city (27). She is making do with the figurations that the global marketplace makes available in the square. Chilean inhabitation of the market is derivative of First World models that prescribe cultural canons and implement criteria of beauty. The aesthetics of the sign yields neither contemporaneity nor novelty but enacts a belated, programmed spectacle. Roles are allotted; scripts are preplanned, as we are told in the second interrogation scene (143). How, then, as the novel proposes, can a bag lady in a Santiago square provide a "model" for the construction of a narrative?

E. Luminata is a reader of her aesthetic environment who is ready to propose errata for the visual forms she registers, effecting creative ruptures in the rule of the sign. "[I]n truth, that lighted advertisement had a defect: the height of the building on which it stood. It was not sufficient and that's why the neons were not being diluted as they ought to have been but, like the sun's rays, painted their surroundings" (198). The sign, E. Luminata notices, relies on antecedent aesthetic modes: It paints. It is supported by an architectural design. It cannot carry its rationality independently but banks on the sun, which produces night as well as day and causes night to be followed by day. In its painterly practice, the sign even mimics the style of the sunshine. E. Luminata creates a reading that historicizes the sign. She situates it in its aesthetic underpinnings, its material and symbolic location in the square.

E. Luminata carries on with her reading. The square assists in shaping her perspective, her voice.[31] She looks at the projections of the sign onto her gray dress. Trying to make them out, she finds the place where the light of the sign is the strongest, "managing to denote some letters that, very diluted, never succeeded in forming words. But the writings open to more than one interpretation occurred there. Each one of them contained more than a single letter" (199). Further interpretive determinacy is not really achieved by changing position. A different viewpoint only allows her to see how the letters that fall onto the center of the square are "presupposed by the reading she made of the ones emanating from above" (199). A supposedly better perspective fails to permit disambiguation. E. Luminata becomes aware of the inescapable equivocality of the sign's emissions.

> She realized . . . that it was impossible for her to specify an accurate combinatorial with certainty. Which two, three, or four letters might fall on her if she stayed in one definite spot. And even more than that: owing to that same distance, some letters piled on top of others, giving rise to complete words, which beyond any clear or precise meaning established links among themselves.
>
> Besides, all this depended on her absolute rigidity, which was totally impossible because of the prevailing cold and each one of her movements would permit the appearance of other signs and that way of various words. (200)

The aesthetic model that the bag lady supplies is a language of ambiguity, fissure, reinvention, and corporeal locatedness. At one level, this form, as Richard observes, restores emotional and bodily excess and failure to the codifications of utilitarian language, seeking out what the marketplace cannot anticipate and what escapes its transparencies (2004a, 12). But at another level, it is a form that parallels the emotional intensities of commodified experience with a far richer and more expansive affective palate.[32] It realizes a pliability and imaginative pluriformity that run athwart both the rigidities and the flows, the minimalisms and the maximalisms projected by neoliberalism's instrumental schemata.

A reader of literature and culture, E. Luminata is also proficient in the cinema. She activates the potentialities of film and other media for the design of the nation and the public square. In the novel's final pages, she does herself up with the instruments she has in her paper bag. She takes out a mirror and cuts her hair with scissors. She puts on a necklace over her gray dress. As she fashions her body, dawn arises. Cars encircle the square. People walk to work. Daybreak follows night. Early and late technologies coexist. E. Luminata's adornment, the urban setting, the streetlights, the walking paths of the passersby, the lettering flowing from the display, and the electricity cables powering the advertisements collaborate to engender the aesthetic constellation that is the square. Satirically reimagined, enlightenment, the public sphere, and the lettered city reveal their corporeal and social investments. Showcasing the previously outcast subaltern female body—indeed, hosting a celebration of their historical other—these structures, newly aestheticized and imagined in alternative terms as the plaza, can also animate the people's powers of reading and self-making.[33] Literature on the model of a ragged bag lady tells them as much. And it communicates this to us, Eltit's readers. Participating in the literary figuration of the plaza, expanding on prods such as the open-ended "Imagine a square space," the reader is spurred to situate literature in the aesthetic location that is the plaza and enlisted in the labor of aesthetic reimagination.

The Public Square as a Site of Aesthetic Agency

The plaza, which hosts the play of light, form, and bodies, is a site of aesthetic bonding and contestation, of memory and forgetting. It is essential to the recuperation of the historical record, which is under threat by the sign. The square can be given over to the sign, but it can also support a historical sensibility, conceived not in a totalizing Hegelian sense but as a state of awareness with jagged edges that both draws from and nourishes contingently emerging experiential horizons. On the one hand, the sign is not entirely foreign to this historical consciousness. On the other hand, literature, as produced, appropriated, and imagined anew in the square, is part and parcel of our ability to grasp the sign's workings and to self-reflexively apprehend its rewriting of the society.

At one point, E. Luminata spells out "WHERE ARE YOU GOING?" in "imaginary calligraphy" on a lamp post. A bit later she chalks it in large letters on the ground (Eltit 1997a [1983], 113). The people rub it out. She writes it again. Together with the people, she scours it off. Subsequently there is more writing, more brushing away. The square upholds these endeavors. They are ongoing. Literature is made and remade, notified of mistakes, blotted out, and reinvented on a new model. The square has resilience; it is multiplicitous. New stories, new meanings can take root there. But to write is to play with fire and to cut into the skin. The ragged bag lady injures herself. Gestures of burning her hand by dunking it into the flames (41–42, 44) and cutting lines into her arm (153–61, 164–65) correlate with moments at which she opens up flows of literary and performative possibility (42, 162–63).[34] Writing is a form of embodiment. Writing a different story is a way of redoing our bodies, of rearranging the plaza.

These endeavors are endless: “Writing piled up on posters, this unbridled proclamation of the square—” (105). A quality of abundance rubs off on the square, coincident with the emergence of a newly invented ordering system. E. Luminata “spread her proclamation in flyers, those same words also produced a ruled floor on the square’s cement—” (105). The people may spot defects in the square (107), but writing, figuration of the square, goes on.

E. Luminata finds pleasure in modalities of discovery, play, and connectedness that circumvent the sign’s indifferent strobing. The square, meanwhile, is in motion. Film gives a frame—or, rather, multiple, evolving frames—for the square, which is itself a frame for creation and participation. The framing, the takes, and the scenes are constantly confronted with errors and adjusted. Taste poses its demands. The public square offers a stage for writing, performance, reading, and display that is liable to editing, redoing, and all manner of uptake. It is a platform of multimodal aesthetic experience, where all formal and sensory modalities can potentially engage one another. Undergirding their interplay, the square is assembled and “reassembled” (181).

Eltit locates subaltern aesthetic agency in her bag lady, offering her ragged protagonist as a mirror image of a technologically advanced consumption society, which never has enough and is always poor. Consumerism, after all, keeps up with the times at the very moment of running already behind them, necessitating the next item, the next purchase. E. Luminata and the people negotiate this paradoxical temporality (178, 197).

The bag lady’s narration both reflects and differs from the story Eltit tells. In one scene, we are reading quotations from E. Luminata’s novel (106), which brings the two texts close to each other while maintaining a difference. This simultaneous connectedness and differentiation speaks also from the following pair of lines, which dismiss restrictive notions of literature as the author’s meaning, a blank page, or a corpse/corpus:

> Her soul is being E. Luminata and offering herself as another.
>
> Her soul is not being called diamela eltit / white sheets / cadaver. (90)

E. Luminata does not equate with Diamela Eltit, the author who created her. The text connects them while maintaining their alterity. Irreducible to the author function diamela eltit, E. Luminata can neither be understood on the model of the blank page or a corpse/corpus, clichéd constructions of literature, which the lettered city shares with the regime of the sign. The novel brings these figures to their limits. E. Luminata's connectedness to people, square, and sign exceeds the scope of what these notions can capture. Literature is neither moribund nor conjured out of nowhere. To see it as such, we need to emplace it in the aesthetic location that is the public square.

Furthermore, by having E. Luminata's tale at once reflect and go aslant the author's text, Eltit embeds her work in the social thematic it problematizes. The very public novel we are reading is not exempt from the workings of the marketplace. In the form of E. Luminata's fiction and, implicitly, Eltit's narrative, literature enacts a decolonial feminist stance. Eltit confronts the output of the marketplace with her invented character's performance, pushing back against the reductions and effacements perpetuated by the global economy. The marketplace requires the aesthetic, and the aesthetic may deploy the marketplace, but the latter cannot wholly control the invention of new forms. The public square harbors the tangle of opposing forces that ensues.

Aesthetic Publicness and the Square

Eltit's square connotes a form of aesthetic publicness that surpasses the models established by the Enlightenment, the lettered city, and the sign. Architecture embodies the frictions on display in the plaza. The square has a dual lighting system (14, 16, 34–35). One is public, feeding the streetlights; the other is implemented by the sign. Both conspire in the making of an aesthetic identity that is at once local and part of a globalized economy. The antagonisms and splits encoded in the urban design are ineradicable elements of the identifications and gatherings that unfold.

The aesthetic dimensions of the square, such as framings, scenography, listenings, gazes, material supports and holdings, interpretations, performances, and displays, are key to the forms of subjectivity, relationality, embodiment, and sexuality that become possible in the nation and the globe. Aesthetic norms and forms shape the registers of autocracy or democracy in which the people can participate and are, in turn, marked by these registers. As the political theorist Bonnie Honig (2017) underscores, public things are items from which democracy is forged. They engender collective attachment and contestation. People constellate around them. Honig has in mind entities such as railroads and national parks. Objects of our care and concern, public things, in her theory, constitute holding environments, allowing democratic citizenship to take form in the trajectories of assembly and conflict that arise around them (4–7, 24–28, 36, 48–57). Eltit, it appears, has been investigating a multimodal aesthetic contest over these politically crucial items while, at the same time, having us reflect on the distinctive features of one of these entities, and a metaphorically highly generative one, at that.

Along the lines of Honig's incisive analysis, the plaza, like the streetlights and electric cables feeding them, is a public thing. Crucially, however, as Eltit's novel impresses on us, it is also an aesthetic thing. While Honig counts films under the umbrella of public things along with cultural artifacts such as poems, concerts, memorials, libraries, sculptures, city pools, and historical narrations, she, by contrast to Eltit, does not explicitly call attention to the aesthetic norms, forms, and traditions instantiated by public things (Honig 2017, 24, 41, 56, 59, 87–88, 92). These elements, however, are part of the resources and forces on which public phenomena such as the plaza and the polity congregating around them draw as they galvanize new ways of coming together and dissenting. Aesthetic publicness enters the scene of people and things as a constellation that forges loops between aesthetic and public modes of responsiveness. Following Eltit, it needs to be reclaimed as such.

Honig's theory must be supplemented with an account of aesthetic publicness. This way, we can both build on her view and advance our understanding of a democratic citizenry. Indeed, by attending to the public aesthetic items that populate constellations of aesthetic publicness, we bring into view aesthetic norms, forms, and patterns of experience that condition our capacities for care and concern and shape collective life in the polity. Aesthetic registers crisscross the relational workings of public things. Theories of democratic subjectivation, embodiment, and local and global collectivity, including the state and other institutional formations, need to take into account the operations of aesthetic relationality that we enact around public things.

The public square, furthermore, is not just any public thing. It carries a distinctive aesthetic and political history. Its metaphorical and conceptual resonance is different from that of a swimming pool, a cinema, a radio station, a pipeline, a waterway, a road system, or a bike lane. We experience the materiality of public and other things in ways that are formative of our relations with them. While public things in the abstract allow for modes of differentiation and identification, the specific material, perceptual, affective, and sensory facets of these items and our engagement with them also enter into the web of relationships we forge around them. In this way, aesthetics recognizes a whole array of further determinants of the inclusions and exclusions that we enact in the sphere of aesthetic publicness, beyond the modalities to which Honig's public thing theory draws attention in such an illuminating fashion.

Considered in aesthetic light, no public thing is a mere public thing. Each public thing carries its distinctive aesthetic histories and potentialities, occupying a node in a web of aesthetic relationships. In the case of the public square, this web of relationships includes governance models such as democracy and autocracy. And the relational lineages that are in play range from historical and contemporary constellations of the agora highlighted in political theory to the reworked urban geography under the Pinochet regime. Given the powerful imaginary of public plazas as sites of democratic interaction and practice, I recognize the plaza's distinctive aesthetic generativity by comprehending it as a platform for aesthetic publicness. The public square, in other words, is a forum where aesthetic address unfolds in shifting structures, in multiple modes and media. This happens in tension and collusion with the scripts of interpellation fostered by the global economy. By understanding the plaza in terms of address, I acknowledge its structural and normative operations, including the manifold aesthetic norms and forms it enacts, as Eltit's novel makes clear. The concept of address creates space to acknowledge all registers of engagement with the square. This notion brings both increased specificity and generality to the framework of modes of public constellation and antagonism advanced by Honig. Thus, it provides the philosophical room we need to acknowledge how the aesthetic enters into the shaping of the public square and into the powers of invention and world making enacted there.[35]

E. Luminata invokes the specter of a totalizing marketplace that appropriates and supersedes the Enlightenment public sphere and the lettered city. Eltit supplements these three figures with the public square where the resulting conflicts and transformations play out. Confronting the Chilean people with two mutually entangled alternatives, she shifts the primary locus of aesthetic agency from the sign's emissions to the bag lady's creativity. The novel counters modernist progressions and their attendant sexual, gender, and class positionings with corporeal imaginaries and temporal disjunctions that reframe the relations among sign, protagonist, and crowd. The bag lady, as we have seen, invents her "own" fiction, toggling between "external" desiderata and internal criteria. The former valorizations introduce cultural exigencies that pertain to global and local hierarchies as well as to the allure of the marketplace. The latter valorizations carry the day in Enlightenment aesthetics. The upshot for public life rings powerfully: Public existence is a fundamentally aesthetic playing field, whose possibilities are caught up with aesthetic norms and forms. We can reap a philosophical takeaway for the notion of aesthetic publicness specifically: In addition to instituting curtailments of subjectivity and cultural engagement, aesthetic publicness features decolonial aesthetic stances that partake of registers of autonomy and heteronomy, interweave aesthetic distance with aesthetic connectedness, and as a result, engender critical reconfigurations of collectivity, signaling necessary lines of democratization.

Aesthetic publicness is a vital work in progress required to counter the encroachments of technologically regulated market rationality on the society. It encompasses the ways in which the aesthetic and the public route through each other in the fashioning of selves and objects; the designing of sociality; and the modes of caring attentiveness, concern, and critique we exercise. To be sure, aesthetic publicness harbors states of indifference to violence and complicity in oppression. It is neither unproblematic nor unwaveringly on the right side of history. But as my reading demonstrates, it is crucial to our attempts to wrestle with the predicaments that tempt contemporary aesthetic discourses to pull away from thick and substantial notions of the public. By jettisoning or diminishing aesthetic publicness, we play into economic frameworks and institutions that must be challenged. We ultimately deprive ourselves of powers needed to contest coloniality. Aesthetic publicness yields forums for aesthetic experience and address that condition the aesthetic activities on which these forums subsequently depend. They are thus of enormous importance to the project of cultural criticism.

While undeniably intertwined with terrorization, sexual violence, and carcerality, a point that merits repeating in the face of enduring forces of denial and forgetfulness, aesthetic publicness, as a historically situated formation, also hosts symbolic and communicative actions that bring to articulation these intertwinements. More than that, it comprises platforms in which actors can give expression to lifeworlds; enter into contact with each other's experiences; ponder categories and schemes of thought, including aesthetic categories and schemes; and intone demands for cultural infrastructures that are conducive to people's flourishing.[36]

The aesthetic is central to publicness. As my analysis has brought out, the contest over the public unfurls in aesthetics terms. It is a struggle over aesthetic forms and contents and their cultural underpinnings and possibilities. People and things exist within aesthetic matrices that mark their relational positionings vis-à-vis other people and things and registers of time and space. We never precede or shake off these matrices. Aesthetic publicness is a pillar of collective existence. While both the Enlightenment and the lettered city ultimately provide inadequate models of aesthetic publicness—ones that are complicitous with coloniality and late capitalist structures of subjectivity, race, gender, and nation—and while these complicities, as I have indicated, require alternative constructions of aesthetic publicness, this does not mean that aesthetics needs to be jettisoned. The same goes for literature. Eltit's novel self-reflexively enacts this awareness. Indeed, my uptake of her thought experiment attests to the centrality of the aesthetic as an encompassing cross-genre, intermedial, multitemporal formal repertoire, at once locally emplaced and global in reach. As such, the aesthetic can encroach on zones of forgetting and enlist material life in the creation of an alternative social body. Backed by the aesthetic, literature can function as a contemporary site of critical political agency. It yields indispensable resources for the actualization of a democratic citizenry and a multivoiced public domain.

Eltit continues the thought experiment at the core of *E. Luminata* in her later novel. I now turn to *The Fourth World* to deepen our inquiry into aesthetic relationality, agency, and publicness.

Taste and the Struggle over Race and Nation

How about taste, that other Enlightenment heritage? In eighteenth-century philosophy, taste becomes a motor and enduring support of aesthetic publicness. Philosophers align it with modes of public comportment. They link aspects of taste or tastelessness with societal positions. Taste holds levers to a system of aesthetic relationships populated by subjects and objects. While underscoring taste's public functioning, David Hume and Immanuel Kant simultaneously inscribe taste into lines of aesthetic racialization and racialized aestheticization that advance white constructions of culture and impede Black ones, while also hindering cultural formations conducive to the flourishing of other racialized and gendered populations (Roelofs 2014).[37] What can we make of taste in view of its ability to elevate some groups of people over others? How should this differential power bear on our understanding of taste's public potentialities?

First published in 1988, *The Fourth World* sports gestures toward an alternative construction of taste. In the vein of *E. Luminata*, the novel brings an aesthetic lens to a state of all-out commodification and contemplates the capacities that literature can exercise under these circumstances. Finance and venture capital provide the setting for a plot that takes as its point of departure the familial, sexual, and gender lineages highlighted by Gabriel García Márquez in his magisterial work *One Hundred Years of Solitude*. As he reveals in some of the novel's most memorable passages, corporate repression and killing of the workers who rise in protest against a banana company are effaced by forgetfulness. History repeats itself. Violent accumulation carries the day in a society that condemns Latin America to a state of solitude, connoted by the Buendía house.[38] Is aesthetics, to speak with some of García Márquez's images, condemned to soldering an interminable series of tiny goldfish? Did each day become a Monday, as a clock made of a mechanical ballerina tells the old Buendía? Eltit rekindles the Buendía family scene to resume García Márquez's questions in the later years of the Pinochet dictatorship.

Eltit's novel spotlights the connections of family, race, and nation. Through this focus, she broaches dimensions of life under the military regime left untouched in *E. Luminata*. A quick dip into political history will help us grasp the novel's framing. As the reader will recall, Salvador Allende's socialist government came to an abrupt end in 1973, when it was overthrown by a military coup financed by the US Central Intelligence Agency. The Pinochet regime, which lasted until 1990, when elections were called, prepared Chile's entry into the global marketplace. A cadre of University of Chicago–educated free-market economists nicknamed the "Chicago Boys," who acted in collusion with the repressive regime, saw Chile as a laboratory for neoliberal policies, strategies that later would be implemented in the United States, among many other countries. *The Fourth World* takes as its immediate backdrop the violent imposition by the US-sponsored dictatorship of a social order that sought to safeguard and intensify corporate control over the nation. While overtly glorifying traditional family values, the authoritarian rule cynically destroyed families by interning, torturing, and killing thousands of citizens. This terror and devastation makes its appearance in the text through states such as anxiety and nightmares; awareness of a normative and institutional vacuum; and a dialectical interplay of expressiveness, affect, and silence. These experiential dynamics, not surprisingly, bring up the operations of the lettered city. Indeed, literature's long-standing ties to (neo)colonial consolidation, nation building, and global capital contribute dense layers of historical meaning to the structures of interlacing sexual, gender, racial, classed, and colonial forces Eltit probes in the novel. The eradication of Amerindian peoples and heritages, as well as the epistemic/cultural disenfranchisement of Indigenous populations, is partially constitutive of the social constellations the novel scrutinizes.[39]

Eltit's deliberate registers of opacity and bewilderment steer away from an explicit foregrounding of either the dictatorship or the colonial legacy. Yet the novel rethinks gender, sexuality, and the family in light of this terrible history. Indeed, the text examines the workings of aesthetic norms, forms, and sensibilities as facets of deeply ingrained patterns of local and global subjectivity, relationality, and agency. A short précis of the work's main structure and thematic helps to clarify the philosophical exigencies that are at issue.

The Fourth World shows art and the marketplace embroiled in a struggle over race and nation. The protagonists are nonidentical male and female twins. The plot follows them from the exact dates they are conceived through their upbringing in a family that, in addition to a father and mother, includes a younger sister. The text consists of two parts, both written in the first-person singular. The first part is told by the brother, who, starting with the siblings' gendered travails in the womb, where he is competing with his sister for space, narrates their childhood and adolescence in the family home and the city. He discusses his bodily sensations and feelings and his understandings of the behavior of his family members. The twins experiment with their sexuality. They discover the desires that bind them to their compatriots—or, as Eltit calls it, repurposing a rarely used European derogatory racial term for South Americans, the *sudaca* race. The second part of the novel, which takes up the final third of the text, is narrated through the twin sister's eyes. The twins' relation has turned incestuous, recalling a thread of intrafamilial liaisons among the Buendías. Things become too much to bear for the parents. They vacate the house. The future of the nation and the race is now in the twins' hands. In the final pages, they give birth to a baby girl that is the novel itself. The twin sister eventually turns out to be "diamela eltit" (Eltit 1995 [1988], 114). Like other discourses and the city itself, her creation is for sale. A position outside the global capitalist order, we can infer, has become impossible to attain for the artist, for the person of taste. Yet art and taste reclaim public territory. They shape a field of aesthetic interaction.

My reading of *The Fourth World* singles out moments in the novel that connote shifting stages of sensibility that range from white European tastes to forms coded by an intermingling of Latin American inflections with globalized experiential templates molded in European terms. Instances of intense intercorporeal contact stimulated by the city lead to attempts to exoticize cultural difference and transcend it. Yet literature, as epitomized by the twins' narratives and our reading of their tales, can enact sensibilities that pass over neither the local nor the global and that initiate pathways toward an alternative future. This understanding unfolds in a trajectory from resignation and hopelessness to expression and agency that we follow by moving from the brother's story, titled "Defeat Will Be Irrevocable," to the sister's, titled "I Have a Terribly Constrained Hand." Surging on the wave of strange taste, aesthetic publicness, as I argue, gives rise to inventive modalities of creativity and political participation that reach beyond established constellations of race, gender, class, coloniality, nation, and the global.

As we learn from the twin brother, the pater familias loves to go clothes shopping. He takes his son on these trips. This is the only time he spends with his offspring. Face to face with the merchandise, the father comments expertly on the materials, delightedly comparing the different varieties of cloth. In the son's words, "His eyes would twinkle when he examined [the clothes], as he demonstrated his wide knowledge of different grades of cloth. He would gently rub the cloth between his fingers and accurately describe its quality and durability. Silk shirts were his preference" (33). Aesthetic theory intuits here the presence of the Humean aesthetic observer. With the figure of the father, Eltit invokes the Enlightenment's subject of taste, who, as Hume saw it, has his pulse on the enduringly good and beautiful in culture and the arts and takes charge of his pleasures.

The son gets the idea: "I shared the same propensity for silk, and it would send chills down my spine when it touched my skin" (33). Dad is even more enraptured than the youngster. In the boy's words, "[H]e would run his fingertips over the surface of the cloth as if he were intimately caressing someone, quivering with implacable impotency" (33). Hours of sensory bliss are passed with the shirts. The aesthetic connoisseur, in his ecstasy, forgets his son is even there—that is, right up to the moment of decision making. When the father has narrowed down the choice to two or three shirts, the son gets to pick. "But it was then that I could see a sense of disappointment in his eyes, as if my body had somehow diminished the quality of the cloth or my face had defiled the splendor of its beauty" (33–34). Latin American embodiment detracts from the disinterested gratification of the beauty experience. The silk shirts drive a wedge between father and son, and the family outing outs the individualism and the colonial outlook that characterize both the marketplace and modern subjectivity, understood on the Enlightenment model of the man of taste.[40]

The father is an aesthete who prefers looking and sensing in a disinterested fashion to buying or using the clothes, at which he balks. He is the modern individual who keeps his surroundings at a desirable distance while accessing them in a purportedly sovereign fashion, shaping the limits of his surrender to the world of objects and other people as he pleases. For Hume, recall, the man of taste controls his existence through the deployment of taste. In Hume's view, this faculty constitutes a globally applicable aesthetic proclivity, an experiential and evaluative disposition that one can bring to any cultural artifact, anywhere on earth, at any time. Frequenting the Santiago stores, the father displays his cosmopolitan flair. The man of taste is a man of the world.

Eltit here allows us to glimpse how aesthetic meaning and agency are pillars of a masculinized, colonial frame of social being. Yet the father's connoisseurship no longer has a place in the city. His apparent autonomy holds only within narrow bounds. The outside world has the patriarch at a loss: "[B]eyond the confines of our house, he was insecure" (54). Indeed, the father is "terrified of the city" (111). He is unprepared for the wider urban regions that outstrip his comfort zone. This is not so for his offspring, which, as we shall see, in this regard takes after the mother. But the son is not yet finished with silk and its mesmerizing potentialities.

Upon reaching puberty, the youngsters become aware that silk lends itself to occupations other than mere reveling. The twin sister takes to the material: "My sister was consumed by silk and glitter. . . . Since she had no style, I was her mentor and audience. I thought purple suited her best. She would paint her cheeks that color and it would ooze down to her lips. Sometimes I preferred red and, if I was feeling calm, I would smear soft rose hues on her" (43–44). The sister's games wildly surpass the father's contemplative absorption in silk's pleats and textures. The twins devise their own rites with the material.

At the same time, their invention relies on precedents. The son reproduces his father's supposed sovereignty to assume his role as an aesthetic authority in a joint performance. The sister, in turn, enlists her brother to mirror herself to herself. Through this relayed aesthetic arrangement, the twins realize their own version of their parents' aesthetic contract, for an intricate ploy connects the adult couple—at least, in the perception of their male offspring, who, before birth, had already been keenly observing them (5). By satisfying the father's wish that his wife wear dresses, jewelry, and perfume—a kind of adornment that left her "indifferent" but in which she, according to her son, nonetheless feigned an interest—the mother at once sought to "please" and "humiliate" her husband (7). Thus, she fed "his illusion of power," as the son had "discovered" from the vantage point of the womb (7). Brother and sister update this aesthetic covenant to accommodate the desires that stir in them in their teens.

The twins' ploy with silk goes back to their earlier childhood games. Back then, the two used to be riveted by an endless role-play that stretched the radius of human possibilities available to them. Their inherited sibling bond inspired this play. At the same time, their closeness was being reshaped in the course of the game, which fed on the concrete circumstances that caught the duo's interest: "Our ancestral pact had definitely brought us together, allowing us to play several unlikely roles: husband and wife, father and daughter, mother and son, brother and sister, friends. Seeking to capture real-life situations, we would play every possible role, from perfect and guilt-ridden parts to hostile and loving ones. We would play until we dropped from exhaustion, then we would begin anew, forming our predestined dyads. We also exchanged roles: if I was the wife, my sister would play the husband while we watched the other rise blissfully to our ideal condition" (24). The twins' interminably renewing games expand the realm of identifications that the teen brother and sister can assume. Symmetrical in organization, however, their childhood performances observe already scripted cultural polarities. Prefabricated oppositions also inform the siblings' play during adolescence. But now a certain fluidity and affective plasticity is lacking. The earlier, reciprocal role switching subsides as inherited stances solidify. In the twin's reenactment of parental aesthetic positions, it falls to the brother to paint his sister's face with makeup and dress her up; the sister, for her part, sees herself reflected in his eyes. Role reversal is no longer part of this rigorously gendered game.

Yet experimentation remains generative. The sister tries on different aesthetically engendered identities: "Attempting desperately to create her own style, her ardent performance would enslave me at her side for hours on end, but I attempted to please her" (44). The brother's compliant fascination foreshadows the transvestite persona that he will assume later on (69).[41] At the same time, the explosion of silk and glitter overwhelms him. He develops an excessive lust that hints at the future.

Out on the Town

At this juncture, the outside world intrudes on the twins' experience. Contrary to the patriarch, his two oldest children crave the city. Encouraged by their mother's reveries, the twin brother and sister roam the streets. "The city, taciturnly benevolent, awoke all kinds of desires and activated fantasies we inherited from my mother. Among the crowded citizenry populating the streets, we could feel the libidinous traffic that consolidated crime and selling. The beautiful, bare torsos of the young sudaca boys were like living sculptures walking down the sidewalks. During our brief outings, our eyes absorbed a seemingly vast orgy" (30). Aesthetic possibilities multiply beyond the confines of the family. Classical and European renaissance statues that one might treasure in a Western colonial museum return in the shapes of the ambulatory, residual bodies relished by the twins in the Santiago streets. A local urban aesthetic employs a sensibility intimating an Enlightenment notion of taste to awaken a cornucopia of unanticipated pleasures.

Subaltern figures inspire desire. The youngsters have flings. They are growing up. Indeed, the year before they started the routine with dresses and makeup, at twelve years old, the brother, to the sister's dismay, had had a sexual encounter in the city, with "a young female beggar or a young male vagabond" (37). Propelled by a chase through the streets, the exchange with this marginal person of uncertain gender had blurred the distinction between pursuer and pursued. At thirteen, her self-fashioning routines witnessed by her brother having fulfilled their ostensible goal, the twin sister is ready to go out into the world for pleasure, dancing, and affairs with the "sudaca beggers" that occupy her fantasies (44). Residual types, again, fuel her longing. She meets a young man with whom she starts a liaison. Her brother swiftly punishes her for her wish to join "the party of the universe" and for her interest in the boy, by having a fling with a "sudaca girl" (45, 49). The outside word spells other adventures for him, as well. He has an encounter with a "mob of angry young sudacas," who practice "a meaningless dialect" and whose "lower-class roots gave them a singular unity" (54–55). The group of subalterns beats him senseless, depositing him in front of the house.

No longer content to gaze at and sense the erotic and sexual display in the street, the twins reach the limits of a European construction of gendered aesthetic subjectivity. Craving more than disinterested perception, they enter into contact with the sudacas populating the city.[42] Their intimate hookups with disposable human beings remain singular and flighty. The games with silk have bred an individualist sensibility. Their mindset never melds into a communal spirit. The twins' engagement with subaltern characters fails to reach beyond exoticist modes of cultural othering. Decoloniality will take another path, a different form.

The next aesthetic stage has the sister haunted by images of mud and "voices that spoke from the black recesses of darkness, clamoring for dead people she didn't know or couldn't remember" (58–59). We intuit a history of disappearances and unspoken absences. Wishing to take her distance both from the family and from the sudacas, she adopts a nonhuman-centric vision of being: "She thought that the family was somewhere behind her and she was standing next to every human species possible, while at the same time enjoying unlimited expanses that made it possible to cast off her passion" (60–61). Alas, the images and voices refuse to vanish. She begins to dig in the soil for slimy worm larvae. "They would slip out of her hands and she knew then she had overcome her fear of death. Each worm was the inverted transformation of her body, which some day would reach that inferior stage, moving the species backwards" (61). Temporal orientation, for the sudaca race, enters into disarray. The future bodes regression, not progress.

At this point, her brother initiates his own embrace of the earth, having struck up a daily dancing routine with the twins' younger sister that enables their "yearning bodies to entwine the universe and to remake it" (52). Performing a "strangely timeless ritual," the sister dances "the history of the world," apparently "expel[ling] her thoughts so they would dance and satiate their contents" (51–52). Thoughtlessness permits transcendence. The older brother, once again, finds himself mesmerized. "While seemingly sensual, I had gone beyond sensuality itself; I felt unreal, as if I were carrying the reality of the human race inside me" (52). Sudaca identity, European identity, and human identity go seamlessly together in this aesthetic condition. Apprehending "life despite death, undulating inside us like a tribute to our roots, our heroes, and our beggars," the siblings' dancing bodies can enter "a celebration of our painful human sorrows and of the uncertainty of our future" (52). This state of joint bodily rapture does not outstrip the domain of the sudaca, the European, or the human but establishes a revitalized register of being: "Without shunning human nature, our bodies exhibited hatred and envy, lust and corruption, with the same emphasis as the amazement of the species of giving birth. Observing ourselves for our capacity to exist, we would disintegrate and be born again, now distant from and outside the world of words, managing to live in a time unfamiliar to time" (52). Temporal experience acquires a new design in the absence of language. The brother has settled on a metamorphic mode of being that assimilates history yet surpasses a cultural dialectic. Paradigms of origin, heroes, and beggars exist in the same ecstatic plane. Colonial difference is effaced. A fluid temporal modality takes effect that exceeds the duality of progression and regression and opens out to uncertain determinations.

The twins, thus, both make their departure from the home. Each envisages a different future for the sudacas. The sister locates the sudacas, along with their other fellow human beings, on the same plane as nonhuman species. The brother emplaces the sudacas in a newly invented order of history and time, apart from thought and words. Neither alternative valorizes the realm of the local, even if the twins have made forays into the city streets and enjoyed moments of closeness to their fellow sudacas or to their sudaca heritage. Visions of transcendence inform both siblings' notions of what the sudaca race can aspire to. Sudaca specificity vanishes in a generalizing affirmation of a universal species-being shared with nonhuman creatures (as enacted by the sister) and a generically human corporeal frenzy (as enjoyed by the brother). The twins settle on an aesthetic that effaces their embodied specificity and the creative thrust of the aesthetic education they have garnered in the streets. A decolonial aesthetic remains as yet out of reach.

Familial impulses rein in the twins. As it turns out, neither twin's aesthetic stance proves to be a viable alternative for the public world and the sphere of domesticity. Traditional persuasions reassert themselves within the confines of the family. In the house, the twins' younger sister reiterates the father's fantasies, which feature her as a "bearer of death" and reduce her to "two opposing poles: success or failure, goodness or badness, life or death" (50–51). The girl's paternal affiliation shuts down any path of growth beyond immiseration: "It was in this very conventional impoverished state that my father had taken root in her so profoundly," observes the twin brother (51). Familiar/familial language and concepts (such as the terminology of the good versus the bad) return with a vengeance, blocking the brother's vision of metamorphic time.[43]

The violence inflicted by the dictatorship makes itself felt in the novel in the first place through experiences such as fragmented dream images and anxieties that grip the twins, along with the twin brother's sense of an absence of "institutions or norms," to give a few examples (27, 58–59). Speaking of the platitudinous and all too easy moral language of the younger sister, the destruction can also be discerned in the overly simple fantasies through which she seeks to keep horror at bay, as in a "story" she voices aloud in her sleep "about goodness, where human beings were able to take advantage of the best they had to offer in order to donate it to the sadness of an inert rock" (60). The benevolence she imagines fails to mitigate the distress that pervades a silent spectacle—barren of humanity but nonetheless carrying traces of sorrow. A still physical object carries affective tonalities that appear to bely its material recalcitrance and noncommunicative self-enclosure. Perhaps we spot here a glimpse of her elder sister's more than human consciousness.

Soon a resurgence of traditional family values effectively shuts down both twins' transgressive stances—the twin sister's post-humanism as well as the brother's intercorporeal rapture in excess of thought and language. Upon the father's discovery that his wife has been committing adultery on the outskirts of the city, the twins retreat into the house to avoid a shameful exposure to other people's gaze. A "cosmic yet personal path" encompasses the "crime" that is the family's lot (64, 66). The outreach to the universe does not take place through their aesthetic spunk and grit but unfolds in the shape of morality and the law, which appoint the mother to the home. She takes her daughters in tow. The scandal bearing down on the home is the junction from which a novel aesthetic setting for narration sprouts forth.

The brother is reaching the end of his story. He is feeling the pressure of time. He concludes his tale with a self-reflexive remark: "As time was becoming critical, I assented to deposit the confession with my twin sister" (66). The brother cites a narrative genre that at once owns up to an ignominy and promises to dispel it. We wonder what a Latin American literature might look like that exemplifies this scenario. Reflecting on the brother's tale, the reader realizes that, regardless of the narrator's allusion to the confessional mode, his revelations emphatically bear the imprint of the European Bildungsroman and the realist novel (e.g., *Madame Bovary*), with their attention to affective development and social process. The brother's exposition also recalls the Latin American testimonial. More than that, the twins' situation is reminiscent of the troubles of several renowned fellow fictional characters. Their place in the house brought to a point of crisis, Eltit's protagonists resemble the reading and knitting brother-sister pair who are banished from the family home in Julio Cortázar's story "House Taken Over," which I discuss in the conclusion of this book.[44] And, as I have indicated, Eltit offers her twins as a continuation of the Buendía family line that came to an end at the close of García Márquez's *One Hundred Years*.[45]

Although the twin brother claims to have composed a confession in his part of the novel, titled "Defeat Will Be Irrevocable," any prospect of redemption strays far afield from his text. If absolution or conversion is to substantiate, it has to occur in the twin sister's part. The twins, it appears, have resumed their role playing. The brother sets his sister up as the recipient of his narration. The confession needs to be received. She obliges, or so it seems. His story ceases. We now get to hear hers. She aptly responds with a tale named "I Have a Terribly Constrained Hand."

Upending a centuries-long literary tradition that spans colonial divides, Eltit places the fate of a Latin American literary identity and cultural lineage in the hands of a female narrator. In a novel that upends conventional gender dichotomies and identifications, the trope of a feminine voice is, of course, far from univocal in its implications. Offering us this open-ended figure through which we can imagine unscripted futures, Eltit makes a feminist intervention into a colonial as well as a decolonial aesthetic history.[46] Cortázar's, García Márquez's, and Eltit's narrations, one by one, move toward views of Latin American art and culture that step aside from the prominent, socially regulative fiction of the nation grounded in the sexually normative couple.[47]

The Twin Sister's Story

The narrating sister regards herself as a chronicler. "[R]eading and translating the sexual activities of this family, [I] knew exactly when the members would speak of possession" (90). She faults her twin brother for his continued attachment to traditional myths of family and nation: "[Y]ou still fear my old father, who hasn't defeated his virility. You still fear the softness of silk. You are afraid of my sister and my mother, and it seems like the multiplicity of your dreams is taking you closer and closer to the most famous and powerful nation in the world" (89–90)—in other words, to dictatorial Chile. The sudacas are living under a stigma (83, 105). The twin sister has had a vision that, as deciphered with the help of her younger sister, recognizes the need for a tribute to dispel the curse inflicted on the people by the supremely powerful nation (83). The vision attests that this nation "change[s] names every century, hiding in new clothing," and "only brotherhood" can "propel [it] into crisis" (83–84). Here we detect the seeds of the sister's plan for the twins, for the race, for the future. She wants to annihilate the "nation of death" and attain freedom from it through the power of "sudaca brotherhood" (93; see also 83–84).

Things at this point become too heated for the parents and the younger sister. They pull out before the twin sister's rebellious program can be executed. They escape the house. The twins remain alone to carry the "sucada stigma" (105). They prepare the tribute to the race that is to break the spell. "It was a tribute to the sudaca species. It was a manifesto" (108). Neither the premature, solitary decampment from the house fantasized by the brother (91) nor his repetitive insistence "I am an honorable sudaca, I am an honorable sudaca" can adequately address the chasm consequent on the twins' having been "born," as the sister puts it, quoting César Vallejo, "on a day that God was sick" (73).[48] Indeed, the sister is plotting a radical "homage" to the race (84): "I want to create a creature that is terribly and scandalously sudaca" (74). Nothing short of an embrace of the outrage of sudaca-being can halt the age-old cycle of denigration channeled through the vortex of race and nation and assert a decolonial feminist alternative.

The turnabout that the sister envisages proceeds in an economic register every bit as much as in an aesthetic and existential one. Compliance with contemporary finance and venture capitalism and a bowing to violent accumulation are unacceptable: "The child will not come into this world to be despised, he will not come demanding something for nothing" (112). The baby the twins are about to give birth to, in short, will not be like the "young sudaca" who stuck out his hand and refused the coin the brother put in it (111). The sister's hope is for a creation—or, as she calls it, "deformity" (92)—that outstrips the schemes of consumption and production. The former mode is condemned to "replenish[ing] the garbage" (111). The latter issues in a selling of the product of labor and other constructive projects, such as "the corn, the wheat, the willow groves," ultimately surrendering all resources to capital and relinquishing the imaginaries they inspire (94, 111). Instead of capitulating to conditions that bring about defeat (94), the twin sister aims to vanquish the nation being created and fortified outside the house through the twins' joint venture—the force of their sudaca companionship. The production-consumption model of the market is vanishing, since workers and buyers now are among the commodities being traded. This is the fate of urban and rural locales alike, including that of literature. How are the twins going to avert it?

The final pages witness the culmination of corporate control over the culture. City and language are losing ground as models of subjective being for the people. "Outside, the devastated city grumbles and is given to useless chatter. With the hope that money will fall from the sky, every kind of rhetorical discourse is heard; like fireflies, the words disappear in weak flashes. The myopic, miserly city doles out the destinies of its sudaca inhabitants. The city, palsied, broken down and irritable, old and greedy, begins to falter" (113). Language dematerializes. Its usefulness vanishes. Neither it nor the city maintains its integrity as a template of identity. Distinctions among varieties of discourse are meaningless. All words have become unmoored from their historical place in the city. They are short-lived, ephemeral. Rather than a center of meaning, history, and corporeal interaction, the city is an urban conglomerate that impassively disburses fates to the sudaca people, and even this civil function is fraying. As we read a bit later, "The city . . . is already a fiction. Only the name of the city remains" (113). Even naming is a matter of indifference. The lettered city no longer can support enduring lines of discourse. Its role as a forum for intellectual/artistic exchanges capable of generating enlarged, far-sighted modes of perception has come to an end. The fate of the race is shifting with the disintegration of the city.

Whereas earlier in the novel desire had already locked into market principles, as attested to by the twin brother's observation that "supply and demand became concentrated in my body, moving back and forth between debasement and exaltation," the aesthetic vicissitudes and affective turmoil that this entailed have lost their dynamism (42). Sexuality is no longer mediated by language, the city, or aesthetic performance, as in the many dress-up rites undertaken by each of the twins, brother as well as sister (see, e.g., 85, 101–102). Desire has ceased to require aesthetic representation or mediation; seduction is redundant: "The money from the sky enters directly through the sex organs, and the ancient voices surrender to wanton adultery" (113–14). Direct sexual contact with money is the norm. The old, aesthetically saturated, sexualized social order dissipates.

Finance capital broadens its grip: "[The] voices [of the sudacas] waver . . . as they squabble over the money that falls from the sky but vanishes into thin air. They sell the wheat, the corn, and the willow groves for nothing, while the young sudacas who planted them look on. Sweat is for sale. Frantic merchants shriek at the buyers, who astutely lower the prices to buy up everything, including the sellers themselves. The money from the sky returns to the sky and the sellers even sell what doesn't belong to them" (113). Racial identity and class and national consciousness undergo a rigorous restructuring under the sway of the marketplace. Traditional discourses briefly flare up before vanishing: "The money that falls from the sky stimulates not only urban fraud but also the false rhetoric about planting a hoax in the fields, which is already sold and now belongs to someone else" (113). Like many other sorts of discourse that are heard, old and new, the once powerful idea that the revolution will come from the countryside is briefly revived. Yet this notion has lost its appeal as the *campo* has already changed hands. Moreover, the belief that the real Latin America is found in the rural areas—as represented by, among others, the figures of the Incas, the gaucho, and Che Guevara—is shown to be no more than a deceptive rhetorical device.[49] Indeed, the dream of the nation is supplanted by hope for economic advancement in a post-national, post-urban marketplace: "[T]he city prostitutes itself, giving itself away at any price to any bidders. The transaction is about to conclude and the contempt for the sudaca race is clearly printed on the money falling from the sky" (114). What mode of linguistic creation might shed the role that all-out corporatism, as Eltit imagines, allots to it? How can discourse cast off the job of servicing financial flows descending onto the people and running away from them? By what means can literature refuse to adorn capital with contempt? What kinds of words might avoid the fate of going into and out of existence as weak, momentary glimmers?

An aesthetically upheld sexual order has fallen apart. The city "has been sold on the open market" (113). The lettered city has morphed into a fiction, a city in name only. Who is entertaining this fiction? In the novel's final paragraph, the twin brother and sister eventually pay their tribute, subverting the stronghold of the family-nation alliance and offering their "manifesto":

"Far away, in a house abandoned to brotherhood, between April 7 and 8, diamela eltit, assisted by her twin brother, gives birth to a baby girl. The sudaca baby will go up for sale" (114). The baby is the book we are reading. As in *E. Luminata*, Diamela Eltit makes a cameo appearance in the double role of the author of the novel and the author in the novel. It is she who is entertaining the fiction of the city, and so are we, her readers. The novel carries the promise of a language that challenges the bonds of the nation to the (re)productive heterosexual family and wrecks the tendency of the global economy to circulate and find fuel in defunct gender constructions and family norms. Like any other being or thing, however, the novel is a commodity in the marketplace. Literature's critical stance is implicated in finance capitalism.

By purchasing the book, the reader partially buys into understandings the novel problematizes, such as socially sedimented gender binarisms and racialized, colonial oppositions between subaltern and First World actors. Yet by invoking a "Fourth World," which satirizes the conventional sequencing of First, Second, and Third ones, the novel simultaneously gestures toward a social vision that shakes off restrictive conceptions of human nature, the body, emotion, love, and chronological development. Superseding the twin's exoticist/generalizing inclinations to pass over local and global specificities, Eltit further calls into question received delineations of gender, class, racial, sexual, and national identity.

If the marketplace recycles and draws its energy from familial/familiar lexicons that carry a ready legibility and instigates fleeting idioms, *The Fourth World* offers us a different kind of language. Eltit's writing, in Richard's (2004a, 12) terms, heightens the "failures and excesses of symbolic imaginaries." In this way, as Richard attests, aesthetic production can restore density of meaning to ostensibly transparent discourse aimed at maximizing profit and create bonds of memory (23–29). The novel plays symbolic ruptures out against traditional values that inform reinvigorated conventional identities under neoliberal capitalism, as well as against market-driven effacements of ideological antagonisms.[50]

Eltit deploys the device of first-person narration to conceive of an array of boundary-suspending movements: between bodies, genders, public and private, city and home, elite and subaltern, historiography and sexual autobiography, experimental writing and political manifesto. Referring less to a univocally identifiable territory than to a zone where a collection of deceptively familiar distinctions governing corporeal, social, geopolitical, and literary practice can undergo unsettlement, *The Fourth World* comprehends aesthetic form as a resource on which we can draw to restructure public existence.

Art and taste turn out to be crucial ways to confront a voracious, all-absorbing marketplace—both grub around in what is left of a model of aesthetic publicness tied to the city and the place of the house within it. The twins tweak their earlier creative practices, their childhood dealings with "silk and glitter," to come up with a solution to the malaise that has set in. The brother paints his face "a golden color," hoping to compete "with the neon stars that twinkle in splendor above" (Eltit 1995 [1988], 85). He puts on "his most outlandish dress," going barefoot, painting his lips, doing up his eyes with mascara (101–2). He glosses his eyebrows and adorns his head with a wrap made from the old, coveted silk. The twin sister, for her part, had gotten her sister to make a "neon halo" for her, "a blue, shining circle" that her pregnancy needed to make her "stand out" (78). The twin sister also had been thinking of "stretching canvas with phosphorescent stripes across the front of the house" (83).[51] Performance and role-play imply the triad of creator, creation, and observer. These acts deploy taste to give shape to a form of aesthetic relationality. They involve registers of publicness that draw on historical performance vocabularies to bring about new experiential possibilities. History carries on in the form of aesthetic experience.

The twin sister's poetics embodies this aesthetic awareness into an ethics, an epistemology, and a sensibility that insists on historicity. She craves an artistic form that is able to carry historical memory. "Knowing the past and bold about the present, I want all the sleepless nights and worms that devour my brain to embellish my song. And I want my brain to be there as well" (86). She aspires to a corporeally, affectively, and rationally supported mode of historical consciousness. She wishes to make a song, a song of terrible beauty, ample enough to hold the trauma of the past and to enter into conversations with the texts of artistic predecessors. Situated in the global marketplace, literature, the novel suggests, can engender a critical response to shifting patterns of production and consumption. It can challenge violent accumulation and extractivism. It can push back against conceptual frameworks that undergird repressive constructions of the nation, race, gender, sexuality, and a postnational, obliviously post-racial globalism that reinstitutes a colonialist order.

For the longest time, the twins keep "looking for a way out" of the house (101–2), one that literary writing ultimately, though with substantial ambivalence, provides: Aesthetic publicness encompasses both the figure of home and the sphere beyond the home. Paradoxically, the house is not a place one can simply leave, and neither can one take it for what it is. In an early scene, old messages, such as the notion of the "indestructible patriarch" who "never veers off track," had insinuated themselves into the young twins' games and dreams, "echo[ing] outward in concentric circles" (28). Although the twins venture far afield from the original, patriarchal home, the echoes have not been called to an abrupt halt. Aesthetic sensibility, in the novel, does not herald a radical overthrow of the Chilean nation, the global marketplace, literature, or aesthetic publicness. Juxtaposing, however, the twin sister's "terribly constrained hand" with the ineluctable "defeat" presaged by her brother (1, 67), *The Fourth World* highlights the potentialities of multimodal aesthetic sensibilities, norms, and forms in devising responses to the cultural overhaul effected by the forced imposition of a market society on the Chilean nation in the years between the 1973 coup and the 1990 election. By activating language afresh, the twins signal who they were, are, and wish to become. Brother and sister, now book, interrupt the symbolic economy of the marketplace that ventures to free itself from mediation. The twins are the aesthetic inventors of our era.

The text's closing episode hints at novel forms of political participation and creativity. Brother and sister have affiliated themselves with the sudacas and yet behave like "entrepreneurs of the self."[52] They incarnate words. They produce language in the shape of human flesh, language designed to generate selves and cultural identities. They replenish words with unanticipated, conflictual meanings, histories, and contexts. In re-embodying language, they remind us that words used to have quite solidly rooted, reliable commercial value in the form of books, magazines, newspapers, and so on. Now, in an epoch in which we encounter the world through the filters of algorithmic capitalism and machine learning technologies, once substantial bodies of words have undergone dematerialization. They have changed into evanescent flashes, pennies from heaven, tokens from the stratospheres, post-human mementos of a past present. At the same time, words along with other aesthetic forms, as we have seen, shore up constellations of social identity and difference. The notion of aesthetic publicness alerts us to the abundant strategies we can devise to invest this constructive labor with unforeseen orientations and points to the manifold aesthetic experiences that we can rally to this effect.

Taste is a faculty for the establishment of relationships. We can deploy it to achieve positionings and repositionings in a public domain. It is an indispensable repertoire of racial strategies. In an era when symbolic productions circulate untethered from public forums such as the square, it is a crucial register of self-fashioning, racial experience, and cultural production. Dislodging taste from the comportment of European connoisseur represented by the father, but maintaining it as a driving force of critical trajectories of aesthetic racialization and racialized aestheticization, Eltit gives it a different construal than the Enlightenment model of publicness provides. Surpassing her father's betrayal of the house, the twin sister orients taste anew toward futural possibilities that remain as yet unscripted. Earlier, she rebuked her brother for his enduring fear of the patriarch, his ultimate inability to shake off the law of the father. The brother, she said, continued to fear the "softness of silk" (89–90). Later, in a satirical twist on Enlightenment imagery, she observes him "measuring the density of light" (89). He remains preoccupied with a model of aesthetic publicness that the twin sister leaves behind. It, thus, is she who takes up the fate of the race and the nation as Eltit's renewed figure of the literary writer. And it is the twin sister with whom Eltit supplants Lispector's male author character in *The Hour of the Star*. Lispector concludes her 1977 novel by having Rodrigo S. M. reflect on the weight of the light before lighting a cigarette. Eleven years later, Eltit rewrites this sexual script by privileging a female narrator who enjoys her own games with soft, shiny, and phosphorescent materials.

In the twin sister's aesthetic vision, the softness of silk no longer is a source of disappointment or trepidation. The sudaca body has ceased to spell aesthetic contamination. Together, silk and body bring into being revitalized possibilities for racial and gendered subjectivity, sexuality, and the nation. The silk is a shareable resource whose attractions and perils stretch across different cultural moments. It is a historically engendered aesthetic creation that contributes its relational impulses and generativity to a zone of aesthetic publicness, a field of experience, value, and desire that we negotiate by way of our evolving tastes.

Conclusion: Creating Aesthetic Connections

Aesthetic materials and fabrics interconnect individual psyche and world, home and city. The bonds between interiority and exteriority unfold in a field of aesthetic publicness. Dropping the house as a schema for identity and fantasy is not an option for aesthetics, but neither can it be left to its own devices: The house needs to be wrenched away from traditionalist constructions of the nuclear family and from restrictively gendered and racialized public-private divides. Taste, likewise, is an ambivalent phenomenon: It lodges in the folds between individual and society yet must be loosened from Enlightenment scripts and delineations of the lettered city. In a similar vein, interiority and exteriority display permutations that require interpretation and refiguration. They don't allow themselves to be grasped in terms of already understood structures, for we are facing unprecedented situations. The volatile interface of psychic life and external reality reflects changing circumstances. Embodiment, desire, fantasy, and sexuality feed on existent aesthetic procedures and occasion new joints and twists in aesthetic constellations. Aesthetic publicness is the territory in which these openings, ruptures, and linkages unfold. Here Eltit makes her intervention.

Expression and agency are out of joint, out of bounds in Eltit's novels. Life is a dispensation of the marketplace. Finance and venture capitalism have remorselessly swallowed cultural performance and elevated themselves to the status of supreme performer, usurping the nation as its proxy. Concern for the body, for the house, for the square, for the people becomes a pathway along which we can animate recalcitrant cultural needs. But the old patterns of valorization don't hold the answers. This is why the people in *E. Luminata*, spearheaded by the bag lady, want to write, to read, to play. And this is also why her fellow female protagonist, the twin sister in *The Fourth World*, assumes a vanguard position ahead of the anxiety-torn twin brother, who is unable to let go of the hold of the father over his emotions.

Satirizing received psychoanalytic scenarios of linguistic and social development and tracing the existential implications of technologically supported, late capitalist constructions of subjectivity and collectivity, *E. Luminata* and *The Fourth World* forge an aesthetic fabric that opens up the ties between house and city, psychic turmoil and political upheaval, to aesthetic figuration and refiguration. Read together, the novels put forth a cultural vision that cherishes public agency while also treasuring the realms of the domestic, the personal, the singular, and the private.

In a move that is reminiscent of the Platonic heritage, Eltit highlights the morally and politically dubious facets of technologically mediated symbolic flows detached from their contexts of creation and reception. Taking a page from critical theory, she challenges the sway of technology and the marketplace over culture from a position within these regimes. She acknowledges that life engulfs us in double binds but, surpassing Spivak's abstract counsel, she embraces phenomenological complexity and renders the experiential and agentic textures of existence in aesthetic terms. Her novels' interest is in the concrete thickets of relational interaction where aesthetic form enacts political meaning and political constellations sustain aesthetic processes. Echoes can be heard with Gloria Anzaldúa's (1999 [1987], 19, 68–73, 101–3; 2015, 17–22) and María Lugones's (2003, 1–3, 13) figurations of the contradictory pulls and intimacies of day-to-day life. Neon and silk, house and street, light and plaza proffer material, affective, and imaginative potentialities. These items are co-creators in the social and political project her female protagonists take on.

The notion of aesthetic publicness suggests an important insight into present-day constellations of authoritarian politics, economic rationality, and content-induced experiential rushes. It furnishes an aesthetic retort to an influential philosophical conception of totalitarianism. In her reflections on 1930s Europe, Hannah Arendt singles out "homelessness on an unprecedented scale, rootlessness to an unprecedented depth" as elements of an affective and existential breeding ground for totalitarianism (2024, xi–xii). Indeed, for Arendt, endemic loneliness, which dissolves feelings of belonging to the world and ruptures a sense of "worldly reality," rendered vast portions of the populace vulnerable to totalitarian control (512–17; 1998, 57–59; 2005, 336–38, 244, 356–60). In her view, the severing of common and shared orientations toward the world, aggravated by widespread feelings of hopelessness and uncertainty, readied masses of people for totalitarian domination.

A spirited sense of aesthetic connectedness provides an antidote to a loss of worldly bondedness. If the marketplace covets totalitarian control over the culture and dictatorial movements coupled with extractivist policies aim to enhance their economic leverage, aesthetic desire and sensibility lend themselves to different types of social and material affiliation. Aesthetic imaginaries of public belonging, both local and global, can touch us in our innermost wishes. Stirring neglected hankerings, they can kindle dormant capacities for care. Where repression and self-abnegation curtail play, newly aroused longings can expand its scope. By awakening unsuspected regions of concern and playfulness, we can fortify our collective world and inoculate it against the authoritarian exploitation of human needs and fears.[53]

Substantive participation in aesthetic publicness, prized loose from traditionally gendered and racialized antitheses of public and private, thus becomes an answer to a marketplace in the grip of totalitarian aspirations. An inventive inhabitation of aesthetic publicness conjoined with an exuberant and daring aesthetic imaginary of belonging forges a necessary counterweight to authoritarian, neoliberal governance models launched by Pinochet's Chile and promulgated across the world ever since. It shields us against the narratives and phantom images favored by autocrats.

Eltit scrutinizes the place of Latin America in a global, technologically driven economy through a feminist lens. She rethinks home and public in a single gesture. Her twins hold the fate of the home. "[W]e will inherit the severity of the walls and the cracks of family guilt," says the twin sister (105). The duo experiences the loneliness of a double abandonment: the desertion of the home by the family and the elusiveness of a socialist vision of solidarity, a "brotherhood" (106). The silk and the shiny neon bands adorning their bodies, gilding their play, and embellishing their fantasies of the house are ciphers of alternative social and political performances. These images communicate at the level of aesthetic publicness because they are part of a web of relationships among humans, among objects, among more than human beings, among places, and among all of these different entities that stretches well beyond the house and its current and previous occupants. Silk and neon channel movements between interiority, both psychic and domestic, and exteriority, both relationally figured and public. They pick up on the light that we can ponder in the company of numerous historical writers and thinkers. They resonate with the dirt and mud that the twin sister at one point may have spread through the house, as a dream vision suggests, and that became stuck under her fingernails (57–58).[54] Silk and neon offer an alternative to the aura of the nation that seeks to bolster its might, its fame. This aura, which, according to the twin brother, pervades the city, resembles "a phosphorescent skull that emits fine, almost imperceptible rays." It encompasses "a large space for death" (93). Conversant with life's terrible sides, neon, silk, and light thus steer away from idealizations. Our play with aesthetic figures is a carrier of a historical consciousness that preserves contact with politically inflicted pain and violence.

Engaging richly interlaced materials and tropes, the twins engender an aesthetic world. They rework local and global history. Eltit points her readers to the manifold powers of aesthetic form and design. In our literary and philosophical readings as well as other creative and productive endeavors, we enact these aesthetic potentialities. This means that content is ours to make. And it is ours to receive, process, digest, distribute, and regulate. It likewise falls to us to fashion content's links to schemas such as the nation and democracy and to give shape to the ways it ties into modes of public participation. Our hands may be "terribly constrained," but there are many of them. We can "extend" them to each other "con el corazón con razón en la mano" (with a reasoned heart in hand), as Anzaldúa urges (2015, 20). These hands have plenty of materials to work with: ample grit and resolve to contribute to the dialogical and coalitional tapestry highlighted in Latinx feminist thought. Aesthetic sensibility and play are buoyant cultural capabilities and critical resources. Everyday objects as well as public things are aesthetic productions. Democracy's destiny, thus, is an aesthetic fate. The generativity of storytelling hinges on aesthetic readings. Let's be alert to the vital powers of our aesthetic agency, lest we give these proclivities over to market forces and the ruthless authoritarian impulses that are clamoring to absorb them.

Conclusion

Singing Unsung Stories, Pivoting Positionalities

In the foregoing chapters, I tracked the production of aesthetic publicness through strange taste. Upending existing sensibilities while participating in their formal, material, and conceptual affordances, strangeness animates feminist social visions and democratizing political stances. Spurred by Jorge Luis Borges's perplexities, I have explored this public turn and strategy from four angles: play and disinterest; poverty and aesthetic exclusion; colonialist and historical effacement; and a technologically ruled, market-based overtaking of publicness. Throughout, strangeness flips and reinvents public frames. Strange taste and aesthetic publicness make up present-day critical modes of making and remaking, reading and rereading, encounter and reencounter. They are junctures in a decolonial feminist aesthetics. In their capacity as historically emergent, experiential, and evaluative dispositions, taste and aesthetic sensibility forge trajectories of cultural agency. Aesthetic publicness, first theorized by the Enlightenment and subsequently reimagined by Gloria Anzaldúa, Stuart Hall, Jean Franco, Nelly Richard, and Coco Fusco, along with the creators in this book's archive, remains an enduringly generative phenomenon. It marks the ways in which aesthetic practices index public domains and summon publicness as a ground for dynamics of normativity and relationality. In this field, the strange exercises its distinctive logic as an aesthetic category—a category of feeling, perceiving, imagining, and becoming—tailored to a changing world.

Anzaldúa comprehends strange taste as a part of an experientially attuned perceptual capacity, la facultad, which gives Latinx queer women and other minoritized people a sharp awareness of their social environments. Aesthetics and politics come together in these subjects' liminal activities and their practices of solidarity and coalition making (Anzaldúa 1999 [1987], 88; 2002; 2015, 53–54). This convergence marks also the geography of strange taste, which is forged by symbolically intricate diasporic entanglements and disparities and densely layered power imbalances. Indeed, by creating, performing, and redefining the strange, Latin American and Latinx writers and artists shed new light on the intersection of aesthetics and politics, giving an anarchic spin to philosophical concepts such as disinterest.

The conclusion distills implications for the notion of the strange and presents a final twist in the argument: By examining two stories by Julio Cortázar that have briefly surfaced in chapters 1 and 4 alongside two poems by Alicia Borinsky from *Frivolous Women* (2009), in addition to those read in chapter 1, I unearth a remarkable connection among strange taste, disinterest, and aesthetic publicness. Play, which has appeared throughout these pages, comes again into focus. In ending, I broaden our institutional frames: Several contemporary visual artworks signal new permutations in the entwinements of strange taste and the public.

The Strange as an Aesthetic Category

The strange is an aesthetic category on par with beauty and the sublime, which, as Borges shows, can hide the strange to the point of making it unrecognizable. Like other aesthetic categories, strangeness hinges on a form of encounter. The encounter is one between a perceiver and material qualities that, while response-dependent and normatively laden, have a footing in objects (Hume 1998e; Ngai 2012; Sibley 1959). The scene of encounter relies on reciprocal modes of address: From the angle of the subject, the relevant qualities are marked by the modes of address and experience that the perceiver assumes toward the object in a given context. These modes include forms of reading and valorization. They are typically multimodal in the sense that they involve a variety of sensory and bodily registers. From the angle of the object, the relevant qualities are marked by the modes of address that it, in the given context, directs at the subject.[1] As an aesthetic concept, the strange indexes a perceptual, imaginative, cognitive, and affective responsiveness that hooks into qualities that are often experienced as belonging to objects. Perceptions and feelings of strangeness have an evaluative facet: They partake of aesthetic normativity. The evaluative element of the experience of the strange can go various ways in the sense that it can encode what are seen as positive as well as negative valorizations and, crucially, express both at the same time. This ambivalence marks many kinds of aesthetic categories and the experiences they channel and inform (Ngai 2012; Roelofs 2014).

Inciting puzzlement, if not bewilderment, the strange provokes questions such as: Where does it come from? What is it about? Where is it going? Keeping the answers open, it sets off a search for meaning. We speculate. We venture framings. We keep contemplating. We weave our own feelings and positionalities into the musings: What is happening to me? What is my role? A back and forth ensues between self and world. Am I strange or is this object strange? If the latter, does that render me strange, too? We question self, other, and institutional and cultural schemas, including frames of public aesthetic interaction. Experiences of strangeness thus lend their condensed interpretive energies to institutions and cultures. The strange upholds a contemplative toggling between singular experiential moments and societal structures, suspending already reaped insights and given positionalities.

To achieve its perplexities, the strange depends on what the subject experiences as ordinary, and what—driven by corporeal habits and lived histories or in the whim of the moment—strikes her as surprising or unexpected. This dissonance resonates affectively. It occasions feelings of the peculiar or odd. It reverberates in aversions and shimmers of loathing, in longings and tinges of joyful bliss. The strange carries comparisons that register in the content and the phenomenal characteristics of the experience. One senses a contrast, an incongruity. There is a feeling of relative difference, relative alterity. This relativity is in motion. It develops, depending on the subject's reference points, which are contingent on epistemic and corporeal positionality. Because these reference points shift during the strangeness experience, the strange is neither stable nor writ in stone. Further reflection on items that are found to be strange and further experiential palpation and feeling of the quality of strangeness can induce altered states of sensibility, where strangeness loses its charge, dissipates, or, for that, matter intensifies. A sense of strangeness often expands into an atmosphere that settles in a place. Or it lodges in uncertain and shifting divides between the normal and foreign, belonging and the alien, as Anzaldúa suggests (1999 [1987], 19; 2015, 55–57). The strange, thus, emphatically is not what is generally found to be strange. By contrast, it involves an in-the-moment, present-to-encounter singularity that philosophers of taste, notably Immanuel Kant, have historically associated with aesthetic experience. Strangeness is a quality that we can catch in its movements by following our sensibilities and inviting them into our reflections.

As an aesthetic quality, the strange belongs neither solely to the object of perception nor to the perceiving subject. In virtue of its specific content, its inherent element of disparity between the usual and unusual, the strange renders acute the question of how things are on each of its constitutive sides—that of the subject and the object. Thus, we experience the strange at the level of splits as well as intimacies between subject and object, self and other, the known and unknown, interiority and exteriority. In strangeness's grip, we traverse this zone of relays and emerging and slipping distinctions. Eve Kosofsky Sedgwick describes this territory in terms of an "across." We might add the "trans." The strange supports a veering "across" and the winding of the "trans": It produces liminal swerves. It imparts its directions and indirections to the field of embodied becoming in-between-and-with-others theorized by scholars such as Anzaldúa (1999 [1987]), María Lugones (2003), and Mariana Ortega (2016, 2025). Its passages suffuse the relational and coalitional practices theorized in Latinx feminist and queer thought.

A curious, historically conscious reflexivity keeps strangeness from reifying and settling in a commodified armor. Thus, the strange requires attentiveness, work, maintenance, and a readiness to go places. As revealed by Claudia Llosa's protagonist Fausta's embrace of life, traced in chapter 3, it involves a willingness to tune in to one's sensibilities and, more than that, to craft and hone them. In following strangeness, we can let it work its spell on us, having it seep into interpretive, experiential, and action-oriented proclivities.

Even in the direst of circumstances, at times of terrible loss, something strange, such as the absence of a potato plant from a garden or some colorful pieces of glass, may catch our attention, elicit a touch of curiosity, and engender further perceptions of strangeness. We may attain a transformed sense of the ordinary. The strange can crack a shell of detachment that encapsulates grief or longing and reawaken the ability to form attachments and affiliations. There are many other ways in which strangeness can modulate our sense of the ordinary and outlandish and get us to encounter ourselves anew on shifting terrain. The aesthetic category of the strange lends itself to the development of a stance toward a changing world—a world that threatens to cut away the social setting and physical or ecological ground we took to hold us up. It signals a form of connectedness across felt distances, including terrifying abysses. A sense of strangeness provides us with modes of experiencing transmuting situations and holding in awareness contradictions, gaps, and rifts, whether with fondness, reluctance, or other kinds of tonalities. Becoming strange can be a way of becoming ordinary in a world that is shifting. In the process, the strange opens up ways of living with or contesting what counts as ordinary and revising or accommodating what is felt to be unusual.

Strange taste, then, enables us to create places in an unsteady, metamorphosing world. It can help render this mutating world an abode of place making, a site where place is lost and left and where a potential recouping can happen in unforeseen forms. The strange thus yields a resource for the creative practices Lugones associates with hanging out, and Ortega with hometactics. The homelessness, rootlessness, and faltering relationality that Hannah Arendt discerns are part of the process of place making but, as she contends, are never the whole because new beginnings, new in-betweens, can arise (2024, 517–18). I am reminded of the frivolous poet's pirouettes in the storm, figured by Borinsky (2009) in "i care for you as if you were my own" and "end of the game" (see chapter 1)—a weather system Arendt invokes in these Benjaminian regions (517). As my readings demonstrate, there is a strangeness we can enter to make different homes, to forge altered roots, to dislodge established aesthetic orders—or, perhaps more minimally, to see and dance anew.

Of course, in addition to sensibility, social positionality is a determining factor of feelings of being in or out of place. But play also has a distinct role in this, for play goes a long way toward developing new strangeness and, hence, toward establishing a new ordinariness or energizing further strangeness. Play jolts sensibility into action. It cajoles it to follow fantasy, to speculate, to invent ways of doing things. Buoyed by aesthetic publicness, alterity can elicit play; play, in turn, can tease out and activate alterities. Meanwhile, the strange is in motion. Criteria of what counts as strange undergo revision. In the plane of feeling, as indicated earlier, the strange then establishes orientations and reorientations between subject and object: Strangeness gives rise to a process of differentiation that modulates self-other boundaries. In Borges's play on an uncanny doubling in "Borges and I," the "I" and its persona occupy this shifty territory. The story infects the reader with the atmosphere of strangeness by getting "I," persona, and reader lost in the attempt to make pivotal distinctions in a zone where these distinctions are being introduced, dissolved, reinstated, and transformed. Publicness, we saw, conditions this zone.

Indeed, the public, as entwined with the aesthetic, is the privileged terrain of the strange. For the strangeness experience, in its perplexity, craves a multiplicity of narrations, perspectives, positionalities, media, and interlocutors held by aesthetic publicness, which can yield parts of a story about the strange that we are telling, and about our—and the world's—place within an encompassing strangeness. In embracing strangeness for what it may be, we desire the public. Our feminist protagonists channel this openness to the public toward the reader. Sparking and connecting with multiplicities, play is a mode of inhabiting this openness.

In an era when commodification routines, information circuits, and performance metrics, as Sianne Ngai (2012, 1, 58, 236–38) demonstrates, confer special pertinence on feelings of the zany, the cute, and the interesting as modes of handling transformed workplaces, human-object relations, and dialogical exchanges, the strange contributes awkward fragilities and powers to our navigation of cultural shifts. It carries the movements of an uncertain, searching aesthetic. The strange is wobbly, delicate, acutely sensitizing, in a way that puts needs and habitual modes of being on the line to the point of calling into question who we are, who we can or might be. It forges not a smooth path "across" places, to return to the preposition through which Sedgwick activates the strange as an impulse of the queer. Jaggedly, teeteringly, the strange queers queering. It runs off course and pushes one over in a way that leaves undecided what the next move will be or if there will even be a next move, rather than stagnation. For Sedgwick, the eddying goes on. But the strange can spell freezing, as it initially does for Fausta. It can occasion a kind of dissolution, reactivity, or rigidification, as in the case of Clarice Lispector's fictional author, who is tripped up by his writing.

Risking states of subjective integrity and intersubjective connectedness with others, the strange moves perilously close to provoking emotions of terror, disgust, shame, or overwhelmingness that shut out or distance alterities. But even here, muted play can spring forth to produce and carry onward a faint strangeness that, triggering further strangeness, reanimates alterity.

The strange shows that the queer is not always "continuing moment, movement, motive—recurrent, eddying, *troublant*," as Sedgwick proposes (2011, 188). Circulations can end up in a knot and become stuck. Churning recurrences can block continuation, inhibit movement, and deplete motive. The troubling can trouble itself into a surge where there is flow but no self any longer that is in flux or struggles with a new strangeness. Tied to the strange, the queer then needs play, labor, love, or plain luck to sustain its queering of polarities of movement and stasis, normalization and alterity. None of these factors keeps Lispector's impoverished aesthetic vanguardist Macabéa alive. Her tragic flaw, as suggested in chapter 2, is her foreclosure of serendipity by way of a princess tale. Fatally, contingency loses its power to speak to her disinterested predilections, whereas Fausta—fortunate for her bonds to sundry fellow community members—warms up to contingency and veers around her stunned terror through muted play. Mutual address between self and world, self and others, persists in her case. In this way, she can let the strange exist and even make it stranger, while Macabéa desperately and vainly attempts to normalize a condition that exceeds her control.

As Macabéa's and Fausta's different fates indicate, the strange is a territory where the queer enacts its vulnerabilities, its opening up and closing off of modes of responsiveness. And as a form of responsiveness, a mode of addressing and being addressed, the strange heightens the potentiality of self-reflexive responses to our own and others' responsiveness, thus introducing additional junctures of mobility and stasis, a further scene of making things strange and ordinary.[2] Meeting the storm with her pirouettes, Borinsky's frivolous poet finds a way to play in the face of threatening devastation. This is also the strategy chosen by Diamela Eltit's characters E. Luminata and the twin sister (see chapter 4). The realm of the strange, for Borinsky and Eltit, is public territory, as I have argued. Play activates the strange as a register of aesthetic publicness, altering responsiveness and shifting the field of people, things, forms, materials, surfaces, narrations, and locations that experience can reach out to during its contingent arising, flow, stabilizations, and stagnations. The strange can animate experience if it doesn't eradicate our capacities for responsiveness and address.

More generally, we see here how the vitality of experience hinges on aesthetic publicness. Experience finds nourishment in the movements between interiority and exteriority, belonging and political agency, interest and disinterest that aesthetic publicness fosters. In these movements, whether incipiently or in a more fully articulated fashion, collective dimensions arise: Aesthetic publicness marks the registers of collectivity that the protagonists who populate these pages inhabit and engender, from specific communities to racialized nations or regions and global frames of attachment and circulation.

Ringing down the curtain on the drama of the normative family conceived as a stand-in for the nation, even for humanity at large, the writers and artists we have followed wield strange taste and devise remarkable kinds of play through which they inflect publicness. They offer works that reflect on their place in a public field, prompting us to rethink this fields' design. The strange yields a public provocation. It challenges us to imagine how public domains and institutions may be aligned with values of justice, equity, and inclusion. It spikes play's imaginative seductions and entrancing sensory meanderings in games that repudiate established familial and societal norms. Our artists and writers use the strange to tell unexpected stories, to design unprecedented aesthetic roles and performances, and to enrich and transform public life: Conditioned by and conditioning cultural productions, aesthetic publicness animates literary and artistic world making.

Public and Play: From Statues to Attitudes

Publicness may be a site of abundant aesthetic potentiality, but what if a girl just wants to read or live a princess tale? What if the ordinary is already more than strange enough?[3] To ponder this question, Borinsky (2009) calls on Cortázar's story "End of the Game," in her poem by the same name, which is dedicated to him. I spend some time with this powerful story, for it intertwines play and strange taste with publicness in a manner that bears on the potentialities of female aesthetic agency in the interval between beginnings and endings.

The game in question is called "Statues and Attitudes." The players are three sisters: Holanda, Letitia, and an unnamed narrator. While drying the dishes after lunch, Holanda and the narrator raise a ruckus so the three of them can leave the house for the train tracks down by the river. Once they get beyond the lemon tree and reach public territory by the willows on the other side of the white gate, they are free. They roam the "kingdom" of play (Cortázar 1967d, 137). Lots are drawn. When the game asks for Statues, the winner is decorated with ornaments chosen by her two sisters so she can strike a pose as, say, "Venus de Nilo" (*sic*), "The Ballerina," or a "Chinese Princess" (141, 143). Attitudes, such as "Charity," "Spite and Jealousy," or "Reproach and Robbery," can dispense with ornaments, but necessitate much "expressiveness" (139, 141). The lucky sister, who sometimes is the unlucky one, for Statues are occasionally "horrible failures" (139), poses for the audience on the train. The other two performers gauge the public's reactions. The hope is that some passengers attend the English school.

One day, a young man sits at the window to enjoy the spectacle. The end of the game is augured when he drops a poorly written note for the threesome, praising their prettiness. The writing style is definitely not English school material, and neither is the grammar. Before long, a note arrives judging Letitia, who suffers from a paralyzing illness, the best of the three. The compliment thrills its beneficiary. Holanda and the narrator let her bask in her glow. When the young man, who goes by the name of Ariel, stops by to say hello a few days later, the latter two have a chat with him. Letitia stays home, for she is not feeling well. Upon her request, Holanda and the narrator pass a letter to the visitor. The day after Letitia's epistolary effort to craft a private line of communication with her admirer, he leans once more out of the train window to look at her. She is a wonderful, "most regal" statue (143), tears running down her face. From now on, the siblings know, the box of ornaments is going to remain shut tight.[4] The three have completed their final performance. The next day, Holanda and the narrator notice that Ariel's usual seat is empty. Grinning at each other "somewhere between relief and being furious" (149), they fancy him riding on the other side of the train.

The story highlights the power and vulnerability of the imagination. Cortázar recognizes the centrality of the audience to the game of representation, narration, and masquerade. Art demands a public and a maker, or group of makers, who take a distance from torpid perceptions of prettiness and slapdash, mechanical beauty judgments. This distance is a necessary condition of aesthetic desire; it is a prerequisite for the spirit of play. Simultaneously, play is thoroughly woven into daily life for the girls. The fireball narrator uses it to cause her mother and aunt to bicker over who gets to do what chores. Surveillance attenuates. Holanda and the narrator throw hot water on the cat to get it to yowl. In the consternation, the three make their exit from the house. They put on a veritable *Tempest*. The mischief is as instrumental as it is fanciful and humorous. Clearly, there is no need that aesthetic distance be pure.[5]

Indeed, because purposefulness and an indeterminacy or absence of purpose typically go together, my argument in this book has often stressed the intertwinements of interest and disinterest. Interest ignites the spirit and gets it to burn in the windswept planes of disinterest. Intrepid disinterest likes to go places where interest flexes its muscle. Spunky, sprightly disinterest piques its own delightful interests when other interests are running the show. Cortázar's story straddles the lines between the two attitudes. He focuses the gaze of aesthetic theory on this stormy territory.

The narrative also contemplates the tumultuous lines between art and life. The only chance that the sisters' game stands to flourish is at a remove from the home, in a zone where social roles loosen; the grip of quotidian identity eases; and pragmatic norms and necessities for the most part fall away. At the same time, customary hierarchies assert themselves by the railroad tracks: Gendered and colonial arrangements and orders of empire, class, and ability make their presence felt. Attitudes allow a remarkable variety, but Statues typically revert to clichéd notions of femininity or female performance, to Orientalist conceptions and Western constructions of canonical art: We meet princesses—Chinese princesses, at that—and dismembered female Greek statues. Why are the Statues standardized while the Attitudes run the whole gamut of feeling? Is art making more like doing Statues or Attitudes? Intriguingly, with a Macabéaesque puff, a touch of the Attitude of Insurgency seems to have passed through the Statues' air of social conformity, wafting through the willows to settle in the botched pronunciation of the Venus de Milo that the girls snuck in, thanks to their aunts' spelling habits. How did the story go on the tangent of right and wrong pronunciations, correct and incorrect spellings? The narrator is writing a story. She epitomizes the figure of the artist.[6] And she is channeling strange tastes. Through the Statues-Attitudes distinction, Cortázar probes the strange from the perspective of the relation between image and expression. The reader wonders, further, how standardization and the singular conspire together in play, in taste, and how this mixture bears on the strange. By virtually slipping the Statues-Attitudes opposition past the reader, Cortázar stresses the precarity and dramatic force of the strange. He intimates that strangeness is at risk of getting quashed even by those who seek it out, those who need it. We notice how fragile strangeness can be. It exercises an almost furtive power. Beauty, as Borges cautioned, needs only to pop up and the strange vanishes.

Apropos the social hierarchies and roles that suffuse the girls' play, Holanda and the narrator are seriously disappointed about Ariel's linguistic fluency and his flimsy handshake, his impassive eyes. As his note foretold, he frequents not the English school but the Industrial High School. The duo pines for a more inspiring audience. The current spectator rigidifies their art: Whatever stirrings it may kindle, Holanda and the narrator remain artistically unmoved by Ariel's presence on the train. Letitia's tight, brittle body epitomizes this stillness, this narrowing. Ariel incites no specific desire to play whatsoever. The nature of aesthetic publicness is in question: Is art really satisfied with a quite abstractly delineated audience—whether universalized or concretely historical—as the Enlightenment conjectured?[7] Or does it want more? The suggestion is that it craves a specific public that is found to be exciting to carry along, to somehow touch, to move someplace. I surmise that the audience that is of interest to Cortázar's dramatic performers—or, more pointedly, of disinterest—must in some sense also hold their interest/disinterest in these creators' actual life: Minimally, the moment of shared engagement must somehow be interesting and simultaneously disinteresting—that is, conducive to disinterest. The question, however, is where the tipping point lies when the fizz goes flat, the charge bleeds off. "End of the Game" teases out these unresolved aspects of performance and publicness and puts them in the balance.

Another set of complexities stems from Letitia's muscular tightening and fatigue. An allegorical reading regards these bodily conditions as symptoms of her efforts at beautification. The project of rendering a character, a type, exacts a price. Certain conventional notions of feminine beauty arguably idolize a body that, in literal and metaphorical terms, can hardly move. These ideals run counter to the imagination. The reach for perfection chooses an idealized, normalized real over fantasy and enforces this preference. For her final performance, Letitia helps herself to her aunt's and her mother's treasured jewelry. The play of ornaments is deemed insufficient. When eroticism and play come apart, the residual no longer entices. Shiny, adult gold is wanted. Play and freedom desert their sovereign province. At this point, the privately and traditionally appealing exercise a more powerful draw than the gambit of public performance and invention.

What is Letitia thinking, who is always reading novels—fantastic Rocambole narratives, at that?[8] What does she find in the stories she consumes day by day, night by night, granted, as the narrator sees it, the prerogative to lounge about as she pleases, to do whatever she wants? Is it all coming down to princess tales? A static, motionless female who takes her lessons from a previous generation that lavishes privileges on her is considered more attractive, more interesting, more generative of disinterest than two live wires. The reader wonders what this says about the notion of the presumptively able or disabled body and about the role of gender and adjacent social categories in spectatorship and artistic creation. The summit of perfection, once again, conceals the strange.

The sisters want a global audience. The public must be riding the train: It should be on the move. The train is a medium for the sisters' performance. It introduces literary innovation to the figure of the aesthetic spectator, converting Ulysses's position of immobilized mobility, his corporeal shielding against the Sirens, into Ariel's static oscillation between rapprochement and flight, progression and repetition. The medium of the train also translates the infamous Three Witches who open Shakespeare's *Macbeth* into the triplet of sisters hovering over the territory among tracks, river, and house. Under the willows extends the girl's dominion. Here, they "spread out upon the world" (137). Their act wildly surpasses the ornamental mode they practice so temptingly. They make theater. They offer prophesies. They instigate crimes.

Like Shakespeare's ghoulishly dressed, wicked schemers and plotters, they boil water and get the cat to yelp. Believe it or not, Letitia sips "special hot broth" at night or really at any moment she wishes (138). The fearsome threesome take their domestic tempest to their hangout by the tracks, shutting the white gate "with a slam like a blast of wind," at which point "it was a freedom which took us by the hands, seized the whole of our bodies and tumbled us out. Then we ran." The storm rages around the willow trees, all right. Inside the house, they had made sure to "get Troy burning" (136).[9] The young terrors are always being warned that they will "end up on the street" (136). This fate, however, seems nothing out of the ordinary to them (138); hence, the prediction fails to impress. Once ignited, the fire burns on. Bubbling, boiling, toil, and trouble spill fast beyond the white gate, engulfing public territory.[10]

No wonder Ariel, that other recoded Shakespeare character, rushes to the opposite window. The girls are putting on technologically mediated art. A random Argentine public won't do: The spectators should be attending English school. Otherwise, how can they engage the Three Witches, these "Weird Sisters," or, as the First Folio edition of *Macbeth* has it, the "Weyward" or "Weyard Sisters" (Shakespeare 2005, 1.3, 4.1)?[11] Strange taste requires literary education or, in its absence, a willingness, a curiosity to play: The public must be open to playing along with the performers. Sheer aesthetic judgment is not play. It even restricts play's radius. Ariel declines to play the game. Evading the three rabble-rousers, these uproarious female Calibans, he terminates his own *Tempest*. He refuses to engage the performance as an orbit of the imagination, a sphere where all sorts of ways of feeling and being become apparent. He balks at the youngsters' fiendish creativity, their aesthetic irreverence, their decolonial rebellion.[12]

Daredevil girls can play princesses, but as soon as an actual amorous scenario infringes on the game, the spell breaks. Disinterest frays. The game is over. This finale is also the end of the story, although the simultaneously relieved and outraged grin on the narrator's and Holanda's faces pronounces any closure to be less final than I am making it out to be here. Their frenzy is unstoppable. Their appetite for the macabre, their demonic relish for subterfuge and chicanery, is not about to be done with in a single blow. This drama demands a vaster aesthetic field where the tragic meets with the comic, fatality with futurity. Aesthetic publicness is art's habitat, the fountain of its play.

The story's compounding endings reemerge in the relation between the frivolous poet's ongoing playacting and the young girl's princess tales in Borinsky's "end of the game." The three youngsters' game demands and produces an expanded and interminable field of aesthetic publicness. Their performance requires a mutuality of play between artist and public in aesthetic creation, participation, and interpretation. Otherwise it ceases. This outcome foreshadows the frivolous poet's continued games.

Before returning to these games I want to pick up the question of feminist agency between beginnings and endings or, perhaps, at points where strange stories, strange tastes have not even begun yet because all a girl wants is a princess tale. Is feminism moot here? How can it begin? Might it, as Lispector suggests, be arriving on the scene with a strangeness rolled out from strange beginnings and endings, ones that are not really beginnings or endings? To reach this possible beginning of feminist agency, we need to go through another Cortázar tale.

Borinsky's poem "end of the game" combines tropes from Cortázar's "End of the Game" with images from that other famous story of his, "House Taken Over." The poem stakes the question of literature's status on the possibilities of female storytelling. But what does this option look like if literature is coming to an end? Cortázar's story toys with this prospect.

"House Taken Over" is set in a large house in Buenos Aires. Its residents are a brother-sister couple who spend their mornings dusting furniture and their afternoons and evenings reading and knitting. On Saturdays, the brother demonstrates his "good taste" by shopping for wool for his sister (Cortázar 1967e [1946], 11). The yarn he brings home is up to her standards. Anxiously awaiting the latest "French literature," he uses the opportunity to satisfy his own tastes, as well, by dropping in at the bookstores (11). Disappointment follows, however: "Nothing worthwhile had arrived in Argentina since 1939" (11). Things get worse. Step by step, the house is requisitioned by unknown occupants, whose actions and purpose make no sense whatsoever to the siblings. The pair vacate the place, upon which the brother throws the house key into the sewer. End of the story.

Again, Cortázar shows himself as the provocative aesthetic theorist he is. The nineteenth-century male reader can no longer serve as the model for literary writing. He is banished by intractable forces. Writing and reading for their own sake—that is, disinterested artistic creation and reception—cannot grasp the heteronomous forces bearing on the vicissitudes and fates of these practices. Faced with the brother's abandonment of the house of literature, the literary enterprise may renew itself or approach its end. It may come upon different strategies of address. The brother's fascination for novelty is not going to be indicative of the new that is yet to emerge. Nothing is as conducive to a fresh beginning as an ending, one might observe.[13] If literature as a whole is not facing its demise, we are, at a minimum, confronting the collapse of literary futures represented by the Europe–Buenos Aires dichotomy. However, any confident, forward-looking take on this temporal organization misses the tale's ominous, uncanny overtones, its resonance with political violence and artistic iconoclasm.[14]

Cortázar offers a literalization of literature's constitutive homelessness, which in this case means that the globe is the limit; the Western canon loses its domicile, its orientation, its consistency. Literature is riddled by opaque, sinister presences. At the same time, literary history and reading refuse to pass on the key to new writers, different readers. Literature demands aesthetic publicness over and above the space of the house that might hold these figures' reading or writing. In a last-ditch effort to salvage his legacy, the brother takes recourse to the sewer. Disposing of the key is the siblings' final hope of preserving the house in a prim state following their departure. In this way, books and knitting will remain in place, safe from petty thieves. External interlopers seem easier to handle than the ones on the inside. Art's proper place is the city streets, a conception that is vintage Cortázar and to which Eltit's twin sister would be more than happy to assent.[15] Agreement rings also from the three demons of "End of the Game," who welcome their destiny in the streets, as the narrator notes in so many words. From the perspective of aesthetic publicness, Cortázar intimates, home and sewer gain equal standing. They are both conditioning forces of the literary enterprise. Indeed, just as Rocambole failed Letitia, the brother's aesthetic education is at a loss when it comes to interpreting these forces. Reading stumbles on its limits. Aesthetic publicness, however, is the terrain where things are happening. The meeting points between the reader *of* the story and the reader *in* the story and between the story's public and the text uphold the frames where reading can reanimate itself outside the casing of the canonical house of literature and the colonialist taste ruling there.

Perhaps the brother has taken to writing in the medium of the sewer. The sewer might end in the Palermo "stretch of coffee-and-cream river" that constitutes the territory of the three sisters' strange tastes (Cortázar 1967d, 137). Things have a way of coming together, and the color has to originate somewhere. Although Cortázar, throughout his writings, overthrows gender delineations in favor of a relational conception of subjectivity, his privileged reader in "House Taken Over," as in many of his other stories and his novels, may well be male. The brother may find an eerie double in his own sister, a twentieth-century Penelope whose ostensibly interminable knitting steers clear of any novelty. But, as we already saw in "End of the Game," even Letitia has been reading up a storm, and perhaps Cortázar's favorite players and artists, at least sometimes, happen to be female.[16] Another literary character, the frivolous poet, has taken note.

Exquisite rummager among leftover objects and substances that she is, frequenter of places that others have left, forgotten, or deemed unworthy, Borinsky's narrator, in "end or the game," recovers the discarded item from the sewer—the frivolous poet, turned evil stepmother, presents the forlorn girl with the key to her cell. The young woman is at liberty to use it as she pleases: to imprison or free herself.

Whichever way the girl chooses—whether she locks herself up in prolix narrations heard over and over again or turns the key another way, hoping to start a story that is yet to be written—the frivolous poet herself makes sure to keep playing. The end of the girl's game doesn't betoken the end of the poet's game. Poetry may lie all it wants, as a Platonic voice opines in "on poetry" (Borinsky 2009). It may embroil the narrator in crimes and land her in prison. But, as discussed in chapter 1, this doesn't cause poetry to desist from insolently trying "another carnival" or proposing "escape voyages around the world."[17] Indeed, the movements of aesthetic publicness, the poem reveals, "send us to another world." What is this other world?

Making and Moving Between Different Worlds: Disinterest and the Strange

Borinsky's poems about reading and writing and her works about erotically poignant encounters, which are often the very same pieces, leave little doubt: The world as we presume to know it is surrounded by an aura of possibilities beyond the ordinary. Disinterested play enlists the imagination in tracing out this simultaneously worldly and otherworldly orbit. Freeing up alternative societal constellations, literary writing and other forms of creation catapult us toward hitherto unenvisaged worlds.

To get a better grasp of the public inhabitance that is so crucial to the poetic venture, we need to look more closely at the slippery language of worlds and world making, for the lines between actual and imaginary or projected worlds are somewhat diffuse—yet, for that matter, not unimportant. Cortázar remains on the philosophical scene with another story, "Continuity of Parks," where the nineteenth-century reader is beheaded in the course of the very tale he is reading. He brings his own tragic fate steadily closer with each word he peruses until, well, the knife slashes at the end (Cortázar 1967c). If the dissolution of the boundaries between the reader's and character's fictional worlds is an effective way of disrupting an absorbed reading for alternate worlds and probing the power of aesthetic appearance and figuration, then this also goes for the assertion of said boundaries, as another Borinsky poem, "visitas médicas / visits to the doctor" (2009, 146–49), indicates. In either case, these frames and the worlds they delineate and set off from each other cannot be taken at face value. For this is to reduce the force of the strange.

The protagonist of "visits to the doctor" consults with her physician about a madness ailing her. The madness consists of her evasion of regular reproductive scripts. It is a matter of her fondness for "seducing keeping the / situation beyond the range of calendars inventing babies." The protagonist dislikes time schedules that regulate the production of offspring. She prefers "nurturing enormous solitary terrains gardens / where her sorcery is unique deserts of aromas." And she has a fondness for "Carnivals without disguises," whose earth-shattering, enigmatic imprint on the heart will manifest itself only centuries later in the form of erotic affections that take the breath away, sweeping up life's familiar outlines. The strange is having a ball. The protagonist's desire is powerful. The usual modesty she witnesses in her surroundings does not satisfy. Her longing goes out to scenes beyond the familiar palate of measured pleasures and predictable transgressions:

she'd like to crumple it all together make it into a shirt
she would wear it during Carnival with polka dots
she will dance in this world and you
will keep on saying she lives in another

The other world to which poetry and dance send us will also be this one. Strange taste has been planning the next act; the dance is going to happen. There is travel from world to world. Disinterested play partakes of either of these worlds. The game goes on, outside the sphere of the regular couple and family, beyond known scripts of love and romance. The distance between worlds is precisely what is necessary, what is productive. Worlds are being made. But the boundaries between them are up to debate, up to reading. Saying too quickly that something belongs to another world rather than the present one is a way to take for granted what is only apparent. It is a way to stay within a conventional narrative about what the world is like. In this fashion, we reinforce received norms. We take a pass on the fury and relief of a good crumpling. We refuse the magic of getting dressed up to do an Attitude (say, Indignation and Escape) or perhaps even a Statue (say, Whispering Witch or Sassy Sorceress). We hold off a game of polka dots. We hem in and confine the strange.

To further reflect on the treacherous tensions and movements between worlds, let's look at the poem "fotografía del matrimonio perfecto / photograph of the perfect couple" (Borinsky 2009, 124–25) Cortázar hasn't entirely left the aesthetic scene because no one is taking any snapshots these days, whether literary or visual, that don't apply a bit of "Blow-Up," especially when the real, the fictional, and the apparent intrude on one another.[18] Borges is around, too, with his uncanny abilities to relieve the strange from its husk of perfection. In the poem, the couple itself, it appears, is responsible for a fusion of the sinister aspect of the Spanish title of Cortázar's story—"Las babas del diablo," which literally means "the devil's drool"—with the explosive inflation expressed by the English title. Having synchronized their behavior into a single unit exemplary of its own "third shared sex," the couple bars the rest of the world from getting through to them, anxious to avoid anything that might expose the pair's nonidentity with each other.

Through the apertures of her camera, Borinsky's narrator, who of necessity has become a photographer—even a spy, owing to the couple's exclusion and mockery of other people—surveys the pair's meticulously orchestrated union. Making a direct address to the couple, she states in her closing stanza:

> As I speak to you my frame invents you
> I threaten new idioms
> A language to exhaust you.

Invention has no patience with a fearful liaison maintained through sameness and merging. A policy of feeding inwardness by warding off "strangers" may guarantee a "voluptuous" selfhood but strangles creativity and growth. This shirking away from the public to find refuge in the private is not to the frivolous poet's liking, just as Cortázar's narrator in "End of the Game" balks at Letitia's choice of a private letter as her preferred form of address to her admirer. Her taste has other aspirations. Once more, poetry and other arts crave aesthetic publicness. The photographer-poet throws herself into it. Witnessing clandestinely, her technologically mediated gaze cuts through insulated, solidified, self-consistent sensibilities. Her words, her camera, her images will click open the forced ties that hold the couple together. Creativity introduces a novel frame. A world is on the verge of collapse. A new one is about to burst forth. Literature borrows lenses and framings from photography to realize scenes where new worlds take off. The verbal snapshot not only rends an idealized, self-enclosed amorous alliance but renews the process of address, of speaking to and with the other, where the production of a static image, an emblem of perfection, had brought it to an end: The frivolous poet employs a frisky Attitude to cast off a Statue's fatal appeal. The strange is in action.

Reading "photograph of the perfect couple" alongside "visits to the doctor," we observe once more the mutually nourishing affiliations between this book's central phenomena: strange taste and aesthetic publicness. Taste wants the strange; it seeks it out. Moreover, it intends to *be* strange, to *bring* strangeness. Taste can't wait to put its own strangeness to work. The new language of the poet's "photograph" will bust a vocabulary that excludes outsiders, that mocks strangers. Strange taste shatters timeworn circulations between inside and outside. It asserts the very aesthetic publicness in which it can thrive. It designs new worlds.

Juggling opacity and clarity, standardization and singularity, generality and intimacy, strange taste finds its material forms and energies in residual zones of publicness. Chapter 1 shows it in action when the aftermath of the planned performance in Borinsky's poem "the show starts when you arrive" (2009) becomes the theatrical setting for the narrator's disinterested play with dust, cobwebs, scents, and other foragers. These characters are primarily human but possibly also more than human. Relationality welcomes the industrious spider that spins its threads under the chairs, which also signals an opening to the sparrows that are the poet's accomplices in another poem. In collaboration with these creatures and items, the frivolous poet transforms a theater gone dark into a site of perplexing writing that attracts as yet unacquainted interlocutors. We imagine curious personalities and other beings dropping in, beguiled by enigmatic signs and gestures that can come into their own once these characters arrive. New expressive forms see the light. Altered webs of aesthetic relationality emerge. Language, communication, and relationality are under production in a displaced forum for aesthetic creation, a platform that redraws institutional bounds. For, as the theatrical setting reveals, the scene of encounter takes place in an institution. The frivolous poet is adamant about this aspect.

Her entries into different worlds occur in concrete historical spaces of literature, performance, and drama. With her pirouettes she weathers a torrential storm blowing from many corners of the culture, as I have argued. Like the relational idioms of a writing in the dust on the floor of the theater, the gusts of wind that are roaring, and the swivels with which the frivolous poet meets these blasts, trespass inside-outside boundaries. She teams up with Cortázar's three tempestuous players who linger nearby. The four of them find their ends in their games' endlessness. And they intuit infinity in the games' provisionary endings. Analogously to the doubling beginnings and endings of Lispector's *The Hour of the Star*, Borinsky's and Cortázar's beginnings and endings are momentary positions that channel stretches of a stream of life. They are porous, impermanent framings traversed by threads of history.

Strange taste brings its agile sensibilities to the field of aesthetic relationality. It is a wellspring of emerging relational forms. Partaking of structures of aesthetic publicness, strange taste feeds and transforms institutionalized patterns of aesthetic relationality. Borinsky's repeated turns to public arenas and aesthetic institutions make this clear.

At the same time, strange taste encounters and draws on historical, structural entanglements between existent tastes and publicness, and between empowered or marginalized tastes and institutionality. What does this imply for the games we play? This question brings us back to Lispector's novel and Claudia Llosa's film and their struggles with old stories. The next two sections briefly revisit these artists' figurations of disinterest and strange taste to uncover remarkable linkages that tie these notions to each other and to aesthetic publicness.

Disinterest as a Lever of Space and Time

In *The Hour of the Star*, recall, Rodrigo and Macabéa struggle over the game they are playing together. Who sets the rules? Although Rodrigo stretches himself beyond his habitual writerly routines, he ultimately wants to play his preferred game. He exercises authorial privilege. As it happens, the games that he and his character are fond of playing resemble each other in many respects, leading him to imagine that the duo are on the same page regarding their aesthetic loves and likes. However, upon visiting the fortune teller, that other narrative strategist, Macabéa changes games. She switches playmates. Rodrigo is not amused. He arranges the end of her game. This portends the end of his game, too: The character's perishing betokens her author's death.

Following Macabéa's demise, Rodrigo falls back on traditional sensibilities. His stubborn authorial gambit trips him up, as he anticipated in the dedication to his text. He halfheartedly tries to recover his balance by changing the topic of his narration to the weight of the light and the present moment, which he hails as that special time of the year when one would do well to eat some strawberries. But although others typically rush to his assistance to keep him up, this move is to no avail, like a "whistling in the dark wind," as one of the novel's titles has it. His final attempt to secure his relevance comes to naught. Once he prevails over his character, he reverts to his old *letrado* habits. He slams the door to the lettered city shut in front of the subaltern. A seasoned writer, trained in methods of temporal ordering and evasion alike, he has already prepared his audience for his defection. He places the responsibility for the crisis represented by Macabéa in the reader's court.

When all is said and done, however, both Rodrigo and Macabéa have been playing games of princes and princesses and getting the short end of the stick. His authorial attempt to give the subaltern her due and find a solution for the problem of aestheticized poverty flops. Nonetheless, the novel refuses to accept the lettered city as it is. While portraying Rodrigo as a cultural actor whose métier requires him to put on a life-and-death struggle with an increasing lack of power, credibility, and relevance, and as a critical thinker who had better rethink his literary strategies lest he be trounced by big business, Lispector satirizes his authority, letting the text get the better of him. Faced with his ultimate cold-heartedness, the female author intervenes.

She takes on the white, masculinist, middle-class constellation of aesthetic publicness constituted by the lettered city. Her voice floats into and out of Rodrigo's narration. A haunting presence in the story, she forges her own pact with the reader, undercutting the lettered order and the social constellation it upholds. The device on which this deconstructive gesture hinges, the reader will remember, is disinterest, that venerable Enlightenment asset that the novel sports in so many permutations. Lispector uses disinterest as an aesthetic lever in her contest with literature's thorny embroilment in a class society.

The Hour of the Star features disinterest as a temporal and spatial pivot, a tool through which we can navigate space and time, as I have argued. It is a springboard for the disjunctive temporalities that Macabéa inhabits. It renders her at once superfast and super-slow, both inside and outside modernity. Assuming this paradoxical position, she upends the normalized aesthetic order with her presence. The novel voices a critical perspective on the system of aesthetic relationality made up by the lettered city. While cultural forms are richly exposed in their phenomenological attraction and their socially ambivalent workings, the problem of the aestheticization of poverty persists. Entrenched lettered alignments resist change, thwarting the endeavor to make room for the subaltern. Aesthetic relationality runs into blockages. It is caught in centuries-old constructions that refuse to budge. At this juncture, Lispector makes an appeal on the reader to do their part of the job.

Throughout, the novel engages in a nimble positioning of the reader. The audience is continually framed and reframed. It is getting their arm twisted, cajoled, placed in different roles. Lispector leaves the lettered city in shambles, but her address to the reader suggests a way out. She responds to the calamity that has crushed Macabéa by activating aesthetic publicness as a site where the capacity to feel and think along uncharted lines and the vision to plot a line of action must be developed. Class difference produces a deadlock that the reader is asked to address. However, the devastating exclusion of Macabéa from the world around her and her profound cultural disenfranchisement do not receive a communal response. The resources for this response have yet to be discovered and hammered out. The reader knows that Macabéa's plight is theirs to address, but philosophy and society remain at a loss for a solution. Lispector brings home this awareness. Her novel is a rich account of the powers and limits of the lettered city. It makes a compelling plea for a revised structure of aesthetic publicness. In its outreach to the reader, it underscores obstacles that need to be addressed and points to an avenue of societal engagement along which such an alternative structure might come about. At the same time, different forms of collectivity are not only possible, but also exist. Women actors and their communities have developed other ways to navigate and counter unbridgeable class disparities. Indeed, we have considered modalities of individual and collective agency that skirt around the terrible restrictions that Lispector brings to our attention.

Taking Charge of the Game of Strange Taste

Llosa's film sketches a communal response and an aesthetic imaginary that outstrip Lispector's and her reader's visions of a collective life world. In *The Milk of Sorrow*, the pueblo joven accommodates the powers and needs of strange taste. Reciprocal interactions arise between Fausta and her community. Her strange taste carries historical codings that go back to past terror and resonate simultaneously with sustaining forms of love realized in the wake of these cruel events. Fausta's sensibility nourishes the community. Moreover, it redefines the community. Relationality evolves. There is a gush of shared feeling, shared care, shared quotidian knowledge, and shared joy and suffering in the pueblo joven. No one is unilaterally laying down the law or sacrificing their values. Fausta engages in a process of negotiation with members of her family and community, during which she shapes her individuality and realizes her singular taste. The contingent movements of her sensibility and creativity give her the flexibility and smarts she needs to combine her commitments to her Andean tradition with a concern for cultural memory and the future of the pueblo joven. We witness a vibrant culture that develops life-enhancing institutional practices around the swimming pool, everyday communicative engagements; societal support networks; celebrations; and representations such as photos, TV shows, music, and dance. The community is home to a multivoiced aesthetic.

For the composer Aída, who briefly employs Fausta, images, things, and people occupy a fixed place circumscribed by sharply defined mnemonic bounds. Fausta's leanings are in the opposite direction, as we have seen. Despite her initial timidity and her state of frozenness, she allows people and items to be fluid: She traverses aesthetic territory as an Attitude. She struggles mightily not to be turned into a Statue, someone's static projection, whether the culprit is her mother, her boss, a suitor, the doctor, her uncle, or just any fellow community member who takes her to have lost her soul, true to her namesake. She is set on telling her own story. When the film poster or a mirroring photograph threaten to fasten her likeness in a prefabricated mold, she dodges. Neither the image of her rising up from her mound of potatoes nor that of her sinking down into it does justice to the game of hide-and-seek that she is playing with the viewer. In a similar vein, neither the figure of a militant nor that of a victim captures her agentic and imaginative energies. Her readerly process and learning elude these alternatives. While appearing in ploys of magical realism, syncretism, and transculturation, she eschews settling there. The positionalities others trace out for her misfire or fall short. She follows the impulses of her own aesthetic experience. This experience, grounded in sensibility, formed by taste, carries her. It unfolds in an ever developing, enlarged imaginative sphere.

In the field of aesthetic publicness, "freedom," to borrow once more from Cortázar, catches Fausta's hand, sweeps up her body, and "tumbles" her out of staid narrative frames. Not surprisingly, she deftly avoids encasement in a marital fantasy into which the viewer, prompted by various characters, may try to slot her. Although she remains vulnerable to mockery, vagaries of taste, and economic conjunctures, Fausta orchestrates the game she is playing. She embeds it into her and her community's course of action. Precarity and vulnerability remain her lot, but she widens the orbit of communal existence to make room for her own game. A two-way street binds her to her counterparts in the world of the fiction.

The tight fist clutching her hard-won pearls renders tangible her determination to hold her destiny in her own hands. The precious items will fund the path she has charted, securing her entry into her game. She puts the magisters of the lettered city behind her. While paying respect to entrenched Andean customs, she reworks them in accordance with her sensibility. Strange taste shows the way. And so Fausta joins the party of Eltit's female creators—E. Luminata and the twin sister. Singer, author, and author/performer alike take charge of their game.

In each case, there is a marked difference with *The Hour of the Star*. Trespassing class barriers leads to a dead end in the worlds of Lispector's novel. These crossings operate differently in Llosa's film and Eltit's texts. World traveling at last enables Fausta to honor her connection with her mother and to strengthen her bond with her community. By giving up on her brother's ability to let go of the aspirations he has inherited from his father, and by having him look for his and his society's salvation in a game with light, Eltit's twin sister in one act dismisses his and Rodrigo's—his predecessor's—claims to contemporary authorship. Their status as creative models is a relic from the past. The white hegemonic template of lettered consciousness is proclaimed defunct. At the end of the day, Lispector's and Eltit's male writers and Llosa's female composer refuse to play it strange. They have no interest in carrying the lessons of the strange to their conclusions. They only go so far before calling things off and making themselves scarce. But aesthetic publicness needs the strange. Indeed, strange taste lithely brings disinterest to public inhabitance: Llosa's and Eltit's female protagonists will sing, write, and perform. How does strange taste carry out this job? And what is the significance of this task?

Strange Taste Brings Disinterest into the Public

Strange taste has ways of drawing out the powers of disinterest and directing them to the urgencies of public life. More specifically, its nimble movements can spur disinterest to channel its energies toward the organization of aesthetic publicness. In other words, by enacting strange taste we can activate disinterest's constructive capacities in response to desires and needs we navigate as participants in structures of aesthetic publicness.

Philosophical aesthetics has influentially theorized disinterest as an aesthetic attitude, a mode of comportment borne toward items of culture and nature.[19] This important idea fails to recognize a whole range of operations of disinterest. Taking a page from Cortázar, however, I suggest that strange taste is a powerful component of a generative aesthetic Attitude. This point hints at vital links among three central foci of this investigation: strange taste, disinterest, and aesthetic publicness. These elements enter into flourishing collaborations. They becomes visible when we put together Lispector's in-depth exploration of the myriad facets of disinterest with Llosa's inquiry into communal life. These ostensibly disparate perspectives, each engaging a different cultural moment, have something valuable to offer one another and aesthetic theory: They provide missing links in the theorization of our key concepts. Lispector unveils disinterest's capacities as a temporal and spatial lever. Llosa registers the reciprocal flow between strange taste and a flourishing pueblo joven. When we read these approaches as complementary, a through line emerges: Strange taste puts aesthetic disinterest in action in support of a vibrant communal life. This is an important cultural operation: Strange taste animates the resources of disinterest and makes them available to the concerns that we juggle as participants in public aesthetic existence.

Strange taste is of crucial significance to the workings of disinterest in the literary and cinematic archive I have examined. While disinterest does not always lodge in the designs of strange taste and serves functions that follow different principles, it is significant that it assumes this role in my archive. The vehicle of strange taste gives disinterest the historical anchorage it requires to make its effects in the lives—and often, but not always, the communities—of our female protagonists. Cortázar's stories help to clarify my gist here because they probe conceptual and aesthetic intricacies that we are coming upon:

Ingeniously, his tales drive a wedge between moments when disinterest enjoys the support of strange taste and when it is left to its own devices.

In "End of the Game," Ariel misrecognizes the bold game of strange taste that the three adventuresome teens are playing. As his kneejerk aesthetic judgments demonstrate, he erroneously interprets their splendid performance as just any regular dress-up act. Letting play slip, he comes to notice only a display, responding to a mere masquerade that lends itself to disinterested perception. By placing this literary outsider in the position of the *letrado* heralded by the name "Ariel," Cortázar intimates that neither the lettered city nor its eradication or sidelining are ways to play a game these days. Unassisted by the operations of strange taste, disinterest abides by traditionally gendered and colonial genres of aesthetic relationality. Its relational politics needs reinforcement from the ruses of strange taste. This is in part a matter of strange taste's historical grit, as "House Taken Over" intimates.

The brother and sister in that tale, which is narrated by the former, devote themselves in all tranquility to a practice of disinterested attention that is out of touch with the world. Their disinterested activities hold off history. The brother awaits the arrival of the latest French novels at the Buenos Aires bookstores, although Europe at the time is in the midst of a war. In his perception, time continues as if nothing has happened, yielding, so he hopes, the latest, as it used to, and sending it his way. Global geography, as he imagines it, remains unchanged. He avoids history. For him, literature has severed its connection with the world. This reader has removed the novel's ability to hook into the society and either glide along with it or grate against it. His sister is in an analogous position. She spends her afternoon knitting garments that pile up in cabinets. On occasion, our modern-day Penelope even engages in unknitting. She aims to manipulate time, like her predecessor. While the ancient character sought to control her own and others' futures, however, her contemporary descendant inhabits a timeless present that insulates her from decisive historical events. The two siblings' disinterested practices, the reader will have noticed, follow a logic that aligns them with the father of Eltit's twins. All three represent conventional taste. What is more, the siblings are two antipodes of strange taste: the brother in a masculinized key, the sister in a feminized one. Their disinterest enacts a politics of the apolitical and affirms traditional gender and class arrangements: The man reads, the woman knits; a steady flow of income supports their lifestyle without demanding any exertion on their part. Banished from the house, kicked out of his vast library, the contemporary Ulysses is cast adrift. He first pays a visit to the sewer. His sister vanishes; she is not heard from anymore. Penelope's thread has come undone. Outside the house, she has no existence to speak of. And after ridding himself of his key in the sewer, this is Ulysses's fate, too. The games of literature and fiber art have unraveled. They are over—for the siblings, at least.

Disinterest is a powerful tool through which one can hope to orchestrate time and space. It can be effectively deployed to give these schemata their desired orientations. Enlightenment philosophy did so with huge success when it rendered disinterest the nucleus of a cosmopolitan aesthetic system and constructed a web of global and cross-historical lineages around it. The brother and sister follow suit with a more modest variation. In their early forties, they see their "quiet, simple" companionship as "the indispensable end to a line established in [the] house by [their] grandparents" (Cortázar 1967e [1946], 11). Their disinterested occupations calmly lead the pair to their last moments, which they plan to live out in the house or elsewhere, should they wisely decide to topple it "before it was too late" (11) in the hope of rescuing it from irresponsible developers or money-grabbing cousins. History and futurity, ironically, are, after all, matters of serious concern to brother and sister. In any event, disinterest ensures that things are in place at the apposite time. It is the tool through which they maneuver time and space. The siblings set an instructive example for the reader. The temporal and spatial agenda of disinterested perception, self-governance, and societal regulation may work well for many of us—until that very instant when strange taste ominously enters the scene and gradually takes over, spreading its strangeness all over the place. At that moment, the inside and outside world turn positively uncanny. Were it not for the missing house key, the barrier between domesticity and external reality would already have buckled in the story, and it is far from clear that it will bear up for any stretch of time to speak of, regardless of the siblings' efforts.

Cut loose from the workings of strange taste, disinterest, as we saw in "End of the Game," enforces a traditional cultural politics. As a part of strange taste, disinterest can critically engage history and the present rather than avert its gaze from them and let things carry on as usual. Strange taste can rescue disinterest from the pull of conventional principles and regular, institutionalized procedures bent on assimilating it. It is needed for the continuation of our games. In "House Taken Over," just as in "End of the Game," narrow constructions of disinterest precipitate the disintegration of the games into which these modes insinuate themselves. Strange taste forges a context in which disinterest can shake off traditional forces and constraints and exercise its critical functions. Cortázar's repeated juxtapositions of instances of strange taste that enact disinterest and instances of classical disinterest unaided by strange taste make this clear.[20]

More than a disposition to effect ruptures in existent structures, strange taste is a sensibility. It embodies modes of connecting with the world and sustains openings toward it. These connections and openings reverberate in other sensibilities, which can assume shifting orientations and engender novel linkages. In this respect, strange taste more closely resembles performing Attitudes than mounting Statues. The brother-and-sister couple of "House Taken Over" are participants in a tradition that installs Statues, even monuments. They are attracted to what they understand to be great works and oeuvres. They prefer these canonical achievements to the rest of history. Strange taste forges new openings and modes of connectedness in the relevant material and symbolic lineages. Disinterest relies for its critical effects on this labor of strange taste. It wants Attitude. Strange taste obliges.[21]

At this point, a further philosophical insight comes to light. Disinterest requires strange taste to lend a hand with its relational operations. Left to its own devices, it is inadequate to the potentialities of aesthetic relationality. While it is an ingenious and indispensable constructive device, it has a hard time buffeting institutionalization, normalization, and other forms of cultural control and entrenchment. Although disinterest constitutes a vital means of relational organization and experiential structuring, there are significant stretches of relational engagement where it falls short of the needs, desires, and values that it enables us to navigate. At these junctures, strange taste rushes in with cobwebs, pirouettes, and an ample helping of dust.

Aesthetic relationality, we find, stands in need of strange taste. For disinterest per se, as "House Taken Over" reveals, is at risk of evading earth-shaking currents of societal history and channeling powers that be. But these situations do not make it necessary for disinterest to go at it alone. Strange taste steps up in support of disinterest's distinctive historical orientations, its ties to concrete historical and material conditions. Indeed, strange taste rallies to furnish disinterest with concrete forms of historical traction. A vehicle for disinterest's historical engagements and interventions, strange taste brings its fundamental historicity and its historical imagination to the structures of aesthetic relationality we realize. Wrapped in strange taste, disinterest displays a spunk and bite it otherwise lacks; it has the wherewithal to circumvent traps that, as we saw in several Borinsky poems in chapter 1, threaten to inhibit its movement or to confine it to restrictive trajectories. Strange taste gives a twist to disinterest's relational engagements.

My take on disinterested perception sides in important respects with influential critiques of the phenomenon in its Kantian iterations, among them Theodor Adorno's. The problem with disinterest, however, is not that it turns art into what Adorno, following Hegel's objections to Horace, calls a "pleasant or useful plaything" (1997, 12). Cortázar's brother and sister employ a more complex aesthetic strategy. They wield disinterested attention as a constructive device. For them, it is a temporal and spatial lever through which they give form to their aesthetic experience and lend aesthetic organization to their lives, their world. Disinterest does not limit itself to the level of reified appearance, as Adorno charges, but structures relationality in a manner that invites already existing aesthetic orders to gain the upper hand in the project of construction. Aesthetic relationality is funneled along predetermined paths. Alternative avenues of relationality are closed off. Here the imaginaries and sensibilities embodied in strange taste make their vital difference.

In "photograph of the perfect couple," the frivolous poet snaps open a private world that has closed itself off to outsiders. In other poems, the frivolous poet interrupts and displaces worlds of commodification. Art, for her, analogously to Fausta's song and her young and old companions' dancing in Llosa's film, takes aesthetic publicness as its domicile. In this domain, aesthetic multiplicity and multivoicedness carry the day. Young women, siblings, and authors may be fond of stories of princes and princesses, but aesthetic publicness is the territory where we find the materials from which we can build different tales, and that can inspire us to sing as yet unsung stories. The public, then, is the terrain where all these stories can play out. Clearly, not all narratives attain actual articulation: Many kinds of stories have been silenced, remain of necessity out of public sight, or are yet to be contrived. Nonetheless, aesthetic publicness constitutes a condition of possibility for flourishing patterns of aesthetic creation and relationality. The artworks we have considered in this book mobilize it as such.

All stories, I have pointed out, carry potential shades of meaning that young girls may want to shed or absorb in their games. By giving the girl of "end of the game," who "only wants to play," the key to her cell and usurping the role of the evil stepmother, Borinsky gestures toward the ambivalent seductions of play. One can encase oneself in a familiar game or venture an escape. This is the choice the young girl is facing. It becomes the reader's choice, too. For by drawing her reader into an old fairytale, a veritable princess story, Borinsky enacts the seductions of play in a manner that appoints the reader to the role of the young girl. Confronted with the dilemmas of taste—do we want the regular princess tales or quirky, loony, offbeat narrations?—the reader is offered something else, to boot: Strange taste, as found in "the show starts when you arrive," carries disinterest into a corporeal, site-specific structure of aesthetic publicness. Here bizarro and wacky intimacies can arise among those who feel drawn to unpredictable gestures and aberrant expressions that institute new modes of reading, listening, smelling, and scratching. Strange tastes enter and take up residence in genders, voices, bodies, relationships.

Like the other protagonists we have gotten to know, the frivolous poet is playing disinterested games. These games are central to our characters' stances in the world and to the individual and collective paths of development on which they embark. Throughout, my analysis has emphasized the aesthetic and political importance of disinterested games: The writers and artists in my archive feature them as strategies of a decolonial feminist world making. The playful and inventive labors of strange taste allow disinterest to realize its constructive and deconstructive movements in the public, where it brings into disarray routine alignments of sociality, materiality, and community.

The games I have singled out in my archive may or may not catch on. For Cortázar's demure sibling pair and his impassive Ariel, these unruly ventures are beyond the pale. Their favored genre of disinterested play either flees or wrecks a game of strange taste. Inevitably, strategies of play that artists devise are bound to misfire with certain publics. When we ourselves want to pass up a game or play some different game from the one we're being hailed into, we can recall Borinsky's gift of the key and the apple. What do we do with these items, these repurposed presents that are poison and remedy in one go and that keep being passed on across places and times? What game, if any, do we want to play? It's our call. We live in societies that have institutionalized various types of play. As we all know, there are a lot of prince and princess tales going around. We even have Borinsky and her cast of characters to thank that we're taking part in one right now. The question, then, is: How do we want to engage this scene of established and emerging games, of games of which we are already part and games that are yet to be devised? Laying out pronounced choices in this regard, the literary and cinematic works we have investigated offer us various considerations to go by when assessing our options. One point stands out loudly and clearly: By playing, by engaging in this imaginative practice that meets interest with disinterest and disinterest with interest, we can activate aesthetic potentialities that are responsible for engrossing and rewarding forms of connectedness.

Much has happened in the current princess game that, inspired by our artists, we have been playing. As illustrated by my final remark in the previous paragraph, abstract philosophical reflection has been a vital impulse of these luxuriant movements. This brings me to Mariángeles Soto-Díaz's multimedia installation *Painting with Fire* (2017), which is featured on the cover of this book. In this work, visual abstraction fuels a practice of feminist image making. The protagonist is Disney's first Latina princess, the animated character Elena of Avalor, who starred in an eponymous TV series that ran for three seasons, starting in 2016. Self-standing sculptural structures occupy the corners of a former nursery room in the Schindler House of the MAK Center for Art and Architecture, in West Hollywood, California. Activating one another and the architecture, they create a play of light with translucent vellum, linen, and iridescent fabric. Pink spaces unfurl within and beyond their frames, establishing dialogues with one another. One piece includes a silent video of an abstract performance (5 minutes, 41 seconds long), a still of which is the cover image. Having replaced Elena's magic wand with a metal torch, the artist's gloved hand, shown in close-up, sets alight the princess's castle. The fire eats away at the palace's lilac grid, first gradually, then with full force. Plastic drips down to settle into an amorphous grey mound on the castle's ground floor. Scorched designs that, the video suggests, remain in place when the flames are doused, yield materials for three-dimensional paintings that rise up in the installation space.

Refiguring what Soto-Díaz describes as Elena's "essentialized 'fiery' nature," the strange, humorous video images spark the painterly, sculptural, and architectural forms making up the rest of the installation.[22] The looping sequence propels playful transformations, not only of the princess's bold adventures filling kids' TV screens at the time, but also of those very screens and, by extrapolation, of the gendered, racial, and capitalist structures buttressing a commercial animation show. Rage blazes through the video's radiant hues. The castle's bright, pink, miniature designs hold the viewer's attention while opening out from the specifics of Elena's story onto enlarged categories of being, feeling, power, and knowing. A strange sensibility, quickened by the literal plasticity of the material and by the register of abstraction, prompts questions: In allegorical terms, What is the castle? Is melting an effective way of softening a confining grid, a reductive stereotype, an imposed narrative? What is Elena burning as the protagonist of her counternarrative? How will the detritus of her palace and the fall-out from her action be dealt with? What else needs to happen for her to invent her tale in freedom, to build a more generous and equitable structure, not just for herself but also for other people and for her more than human fellow creatures? The strange keeps us musing on these mysterious questions, which encounter matters of grave public significance with a slightly absurd whimsicality produced through abstraction.

Feminist Reclamations of Aesthetic Publicness

Feminist artists reclaim public space through disinterested play. My juxtaposition of Lugones and Gayatri Spivak with Borinsky reveals that this play is not insulated from gender, class, racial, and colonialist oppression. Moreover, it interweaves disinterest and interest, as I have shown. The girl, after all, wants her princess tales. We want ours, perhaps. But public inhabitance abundantly surpasses these narrations with other stories. The artists and writers discussed in this book are not alone in their pursuit of different narratives. Analogous strategies can be found in the work of other contemporary Latin American and Latinx artists. Across contexts, acts of play create public intimacies that call forth selves and others and that enrich and shape aesthetic relationality and publicness. In this spirit of play, I offer a few examples in a range of media and genres. My first three cases bring out angles of homeplaces left untouched by Cortázar and Borinsky.

The house of the brother and sister in Cortázar's story may be up against strange taste or against an invasion by a sinister military presence, but in Melissa Calderón's embroidered linen *Bronx Housing Court Monster* (2018) (figure C.1), the force that threatens to take over is a public institution and economic system with relentless strictures that favor homeowners' over renters' interests. A couch's unraveling in *Change*, a work in the artist's *My Underemployed Life* series (2023), threatens to take down the whole material support of a domestic lifeworld, if not the house itself. Tropes of fiber art and home in Calderón's linens cast publicness in an atmosphere of precarity engendered by forms of displacement and undoing—at once urban, political, economic, and legal—that differ from what we see in Cortázar.

Consuelo Jimenez Underwood's installation *Undocumented Tortilla Happening* (2015) (figure C.2) dramatizes the utterly public threat of deportation. The threat invades the intimacy of the kitchen. Terrorized, the tortillas fly away from their wire cloth and barbed wire basket, including the last tortilla, which has a protective Virgin of Guadalupe image sewn into it. Aesthetic publicness faces the challenge of providing refuge.

Beatriz Cortez opens the aesthetics of home to temporal and spatial framings that underscore the planetary dimensions of our immediate lifeworlds and expand the historical resonance of places we may regard as home. Her life-size steel sculpture *Stela XX (Absence)* (2024) bears imprints, cracks, and elevated figurations that resonate in multiple registers of time and space. One side represents the ash-covered land following a volcano outburst in the fifth century CE that formed Lake Llopango in El Salvador, where she used to

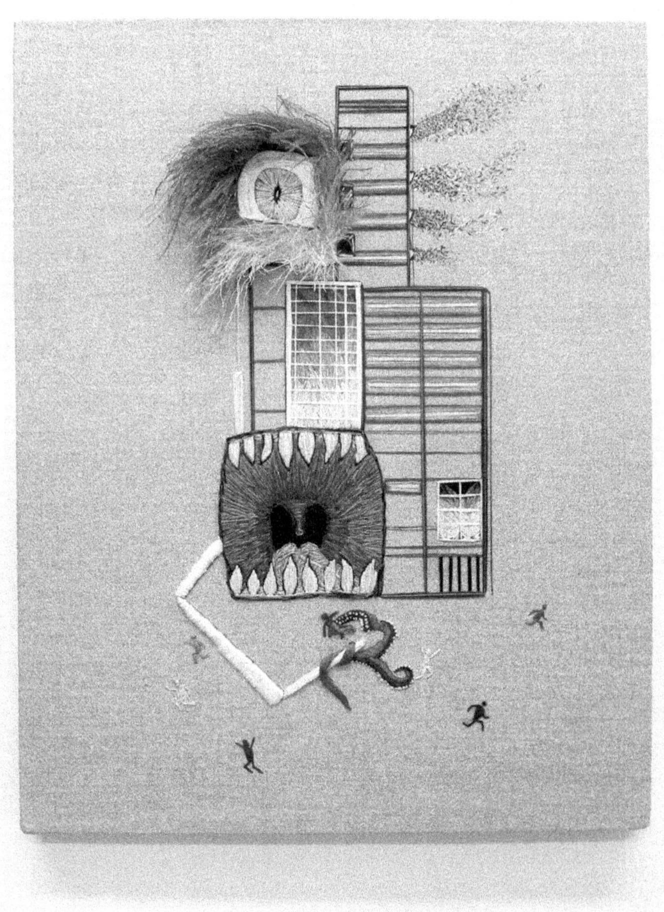

FIGURE C.1. Melissa Calderón, *The Bronx Housing Court Monster*, 2018. Embroidery on linen, 16 × 20 in. Courtesy of the artist.

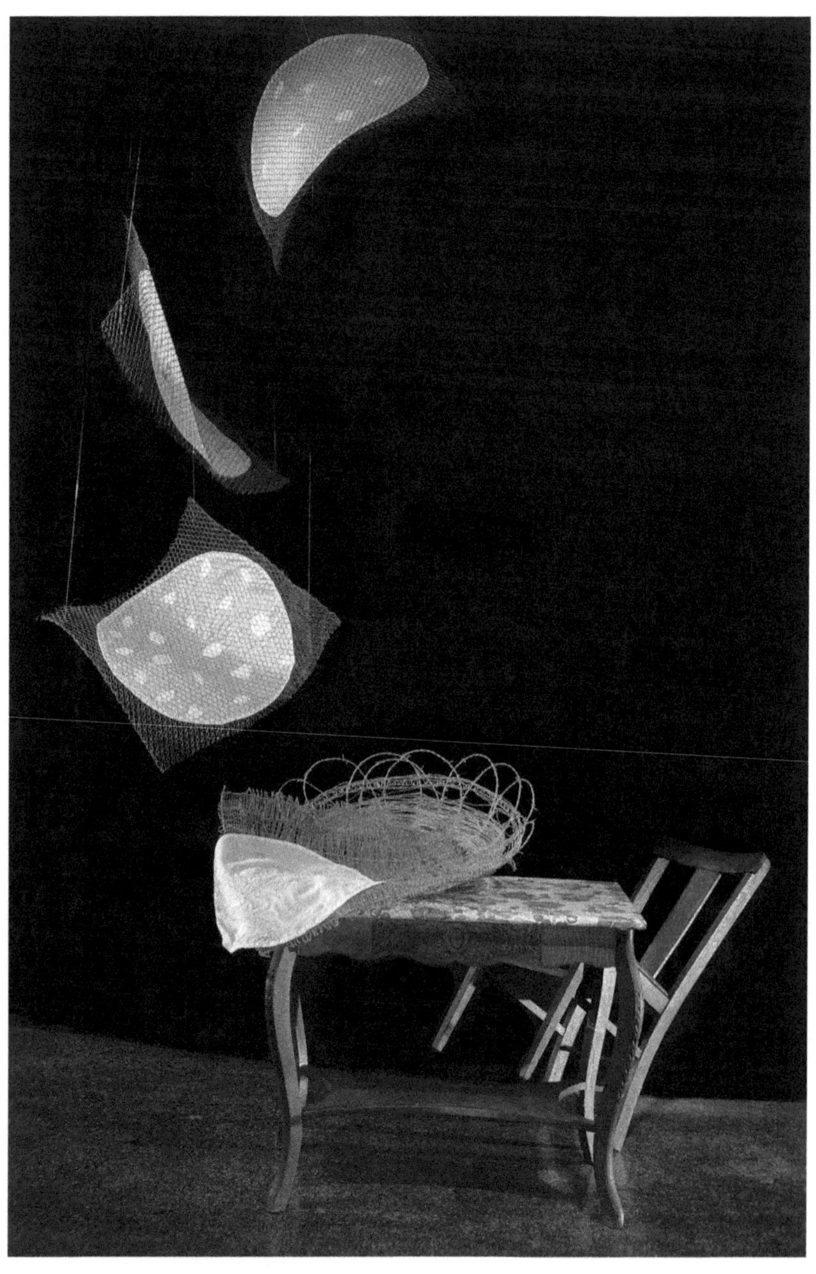

FIGURE C.2. Consuelo Jimenez Underwood, *Undocumented Tortilla Happening*, 2015. Mixed-media installation. ArtRage Gallery, Syracuse, NY. Photograph courtesy of ArtRage Gallery.

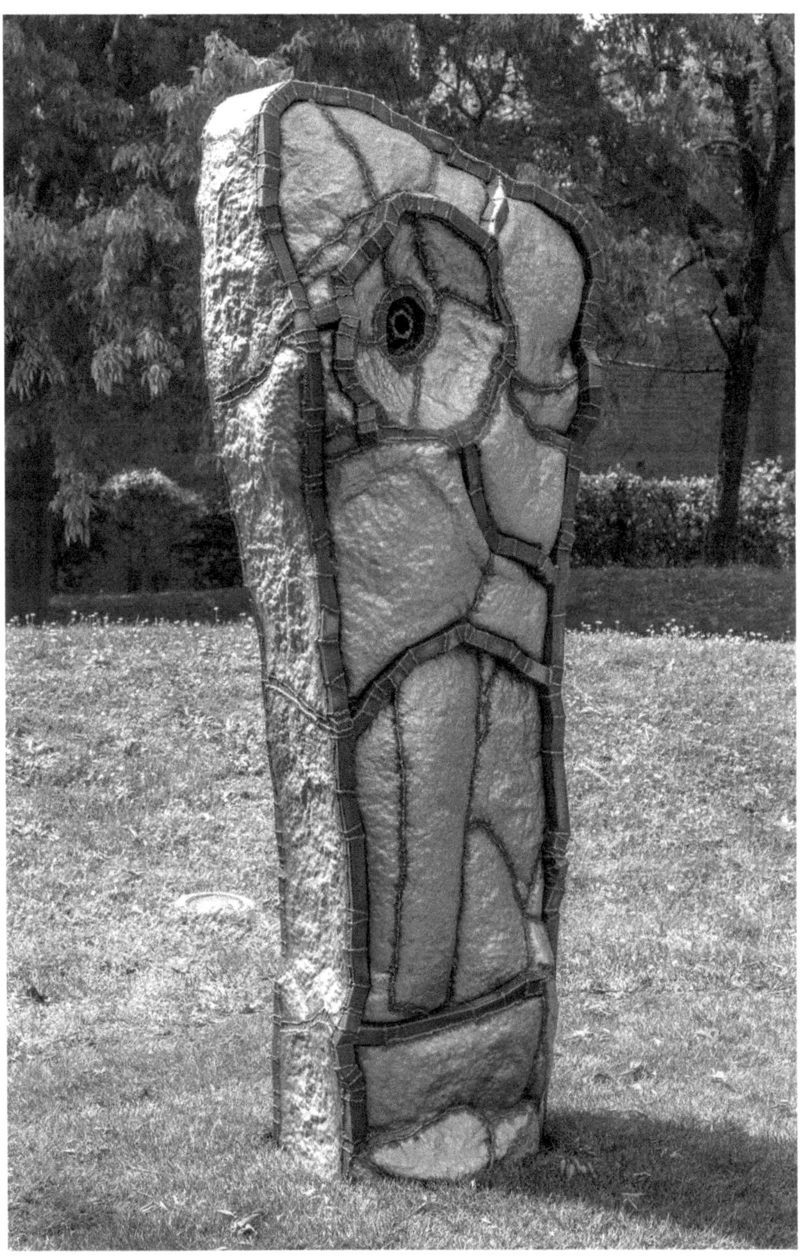

FIGURE C.3. Beatriz Cortez, *Stela XX (Absence)*, 2024. Steel, approx. 96 × 40 × 23.5 in. Installation view, 60th International Art Exhibition, Biennale Arte, Venice, 2024: *Stranieri Ovunque—Foreigners Everywhere*. Photograph by Marco Zorzanello. Courtesy of the artist, Archivio Storico della Biennale di Venezia, Archivio Storico delle Arti Contemporanee (ASAC), and Commonwealth and Council.

swim as a child (figure C.3). The other side depicts various Mesoamerican stelas that were removed from their places of origin for incorporation in Western art museums. Aesthetic publicness encompasses the resulting disjunctive temporal and spatial registers. In a similar vein, the artist's sculpture *Migrante* (2024) reminds the viewer of the fact that the Baja California peninsula was once an ocean. The presence of whale bones on dry land calls to mind the victims not only of the whale trade but also of climate change while resonating with other dead bodies strewn in the borders regions between Mexico and the United States—the bodies of courageous and desperate migrants who risked the perilous voyage north. Aesthetic publicness holds memory, sheltering it as a part of the present.

To spot a point of contrast between different modes of public inhabitance, recall Las Tesis's performance *Un violador en tu camino*. As I pointed out in the introduction, this performance, which occurred in numerous places across the globe, adopts a direct form of address to institutions and authorities. The performance exemplifies the widely acclaimed feminist aesthetic script that purports to expand the public arena to bring to awareness systemically invisibilized realities, needs, and claims. This mode is valorized by feminist critics from Franco to Richard and Fusco. However, formations of aesthetic publicness are complex structures of address between artworks and audiences and among other subjects, objects, and materials. These constellations deploy, bear the marks of, and give rise to a whole array of strategies of address, many of which are quite indirect and follow intricate imaginative and interpretive paths. By exploring an archive that includes but also exceeds direct modes, I have teased out pressures and potentialities that pervade the webs of address that make up systems of aesthetic publicness. Among the relatively indirect strategies, we have encountered modes that enact disinterest and strange taste, registers that thrive on obliqueness. Elements of peculiarity and distance, in these cases, conspire to give pause. A space emerges for curiosity and for avenues of experience and address that detour around expected forms. Artistic strategies that are difficult to make sense of lead us to suspend reading as usual. Regular sensibility is held off. A tension arises between stretches of engagement where meaning emerges and where it disappears or remains as yet ungraspable. The strange thus cracks open spaces where received sensibilities are held at bay to make room for different tastes. My next case follows this involved path.

Eating dirt mixed with salt water in her performance *El peso de la culpa* (*The Burden of Guilt* [1997–99]), Tania Bruguera enacts historicity as a mode of corporeal ingestion and public mourning (figure C.4). Her gesture recalls

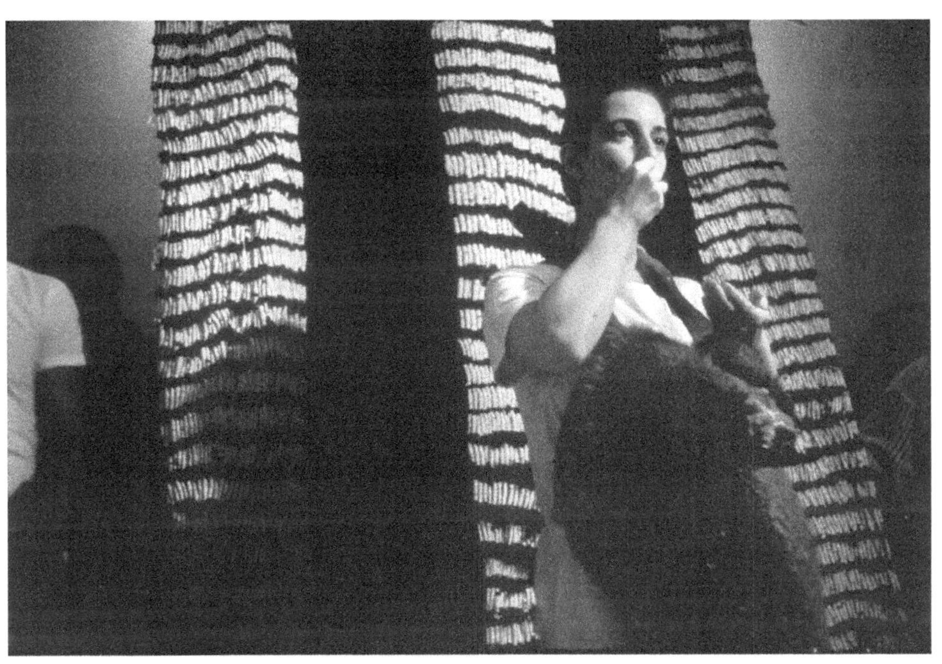

FIGURE C.4. Tania Bruguera, *El peso de la culpa* (*The Burden of Guilt*), 1997–99. Performed in 1997. Decapitated lamb, rope, water, salt, and Cuban flag made out of human hair on fabric. Courtesy of Estudio Bruguera. Photograph by Robert Schweitzer.

the eradication of Native American populations and the effacement of their practices of resistance, which reportedly included the eating of soil. Bruguera corporeally stages this strategy while also alluding to tears of sorrow. A lamb carcass hanging from her neck invokes Afro-Cuban sacrificial customs that, in her reading, "charge [it] with energy" at the same time that it resonates with more generally shared vocabularies of "submission" (Bruguera, quoted in Muñoz 2020, 91). As signaled by a Cuban flag made of human hair, suspended behind her in the 1997 version, the performance embodies its contrastive dimensions of violence, protest, loss, and affective internalization and incorporation into the artist's body, as well as into the broader body politic actualized by the Cuban population within and beyond the nation (Muñoz 2020).

Both Bruguera's performance and Doris Salcedo's sculptural installation *A flor de piel* (2011–12) weave a delicate web of social connections around historical loss and destruction that expands the scope of those whom we publicly honor and mourn. In Salcedo's piece, a membrane of fragile, dark-red rose petals threaded together by hand extends in gentle folds on the gallery floor (figures C.5 and C.6). The petals' branching ribs connote the veins of blood of a disappeared woman. The tapestry's soft waving resonates with the blood flows coursing through existence in the flesh, as if newly animating her life. The finely crafted shroud brings her violent death, the very corporeal, spiritual aliveness that was destroyed, to public consciousness while also communicating protection, dignity, and care and avoiding being overwhelmed by the spectacular. A zone of aesthetic publicness gains in complexity and subtlety. It becomes richer, more humane.

Lucrecia Martel's film *La mujer sin cabeza* (*The Headless Woman* [2008]) starts with the play of Amerindian teens by the roadside (figure C.7). The play is strange: It involves a bicycle that inexplicably—and, to the viewer, invisibly—hangs high on a roadside billboard on which the kids are climbing. One of them is killed, possibly by the eponymous protagonist, but all traces are effaced by her family in a manner that resonates with historical disappearances. Martel's film enlists strange play in an unsettling exploration of the entanglements of interiority, historicity, and the nation. Aesthetic publicness undergoes destabilization. Her TV documentary *Terminal Norte* (*North Terminal* [2021]) features a group of queer and nonbinary female musicians bonding around a house in the country, envisioning this location not as the private domain of the heterosexual family but as the site of an inclusive form of aesthetic publicness that welcomes a pejoratively dismissed strangeness

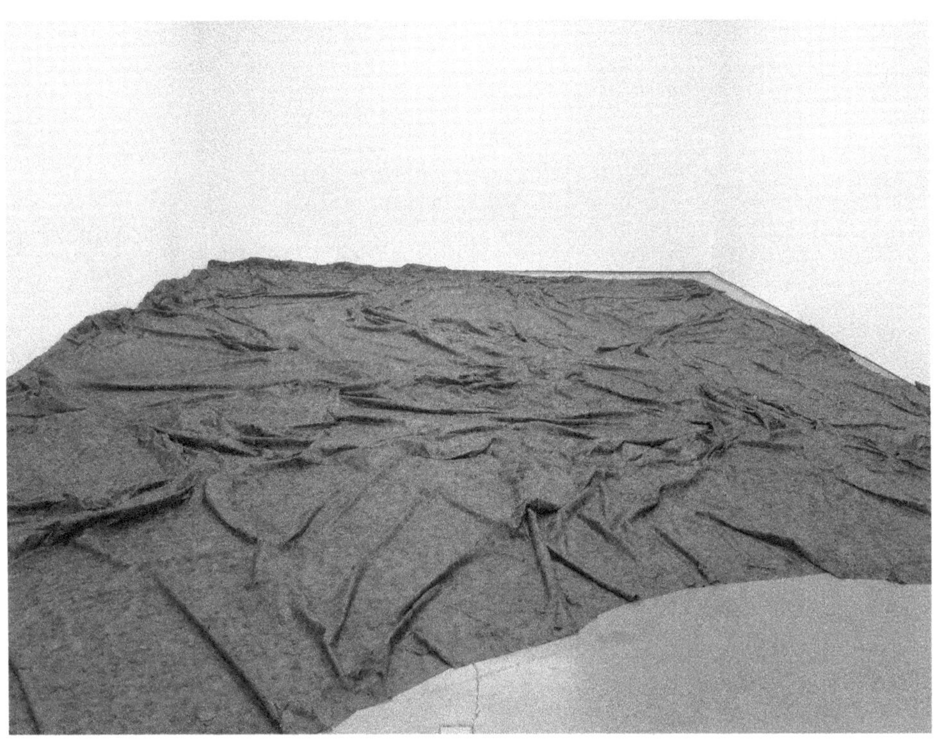

FIGURE C.5. Doris Salcedo, *A flor de piel*, 2011–12. Rose petals and thread, approx. 246⅞ × 433$^{1}/_{16}$ in. (627 × 1,100 cm). © Doris Salcedo. Photograph © White Cube (Ben Westoby).

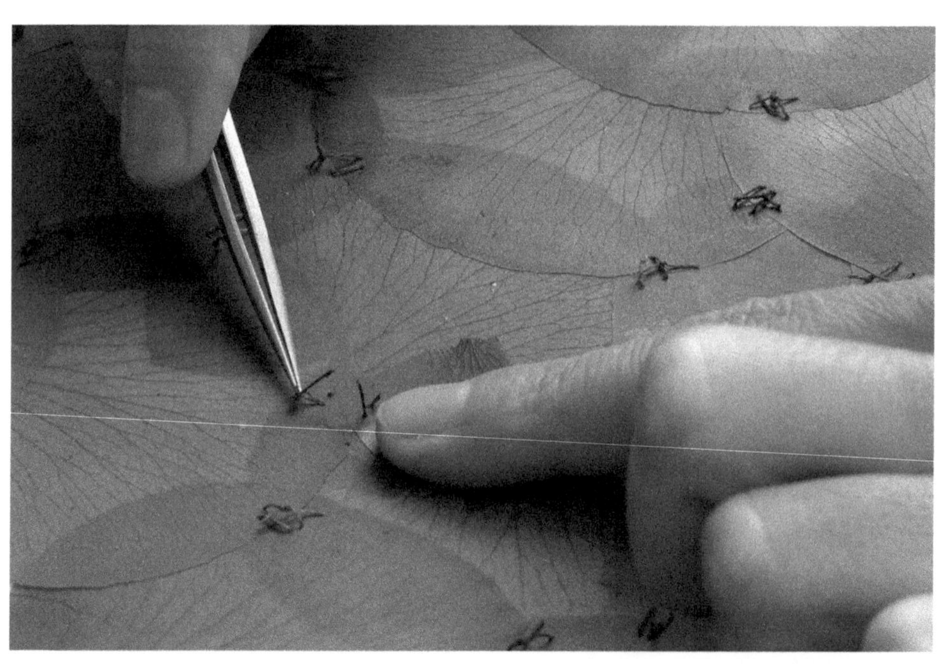

FIGURE C.6. Doris Salcedo, *A flor de piel*, 2011–12. Rose petals and thread, approx. 246⅞ × 433¹⁄₁₆ in. (627 × 1,100 cm) © Doris Salcedo. Photograph © White Cube (Ingrid Raymond).

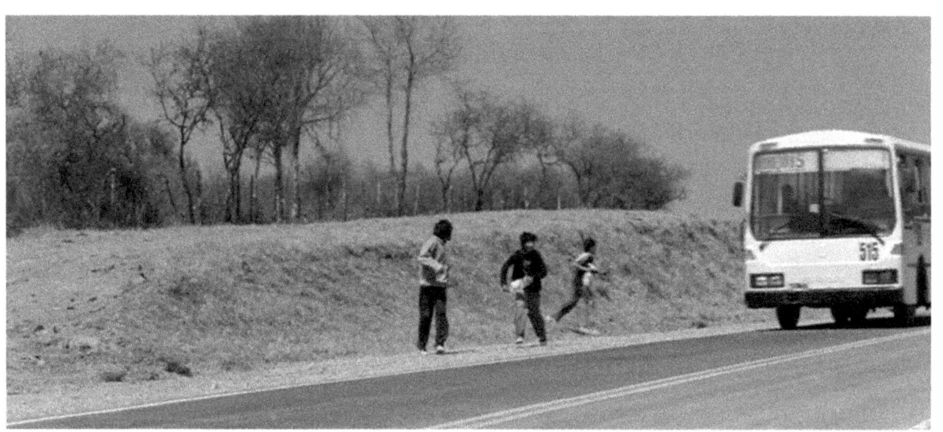

FIGURE C.7. Lucrecia Martel, *La mujer sin cabeza* (*The Headless Woman*), 2008, film still. Three Indigenous teens from a poor neighborhood, two of whom are brothers, play by the side of a road at the start of the film.

into a desirably strange ordinariness, dislodging normalized bounds between the familiar and the strange.

The multimedia artist María Magdalena Campos Pons, likewise, realizes an artistic gathering. Her collaborative performance *When We Gather* (2022), held in the National Gallery in Washington, DC, turns a traditionally white art institution into a forum of aesthetic publicness that consists of a holding environment for the work of women-of-color artists and cultural practitioners (figure C.8). By reconstructing her pioneering installation *El partenón de los libros* (*The Parthenon of Books*) in 2017 at Documenta 14 in Kassel, Germany—which she had originally mounted in Buenos Aires in 1983 in the days following the fall of the Argentine dictatorship—Marta Minujín countered with her monumental structure of banned books collected through worldwide crowdsourcing, a lengthy, ongoing history of state-supported measures to pare down aesthetic publicness to a narrow niche of politically convenient expression (figure C.9). Intervening into a variety of institutional frames—from the public square, democratic culture, the Western art museum, the concert hall, the library, and the milonga to the streets, natural environments, and the nation—feminist artists work to conceptualize spaces of aesthetic publicness as sites of community making and storytelling.

Playing with Dust, Playing with Stars, Inventing Unsung Stories

Aesthetic publicness holds abundant resources—affective, material, and political—that we can draw on to encounter already given games with different games. Entering publicness, our imaginaries and sensibilities can put themselves to work to tell unsung tales. We can sow the seeds of change in established structures of relationality. The institutional gesture is indispensable to a flourishing aesthetic existence. After all, aesthetic relationships and the forms and values they embody require organizational bolstering. They yield wonderfully evanescent moments, but these ephemeral instances emerge in the context of more enduring social and symbolic formations. Orders such as the lettered city and the Enlightenment model of aesthetic publicness and normativity historically have funneled institutional support toward an overly restrictive scope of aesthetic endeavors. These structures need significant overhauling. While aesthetic publicness conditions and shapes aesthetic life, it is and always will be a work in progress. It is a tempestuous setting where traditional patterns meet with emerging structures.

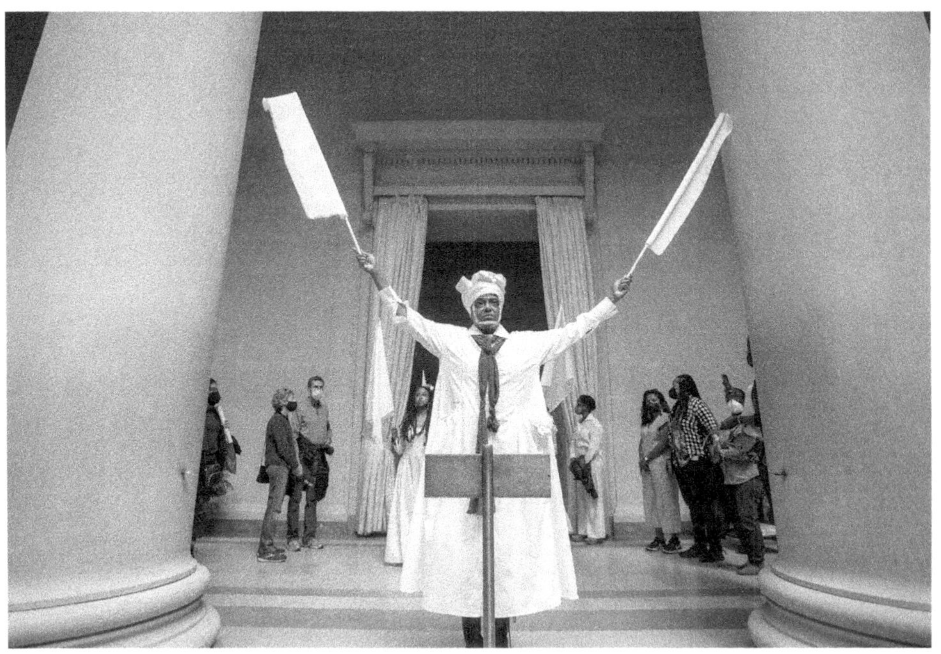

FIGURE C.8. María Magdalena Campos-Pons, *When We Gather*, 2022. Performance documentation, National Gallery, Washington, DC, April 30, 2022. Campos-Pons with Dell Marie Hamilton, Jana Harper, Sue-Ann Letta Forde, Stephanie Mercedes, Helina Metaferia, and Jessica Sandhu. Photograph by Mariah Miranda.

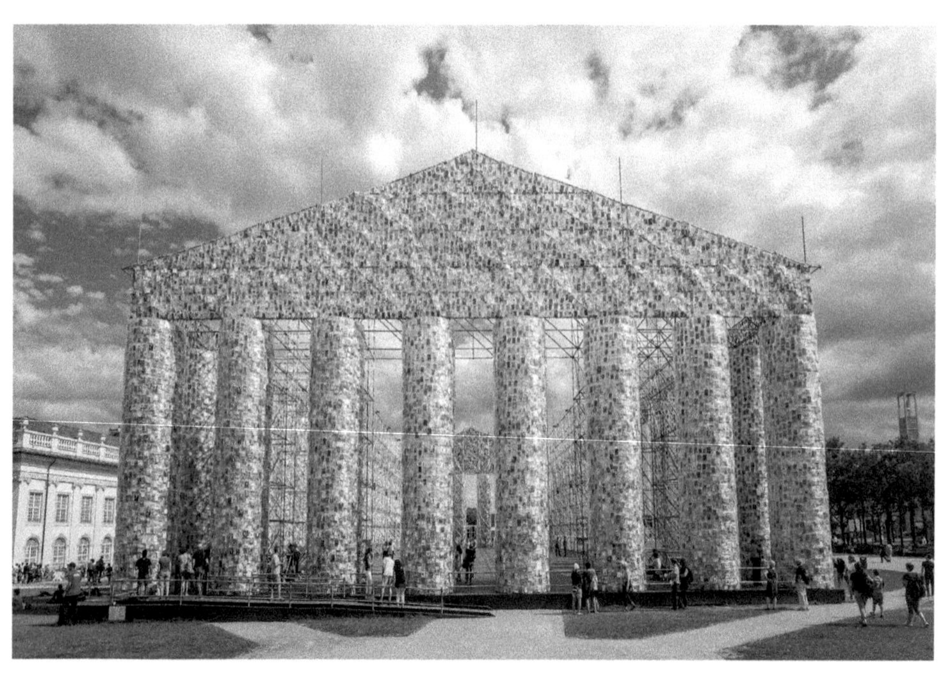

FIGURE C.9. Marta Minujín, *El partenón de los libros* (*The Parthenon of Books*), 2017. Installation view, Friedrichsplatz, Kassel, Germany. Steel, books, and plastic sheeting. © Marta Minujín. Photograph by Mathias Völzke.

By coaxing the reader back into the theater after the performance, by upending the normatively aestheticized social order, by highlighting the dynamism of quotidian life in the pueblo joven, and by reclaiming the public plaza for art and literature, the four artists and writers we have considered insist on the importance of aesthetic publicness. Reading for publicness, accordingly, is a necessary dimension of our participation in decolonial world making and future building. Practices of reading, writing, image making, song, and philosophy share a habit of passing around princess tales. As long as these stories also feature dust, stars, tricks of the light, and spiders, let's be game.

Notes

INTRODUCTION. AESTHETICS, TASTE, AND PUBLIC INHABITANCE

1 A condensed sample of these views includes Dávila 2020; Hall 1996a, 1996b; Levinson 2001, 25–28; Alcoff 2006; Milian 2019; Milian and Romera-Figueroa 2024; Muñoz 1999; Ramírez et al. 2012.

2 Judith Butler (1988, 523, 529–31) and Ellen Rooney (2017, 446) underscore the political project of feminist subject formation. Butler's invocations of theater and play and Rooney's deployment of aesthetic categories signal an aesthetic generativity that must be theorized more fully, an agenda this book aims to advance.

3 For their detailed theorizations of these dimensions, see Anzaldúa 1999 [1987]; Lugones 2003, 2006, 2010; Ortega 2016, 2025.

4 Anzaldúa's critique of dualities (1999 [1987], 68–73) and notions of border crossing and border culture (25–35, 37–45) and Lugones's critique of purity (2003, 121–46) and her decolonial feminist critique of dichotomies (2010, 742) are central here. So are Hall's critiques of cultural purity and binaries (1994, 400; 1996c, 170–71).

5 Like Pérez (2019, 136), I read art as proposing cutting-edge theoretical insights.

6 For a qualified, nonbinary view of publicness, see Lugones (2003, 136–39, 210; 2010, 746). Milian (2019, 11), as already noted, marks the public register of "Latinx." As a relational phenomenon, publicness in my usage is intertwined with interiority. On such entanglements, see Kelly and Roelofs (2024, 12–17).

7 For the notion of multimodal address employed in this book, see Roelofs 2014, 2020.

8 For an approach to the public that acknowledges these dimensions while distinguishing publicness from what falls under the categories of the state, shared space, and the commons, see Honig 2017. On the entanglements of human and ecological forces and conditions, see Connolly 2017.

9 Borges's take on aesthetic publicness invokes the notions of Homer and "the classics" (2000, 6, 14) in a problematic, Eurocentric manner that others African culture and yet pushes back against this move, as I clarify momentarily (see note 11).

10 Since it was Vasco Núñez de Balboa, not Hernán Cortés, who colonized Darién and spotted the Pacific from a mountain peak in 1513, Keats is overlaying different conquistadores.

11 Borges displaces and reconceptualizes traditional views of Homer and "the classics" by extending the scope of beauty well beyond these authors, as we have seen, and by inscribing a strange, "lurking" kind of beauty into their texts (2000, 15). In this way, he attains a self-reflexive stance on the idea of such "great or famous writer[s]" and the Western canon. With his self-displacing invocation of Homer

and "the classics," he then locates himself in a position analogous to Keats's: Both dwell in the strange.

12 On Borges's anticipation of digital forms such as hyperfiction, though not in the present story, see Sassón-Henry 2007.

13 With the proviso that Borges sheds light on the ties between information/ language and identity. My point also needs complication in view of the many figurations of the marketplace pervading his stories. Think, for example, of the stockbroker in Borges 1999b, 232.

14 My approach rests on the shoulders of theorists such as Audre Lorde, Sylvia Wynter, Chela Sandoval, Achille Mbembe, Okwui Enwezor, Anne Anlin Cheng, Gayatri Gopinath, and Denise Ferreira da Silva, among others.

15 See, e.g., Ahmed's take on the prefix (2000, 9–14). While some theorists sharply contrast these approaches (see, e.g., Mignolo 2007, 452), the proposed distinctions are often quite loose and slippery. My primary interest is in forging a conceptual apparatus needed to carry out the necessary critical and constructive work, less in pinpointing the relevant differentiations.

16 For detailed cases, see Roelofs 2014, chaps. 5–6.

17 On this intertwinement, see Gopinath 2018, 8–10, 16–17, 169–70; Alcoff 2020, 18, 26; Mignolo 2012; Wynter 1992.

18 These facets are important to call out here, although they are not all-determining but operate in tandem with registers of clarity, certainty, and determinacy, which also fulfill important functions in a decolonial aesthetics. On the centrality of opacity and uncertainty, see Lugones 2003, 196, 231; 2006; 2010. On the undetermined aspect of border dwelling, see Anzaldúa 1999 [1987], 25. On opacity, see also Glissant 1997.

19 In large outlines, contemporary analytical aesthetics follows on this point in the footsteps of Ted Cohen's (1973, 2018), Arthur Danto's (1998), and Noël Carroll's (2022) reservations about the philosophical significance of taste and their (to my mind, partial) displacements of taste at the level of art criticism and aesthetic experience (see also Horowitz and Huhn on taste in Danto's philosophy [Danto 1998]). Benjamin's critique of the aestheticization of politics has further contributed to taste's dismissal in many strands of continental aesthetics.

20 Jodi Dean underscores the limitations of discursive structures that emerged with the ascendance of the web and networked media. Protecting market principles from political contestation, these communicative formations, she argues, foster a class society and empty out democracy, leaving it in an impasse (2009, 76, 93–94).

21 For a theoretical approach that ascribes a crucial role to sensitivity and the strange in political contexts, see Connolly 2013, 7–11, 50, 133; 2017, 7, 56–57, 61–62. The strange suffuses Walter Benjamin's aesthetics, limning the aura (2002b, 104), the novel, information circuits (2002a, 147), and the modern city, whether directly (2003a, 321–22) or in a familiarized form through cinematic play and training (2002b, 117–120, 132n33). For Francine Masiello (2018), the strange is a part of a wide-ranging politics of the senses that shapes democratic practice. In Melvin Rogers's reading (2023, chap. 5), Billie Holiday's *Strange Fruit* exemplifies an activist, democratizing

aesthetics of the strange that awakens the horror of anti-Black lynchings alongside hope for social transformation. Holiday's poignant adjective recalls W. E. B. Du Bois's description of the spirituals, or "Sorrow Songs," as strange and "strangely" moving (1986, 536, 542). James Baldwin picks up on both interventions with his notion of the "strange vividness that is life" (2010, 286), and by often, like Du Bois, using the strange as a starting point for narration. Touching on strange narrations, Alva Noë (2015) associates art in general with the strange. James Haile (2025, v–vi, 139–40, 159) invokes the strange as a register of Black speculative fiction. On perplexity, which suffuses Borges's strange, see Benjamin (2002a, 146). On perplexity's epistemic and correlative societal potentialities, see Medina (2013, 18–21).

22 For a Latinx feminist aesthetic of carnalities, see Ortega 2025.

23 For examples and discussion, see Korsmeyer 2006; Roelofs 2021a, 40–43, 45.

24 Strange tastes differ from Sianne Ngai's ugly feelings (2005) in that Ngai's ugly feelings tend more heavily in the direction of negative and dysphoric states, while strange tastes include both positive and negative affects and, as it happens, often are quite euphoric in character. As an aesthetic category, the strange is frequently ambivalent in a way that is closer to the zany, cute, and interesting, which Ngai analyzes elsewhere (2012), than to ugly feelings, which, although they encode political ambivalences (2005, 6) and link to ambivalences at the level of agency (1–5, 14, 27), remain in Ngai's analysis definitionally tethered to negative affects.

25 Yuriko Saito (2017, 14) gives sensibility a central role in everyday aesthetics. Kant considers singularity crucial to the beauty judgment (2000 [1790], 100), which requires immediate perception and invites experiential dwelling (107), rather than being rule-bound (101).

26 For a reading of the historical emergence of certain cinematic publics informed by Benjamin's notion of experience, see Hansen 1991. Hume and Kant theorize different kinds of publics—namely, historical as well as universally accessible ones. On their interplay, see Roelofs 2020, 66–86. On the cultural workings of aesthetic norms and codes, see Ngai 2012.

27 Hume and Kant are proponents of this approach. For analysis, see Roelofs 2014, 5, 29–56, 195, 202, 205–6; 2020, 60–87.

28 On these and other locally specific references, see Vanessa Barbara, "Latin America's Radical Feminism Is Spreading," *New York Times*, January 28, 2020; Liinason 2024; Martin and Shaw 2021.

29 For these dates, see Aunye Boone, "A Conversation with Fiber Artist: Consuelo Jimenez Underwood," *National Endowment for the Arts Blog*, September 28, 2023, https://www.arts.gov/stories/blog/2023/conversation-fiber-artist-consuelo-jimenez-underwood.

30 On Hume, see Roelofs 2014, 35; 2020, 85. On Kant, see Roelofs 2014, 36–37; 2020, 61, 64.

31 On these notions in Borges's lecture and stories, see Roelofs forthcoming.

32 My reading here is indebted to Jerrold Levinson's (2002) interpretation of the functioning of canonical works in Hume's theory.

33 See Korsmeyer 1995, 1998.

34 I document these interconnections extensively in Roelofs 2014, 31–36.

35 See Roelofs 2014, 1, 8, 10, 210–11.

36 See Hume 1998a, 1998b, 1998d.

37 I develop the theoretical concepts deployed here and argue for their pertinence to the notion of the aesthetic in Roelofs 2014.

38 Illuminating readings of Kant's views of race and coloniality in difference sources include Bernasconi 2002, 2003, 2011; Kleingeld 2024; Larrimore 2008; Lu-Adler 2023. On some of the aesthetically pertinent issues, see Kelly and Roelofs 2024, 2, 20–21n2; Roelofs 2014, 36–37; 2022, 61–78.

39 This is visible in the deployment of a Humean framework by analytical philosophers such as Noël Carroll and Kendall Walton. In continental thought, this tendency appears in the work of Jacques Rancière, who, despite his critical approach to various dynamics of aesthetic power, subscribes to the notion of the "indifferent democracy" (2004, 15) or "undifferentiated public" (2009, 9–10) within the aesthetic regime of the arts, thus preserving Kantian persuasions.

40 On aesthesis as an antidote to the problems of the aesthetic, described as a hegemonic, exclusionary, Eurocentric regime of art, beauty, sublimity, normativity, sensory regulation, and mimesis, see Mignolo 2012, xvi–xvii; 2021, xii, xvi–xvii, 5, 55–56; Mignolo and Vázquez 2013. For different approaches to aesthesis, see Ortega 2025; Rancière 2013. On aesthesis and taste, see Probyn 2012.

Approaches to publicness in postcolonial and decolonial scholarship include Franco 1992; Muñoz 1999. Drawing on José Esteban Muñoz, among others, Gopinath offers rich cultural analyses that home in on public cultures and eschew neocolonial public–private divides and their attendant dynamics of inclusion and exclusion, visibility and invisibility (2005, 20–23, 30, 188; 2018, 33, 65, 78). While there is much to appreciate in these approaches, the aesthetic and the public enter into more extensive entanglements than Franco recognizes, necessitating further exploration of aesthetic publicness (Roelofs 2014, 2020). Furthermore, aesthetic publicness encompasses social and aesthetic formations that fall through the mazes of Muñoz's (and Gopinath's) analytics of majoritarian and counterpublic spheres (see, e.g., Muñoz 1999, 147–48). The same goes for Rancière's (2004) conception of the distribution of the sensible, which fails to acknowledge structural dynamics of aesthetic publicness that stand in need of analysis.

41 Hall specifically emphasizes the role of black popular cultural spaces and repertoires (1996c, 471).

42 For different angles on the public in Anzaldúa, see Ortega 2025, 58–62; Pitts 2021, chap. 2.

43 Importantly, Lugones follows Anzaldúa's move away from normalcy, and links this to "an unsettling quality of being a stranger in . . . society" (2003, 143–44; see also 231).

44 For a phenomenologically expansive and profound reading of Anzaldúa's corporeal and political aesthetics, see Ortega 2025.

45 Under the rubric *carnalities*, Ortega (2025) highlights the aesthetics of these extended intercorporeal movements. Meanwhile, in reading Borges, it is of course crucial to realize how a figure such as the hourglass poignantly and ominously

situates the body in relation to life and death, introducing complex corporeal registers.

46 This involves explicitly recognizing the historical dimension of enlightenment hypothesized and acknowledged by Kant, a point that I argue elsewhere is of major significance to his aesthetics (Roelofs 2020, 61–62, 69), although it has been downplayed by influential strands of Kant scholarship.

47 I agree with Lauren Berlant's (2008, viii) observation that "publics presume intimacy." Aesthetic publicness differs from Berlant's intimate publics in that it comprises a more general, historically emerging structure of address that is less centered in affect and expectations of a shared worldview.

48 As the national and international debates around the 2023 pro-Pinochet demonstrations during the fiftieth anniversary of the coup made abundantly clear.

CHAPTER 1. DUST: A SNIFF OF GETTING TOGETHER

An earlier version of a part of chapter 1 appeared in my "Decoloniality, Identity, and Aesthetic Publicity," *Contemporary Aesthetics*, special volume 10 (2022).

1 Quotations from this collection (Borinsky 2009) are reprinted by permission of Swan Isle Press.

2 Lugones further elaborates the notion in a critique of Danto's take on resistant feminist expression, arguing that his conception of worlds misrecognizes feminist resistance, complex communication, and the tense and fractured multiplicity of the social (2003, 21–26). Her view is a major contribution to a decolonial feminist aesthetics.

3 On these traveling tongues, see Roelofs 2016, 383–85.

4 On humor as a tool of feminist social criticism, see Willett and Willett 2019. On play's subtle element, see Benjamin 2019, 69.

5 Benjamin (2006, 54, 123) voices an analogous perception.

6 Although Lugones sometimes uses the term *political* in related contexts (see, e.g., 2003, 28), she here might prefer *infrapolitical* (2006, 77, 83). In my usage, which is broader than hers, the political exceeds the transparently legible and publicness understood as the universally accessible. Relatedly, I employ a broader notion of agency than she, one that surpasses the realm of autonomous intentional action.

7 With the figure of the key, Borinsky reimagines the dilemmas of two Cortázar stories (1967d, 1967e [1946]) activating linkages I elaborate in this book's conclusion.

8 Lugones (2003, 17–18) criticizes the hierarchical distribution of world traveling, which is demanded of women of color to a much greater extent than of white men and women (depending also on intersecting social categories). This critique leaves the practice of playful world traveling itself untouched, however.

9 While I later consider elements of Lugones's social philosophy that speak to this limitation, my focus here is on the aesthetic state of play.

10 For Spivak, this process involves embracing an intended mistake (2012, 14–15, 20, 25–28).

11 On her commitment to theorizing the cultural world "in its tense multiplicity," see Lugones 2003, 25; 2010, 754.

12 Paul de Man contrasts Schiller's allegedly unreflective embrace of figuration and hence his celebration of aesthetic ideology with a conception of language's iterative workings that Schiller elides and that also informs Spivak's account, yielding what she terms a double bind (de Man 1996; Spivak 2012, 27).

13 Numerous feminist scholars reject this binary. On critical and historical dimensions of this debate, see Korsmeyer and Brand Weiser 2021. Spivak's notion of a double bind between interest and disinterest (2012, 8) doesn't prevent her from mobilizing it at crucial junctures as a binary.

14 Both scholars offer other productive avenues of approach to these concrete dimensions. Lugones embraces concrete, historical life in the flesh, a creative defiance of norms and scripts, and "playful reinvention" (2003, 144–45, 196; 2010, 753–54). Spivak envisions readings attuned to alterity. Nonetheless, play's distinctively aesthetic elements must be recognized, too.

15 Borinsky's interlocutor Cortázar, likewise, deploys play in this critical role, challenging Western canonical cultural constellations and venturing decolonial strategies that her poems will take into new directions (Roelofs 2021b, 2022).

16 On the inscription of the mother-child relation and a masculinized subject position in Benjamin's critical epistemology, see Hansen 1987, 190, 214–16. This subject position, I would add, is at the same time fundamentally white, Western, heterosexual, and cisgendered. On the philosophical implications of several figurations of the mother in Benjamin, see Weigel (1998). On a mobile constellation of mother, whore, and Sybil, see Damião (2016).

17 Benjamin's flaneur is basically a white, male bourgeois subject who saunters through a commercial world mediated by empire. The aesthetic politics of the flaneur's strategy of address both marks and is marked by Benjamin's notions of collective experience, allegory, dialectical images, and constellations, yielding complexities that I take steps to rethink in the context of play through my reading of Borinsky's poems.

18 On these figures of play, see Benjamin 2002b, 107, 117–18, 124n10; 2003a, 319–30, 337–43; 2006, 23–27, 50–56, 74–75, 81–82, 113, 120–26. A reciprocal imbrication of seeing and being seen, for him, is shot through with otherness and involves "productive" forms of modern "self-alienation" (2002b, 113). For an incisive analysis of Benjamin's aesthetically pivotal notion of play, see Hansen 2012, 132–204.

19 Notwithstanding the dimension of alterity that marks Benjaminian play, aesthetic mediation, in his epistemology, encodes racialized and gendered constructions that remain untheorized. On intersecting gender, racial, and colonialist figurations, see notes 16 and 17. Hansen (2012, 167) recognizes white projections of Blackness in Mickey Mouse. Benjamin's drug experiments, furthermore, are replete with racialized and colonialist imagery and formations of space and time, including tropes that associate Black and Brown subject positions with silence and trance-induced white fantasies of becoming Black or resembling Arab people in spirit (Benjamin 2006, 109–10, 115, 140). The repressive and critical potenti-

alities and methodological implications of these sorts of constructions remain untheorized by Benjamin, leaving fundamental shortcomings in his view of play.

20 Play, for Borinsky, involves risk, as it does for Lugones (2003) and Gadamer (2000, 106), which, as Gadamer would affirm, is part of its allure. I surmise that running this risk can reduce risks of publicness. Further, through its self-reflexive stance—especially her questioning not only of stories, but also specifically of stories about games, about publicness, and about stories themselves—Borinsky's poetry challenges existent distributions of the risk of publicness. Rendering publicness something that is to be construed on alternative terms, the poems push back against given systems of social othering and their concomitant allocations of threats and promises, of desirability and repulsion.

21 This figure connotes a privileged mode of white, Western, heterosexual masculinity.

22 In her analysis of the structure of a Black gaze in contemporary visual art and culture, Campt (2021, 7, 99, 102–6) observes that the realization of intimacy as a dimension of aesthetic experience often involves the audience's labor of making and maintaining connections.

23 The notion of aesthetic autonomy is closely affiliated with that of disinterested attention. Autonomy and disinterest denote corollary conditions, with autonomy often referring to the aesthetic object and disinterest to the observer's experience. Several Borinsky poems under consideration in this chapter invoke aesthetic autonomy through signifiers of distance and freedom. In my discussion of the pitfalls of disinterested attention I sometimes emphasize autonomy with the understanding that disinterest is at issue, as well.

24 The frivolous poet charges the gamers with bad taste: They need an excess of sugar in their tea to eradicate a bitterness they cannot stomach, just as they cannot stomach the poet's stories. The frivolous poet puts the censors of strange taste in their place.

25 I'm not claiming that the notion of aesthetic autonomy inevitably produces these impasses or produces them on its own. Neither do I want to imply that Borinsky's poems suggest this. Rather, through tropes of artistic freedom, self-determining exploration, uselessness, and distancing, several poems explore both the capabilities and hazards of aesthetic autonomy and investigate the nature of this concept as an element of aesthetic practices under current colonialist and capitalist conditions.

26 Lauren Berlant illuminatingly connects play with various kinds of intimacy (2022, 49–50, 66, 125, 158–59).

27 In Roelofs 2014, I make the case for the centrality to the aesthetic of such ambivalence and the undiminished promises and threats it entails and argue that the public is a central participant in aesthetically mediated constellations of promises and threats.

28 Quotations from this poem are reprinted with the poet's permission.

29 Analogously to Benjamin's and Cortázar's play, it unfolds in residual and public territory (Benjamin 2002b, 117; Benjamin 2003a, 321, 336; Cortázar 1967d, 1967e [1946]) and pushes back against (heterosexual) constructions of national culture

(Benjamin 1996, 487; see also Roelofs 2021b; Sommer 1991). Simultaneously, Benjamin's objections to interiority (1999a) transfer in various ways to his understanding of intimacy.

CHAPTER 2. PINGS: SOUNDING OUT THE CITY

1 See Glissant 1997; Lugones 2003; Lugones 2006, 76–77, 79, 83–84. On the limitations of polarities such as modernity and tradition, coloniality and postcoloniality, and Europe and non-Europe, see Spivak 2012, 3, 21.

2 See, among others, Braidotti 2002; Cixous 1990, 1991.

3 While Edson Costa Duarte (2017), Daae Jung and João Paulo Guimarães (2023), Lúcia Sá (2004), and Nelson Vieira (2022), among others, perspicaciously trace registers of subjectivity, migration, gender, class, language, and humor, the aesthetic inflects these registers in a manner that remains to be scrutinized.

4 On the powers of listening in relation to racialized constructions of sound and subjectivity, including figurations of Latina identity, see Nina Sun Eidsheim's (2019) argument that multisensory engagements, including literary ones, are partially constitutive of sounds in a political manner. Read along these lines, the novel intervenes politically into a quotidian aesthetic lifeworld: Entering into the pings' constitution, it alters and displaces their normalized institutional status. See also note 16.

5 I cite the Portuguese in this section because my reading turns on the specificities of the language.

6 Franco (1992, 76) observes that the idea that "all forms of life are equal" appears repeatedly in Lispector's narratives, aptly noting that it incites the contrary awareness of random inequality. See also note 14. For Braidotti, boundary crossings in Lispector's *Passion* activate multiplying becomings and enact the interconnectedness and interdependence of living matter (2002, 160–67). While Braidotti, drawing on Luce Irigaray, Gilles Deleuze, and Adriana Cavarero, finds here a specifically feminine form of immanent transcendence, she downplays *Passion*'s registers of coloniality, class, and race. In my reading of *The Hour of the Star*, the aesthetic effacement of ontological distinctions is one of several strategies through which Lispector rethinks gendered aesthetic agency and aesthetic gendering along with intersect modalities of difference (on these concepts, see Roelofs 2014).

7 Vieira (2022, 174–78) underlines the novel's "ethics of address."

8 The adjective *black* invokes racial dimensions, which I analyze in Roelofs 2014, 91, 104, 182–83.

9 On the death toll of the February 4, 1976, Guatemala earthquake, see "'76 Termed Among Worst in Toll from Earthquakes," *New York Times*, January 24, 1977.

10 Renowned cases are Adorno 1997, 5–8; Schiller 1967, esp. his 27th Letter.

11 Rodrigo, who also appreciates gold, takes a more roundabout approach. For our novelistic craftsman or alchemist, it will gild truth in the course of a slow artistic process: "I'll try to wrest gold from charcoal" (8). He doesn't just buy it.

12 See Benjamin 1999a, 2002a. The Benjaminian motifs in the quotation stand also in conversation with other Benjaminian themes in the novel. Rodrigo's anti-

ornamental poetics of coldness and his insistence on his story's poverty (9) recall Benjamin's take on nineteenth-century decorative, European-bourgeois domestic aesthetics and the new barbarism with which he counters it (1999a). Repeated invocations of Technicolor resonate with the (unstable) contrast between a multicolored narrative fabric Benjamin associates with a profane worldview and the golden texture of a story he associates with a religious orientation (2002a, 153). Another parallel concerns the storyteller's role as the chronicler of death and natural order. This also ties into the shared trope of an absence of history (Benjamin 2003a, 336).

13 Kafka's *Metamorphosis*, like Lispector's novel, is another treatise of strange tastes (see Roelofs 2013).

14 In this instance, the idea of equality, in Franco's (1992, 76) terms, "shockingly foregrounds arbitrary inequalities."

15 Cixous mentions that the novel doesn't begin, yet reads this as inaugurating a merging of present, past, and future (1990, 160–61).

16 Eidsheim's (2019) analysis of sonic cultures illuminates how the manifold dimensions of listening participate in constructing what sounds actually are.

17 By endowing Macabéa with a capacity for disinterested perception, Lispector emphasizes that disinterest can be a source of pleasure and understanding in a state of destitution and a position outside lettered institutionality and contemplates the philosophical implications of this insight. I further discuss the novel's critical exploration of Enlightenment constructions of disinterest in Roelofs 2014, 180.

18 In her important essay on what I call aesthetic publicness, Franco (1992) argues that the novel, among other texts by Latin American women writers, challenges the public-private opposition and engages its protagonist in negotiations of public space.

19 In multiple contexts, scholars highlight the dynamics of such assemblages. Deleuze and Guattari (1987, 406) understand assemblages, such as cultures or ages, as more or less fluid constellations of heterogeneous elements involving contingent orderings of elements. Stuart Hall (2005) uses the notion of assembly to capture the heterogeneous, only partially cohering elements of historical conjunctures, specifically of 1980s Black art in Britain. For him, assemblies are constellations brought out through genealogical modes of interpretation that mark interconnections between disparate phenomena. Paul Taylor (2016, 3–5) deploys Hall's view to argue that Black aesthetics is at once multiple and characterized by what Hall describes as a distinctive "horizon" or "problem space" (4, quoting Hall). As I indicate in Roelofs 2014, 2, the aesthetic itself is usefully seen as a kind of assembly.

CHAPTER 3. SONG: A NEW LIFE

Earlier versions of portions of chapter 3 were published in two essays I coauthored with Norman S. Holland: "Indigeneity at the Limits of Transculturation: Decolonial Aesthetics in Claudia Llosa's *The Milk of Sorrow*," *PhiloSOPHIA: A Journal of transContinental Feminism* 14 (1–2) (2024): 1–30; and "The Role of the Aesthetic in Decolonial Critique: Claudia Llosa, *The Milk of Sorrow / La teta asustada*," *Latin American and Latinx Visual Culture* 7 (1) (2025): 26–47.

1 The film, among other Llosa movies, figures in a polemic over magical realism. Franco (1992, 73) critiques magical realism as a marketing category. Dolores Tierney links it to colonialist forms of art criticism and artistic production in "Against (Coloniality in) Anglophone Film Criticism," *Mediático* (blog), July 4, 2023, https://reframe.sussex.ac.uk/mediatico/2023/07/04/against-coloniality-in-anglophone-film-criticism-bardo-false-chronicles-of-a-handful-of-truths-bardo-falsa-cronica-de-unas-cuantas-verdades-alejandro-gonzalez-inarritu-2022/. Magical realism holds a powerful grip on readings of Latin American art and culture. In an interview with Isabel Allende about her novel *The Wind Knows My Name* (2003), the journalist Christiane Amanpour wonders whether it was a "deliberate" choice or part of the author's "evolution" that "the magic is cast off, there is no fairy dust being sprinkled over your latest book." The expectation of magical realism is so ingrained that its absence is thought to require explanation. Indeed, the North American and Brazilian releases market Allende's novel under this rubric, with their cover image of a Latin American, possibly Indigenous, woman surrounded by a pink sky and tropical plans and sporting a blue butterfly in her hair, although, in the author's words, "Magic realism is not like salt and pepper that you can sprinkle everywhere" and *The Wind Knows My Name* "doesn't allow it, it is a very realistic story." Isabel Allende, interview by Christiane Amanpour, *Amanpour*, CNN, September 27, 2023.

2 This chapter draws on two previous, coauthored explorations of the film's decolonial aesthetics and its take on magical realism, transculturation, and syncretism (Roelofs and Holland 2024, 2025), while further advancing the angles of play, taste, and publicness.

3 The film explores aesthetic dimensions of what Silvia Rivera Cusicanqui describes as the contemporaneity of the Indigenous and an Indigenous notion of modernity that engages current economic and social conditions (2012, 96, 106).

4 On the importance of the potato to present-day Indigenous communities, see Stephenson 2012.

5 Films such as *La ciénaga* (*The Swamp* [2001]), *La niña santa* (*Holy Girl* [2004]), and *La mujer sin cabeza* (*The Headless Woman* [2008]) have won Martel major critical acclaim for, among other things, their portrayal of their female protagonists.

6 The film investigates modes of address toward and by these substances, including sensory, interpretive, and linguistic modes.

7 On the limitations of representations of slums, notably in Global North-South cinematic coproductions, see Dasgupta 2013, 150.

8 Adriana Laura Massidda (2023) traces the shifting vocabulary around low-income communities in Latin America, usefully problematizing *slums* yet uncritically reverting to *shantytowns*.

9 Carolyn Wolfenzon (2022) insightfully interprets the film as a critique of the role of the lettered city in contemporary Latin America. She contends that it is

the slum dwellers, conceived of as *el tercer anillo* (following Rama), who sustain the nation and currently constitute the center of culture, and observes that the lettered class fundamentally depends on the cultural innovation of the Andean populations in Lima's periphery (22). While, according to Wolfenzon, the lettered city is reduced to a small, arcane space ruled by racism, she regards transculturation as an inevitable and indispensable force of cultural development (22–23). In what follows, I signal the limits of a transcultural reading.

10 Contesting the film's representation of trauma, several critics denounce Llosa's portrayals of the transmission of trauma through breast-feeding and of a potato as a prophylactic device as exoticist (e.g., Vich 2014). Similarly emphasizing trauma, Adriana Rojas (2017) and Carolina Rueda (2015) defend the significance of the milk of sorrow by reference to Kimberly Theidon (2004), on which the film is partly based.

11 The painting is a version or copy of Mateo Pérez de Alesio's *Virgen de la Leche*. Pérez de Alesio painted multiple variations of the Madonna Lactans, including, besides other images in Lima, a 1604 version on display in the Lima Art Museum and one dated about 1600 in the Denver Museum of Art.

12 See, e.g., Anzaldúa 2009; Aparicio and Chávez-Silverman 1997; Hall 1994; Mbembe 2021; Pratt 2008.

13 Nelly Richard (2004a) stresses in this context the importance of aesthetic ruptures in economic rationality. When employed as commodifying tools, notions of transculturation threaten to efface difference while simultaneously figuring it (Acosta 2014, 5), eliding what Sara Ahmed (2000) would call strange strangeness and asserting a coercive promise of happiness (Ahmed 2010).

14 Aparicio (1998), among others, stresses resistance.

15 On the globalization and commercialization of cultures and their effects on the positioning of postcolonial and transcultural/multicultural aesthetic production, see Lazarus 2012, esp. 21–25. On the effacement of social antagonism under globalization, see Richard 2004a.

16 At the end of the Reconquista, the campaigns by Christian kingdoms to recover Iberian territory from Muslim rule extending from the eighth through the fifteenth century, anyone living on the Iberian Peninsula had to be Christian or convert to Christianity. Many Jews and Muslims did. Accusations of false conversions abounded. Laws demanding proof of purity of blood were instituted. Ancestry became a determining social factor. Within Spain's colonies the concept of limpieza de sangre evolved to connote racial purity for both Spaniards and Indigenous peoples.

17 Peru's 2017 national census recognizes the country's Afro-Peruvians population for the first time since the early 1940s. This group, totaling 9 percent of the nation (a reportedly grossly underestimated number), includes "Blacks," signifying unmixed African descent; "Mulatos," connoting mixed African and European ancestry; and "Zambos," marked by mixed African and Indigenous ancestry. (See Instituto Nacional de Estadística e Informática 2018, 222; Néstor David Pastor, "After Decades of Erasure, Afro-Peruvians Will Finally Be Counted in the National Census," *OkayAfrica*, October 19, 2018, https://www.okayafrica.com/census-to-count-afro-peruvians.) As these categories suggest, limpieza de sangre

doctrines persist in Peru and throughout Latin America. Llosa's film inventively engages the bonds between interrelated fluids and racial categories that are also complexly gendered via corporeal processes that involve milk, blood, and semen and their presumed capacities to pollute and purify.

18 As this moment indicates, the film, which aspires to intelligibility by a public proficient in Spanish and not necessarily in Quechua, situates itself explicitly within global cinema.

19 Their singing invokes the Quechua convention of deploying myth, often in the form of songs, to cope with current predicaments. The Indigenous writer and scholar José Maria Arguedas (1969) documents and participates in this practice.

20 Since the conquest, Andean culture has absorbed but also transformed Christian symbols and imagery (Yetter 2017, 1–14). Possibly, the mother is following this tradition. For contemporary uses of syncretism, see Taussig 2010 (1980).

21 Indigenous and Marian imagery converge and diverge as elements of manifold aesthetic trajectories fueled by potato and song. In navigating confluences and differences between milk and blood and linking these substances with Fausta's, Perpetua's, and Aída's positions in the story, Llosa elaborates a decolonial aesthetic perspective that rethinks the racial, gender, and class implications of a series of material and symbolic connections whose locus in the West is Mary's body (Kristeva 1987, 234–63; Warner 2016 [1976], 195–222) and that, in colonial Spanish and Spanish American art, broaches Augustinian tensions between Mary's milk and Christ's blood. These fluids' racial connotations shift during the film.

22 Focusing on this instance, Irma Vélez (2011) observes that the Virgin nourishes Fausta throughout her journey. She notes that "the encounter of the woman with art . . . gives light to the breast, and shadow to the fear" (48, my translation). I challenge this reading, which fails to imagine a future for Fausta outside a discourse of maternity and beyond modern colonial parameters. For Vélez, "The hallway that Fausta traverses [symbolizes] her rebirth to another type of motherhood, definitely her own to come" (48, my translation). Rojas also cites this moment as evidence that, once cured of her trauma, Fausta faces a future of marriage and motherhood (2017, 306). See also notes 31 and 38.

23 Semen, blood, and milk meet in this overlay of images, lodging the film in the turbulent encounters among these elemental substances.

24 Llosa may be paying sly tribute to the Chilean bestseller *Para leer al pato Donald* (1971). This book views the comics as corporate propaganda that furthers cultural imperialism (Dorfman and Mattelart 2018 [1971]).

25 Curiously, Ariel Dorfman and Armand Mattelart (2018 [1971]) begin their polemic by focusing on the sexual undercurrents of these fluids in Disney cartoons in chapter 1, aptly titled, "Uncle, Buy Me a Contraceptive . . ." They start the chapter by stressing the absence of parental figures amid the proliferation of ducks that are relatives of Donald and one another. Neither Fausta nor the duck has parents.

26 This rewriting is part of the logic of aesthetic promises (and their attendant threats). See Roelofs 2014, 23.

27 With Fausta's gift to Aída, the film counters limitations that coloniality, as Nelson Maldonado-Torres (2007, 258–61) argues, places on the subaltern's capacity for

giving. Insisting on Fausta's aesthetic gift, the film counters extractivist aesthetics with a specifically decolonial aesthetics. The aesthetic dimension proves to be crucial to the film's figuration of coloniality and to its decolonial strategies. Lugones's (2003, 72–74) view of white women's blocked identification with women of color points to other facets of the women's interaction. For a rich discussion of whiteness and coloniality in the film, including Llosa's own positioning within these formations, see Renker 2024.

28 Marking but foreclosing opportunities for shared joy, the film highlights the racially asymmetrical desirability of transculturation and brings this to bear on the construction of cultural agency and aesthetic futurity associated with the paradigm of transculturation. While Wolfenzon (2022, 25–26) interprets the concert as an instance of transculturation, in my reading Llosa's representation of the performance and the subsequent betrayal attests to that notion's inadequacy.

29 In his analysis of the lettered city as a motor of alleged civilization since the conquest, Rama notes that writing acquired "an almost sacred aura," on account of the lettered classes' ability to control it in predominantly illiterate societies (1996 [1985], 24). For Franco, the Cold War marks a sea change in this history. Supported by the ruling classes in its fight against communism, she indicates, the military establishment in Latin America undercut notions of art and literature "as agents of 'salvation and redemption'" (2002, 12). The changes military governments wrought in the structure of civil society brought artists' utopian visions to an end and diminished the role of the arts in the nation-building project (12). From the angle of elite culture and its status within the nation, Aída exemplifies this moment. Simultaneously, the aesthetic strategies I highlight in this chapter go beyond utopian visions or a nation-building project, and so do many of the literary strategies under discussion in this book. Accordingly, it is too hasty to call the shots on the historical construct Rama and Franco theorize so illuminatingly. This point also speaks from my analyses in the previous and subsequent chapters: The lettered city has potentialities that Franco's metaphor of its "decline and fall" fails to capture, although they glisten brightly in the subtext of her account.

30 For Deborah Shaw, the potato image exemplifies magical realism and thus diminishes Indigenous agency (2018, 93–94). This reading, however, elides aesthetic complexities that mark Llosa's treatment of Fausta and the potato.

31 While Rojas (2017) argues persuasively that Fausta honors her mother's memory by means of song, potato, and pearls, she sidesteps Fausta's need to rewrite these metaphors to create a livable alternative to the mother's narrative.

32 The idea of a distorted modernity holds that Western epistemology and society stand for modernity, while frames of thought and social organization placed on the other side of a colonial divide fall short of this, a persuasion contested by decolonial and critical race theory. The film considers the aesthetic dimensions of this construction.

33 The flying scene humorously alludes to the famous moment in Gabriel García Márquez's *One Hundred Years of Solitude* when Remedios La Bella ascends to heaven (2006 [1967]). As in other instances in the film, Llosa employs a magical realist trope while simultaneously distancing it.

34 The capitalist marketplace, clearly, has a heavy hand in the violent history whose aftermath the film explores. Further, setting off Máxima against Aída, Llosa emphasizes the temporal frictions that mark the composer, who is both an effective present-day economic operator and an inheritor of a colonial tradition, a point foreshadowed by the interior of her house and that I return to later.

35 This sociality evolves during the film in a manner that imbricates a conviviality among the living with a relation to death. For the longest time, Fausta's immediate family refrains from expressing sympathy at her mother's death. The young woman's relationship with her uncle, her mother's brother, is tense in the period the corpse is in the house. Yet, at last he transports the corpse along with other family members in a show of support and compassion, underscoring people's shared mortality. Lugones's view of collaborative intention formation speaks to the unfolding of aesthetic sociality the film reveals (2003, 216–20).

36 Fausta's anguish, underlined by the film poster, cannot be read as a trauma-induced fear of men specifically, which would belie her basic trust of uncle Lúcido, her growing trust of Noé, and her dread of Aída, figures that complicate gender issues away from binary thinking. Fausta's fear is of (sexual) violence broadly. It involves her aesthetic and political suspicions about systems that are biased against her: a colonial value system, the military, institutionalized medicine, and, as I indicate shortly, selective botanical classifications.

37 Through the figures of Fausta, Lúcido, the doctor, and the duck, Llosa offers a set of halting translations among different kinds of biopolitics, which she renders readable in aesthetic terms—that is, in relation to the potato, milk, and the cranes. On the biopolitical regulation of life and death, see Foucault 1978. Lúcido's pained and fragmentary interlopings between various biomedical/aesthetic systems point to the epistemic, affective, and aesthetic labor involved in the encounters between these systems and signals gaps in readings in terms of transculturation. For example, Ortiz's idea that "when cultures encounter each other, each of the parties invariably exerts a strong influence on the other(s)" (1995 [1940], 100) fails to capture the specificities of the relevant interactions.

38 For Rojas, among others, Fausta recovers from her trauma; she reads the ending as signifying health and readiness for marriage in a resilient community (2017, 299–300, 305, 310, 312). Gastón Lillo (2011) is skeptical of Fausta's liberation. While witnessing a trajectory leading from trauma to cure, he finds that Fausta, instead of remembering to overcome trauma, keeps living the memory.

39 The North American DVD cover promotes the film with this representation of an Indigenous woman in the tradition of Carmen Miranda.

40 Yuriko Saito (2017) underscores the world-making capabilities of everyday aesthetic existence. On the lived reality of coloniality and decolonization, see Lugones 2003, 2010; Maldonado-Torres 2007. On the centrality of the quotidian to decolonial feminisms, see Alcoff 2020.

41 This is not to say that the film doesn't feature forms of resistance. It is to de-emphasize these facets to focus on aesthetic dimensions that tend to elude the frames of resistance currently given so much weight in the aesthetic field. While

I recognize the importance of strategies of resistance, inspired by Acosta (2014), Anzaldúa (1999 [1987], 100–101), and Quashie (2012, 2021), this chapter elaborates an aesthetic framework that avoids lending them the critical and analytical prevalence they now enjoy at the cost of different kinds of aesthetic registers. For further discussion, see this chapter's conclusion. For useful reservations about racially binary notions of resistance within an aesthetic approach that otherwise emphasizes resistance, see Vallega 2014, 123–24. For a take on resistance as an ontological condition in contrast to a political exigency, drawing on Quashie's account, see Kelly and Roelofs 2024, 12–16.

42 Probing further where Lugones (2003, 2010) and Walter Mignolo (2007) leave off, the film notes an Afro-Peruvian presence through the figure of the Black domestic worker and hints lightly at an Asian Peruvian presence by way of the origami cranes. We are shown how the upper classes deploy a biopolitics that pits the Afro-Peruvians against the Indigenous, asking them to do the dirty work. The song "La Negra, La China, La Chola, La Rubia" (The Black, the Asian, the rural Indigenous, the blonde), by Luis Javier Amorrorto and Gustavo Aranibar, played while Lúcido is comforting Fausta after she has fainted during the communal wedding festivities and continuing while she is waiting in a long line of women in the hospital, points to the interrelations among these racial stratifications.

43 For a philosophical account of the role of threats and promises in aesthetically mediated constellations of race and gender and aesthetic life broadly conceived, see Roelofs 2014. On the gendered and racializing functioning of cinematic promises of happiness, see Ahmed 2010.

44 On this logic, which marks aesthetic promises and threats generally, see Roelofs 2014, 207.

45 On an ethically grounded aesthetics of care that is also an aesthetically guided care ethics, see Saito 2022. Saito stresses the role of imagination in care (35–37, 40–45), which can involve joining an imaginary community of people who care or of those who share in a common humanity (158–59).

CHAPTER 4. LIGHT: SENSIBILITY ON SALE

Earlier versions of portions of chapter 4 appeared in my "Selling Literature / Selling the Race: Diamela Eltit's Decolonial Feminist Critique of the Neoliberal Marketplace," *Journal of Aesthetics and Art Criticism* 77 (4) (2019): 461–73; and "Public Things, Public Squares: Aesthetic Democracy in Diamela Eltit's *E. Luminata*," *Parallax* 30 (1) (2024): 62–81.

1 See Anzaldúa 1999 [1987], 104–10; 2002; 2015, 19, 123; Lugones 2003; Pérez 2019, 6–16, 122; Alcoff 2020; Ortega 2025.

2 On Plato's view of enthusiasm, see Gadamer 1980, 42–43.

3 Gadamer underscores the poetic character of Plato's work (1980, 46, 67–68).

4 Hans-Georg Gadamer and Jacques Derrida identify aporias in Plato's texts. For Gadamer, myths in Plato acquire "new meaning as magnifications, inversions, views from afar, and ironic counterimages (1980, 68; see also 67, 69–70). Derrida (1981) emphasizes the centrality of myth to Plato's philosophical endeavor in the *Phaedrus*.

5 Gadamer (1980) provides a richly contextualized analysis of poetry's role in the *Republic*. In his famous discussion of Plato's division between speech and writing, Derrida underscores philosophy's worries about straying significations and uncovers conceptual hierarchies that Plato both posits and undermines through a series of interconnected binaries (1981, 85, 91–94, 129, 168).

6 At a minimum, economic valorizations are part of Plato's rhetoric. On such financial dimensions, see also Derrida 1981, 82.

7 The soul, which Plato divides into appetitive, spiritual, and rational parts, must be governed by the latter part, whose pleasures are the truest and whose judgment is decisive (2004, 580d–583b6). Plato's exclusion of poetry from the city in the *Republic* makes an exception for "hymns to the gods and eulogies of good people" (607a2). He also allows that if lovers of pleasure-seeking, imitative poetry muster a defense of its beneficial effects (607c3–6) and its serious, truthful character (608a6–7), poetry can be readmitted to the "well-governed city" (607c4–5).

8 See Derrida 1981; Gadamer 1980; Griswold 2024.

9 Gadamer (1980, 70–72) stresses this dimension of the genre of play exemplified by Plato's dialogues.

10 Plato 2004, 536c1–c7, 558b; see also 2005b, 265c2–c8. Simultaneously, unless one is a youngster who is just getting a taste of argument, dialectic shouldn't be used as if one is playing a game of disputation (2004, 539b–c) or an eristic type of verbal exchange that valorizes debate over getting at the truth (453e7–454b1).

11 Play is an alternative to coerced learning, which rapidly takes flight from the soul (Plato 2004, 536e). It allows the educator to gauge each child's specific aptitudes (536e7–537a1).

12 Derrida's reading of play in the *Phaedrus* emphasizes how textual play deconstructs the binaries the dialogue articulates (1981, 93, 127, 129, 130, 156–58, 169–71). While Derrida stresses play's indeterminacy, I highlight its seductive workings and aesthetic dimensions. For Derrida, the pharmakon employs seduction (70).

13 Groundbreaking critiques along these lines include Adorno 1991; Horkheimer and Adorno 2002.

14 On the public functioning of concern and care, see Arendt 1998; Honig 2017.

15 On the ties between the military dictatorship, the horrific repression and destruction it wielded, and the neoliberal market policies it instituted, see Franco 2002, 260–61, 268; Richard 2019, 139–40, 146.

16 Discussing her novel and the poetics and politics of her writing, Eltit (1997b, 11) voices her interest in connecting "the individual with the public, the subjective with the social." She underscores the centrality of the square in the novel (Eltit 2020, 150, 153). For Mary Louise Pratt (1996, 159, 163), the novel reenvisions possibilities for "public life and the plazas" in response to the military regime's "rearrangement and resymbolization of public space." Amanda Holmes links the plaza to the Athenian agora (2007, 129–30). Eltit notes that her interest in the public includes its limits as well as possibilities (Morales Rodríguez 2021, 162).

17 For a discussion of the novels in relation to violent, right-wing extremist mobilizations in Europe and in the context of figurations of aesthetic publicness and

identity in a range of artworks, including performance, installation, and so-called "public" art, see Roelofs 2024a.

18 I read this as a riff on Kant's (1991) essay on enlightenment and Michel Foucault's (2007) association of enlightenment with a critical attitude exemplified by Kant among others. While challenging a propagandistic, dictatorial figuration of enlightenment as "flames in the night," as Pratt (1996, 160) notes, Eltit simultaneously anticipates what Wendy Hui Kyong Chun (2006, 299) calls the "literalization of 'enlightenment'" by fiber-optic systems.

19 Eltit (1995 [1988], esp. 112–14) explores these convergences further, which, fascinatingly, prefigure linkages we activate when accessing the worldwide web (see Chun 2006, 3–5).

20 Modes of individuation erode within what Gilles Deleuze (1992 [1990]) some years later would comprehend as contemporary mechanisms of control.

21 On the supplantation of the Latin American state and civic society by consumerism as a model for belonging and identification under global corporatism, see García Canclini 2014, 137–50.

22 The debates around the coup's 50th anniversary in 2023, which featured pro-Pinochet demonstrations, reflect the conflicting positionalities of the deceased dictator's advocates and detractors. Regarding the dictator's 2006 funeral, which was attended by right-wing groups of supporters, Eltit (2023, 93–94) identifies a "Pinochet machine," meaning, a cultural apparatus that "keeps churning, a machine of destruction and abuse whose every facet bears the name Pinochet." Despite his death and burial, the general remains "latent." Eltit imagines that "the same political right that showed up for his funeral has a secret identity named Pinochet and that the army incubates Pinochet in its weapons and medals. We've survived one Pinochet, but there's another, and another, and another. That's why we'll never rest in peace. Never" (94). See also Richard 2019, 115–52, for a reading of the aesthetics and politics of memory around the coup's 40th anniversary in 2013. On the gendered dynamics of the right's enshrinement and adulation of Pinochet, see Richard 2019, 12–23.

23 Richard (1993) and Julio Ortega (1993) offer more extensive readings of the novel's literary strategies. Through ambiguity, a "slow attention to language," and a "celebration of lettered culture" linked to the foregrounding of "an aestheticized popular subject," Eltit's fiction, in Masiello's important account (2001, 138–39, 208, 218), offers a critique of the marketplace and insists on "a resemanticization of the public sphere." Here, feminine writing and the aesthetic, Masiello argues, are sites of ethical questioning. These modalities "reconstruct an arena for debate" and dislodge neoliberal North/South logics while satirizing "our preferences for mass culture" (138). My reading pushes further the relevant aesthetic dynamics.

24 Robert Neustadt (2003, 124–25) discusses continuities between Eltit's novel and the performance it informed.

25 See Eltit 1997a [1983], chaps. 8–9.

26 Diamela Eltit, *Maipú*, performance on Maipú Street, Santiago, Chile, 1980.

27 Though not specifically focused on *E. Luminata*, Richard's (2004a) discussions of Eltit's fiction offer this reading in an analysis of the dictatorship and the subsequent dictated transition. See also Eltit 1997b.

28 On this point, among others, Eltit's reading of contemporary society goes well beyond Deleuze's (1992 [1990]) analysis of the epistemic and political dynamics of control.

29 See, e.g., Eltit 1997a [1983], 21–23, 29–33, 87–90.

30 See also Eltit 1997a [1983], 188. This engagement with Mapuche idioms, images, and ceremonies has precedents in her work. On her collaboration in the publication of Mapuche testimonials, see Eltit 2020, 153. For a helpful reading, see also Christ 1997, 227–28.

31 See also Eltit 1997a [1983], 101.

32 The novel, crucially, challenges not only neoliberalism's affective flattening analyzed so perspicaciously in Richard 2004a but also its affective intensities. For Masiello (2001, 68–69), E. Luminata's self-fashioning evinces a mode of perception that eludes the sign. Thus, she observes, it heralds alternative forms of gendering and congregation, and exemplifies art's power to change history.

33 E. Luminata "celebrates herself" (Eltit 1997a, 17) and is being celebrated in the bodies of each of the people in the square (19). The narrative for which the people look to E. Luminata is "transitory" (105), not definitive, and hence supplies a model that can be displaced by different stories told by members of the crowd.

34 Pratt (1996, 161–62) signals here a critical reclamation of pain and torture in engagement with state violence. However, these figurations also invite less literal readings. Franco (2002, 180–81) reads in Eltit's cuts and burns "a codified reference" to other tortured bodies" and a questioning of narrative coherence.

35 Eltit (1997b, 5) observes regarding the dictatorship that "[w]hen my freedom—I don't mean *freedom* in the literal sense but in its whole symbolic range—was threatened, then I took the liberty of writing freely." She emphasizes her investment in a "politics of writing," which she associates with her texts' deployment of "linguistic materials" (10). Through writing, she aims to "establish a field of questions" (11). Addressing themes of marginality and the organization of "structures of meaning" this engenders, she regards literature as a site of "disjunction rather than as a zone of answers" and as a "generator of conflict" (7–8). This approach demands readers who engage in "serious work" and become "partners in dialogue, accomplices in a certain disconformity" (8). Accordingly, Eltit seeks to activate a specific scenario of address between novel and reader. Formal, linguistic innovation meanwhile is central to her poetics (7–8, 10). She explicitly conceptualizes her writing in terms of the aesthetic—as a figuration of "aesthetic spaces" (7) and a creation of a "scene of aesthetic and social unrest" (8). Articulating a feminist outlook in her work although without adumbrating a social program (8–12), she understands literature as "a revolutionary activity: comparable to that of certain household appliances which rotate their gears in order to shake up their own contents" (11). She thus emphatically ties literature to everyday material and embodied configurations into which it purports to intervene and to

the social "codes" and registers of "power or regulation" they imply (8). Eltit's literary output, furthermore, must be seen in the context of her multimedia artistic practice, which includes performance, film, and video, and actively participates in dialogues with other artists and writers (5–6).

36 While *E. Luminata*, as I have argued, casts doubt on the consistency of aesthetic categories, it also signals the need to critically reflect on them and to explore their workings and relevance to the current era, a project that the novel itself and this book engage in.

37 See also the introduction to this book.

38 For the twin sister, the rooms and walls of the house exude an aura of loneliness and the sense of a "perverted humanity" (Eltit 1995 [1988], 59–60).

39 The enslavement and forced labor of Amerindians must also be mentioned in this regard. Tropes related to Amerindian populations emerge more explicitly in *E. Luminata* than in *The Fourth World*. Yet images of dancing in the latter (Eltit 1995 [1988], 52) resonate with the trope of an Amerindian dance in the former (1997a [1983], 95–96). I leave aside here the treatment of Black (and Polynesian) slaves and forced laborers, which neither novel substantially engages apart from the occasional reference to exoticizing images of Blackness (or Asian origins).

40 Regenia Gagnier (2000, chap. 3) elaborates the notion of the man of taste as an individual consumer and emphasizes this figure's centrality to Western modernity. On taste's dimensions of individual control and autonomy in Hume's aesthetics, see Roelofs 2014, 33–34, 71. For an intersectional reading of the racializing implications of the Humean man of taste who takes command of his pleasures, see Roelofs 2014, 29–36, 59–71, 118–20.

41 It also picks up on the father's "implacable impotency" when stroking the silk.

42 Because the term *sudaca*, or "south-shit" (Masiello 2001, 208), in Eltit's novel serves to reclaim a pejorative denomination and ironically engages it to dispel its deprecatory force, as in the case of *queer*, I use it without quotation marks, while of course dissenting from the disparagement encoded in the term. The name sudaca in this chapter embodies a movement from denigration to an aesthetically envisioned, if ambivalent affirmation of a Latin American identity, a movement my usage is designed to explore. According to Masiello, Eltit, through this term, stresses the circumstances of the decentered poor and "resemanticize[s] the language of violence" (208). In *The Fourth World*, like other works by the artist, Masiello observes, marginalized subjects then exercise the capacities of the aesthetic.

43 Eltit, here, plays with ethical views (such as Aristotle's) that construe the home as a site of moral agency.

44 The brother in Cortázar's story, which is a precursor to *The Fourth World*, is a reader dedicated to the latest French literature (Cortázar 1967e [1946], 11). Cortázar's brother-sister duo, which stands outside the conventionally (re)productive social order, fuels a decolonial aesthetic inquiry: His siblings gesture toward a Latin American literature and cultural identity conceived in terms other than those circumscribed by European definitions of the "new" or—by contrast—the

culturally archaic. Eltit parallels and updates this strategy in view of the increased cultural dominance of capitalist accumulation and market rationality.

45 The reader will recall the incestuous family lineage passing through the Buendía house in Macondo. *One Hundred Years*, in turn, stands in conversation with "House Taken Over" in its exploration of the potentialities of a decolonial Latin American literature and identity through the tropes of the house and the sexually non-normative family that alternately inhabits, leaves, returns to, or is partially banished from its domicile. Eltit, again, further explores the exploitative global economic politics that García Márquez also challenges and that in his novel culminates in the figure of the banana company, the changes it brings to the town, the massacre it wreaks on its protesting workers, and its immediate pull-out when things get rough (García Márquez 2006 [1967], 225–29, 237, 293–310).

46 In Roelofs 2019, I further elaborate Eltit's (1995 [1988]) decolonial feminist aesthetics.

47 On the figure of the heterosexual couple at the basis of the nation in Latin American literature, see Sommer 1991. On manifold connections between sexual formations and nationalist stances, see Parker et al. 1992. On relevant links within European modernity, see Mosse 1985. Cortázar and Eltit, meanwhile, move farther away from heteronormative conceptions of the nation than García Márquez.

48 Eltit, here, alludes to César Vallejo's famous poem "Espergesia," in Vallejo 1969 [1918].

49 This vision, notably, also has a great deal of traction in US politics.

50 See Richard 2004a, 16.

51 This is a part of the content of a vision she has that her sister helps her decipher.

52 Eltit's novel engages the entwined registers of power, economic rationality, and sexuality that Foucault (2010, 226, 230) stresses in his argument that neoliberal governmentality posits the entrepreneurship of self as its driving mode of subject formation and sociality. Thus, Foucault observes how neoliberalism occasions a shift in historical configurations of *homo œconomicus* (see note 40). Eltit explores this changing constellation through a decolonial feminist aesthetic lens.

53 Fear is among the factors Arendt takes to be conducive to totalitarianism (2005, 336–38, 344), even as it ties into freedom, albeit in a warped manner.

54 The image of the mud-covered house resonates with Cortázar's image of the dust hanging in the city air and collecting on the furniture inside the house in "House Taken Over" (Cortázar 1967e [1946], 13).

CONCLUSION. SINGING UNSUNG STORIES, PIVOTING POSITIONALITIES

1 David Hume (1998e) champions this view of aesthetic qualities with his account of the mutual address between artwork and public (Roelofs 2020, 78–87).

2 This reflexivity includes reflection on the role of other aesthetic categories.

3 For Yuriko Saito (2017, 30), everyday aesthetic life involves balancing familiarity and unfamiliarity.

4 On Cortázar's repeated motif of perfection's deadly effects as a dimension of the production of idealized images and completed narrations, see Sommer 1998, 223–27.

5 See Adorno 1997; Brand 1998; Dewey 1934; Jones 2003; Levinson 1996.

6 Since the game of Statues and Attitudes, on the surface, involves neither spelling nor writing, the three sisters exemplify the figure of the artist or writer. With this gesture, Cortázar differentiates art and writing from the norms of the lettered city, as Lispector will do roughly two decades later. In the same act, he invokes an extended philosophical tradition, emblematized by Kant, that distinguishes aesthetics from rule-governed contemplation and agency. What is more, the reader wonders whether the narrator is taking us on a stroll through the meticulously groomed parks of another famous Cortázar story to be discussed momentarily (Cortázar 1967c).

7 On Hume's and Kant's reliance on both notions of historically situated publics and notions of ideal, nonsituated publics conceived of as open to anyone, see Roelofs 2020, 66–86.

8 Cortázar here blurs the distinction between character and author because Rocambole is said to be both. This purposeful conflation of reality and fiction complicates the status of Letitia's reading.

9 This is how the three agitators shake up Ulysses and get him to board his ship, the modern train running on the "Argentine Central tracks" (136), so he can meet the irresistible Sirens.

10 With his delightful play on these Shakespearean signifiers and other classical Western tropes, Cortázar is preparing his own "charmed" concoction, stirring his steamy cauldron, and "enchanting all that [he] put[s] in[to]" his subversively Baroque tale, to borrow the playwright's words (Shakespeare 2005, 4.1).

11 These predicates go back to the Old English "wyrd," which refers to fate or destiny. Cortázar's tale spins, reworks, and amplifies these meanings through the three youngsters' art and play: Their dress-up act raises the question of what the future will bring. In the First Folio edition, the sisters are repeatedly called "weyward" or "weyard," as in *Macbeth,* 1.3.216v (Shakespeare 1623, *Tragedies,* 132) and 4.1.2n1r (145), respectively. Later editions typically replace both terms with "weird" (see, e.g., Shakespeare 2005). A rarer usage is the Scottish "weïrd" (Shakespeare 2013).

12 For a rich reworking of the extended Latin American and Caribbean cultural tradition on which Caliban emblematizes the postcolonial actor and Ariel a traditionally lettered subject or *letrado,* see Beverley 1993, chap. 1. Read in light of these figures' struggle, Cortázar's story, ironically, does not displace Ariel in favor of Caliban but calls into question the opposition between literature and its outside, between the disinterested pleasure of autonomous games and a heteronomous world of practical rationality.

13 An odyssey, however, isn't in the books for the unhoused brother. This modern-day Ulysses is more interested in preservation than in adventure, in novelty, as I indicate.

14 For a multifaceted, historicized approach to the story's perspective on the aesthetics-politics relation, see Levinson 2004.

15 For a more detailed discussion of figurations of the street in various Cortázar narratives, see Roelofs 2020, chap. 3. Eltit's twin sister wants the public, but not at

the price of surrendering the home in order to maintain the domestic as morally pure rather than strange.

16 Notably, his famous celebration of the male reader in *Hopscotch* is countered by the figure of La Maga in the streets, who is all play. Shifting gender play and performance characterizes much of Cortázar's fiction, as Anzaldúa acknowledges (2009, 83). See also Pitts 2021, 168.

17 Quotations from *Frivolous Women* (Borinsky 2009) are reprinted with permission of Swan Isle Press.

18 As in Cortázar 1967b.

19 For an influential view of disinterested attention as an, even *the*, aesthetic attitude and a defense of its significance as a component of taste within modern aesthetics, see Stolnitz 1961, 1978.

20 The point is all the more forceful since it applies both in the case of the working-class character Ariel of "End of the Game" and that of the upper-middle-class siblings of "House Taken Over."

21 An Attitude of magnanimity, thus, is among its offerings.

22 Mariángeles Soto-Díaz, *Painting with Fire* (artist's statement), accessed December 10, 2025, https://www.sotodiaz.com/painting-with-fire/.

References

Acosta, Abraham. 2014. *Thresholds of Illiteracy: Theory, Latin America, and the Crisis of Resistance*. Fordham University Press.

Adorno, Theodor W. 1991. "Culture Industry Reconsidered." Translated by Anson G. Rabinbach. In *The Culture Industry*, edited by J. M. Bernstein. Routledge.

Adorno, Theodor W. 1997. *Aesthetic Theory*. Translated by Robert Hulot-Kentor. University of Minnesota Press.

Ahmed, Sara. 2000. *Strange Encounters: Embodied Others in Post-Coloniality*. Routledge.

Ahmed, Sara. 2005. "The Skin of the Community: Affect and Boundary Formation." In *Revolt, Affect, Collectivity: The Unstable Boundaries of Kristeva's Polis*, edited by Tina Chanter and Ewa Ptonowska Ziarek. State University of New York Press.

Ahmed, Sara. 2010. *The Promise of Happiness*. Duke University Press.

Alcoff, Linda Martín. 2006. *Visible Identities: Race, Gender, and the Self*. Oxford University Press.

Alcoff, Linda Martín. 2020. "Decolonizing Feminist Theory: Latina Contributions to the Debate." In Pitts et al., *Theories of the Flesh*.

Amaral, Suzana, dir. 1985. *A hora da estrela* (*The Hour of the Star*). Raíz.

Anzaldúa, Gloria. 1999 [1987]. *Borderlands/La Frontera: The New Mestiza*. 2nd ed. Spinsters/Aunt Lute.

Anzaldúa, Gloria E. 2002. "Speaking in Tongues: A Letter to Third World Women Writers." In *This Bridge Called My Back: Writings by Radical Women of Color*, 3rd ed., edited by Cherríe L. Moraga and Gloria E. Anzaldúa. Third Woman.

Anzaldúa, Gloria E. 2009. *The Gloria Anzaldúa Reader*. Edited by AnaLouise Keating. Duke University Press.

Anzaldúa, Gloria E. 2015. *Light in the Dark / Luz en lo oscuro: Rewriting Identity, Spirituality, Reality*. Edited by AnaLouise Keating. Duke University Press.

Aparicio, Francis R. 1998. *Listening to Salsa: Gender, Latin Popular Music, and Puerto Rican Cultures*. Wesleyan University Press.

Aparicio, Francis R., and Susana Chávez-Silverman, eds. 1997. *Tropicalizations: Transcultural Representations of Latinidad*. University Press of New England.

Arendt, Hannah. 1998. *The Human Condition*. 2nd ed. University of Chicago Press.

Arendt, Hannah. 2005. "On the Nature of Totalitarianism: An Essay in Understanding." In *Essays in Understanding 1930–1955: Formation, Exile, and Totalitarianism*, edited by Jerome Kohn. Schocken.

Arendt, Hannah. 2024. *The Origins of Totalitarianism*. Mariner Classics.

Arguedas, José Maria. 1969. *El sueño del pongo: Cuento quechua y canciones quechuas tradicionales*. Editorial Universitaria.

Baldwin, James. 2010. *The Cross of Redemption: Uncollected Writings*. Edited by Randall Kenan. Pantheon.

Benjamin, Walter. 1996. "One-Way Street." Translated by Edmund Jephcott. In *Selected Writings*, vol. 1. Edited by Marcus Bullock and Michael W. Jennings. Harvard University Press.

Benjamin, Walter. 1999a. "Experience and Poverty." In *Selected Writings*, vol. 2, pt. 2. Edited by Michael W. Jennings, Howard Eiland, and Gary Smith. Translated by Rodney Livingstone et al. Harvard University Press.

Benjamin, Walter. 1999b. "Old Toys: The Toy Exhibition at the Märkisches Museum." In *Selected Writings*, vol. 2, pt. 1. Edited by Michael W. Jennings, Howard Eiland, and Gary Smith. Translated by Rodney Livingstone et al. Harvard University Press.

Benjamin, Walter. 1999c. "On the Mimetic Faculty." In *Selected Writings*, vol. 2, pt. 2. Edited by Michael W. Jennings, Howard Eiland, and Gary Smith. Translated by Rodney Livingstone et al. Harvard University Press.

Benjamin, Walter. 1999d. "Program for a Proletarian Children's Theater." In *Selected Writings*, vol. 2, pt. 1. Edited by Michael W. Jennings, Howard Eiland, and Gary Smith. Translated by Rodney Livingstone et al. Harvard University Press.

Benjamin, Walter. 2002a. "The Storyteller: Observations on the Work of Nikolai Leskov." In *Selected Writings*, vol 3. Edited by Howard Eiland and Michael W. Jennings. Translated by Edmund Jephcott, Howard Eiland, et al. Harvard University Press.

Benjamin, Walter. 2002b. "The Work of Art in the Age of Its Technological Reproducibility." Second Version. In *Selected Writings*, vol. 3. Edited by Howard Eiland and Michael W. Jennings. Translated by Edmund Jephcott, Howard Eiland, et al. Harvard University Press.

Benjamin, Walter. 2003a. "On Some Motifs in Baudelaire." Translated by Harry Zohn. In *Selected Writings*, vol. 4. Edited by Howard Eiland and Michael W. Jennings. Harvard University Press.

Benjamin, Walter. 2003b. "On the Concept of History." Translated by Harry Zohn. In *Selected Writings*, vol. 4. Edited by Michael W. Jennings et al. Harvard University Press.

Benjamin, Walter. 2006. *On Hashish*. Edited by Howard Eiland. Translated by Howard Eiland et al. Harvard University Press.

Benjamin, Walter. 2019. *Origin of the German Trauerspiel*. Translated by Howard Eiland. Harvard University Press.

Berlant, Lauren. 2008. *The Female Complaint: The Unfinished Business of Sentimentality in American Culture*. Duke University Press.

Berlant, Lauren. 2022. *On the Inconvenience of Other People*. Duke University Press.

Bernasconi, Robert. 2002. "Kant as an Unfamiliar Source of Racism." In *Philosophers on Race: Critical Essays*, edited by Julie K. Ward and Tommie L. Lott. Blackwell.

Bernasconi, Robert. 2003. "Will the Real Kant Please Stand Up: The Challenge of Enlightenment Racism to the Study of the History of Philosophy." *Radical Philosophy* 117: 13–22.

Bernasconi, Robert. 2011. "Kant's Third Thoughts on Race." In *Reading Kant's Geography*, edited by Stuart Elden and Eduardo Mendieta. State University of New York Press.

Beverley, John. 1993. *Against Literature*. University of Minnesota Press.

Borges, Jorge Luis. 1998a [1966]. "Borges and I." In *Collected Fictions*. Translated by Andrew Hurley. Penguin.

Borges, Jorge Luis. 1998b. "Pierre Menard, Author of the *Quixote*." In *Collected Fictions*. Translated by Andrew Hurley. Penguin.

Borges, Jorge Luis. 1999a. "The Argentine Writer and Tradition." In *Selected Non-Fictions*. Edited by Eliot Weinberger. Translated by Esther Allen, Suzanne Jill Levine, and Eliot Weinberger. Penguin.

Borges, Jorge Luis. 1999b. "John Wilkins' Analytical Language." In *Selected Non-Fictions*. Edited by Eliot Weinberger. Translated by Esther Allen, Suzanne Jill Levine, and Eliot Weinberger. Penguin.

Borges, Jorge Luis. 2000. "The Riddle of Poetry." In *This Craft of Verse: The Charles Eliot Norton Lectures, 1967–68*, edited by Călin-Andrei Mihăilescu. Harvard University Press.

Borinsky, Alicia. 2007. *Golpes bajos / Low Blows: Instantáneas / Snapshots*. Translated by Cola Franzen and the author. University of Wisconsin Press.

Borinsky, Alicia. 2009. *Frivolous Women and Other Sinners / Frívolas y pecadoras*. Translated by Cola Franzen and the author. Swan Isle.

Braidotti, Rosi. 2002. *Metamorphoses: Towards a Materialist Theory of Becoming*. Polity.

Brand, Peggy Zeglin. 1998. "Disinterestedess and Political Art." In *Aesthetics: The Big Questions*, edited by Carolyn Korsmeyer. Blackwell.

Butler, Judith. 1988. "Performative Acts and Gender Constitution: An Essay in Phenomenology and Feminist Theory." *Theatre Journal* 40 (4): 519–31.

Butler, Judith. 2015. *Notes Toward a Performative Theory of Assembly*. Harvard University Press.

Campt, Tina M. 2021. *A Black Gaze: Artists Changing How We See*. MIT Press.

Carroll, Noël. 2022. "Forget Taste." *Journal of Aesthetic Education* 56 (1): 1–27.

Cervantes, Miguel de. 2003. *Don Quixote*. Translated by Edith Grossman. HarperCollins.

Chayka, Kyle. 2024. *Filterworld: How Algorithms Flattened Culture*. Doubleday.

Christ, Ronald. 1997. "Extravag(r)ant and Un/erring Spirit." In Diamela Eltit, *E. Luminata*. Translated by Ronald Christ. Lumen.

Chun, Wendy Hui Kyong. 2006. *Control and Freedom: Power and Paranoia in the Age of Fiber Optics*. MIT Press.

Cisneros, Sandra. 2009 [1984]. *The House on Mango Street*. Vintage.

Cixous, Hélène. 1990. *Reading with Clarice Lispector*. Edited and translated by Verena Andermatt Conley. University of Minnesota Press.

Cixous, Hélène. 1991. "The Author in Truth." Translated by Deborah Jenson. In *"Coming to Writing" and Other Essays*, edited by Deborah Jenson. Harvard University Press.

Cohen, Ted. 1973. "Aesthetic/Non-Aesthetic and the Concept of Taste: A Critique of Sibley's Position." *Theoria* 39 (1–3): 113–52.

Cohen, Ted. 2018. "Liking What's Good: Why Should We?" In *Serious Larks: The Philosophy of Ted Cohen*, edited by Daniel Herwitz. University of Chicago Press.

Coles, Kimberly Anne, Ralph Bauer, Zita Nunes, and Carla L. Peterson, eds. 2015. *The Cultural Politics of Blood, 1500–1900*. Palgrave Macmillan.

Connolly, William E. 2005. *Pluralism*. Duke University Press.

Connolly, William E. 2013. *The Fragility of Things: Self-Organizing Processes, Neoliberal Fantasies, and Democratic Activism*. Duke University Press.

Connolly, William E. 2017. *Facing the Planetary: Entangled Humanism and the Politics of Swarming*. Duke University Press.

Cortázar, Julio. 1967a. "Axolotl." In *Blow-Up and Other Stories*. Translated by Paul Blackburn. Pantheon.

Cortázar, Julio. 1967b. "Blow-Up." In *Blow-Up and Other Stories*. Translated by Paul Blackburn. Pantheon. Originally published as "Las babas del diablo."

Cortázar, Julio. 1967c. "Continuity of Parks." In *Blow-Up and Other Stories*. Translated by Paul Blackburn. Pantheon.

Cortázar, Julio. 1967d. "End of the Game." In *Blow-Up and Other Stories*. Translated by Paul Blackburn. Pantheon.

Cortázar, Julio. 1967e [1946]. "House Taken Over." In *Blow-Up and Other Stories*. Translated by Paul Blackburn. Pantheon.

Damião, Carla Milani. 2016. "Women as Constellation in Walter Benjamin's Aesthetics." *Estetyka i Krytyka: Polish Journal of Aesthetics* 41 (2): 119–34.

Danto, Arthur C. 1998. *The Wake of Art: Criticism, Philosophy, and the Ends of Taste*. Edited by Gregg Horowitz and Tom Huhn. Gordon and Breach.

Dasgupta, Sudeep. 2013. "Permanent Transiency, Tele-Visual Spectacle, and the Slum as Postcolonial Monument." *South Asian Studies* 29 (1): 147–57.

Dávila, Arlene. 2020. *Latinx Art: Artists, Markets, Politics*. Duke University Press.

Davis, Mike. 2006. *Planet of Slums*. Verso.

Dean, Jodi. 2009. *Democracy and Other Neoliberal Fantasies: Communicative Capitalism and Left Politics*. Duke University Press.

Deleuze, Gilles. 1992 [1990]. "Postscript on the Societies of Control." *October* 59: 3–7.

Deleuze, Gilles, and Félix Guattari. 1987. *A Thousand Plateaus: Capitalism and Schizophrenia*. Translated by Brian Massumi. University of Minnesota Press.

de Man, Paul. 1996. "Kant and Schiller." In *Aesthetic Ideology*, edited by Andrzej Warminski. University of Minnesota Press.

Derrida, Jacques. 1981. *Dissemination*. Translated by Barbara Johnson. University of Chicago Press.

Derrida, Jacques. 2005. "Rams: Uninterrupted Dialogue—Between Two Infinities, the Poem." In *Sovereignties in Question: The Poetics of Paul Celan*, edited by Thomas Dutoit and Outi Pasanen. Fordham University Press.

Dewey, John. 1934. *Art as Experience*. New York: G.P. Putnam.

Dorfman, Ariel, and Armand Mattelart. 2018 [1971]. *How to Read Donald Duck: Imperialist Ideology in the Disney Comic*. 4th ed. Translated by David Kunzle. OR Books. Originally published as *Para Leer al Pato Donald: Comunicación de Masa y Colonialismo* (Ediciones Universitarías de Valparaíso).

Duarte, Edson Costa. 2017. "O riso em *A hora da estrela*, de Clarice Lispector." *Literatura e Sociedade* 25: 38–52.

Du Bois, W. E. B. 1986. *The Souls of Black Folk*. In *W. E. B. Du Bois: Writings*, edited by Nathan Higgins. Library of America.

Eidsheim, Nina Sun. 2019. *The Race of Sound: Listening, Timbre, and Vocality in African American Music*. Duke University Press.

Eltit, Diamela. 1995 [1988]. *The Fourth World*. Translated by Dick Gerdes. University of Nebraska Press. Originally published as *El cuarto mundo* (Planeta).

Eltit, Diamela. 1997a [1983]. *E. Luminata*. Translated by Ronald Christ. Lumen. Originally published as *Lumpérica* (Planeta).

Eltit, Diamela. 1997b. "Errant, Erratic." In *E. Luminata*. Translated by Ronald Christ. Lumen.

Eltit, Diamela. 2020. "Writing, Plot, and Desire." Translated by Ramsey McGlazer. *Critical Times* 3 (1): 148–56. https://doi.org/10.1215/26410478-8189889.

Eltit, Diamela. 2023. "Pinochet Machine." Translated by Michael J. Lazzara. In *Diamela Eltit: Essays on Chilean Literature, Politics, and Culture*, edited by Michael J. Lazzara, Mónica Barrientos, and María Rosa Olivera-Williams. Latin America Research Commons.

Evaristo, Conceição. 2023. *Macabéa: Flor de Mulungu*. Illustrated by Luciana Nabuco. Oficina Raquel.

Feros, Antonio. 2017. *Speaking of Spain: The Evolution of Race and Nation in the Hispanic World*. Harvard University Press.

Foucault, Michel. 1970. *The Order of Things*. Pantheon.

Foucault, Michel. 1978. *The History of Sexuality, Volume 1: An Introduction*. Translated by Robert Hurley. Vintage.

Foucault, Michel. 2007. "What Is Critique?" In *The Politics of Truth*, edited by Sylvère Lotringer, translated by Lysa Hochroth and Catherine Porter. Semiotext(e).

Foucault, Michel. 2010. *The Birth of Biopolitics: Lectures at the Collège de France, 1978–1979*. Edited by Michel Senellart. Translated by Graham Burchell. Palgrave Macmillan.

Franco, Jean. 1992. "Going Public: Reinhabiting the Private." In *On Edge: The Crisis of Contemporary Latin American Culture*, edited by George Yúdice, Jean Franco, and Juan Flores. University of Minnesota Press.

Franco, Jean. 2002. *The Decline and Fall of the Lettered City: Latin America in the Cold War*. Harvard University Press.

Fusco, Coco. 2000. "Introduction: Latin American Performance and the Reconquista of Civil Space." In *Corpus Delecti: Performance Art of the Americas*, edited by Coco Fusco. Routledge.

Gadamer, Hans-Georg. 1980. "Plato and the Poets." In *Dialogue and Dialectic: Eight Hermeneutical Studies on Plato*. Translated by P. Christopher Smith. Yale University Press.

Gadamer, Hans-Georg. 2000. *Truth and Method*. 2nd revised ed. Translated by Joel Weinsheimer and Donald G. Marshall. Continuum.

Gagnier, Regenia. 2000. *The Insatiability of Human Wants: Economics and Aesthetics in Market Society*. University of Chicago Press.

García Canclini, Néstor. 2001. *Consumers and Citizens: Globalization and Multicultural Conflict*. Translated by George Yúdice. University of Minnesota Press.

García Canclini, Néstor. 2014. *Imagined Globalization*. Translated by George Yúdice. Duke University Press.

García Márquez, Gabriel. 2006 [1967]. *One Hundred Years of Solitude*. Translated by Gregory Rabassa. HarperCollins.

Glissant, Édouard. 1997. *Poetics of Relation*. Translated by Betsy Wing. University of Michigan Press.

Gonzáles Iñárritu, Alejandro, dir. 2000. *Amores perros*. Altavista Films and Zeta Film.

Gopinath, Gayatri. 2005. *Impossible Desires: Queer Diasporas and South Asian Public Cultures*. Duke University Press.

Gopinath, Gayatri. 2018. *Unruly Visions: The Aesthetic Practices of Queer Diaspora*. Duke University Press.

Griswold, Charles L. 2024. "Plato on Rhetoric and Poetry." In *Stanford Encyclopedia of Philosophy*, Spring ed., edited by Edward N. Zalta and Uri Nodelman. https://plato.stanford.edu/archives/spr2024/entries/plato-rhetoric.

Haile, James B., III. 2025. *The Dark Delight of Being Strange: Black Stories of Freedom*. Columbia University Press.

Hall, Stuart. 1994. "Cultural Identity and Diaspora." In *Colonial Discourse and Post-Colonial Theory: A Reader*, edited by Patrick Williams and Laura Chrisman. Columbia University Press.

Hall, Stuart. 1996a. "Introduction: Who Needs 'Identity'?" In *Questions of Cultural Identity*, edited by Stuart Hall and Paul du Gay. Sage.

Hall, Stuart. 1996b. "New Ethnicities." In *Stuart Hall: Critical Dialogues in Cultural Studies*, edited by David Morley and Kuan-Hsing Chen. Routledge.

Hall, Stuart. 1996c. "What Is This 'Black' in Black Popular Culture?" In *Stuart Hall: Critical Dialogues in Cultural Studies*, edited by David Morley and Kuan-Hsing Chen. Routledge.

Hall, Stuart. 2005. "Assembling the 1980s: The Deluge—and After." In *Shades of Black: Assembling Black Arts in 1980s Britain*, edited by David A. Bailey, Ian Baucom, and Sonia Boyce. Duke University Press.

Hansen, Miriam. 1987. "Benjamin, Cinema and Experience: 'The Blue Flower in the Land of Technology.'" *New German Critique* 40: 179–224.

Hansen, Miriam. 1991. *Babel and Babylon: Spectatorship in American Silent Film* Harvard University Press.

Hansen, Miriam. 2012. *Cinema and Experience: Siegfried Kracauer, Walter Benjamin, and Theodor W. Adorno*. University of California Press.

Holmes, Amanda. 2007. *City Fiction: Language, Body, and Spanish American Urban Space*. Bucknell University Press.

Honig, Bonnie. 2017. *Public Things: Democracy in Disrepair*. Fordham University Press.

Horkheimer, Max, and Theodor W. Adorno. 2002. "The Culture Industry: Enlightenment as Mass Deception." In *Dialectic of Enlightenment: Philosophical Fragments*, edited by Gunzelin Schmid Noerr; translated by Edmund Jephcott. Stanford University Press.

Huizinga, Johan. 1949. *Homo Ludens: A Study of the Play-Element in Culture*. Routledge and Kegan Paul.

Hume, David. 1998a. "Of Commerce." In *Selected Essays*. Edited by S. Copley and A. Edgar. Oxford University Press.

Hume, David. 1998b. "Of Refinement in the Arts." In *Selected Essays*. Edited by S. Copley and A. Edgar. Oxford University Press.

Hume, David. 1998c. "Of the Delicacy of Taste and Passion." In *Selected Essays*. Edited by S. Copley and A. Edgar. Oxford University Press.

Hume, David. 1998d. "Of the Rise and Progress of the Arts and Sciences." In *Selected Essays*. Edited by S. Copley and A. Edgar. Oxford University Press.

Hume, David. 1998e. "Of the Standard of Taste." In *Selected Essays*. Edited by S. Copley and A. Edgar. Oxford University Press.

Instituto Nacional de Estadística e Informática. 2018. *Perú: Perfil Sociodemográfico Informe Nacional*. https://www.inei.gob.pe/media/MenuRecursivo/publicaciones_digitales/Est/Lib1539/libro.pdf.

Jones, Amelia. 2003. "Meaning, Identity, Embodiment: The Uses of Merleau-Ponty's Phenomenology in Art History." In *Art and Thought*, edited by Dana Arnold and Margaret Iverson. Blackwell.

Jung, Daae, and João Paulo Guimarães. 2023. "Lispector's Halo: Life Contemplating Itself in *The Hour of the Star*." *Angelaki* 28 (2): 33–44.

Kant, Immanuel. 1991. "An Answer to the Question: 'What is Enlightenment?'" In *Political Writings*. 2nd enlarged ed. Edited by Hans Reiss. Translated by H. B. Nisbet. Cambridge University Press.

Kant, Immanuel. 2000 [1790]. *Critique of the Power of Judgment*. Edited by Paul Guyer. Translated by Paul Guyer and Eric Matthews. Cambridge University Press.

Kant, Immanuel. 2011 [1764]. *Observations on the Feeling of the Beautiful and Sublime*. Translated by Paul Guyer. In *Observations on the Feeling of the Beautiful and Sublime and Other Writings*. Edited by Patrick Frierson and Paul Guyer. Cambridge University Press.

Kant, Immanuel. 2012a. *Lectures on Anthropology*. Edited by Allen W. Wood and Robert B. Louden. Translated by Robert R. Clewis et al. Cambridge University Press.

Kant, Immanuel. 2012b. *Physical Geography*. Translated by Olaf Reinhardt. In *Natural Science*. Edited by Eric Watkins. Translated by Lewis White Beck et al. Cambridge University Press.

Kelly, Michael, and Monique Roelofs. 2024. "Introduction: Revalorizing Black Aesthetics." In *Black Art and Aesthetics: Relationalities, Interiorities, Reckonings*, edited by Michael Kelly and Monique Roelofs. Bloomsbury.

Kleingeld, Pauline. 2024. "Anti-Racism and Kant Scholarship: A Critical Notice of *Kant, Race and Racism: Views from Somewhere*, by Huaping Lu-Adler." *Mind*. http://doi.org/10.1093/mind/fzae022.

Korsmeyer, Carolyn. 1995. "Gendered Concepts and Hume's Standard of Taste." In *Feminism and Tradition in Aesthetics*, edited by Peggy Zeglin Brand and Carolyn Korsmeyer. Pennsylvania State University Press.

Korsmeyer, Carolyn. 1998. "Perceptions, Pleasures, Arts: Considering Aesthetics." In *Philosophy in a Feminist Voice: Critiques and Reconstructions*, edited by Janet A. Kourany. Princeton University Press.

Korsmeyer, Carolyn. 2006. "Terrible Beauties." In *Contemporary Debates in Aesthetics and the Philosophy of Art*, edited by Matthew Kieran. Blackwell.

Korsmeyer, Carolyn, and Peg Brand Weiser. 2021. "Feminist Aesthetics." In *Stanford Encyclopedia of Philosophy*, Winter ed., edited by Edward N. Zalta. https://plato.stanford.edu/archives/win2021/entries/feminism-aesthetics/.

Kristeva, Julia. 1987. "Stabat Mater." In *Tales of Love*. Translated by Leon S. Roudiez. Columbia University Press.

Kristeva, Julia. 1991. *Strangers to Ourselves*. Translated by Leon S. Roudiez. Columbia University Press.

Larrimore, Mark. 2008. "Antinomies of Race: Diversity and Destiny in Kant." *Patterns of Prejudice* 42 (4–5): 341–63.

Lazarus, Neil. 2012. *The Postcolonial Unconscious*. Cambridge University Press.

Levinson, Brett. 2001. *The Ends of Literature: The Latin American "Boom" in the Neoliberal Marketplace*. Stanford University Press.

Levinson, Brett. 2004. "Populism, Aesthetics, and Politics for Cortázar and for Us: Houses Taken Over." *Latin American Literary Review* 32 (63): 99–112.

Levinson, Jerrold. 1996. "Pleasure and the Value of Works of Art." In *The Pleasures of Aesthetics*. Cornell University Press.

Levinson, Jerrold. 2002. "Hume's Standard of Taste: The Real Problem." *Journal of Aesthetics and Art Criticism* 60 (3): 227–38.

Liinason, Mia. 2024. "The Performance of Protest: Las Tesis and the New Feminist Radicality at the Conjunction of Digital Spaces and the Streets." *Feminist Media Studies* 24 (3): 430–47. https://doi.org/10.1080/14680777.2023.2200472.

Lillo, Gastón. 2011. "*La teta asustada* (Perú, 2009) de Claudia Llosa: ¿Memoria u olvido?" *Revista de Crítica Literaria Latinoamericana* 37 (73): 421–46.

Lispector, Clarice. 1998 [1977]. *A hora da estrela*. Rocco.

Lispector, Clarice. 2011. *The Hour of the Star*. Translated by Benjamin Moser. New Directions.

Llosa, Claudia, dir. 2009. *La teta asustada* (*The Milk of Sorrow*). Olive Films.

Llosa, Mario Vargas. 2011. *The Time of the Hero*. Translated by Lysander Kemp. Farrar, Straus and Giroux.

Lorde, Audre. 1984. "Uses of the Erotic: The Erotic as Power." In *Sister Outsider: Essays and Speeches*. Crossing Press.

Lu-Adler, Huaping. 2023. *Kant, Race, and Racism: Views from Somewhere*. Oxford University Press.

Lugones, María. 2003. *Pilgrimages/Peregrinajes: Theorizing Coalition Against Multiple Oppressions*. Rowman and Littlefield.

Lugones, María. 2006. "On Complex Communication." *Hypatia* 21 (3): 75–85.

Lugones, María. 2007. "Heterosexualism and the Colonial / Modern Gender System." *Hypatia* 22 (1): 186–209.

Lugones, María. 2010. "Toward a Decolonial Feminism." *Hypatia* 25 (4): 742–59.

Lunsford, Andrea A. 1998. "Toward a Mestiza Rhetoric: Gloria Anzaldúa on Composition and Postcoloniality." *JAC* 18 (1): 1–27.

Maldonado-Torres, Nelson. 2007. "On the Coloniality of Being: Contributions to the Development of a Concept." *Cultural Studies* 21 (2–3): 240–70.

Martel, Lucrecia, dir. 2001. *La ciénaga* (*The Swamp*). Wanda Visión.

Martel, Lucrecia, dir. 2004. *La niña santa (The Holy Girl)*. El Deseo.

Martel, Lucrecia, dir. 2008. *La mujer sin cabeza (The Headless Woman)*. El Deseo.

Martel, Lucrecia, dir. 2021. *Terminal Norte (North Terminal)*. Rei Cine.

Martin, Deborah, and Deborah Shaw. 2021. "Chilean and Transnational Performances of Disobedience: LasTesis and the Phenomenon of *Un violador en tu camino*." *Bulletin of Latin American Research* 40 (5): 712–29.

Martínez, María Elena. 2008. *Genealogical Fictions: Limpieza de Sangre, Religion, and Gender in Colonial Mexico*. Stanford University Press.

Masiello, Francine. 2001. *The Art of Transition: Latin American Culture and Neoliberal Crisis*. Duke University Press.

Masiello, Francine R. 2018. *The Senses of Democracy: Perception, Politics, and Culture in Latin America*. University of Texas Press.

Massidda, Adriana Laura. 2023. "Slums, Villas Miseria, and Barriadas: Why Terms Matter." *Journal of Urban History* 49 (3): 552–70.

Mbembe, Achille. 2021. *Out of the Dark Night: Essays on Decolonization*. Columbia University Press.

Medina, José. 2013. *The Epistemology of Resistance: Gender and Racial Oppression, Epistemic Injustice, and Resistant Imaginations*. Oxford University Press.

Meirelles, Fernando, and Kátia Lund, dirs. 2002. *Cidade de Deus* (*City of God*). O2 Filmes.

Mignolo, Walter D. 2007. "Delinking: The Rhetoric of Modernity, the Logic of Coloniality and the Grammar of De-Coloniality." *Cultural Studies* 21 (2–3): 449–515.

Mignolo, Walter D. 2012. *Local Histories, Global Designs: Coloniality, Subaltern Knowledges, and Border Thinking*. Reprint ed. Princeton University Press.

Mignolo, Walter D. 2021. *The Politics of Decolonial Investigations*. Duke University Press.

Mignolo, Walter, and Rolando Vázquez. 2013. "Decolonial AestheSis: Colonial Wounds / Decolonial Healings." *Social Text, Periscope*. https://socialtextjournal.org/periscope_article/decolonial-aesthesis-colonial-woundsdecolonial-healings/.

Milian, Claudia. 2019. *LatinX*. University of Minnesota Press.

Milian, Claudia, and Elia Romera-Figueroa. 2024. "Transatlantic LatinX studies, Iberian Studies, and the Global South." *Cultural Dynamics* 37 (1–2): 3–62.

Morales Rodríguez, Luvia Estella. 2021. "'La letra no es inocente ni menos neutral': Una conversación con Diamela Eltit." *Confluencia* 36 (2): 160–66.

Mosse, George L. 1985. *Nationalism and Sexuality: Respectability and Abnormal Sexuality in Modern Europe*. Fertig.

Muñoz, José Esteban. 1999. *Disidentifications: Queers of Color and the Performance of Politics*. University of Minnesota Press.

Muñoz, José Esteban. 2020. "Performing Greater Cuba: Tania Bruguera and the Burden of Guilt." In *The Sense of Brown*, edited by Joshua Chambers-Letson and Tavia Nyong'o. Duke University Press.

Neustadt, Robert. 2003. "Diamela Eltit: Performing Action in Dictatorial Chile." In *Holy Terrors: Latin American Women Perform*, edited by Diana Taylor and Roselyn Costantino. Duke University Press.

Ngai, Sianne. 2005. *Ugly Feelings*. Harvard University Press.

Ngai, Sianne. 2012. *Our Aesthetic Categories: Zany, Cute, Interesting*. Harvard University Press.

Noë, Alva. 2015. *Strange Tools: Art and Human Nature*. Farrar, Straus and Giroux.

Ortega, Julio. 1993. "Diamela Eltit y el imaginario de la virtualidad." In *Una poética de literatura menor: La narrativa de Diamela Eltit*, edited by Juan Carlos Lértora. Cuarto Proprio.

Ortega, Mariana. 2016. *In-Between: Latina Feminist Phenomenology, Multiplicity, and the Self*. State University of New York Press.

Ortega, Mariana. 2025. *Carnalities: The Art of Living in Latinidad*. Duke University Press.

Ortiz, Fernando. 1995 [1940]. *Cuban Counterpoint, Tobacco and Sugar*. Translated by Harriet de Onís. Duke University Press.

Palma, José-Alberto, and Fermin Palma. 2020. "Maternal Breastfeeding or Wet Nursing? Religion, Persecution, and Ideology in the 17th Century." *Breastfeeding Medicine* 15 (12): 756–58. https://doi.org.10.1089/bfm.2020.0255.

Parker, Andrew, Mary Russo, Doris Sommer, and Patricia Yaeger, eds. 1992. *Nationalisms and Sexualities*. Routledge.

Pérez, Laura E. 2019. *Eros Ideologies: Writings on Art, Spiritualities, and the Decolonial*. Duke University Press.

Pérez, Laura M. 2020. "Enrique Dussel's *Ética de la liberación*, US Women of Color Decolonizing Practices, and Coalitionary Politics amid Difference." In Pitts et al., *Theories of the Flesh*.

Pitts, Andrea J. 2021. *Nos/Otras: Gloria E. Anzaldúa, Multiplicitous Agency, and Resistance*. State University of New York Press.

Pitts, Andrea J., Mariana Ortega, and José Medina, eds. 2020. *Theories of the Flesh: Latinx and Latin American Feminisms, Transformation, and Resistance*. Oxford University Press.

Plato. 1997a. *Ion*. Translated by Paul Woodruff. In *Plato: Complete Works*. Edited by John M. Cooper and D. S. Hutchinson. Hackett.

Plato. 1997b. *Symposium*. Translated by Alexander Nehamas and Paul Woodruff. In *Plato: Complete Works*. Edited by John M. Cooper and D. S. Hutchinson. Hackett.

Plato. 2004. *Republic*. Translated by C. D. C. Reeve. Hackett.

Plato. 2005a. *Meno and Other Dialogues*. Translated by Robin Waterfield. Oxford University Press.

Plato. 2005b. *Phaedrus*. Translated by Christopher Rowe. Penguin.

Pratt, Mary Louise. 1996. "Overwriting Pinochet: Undoing the Culture of Fear in Chile." *Modern Language Quarterly* 57 (2): 153–63.

Pratt, Mary Louise. 2008 [1992]. *Imperial Eyes: Travel Writing and Transculturation*. 2nd ed. Routledge.

Probyn, Elspeth. 2012. "In the Interest of Taste and Place: Economies of Attachment." In *The Global and The Intimate: Feminism in Our Time*, edited by Geraldine Pratt and Victoria Rosner. Columbia University Press.

Quashie, Kevin. 2012. *The Sovereignty of Quiet: Beyond Resistance in Black Culture*. Rutgers University Press.

Quashie, Kevin. 2021. *Black Aliveness, or A Poetics of Being*. Duke University Press.
Quijano, Aníbal. 2007. "Coloniality and Modernity/Rationality." Translated by Sonia Therborn. *Cultural Studies* 21 (2–3): 168–78.
Rama, Ángel. 1996 [1985]. *The Lettered City*. Translated and edited by John Charles Chasteen. Duke University Press.
Rancière, Jacques. 2004. *The Politics of Aesthetics*. Translated by Gabriel Rockhill. Continuum.
Rancière, Jacques. 2009. *Aesthetics and Its Discontents*. Translated by Steven Corcoran. Polity.
Rancière, Jacques. 2013. *Aesthesis: Scenes from the Aesthetic Regime of the Arts*. Translated by Zakir Paul. Verso.
Renker, Tess. 2024. "Whiteness, Coloniality and Distributive Justice in Claudia Llosa's *La teta asustada* (2009)." *Hispanic Review* 92 (2): 201–21.
Rich, Adrienne. 1980. "Compulsory Heterosexuality and Lesbian Existence." *Signs* 5 (4): 631–60.
Richard, Nelly. 1993. "Tres funciones de escritura: Desconstrucción, simulación, hibridación." In *Una poética de literatura menor: La narrativa de Diamela Eltit*, edited by Juan Carlos Lértora. Cuarto Proprio.
Richard, Nelly. 2000 [1986]. "Margins and Institutions: Performances of the Chilean Avanzada." Translated by Paul Foss and Juan Davila. In *Corpus Delecti: Performance Art of the Americas*, edited by Coco Fusco. Routledge.
Richard, Nelly. 2004a. *Cultural Residues: Chile in Translation*. Translated by Alan West-Durán and Theodore Quester. University of Minnesota Press.
Richard, Nelly. 2004b. *The Insubordination of Signs: Political Change, Cultural Transformation, and Poetics of the Crisis*. Translated by Alice A. Nelson and Silvia R. Tandeciarz. Duke University Press.
Richard, Nelly. 2009. "City, Art, Politics." Translated by Samuel Lockhart and Rebecca E. Biron. In *City/Art: The Urban Scene in Latin America*, edited by Rebecca E. Biron. Duke University Press.
Richard, Nelly. 2019. *Eruptions of Memory: The Critique of Memory in Chile, 1990–2015*. Translated by Andrew Ascherl. Polity.
Rivera Cusicanqui, Silvia. 2012. "Ch'ixinakax utxiwa: A Reflection on the Practices and Discourses of Decolonization," *South Atlantic Quarterly* 111 (1): 95–109.
Roelofs, Monique. 2013. "Taste, Distaste, and Food." In *Encyclopedia of Food and Agricultural Ethics*, edited by Paul B. Thompson and David M. Kaplan. Springer. https://doi.org/10.1007/978-94-007-6167-4_22-2.
Roelofs, Monique. 2014. *The Cultural Promise of the Aesthetic*. Bloomsbury.
Roelofs, Monique. 2016. "Navigating Frames of Address: María Lugones on Language, Bodies, Things, and Places." *Hypatia* 31 (2): 370–87.
Roelofs, Monique. 2019. "Selling Literature / Selling the Race: Diamela Eltit's Decolonial Feminist Critique of the Neoliberal Marketplace." *Journal of Aesthetics and Art Criticism* 77 (4): 461–73.
Roelofs, Monique. 2020. *Arts of Address: Being Alive to Language and the World*. Columbia University Press.

Roelofs, Monique. 2021a. "Philosophy and the Politics of Beauty." In *The Routledge Companion to Beauty Politics*, edited by Maxine Leeds Craig. Routledge.

Roelofs, Monique. 2021b. "Playing with the Rules of the Game: Imagination, Normativity, and Address in Aesthetics." In *Art, Representation, and Make-Believe: Essays on the Philosophy of Kendall L. Walton*, edited by Sonia Sedivy. Routledge.

Roelofs, Monique. 2022. "Decoloniality, Identity, and Aesthetic Publicity." *Contemporary Aesthetics*, special volume 10.

Roelofs, Monique. 2024a. "Identity, Art, and the Aesthetic Effusiveness of Racialised Possibility." In *Public Art: Das Recht auf Erinnerung und die Realität der Städte / The Right to Remember and the Reality of Cities*, edited by Baureferat Nürnberg with Jörg Heiser, Gürsoy Doğtaş, and María Inés Plaza Lazo. Distanz.

Roelofs, Monique. 2024b. "Public Things, Public Squares: Aesthetic Democracy in Diamela Eltit's *E. Luminata*." *Parallax* 30 (1): 62–81.

Roelofs, Monique. Forthcoming. "The Lurking Universal and the Tingly Particular: Borges's Aesthetics of the Strange and Perplexing." *New Literary History* 57 (2).

Roelofs, Monique, and Norman S. Holland. 2024. "Indigeneity at the Limits of Transculturation: Decolonial Aesthetics in Claudia Llosa's *The Milk of Sorrow*." *PhiloSOPHIA* 14: 1–30.

Roelofs, Monique, and Norman S. Holland. 2025. "The Role of the Aesthetic in Decolonial Critique: Claudia Llosa, *The Milk of Sorrow / La teta asustada*." *Latin American and Latinx Visual Culture* 7 (1): 26–47.

Rogers, Melvin L. 2023. *The Darkened Light of Faith: Race, Democracy, and Freedom in African American Political Thought*. Princeton University Press.

Rojas, Adriana. 2017. "Mother of Pearl, Song and Potatoes: Cultivating Resilience in Claudia Llosa's *La teta asustada / The Milk of Sorrow* (2009)." *Studies in Spanish and Latin American Cinemas* 14 (3): 297–314.

Rooney, Ellen. 2017. "Feminists Reading Novels, Now, and Again, and Again." *Novel: A Forum on Fiction* 50 (3): 441–51.

Roth, Norman. 1995. *Conversos, Inquisition, and the Expulsion of the Jews from Spain*. University of Wisconsin Press.

Rueda, Carolina. 2015. "Memory, Trauma, and Phantasmagoria in Claudia Llosa's *La teta asustada*." *Hispania* 98 (3): 452–61.

Sá, Lúcia. 2004. "*A hora da estrela* e o mal estar das elites." *Estudos de Literatura Brasileira Contemporânea* 23: 49–65.

Saito, Yuriko. 2007. *Everyday Aesthetics*. Oxford University Press.

Saito, Yuriko. 2017. *Aesthetics of the Familiar*. Oxford University Press.

Saito, Yuriko. 2022. *Aesthetics of Care: Practice in Everyday Life*. Bloomsbury.

Sassón-Henry, Perla. 2007. *Borges 2.0: From Text to Virtual Worlds*. Peter Lang.

Schiller, Friedrich. 1967. *On the Aesthetic Education of Man: In a Series of Letters*. Translated by Elizabeth M. Wilkinson and L. A. Willoughby. Oxford University Press.

Schroeder, Barbet, dir. 2000. *La virgen de los sicarios (Our Lady of the Assassins)*. Tornasol.

Sedgwick, Eve Kosofsky. 2011. *The Weather in Proust*. Edited by Jonathan Goldberg. Duke University Press.

Serafini, Paula. 2020. "'A Rapist in Your Path': Transnational Feminist Protest and Why (and How) Performance Matters." *European Journal of Cultural Studies* 23 (3): 290–95. https://doi.org/10.1177/1367549420912748.
Shakespeare, William. 1623. *Mr. Wiliam Shakespeares Comedies, Histories, and Tragedies: Published According to the True Originall Copies*. First folio ed. Isaac Iaggard and Edward Blount.
Shakespeare, William. 2005. *Macbeth*. Edited by Burton Raffel. Yale University Press.
Shakespeare, William. 2013. *Macbeth*. In *Folger Shakespeare Library Updated Edition*, edited by Barbara A. Mowat and Paul Werstine. Simon and Schuster.
Shaw, Deborah. 2018. "European Co-Production Funds and Latin American Cinema: Processes of Othering and Bourgeois Cinephilia in Claudia Llosa's *La teta asustada*." *Diogenes* 62 (1): 88–99.
Sibley, Frank. 1959. "Aesthetic Concepts." *Philosophical Review* 68 (4): 421–50.
Sommer, Doris. 1991. *Foundational Fictions: The National Romances of Latin America*. University of California Press.
Sommer, Doris. 1998. "Pursuing a Perfect Present." In *Julio Cortázar: New Readings*, edited by Carlos J. Alonso. Cambridge University Press.
Spivak, Gayatri Chakravorti. 2012. *An Aesthetic Education in the Era of Globalization*. Harvard University Press.
Stephenson, Amanda. 2012. "The Quechua: Guardians of the Potato." *Cultural Survival Quarterly* 36 (1). https://www.culturalsurvival.org/publications/cultural-survival-quarterly/quechua-guardians-potato.
Stolnitz, Jerome. 1961. "On the Origins of 'Aesthetic Disinterestedess.'" *Journal of Aesthetics and Art Criticism* 20 (2): 131–43.
Stolnitz, Jerome. 1978. "'The Aesthetic Attitude' in the Rise of Modern Aesthetics." *Journal of Aesthetics and Art Criticism* 36 (4): 409–21.
Swanson, Kara W. 2014. *Banking on the Body: The Market in Blood, Milk, and Sperm in Modern America*. Harvard University Press.
Taussig, Michael. 2010 [1980]. *The Devil and Commodity Fetishism in South America*. 2nd ed. University of North Carolina Press.
Taylor, Paul C. 2016. *Black Is Beautiful: A Philosophy of Black Aesthetics*. Wiley Blackwell.
Theidon, Kimberly. 2004. *Entre prójimos: El conflicto armado interno y la política de la reconciliación en el Perú*. Instituto de Estudios Peruanos.
Vallega, Alejandro A. 2014. "Fecund Undercurrents: On the Aesthetic Dimension of Latin American and Decolonial Thought." In *Latin American Philosophy from Identity to Radical Exteriority*. Indiana University Press.
Vallejo, César. 1969 [1918]. *Los heraldos negros*. Losada.
Vélez, Irma. 2011. "Matricidio y ob-scenidad en la (est)ética de Claudia Llosa." *Lectures du Genre* 8: 28–52.
Vich, Cynthia. 2014. "De estetizaciones y viejos exotismos: Apuntes en torno a *La teta asustada* de Claudia Llosa." *Revista de Crítica Literaria Latinoamericana* 40 (80): 333–44.
Vieira, Nelson H. 2022. "Clarice Lispector and World Literature: Is *The Hour of the Star* a Global Novel?" In *After Clarice: Reading Lispector's Legacy in the Twenty-First*

Century, edited by Adriana X. Jacobs and Claire Williams. Modern Humanities Research Association and Legenda.

Warner, Marina. 2016 [1976]. *Alone of All Her Sex: The Myth and Cult of the Virgin Mary*. Oxford University Press.

Weigel, Sigrid, 1998. "From Gender Images to Dialectical Images in Benjamin's Writings." Translated by Rachel McNicholl. In *The Actuality of Walter Benjamin*, edited by Laura Marcus and Lynda Nead. Lawrence and Wishart.

Willett, Cynthia, and Julie Willett. 2019. *Uproarious: How Feminists and Other Subversive Comics Speak Truth*. University of Minnesota Press.

Wolfenzon, Carolyn. 2022. "*La teta asustada* de Claudia Llosa y *Dioses* de Josué Méndez: Una lectura crítica de *La ciudad letrada* desde el cine peruano." *Latin American Literary Review* 49 (98): 21–32.

Wynter, Silvia. 1992. "Rethinking 'Aesthetics': Notes Towards a Deciphering Practice." In *Ex-Iles: Essays on Caribbean Cinema*, edited by Mbye Cham. Africa World Press.

Wynter, Silvia. 2003. "Unsettling the Coloniality of Being/Power/Truth/Freedom: Towards the Human, After Man, Its Overrepresentation—An Argument." *New Centennial Review* 3 (3): 257–337.

Yetter, Lynette. 2017. "Virgin Mary/Pachamama Syncretism: The Divine Feminine in Early-Colonial Copacabana." *Western Tributaries* 4: 1–14.

Index

Page locators in italics indicate figures.

www.ingramcontent.com/pod-product-compliance
Lightning Source LLC
LaVergne TN
LVHW052339100826
845147LV00021B/1115

* 9 7 8 1 4 7 8 0 3 8 6 5 8 *